Working in Tourism

The UK, Europe & Beyond

For seasonal and permanent staff

Verité Reily Collins
Revised by Susan Griffith

Distributed in the USA by
The Globe Pequot Press, Guilford, Connecticut

Published by Vacation Work, 9 Park End Street, Oxford
www.vacationwork.co.uk

WORKING IN TOURISM
Verité Reily Collins

First Edition 1995
Second Edition 1999 (revised by Munira Mirza)
Third Edition 2004 (revised by Susan Griffith)

Copyright © Vacation Work 2004

ISBN 1 85458 311 5 (softback)

Cover Design by mccdesign ltd

Publicity: Roger Musker

Illustrations by John Taylor

Typeset by Brendan Cole

Printed and bound in Italy by Legoprint SpA, Trento

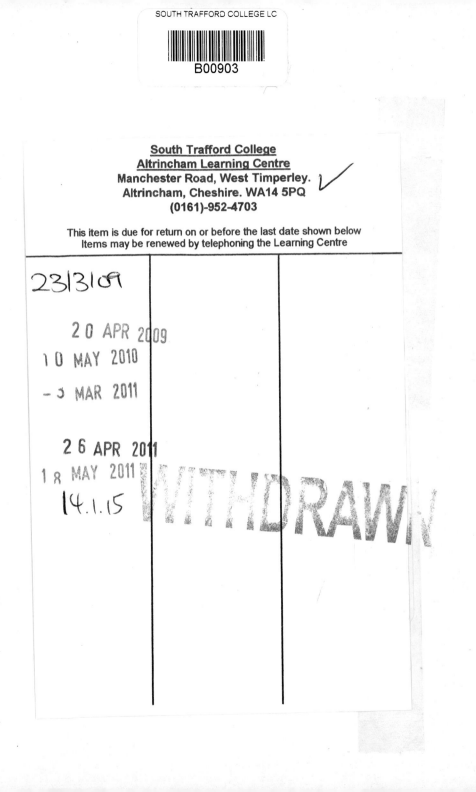

CONTENTS

PART I THE JOBS & HOW TO FIND THEM

PART II COUNTRY BY COUNTRY GUIDE

PART III   DIRECTORIES OF EMPLOYERS

PART IV   APPENDICES

Acknowledgments

Colleagues (who are usually friends, unless I have stretched the bounds of their goodwill too far) helped by passing on their expertise, information and tips, as well as giving permission to publish their stories. To all of them a heartfelt thank you. Many people have helped, including the Press Officers of the National Tourist Offices.

The editor would also like to thank the following for supplementing our research and providing first-hand accounts of their trials and triumphs working in the tourist industry:
Susan Beney, Jennie Cox, Carisa Fey, Debra Fuccio, Debbie Harrison, Keith Leishman, Colm Murphy, James Nibloe and Juliet Radford.

While every effort has been made to ensure that the information contained in this book was accurate at the time of going to press, some details are bound to change within the lifetime of this edition. Tourism companies move, close and change, while wages, exchange rates and government policies are particularly susceptible to fluctuations. The ones quoted here are intended merely as a guide.
If in the course of your job hunt or while working in the tourist industry, you come across anything which might be of interest to readers of the next edition, please write to the author or editor at Vacation-Work, 9 Park End Street, Oxford OX1 1HJ; susan@vacationwork.co.uk. The best contributions will be rewarded with a free copy of the next edition.

Note: Companies and organisations mentioned in the text in italics and without an accompanying address or cross-reference can be located in one of the two directories in Part III: Placement and Recruitment Agencies followed by the Directory of Tour Operators.

PREFACE

Tourism is firmly established as the world's largest industry, employing a staggering 72 million people worldwide. The negative impact that world terrorism has had on travel and tourism since September 11th 2001 has failed to stem the tidal flow of people joining this exciting sector. In fact skills shortages, especially of chefs and managers, continue to be of serious concern. Shifting trends and tastes in travel have created many new opportunities that might not immediately spring to mind, for example in the fields of eco-tourism and heritage, for conference organisers and cabin crew. Job vacancies with cruise lines have escalated in the past five years faster than in almost any other branch of employment.

As consumer legislation has resulted in greater protection for the holidaymaker so it has brought changes for those working in the industry. Tour operators have been forced to adopt a more professional approach or risk going out of business, which has encouraged many more people to seek formal training before entering the job market. Details are given in the following pages of a whole range of courses that will improve your chances of finding a job in tourism.

Although it helps to speak another language, probably 80% of the world's tourism business is conducted in English. The annual pilgrimage in search of sun and sand still relies on an army of tour reps, but has been joined by a thirst for special interest holidays. Tour operators are looking to recruit specialists in a range of diverse activities, from cycling to opera, tropical birds to vineyards. Working in tourism can provide a unique opportunity to experience the lifestyle of the rich (and possibly famous) on ordinary wages, stay in top hotels, meet interesting people and visit the wonders of the world – all as part of your job. In addition, helping people to enjoy the holiday of their dreams is a source of great job satisfaction.

When the first edition of *Working in Tourism* came out, kind readers sent me letters about how the book had helped them find work. It has found its way into classrooms and public libraries as a store of useful information about the ever-growing industry. This new edition has taken into account the massive changes that have taken place since then, including the accession of ten new countries into the European Union and the inexorable rise of on-line booking and no-frills airlines. I am confident that this updated and expanded edition will continue to provide practical and realistic advice about where and how to find work in the industry, as well as helping newcomers and those hoping to build a career in tourism to avoid the rough introduction so many of us experienced in our first jobs. Most will agree that the advantages far outweigh the frustrations.

Bon voyage to both you and your future clients.

Verité Reily Collins
London

PART I

The Jobs and How
to Get Them

INTRODUCTION

Ever since the Second World War, the travel and tourism industry has been expanding to encompass all social classes in the developed world and the privileged classes in the developing world. The proliferation of hotel and resort accommodation together with the affordability of air transport and the increase in leisure time mean that travel is the preserve of the majority, even in these days of terrorist threats. The World Travel & Tourism Council estimated at the beginning of 2004 that the industry is the world's largest employer, providing a staggering 200 million jobs worldwide.

Whenever the topic of international tourism crops up, statistics involving tens of millions are always bandied about and it is not always easy to understand how these statistics are compiled. How can anyone count all those people who move away from their homes in search of novelty and entertainment? Of course the tens of thousands of Britons who take a package holiday abroad and their counterparts in North America who go south in the winter are tourists. But so are the daytrippers who go on a cross-Channel shopping spree, a day trip to the seaside, a theme park or a National Trust property, and so are the business people and scientists who regularly attend conferences away from home. All these travellers require an army of people to service their needs. The tourist industry holds out an immense potential for job creation and imposes relatively low barriers to entering it compared to other industries.

SOME DEFINITIONS

The tourism industry is so diverse that job definitions are not always precise. In this book we have adopted a very broad definition of tourism, though in some contexts we have necessarily dealt with a narrower view.

Although the great majority of tourists stay in hotels and eat in restaurants, the hotels and catering industry is not always considered to be part of the tourist industry. Typically, the Association of Graduate Careers Advisory Services in the UK, publishes separate booklets on 'Working in Tourism' and 'Working in Hospitality'. Certainly someone who trains to be a chef will follow a very different career path from someone who works as a guide or rep. Yet some of the key areas of tourism, such as cruise ships or ski resorts, require both. Vacancies for cooks and assorted hotel staff abound in these industries, as well as for more mainstream tourism personnel. Therefore this book also contains some advice for people who are interested in this aspect of the tourist business.

The classic tourism job is that of guide or representative (formerly known as couriers), the person who looks after holidaymakers. Guides work in a town, city or area and usually return to base each evening whereas tour managers/directors travel round with their clients staying in a different place most nights. Travel is generally by coach but can be by rail, plane, private car or limousine or any of these in combination.

A tour operator puts together the components of a holiday package or tour, booking accommodation, travel and services. The people who work in the office in charge of the bookings, budget, etc. are 'destination managers', most of whom were once reps or guides themselves. A ground handler is the term for a company which looks after visitors at a destination.

Travel agents (or consultants as they prefer to be called in the US) have the job of selling the packages created by tour operators. Travel agencies are like any high street store rather than designer studios. They are retail outlets which, like high-street stores, are often part of a national chain. Contrary to popular belief, working in a travel agency does not lead directly to jobs in other tourism sectors, though it is useful training for other things.

Tourist information centres (TICs) employ a vast number of people. There are more than 550 in the UK alone. Tourist boards are generally a government or local authority funded organisation which promotes an area, region or country to visitors and local people.

Incentive conferences serve as bonuses to the high-achieving staff in big companies, and provide a surprising amount of work within the industry. For example a multinational electronics company might organise a luxury island holiday for those employees who have been responsible for increasing turnover in the previous financial year.

Before turning our attention to the scope of employment opportunities available, it is worth pausing to consider the wider issues. Tourism has undoubtedly been guilty of harming local economies, particularly in developing countries. From the point of view of the locals in the tourist destination, foreign tour operators employ foreign staff to look after foreign holidaymakers who pay for most of their holiday in foreign currency. Some trickles down to the local community but not nearly as much as there would be if the locals themselves provided the services to travellers and tourists. On the other hand, packaged tourists can be better controlled, and if the company looking after them is sensitive to local concerns, this can be less intrusive than a mass invasion of independent travellers.

SCOPE OF OPPORTUNITIES

The range of jobs subsumed under that all-encompassing heading 'Tourism' is staggering, from fourth pursers on cruise ships to children's reps on European campsites, guides in national parks to ski chalet cooks. Of course the tourist industry provides holiday jobs, but it also provides careers in marketing, promotions, public relations, etc. and for people with degrees in archaeology, business administration, history of art or a host of other subjects.

No clear line demarcates seasonal and permanent jobs in the world of tourism. Although many companies offer employment for only six months of the year, they are not necessarily looking for drifters and dabblers. In many cases they are seeking professionally minded candidates who intend to make a career in the industry. A substantial percentage of those filling administrative jobs in tour operations started as reps or guides and worked their way up, often by accepting part-time or badly paid administrative work over the winter for the first year or two. The large tour operators employ an army of people in accountancy, personnel, marketing, brochure production, design, contracting, reservations, etc. At one time the major UK tour operators were all based in London. But when a small company set up in a village in Lancashire and grew to become the giant tour operator Airtours (now part of the troubled MyTravel Group), other companies moved out of London too.

Almost all countries now feature on the tourist map of the world, from Albania to Zambia. Formerly unvisited countries like Laos and the Central Asian Republics have opened their frontiers to tourism, and even the moon is earmarked as a future destination with some potential visitors having paid upfront already. Opportunities are legion to work in another country, and with the free movement of labour within an expanding European Union, it has become easier to cross European boundaries in the job hunt (see section *Red Tape* below).

Jobs in tourism exist for young and old, male and female, school leavers and university graduates, people of all nationalities. An ability to remain calm in the face of a crisis, crack jokes and solve practical problems knows no limits of age, nationality, gender or background. It is one of the few industries where sex discrimination is minimal. Many heads of companies are women, particularly in conference organising, and the only jobs which women don't seem to want are as coach drivers with Japanese or American clients, since lifting their enormous suitcases can be a challenge.

Opportunities exist for people working from home (see separate section *Working for Yourself*), for people who want to work part-time and for people with disabilities. For instance, being partially sighted or dyslexic may not hinder a guide. People with wheelchairs may have trouble getting insurance for jobs that require mobility and the potential need for helping to evacuate passengers, but there are suitable jobs in hotels and museums.

It doesn't matter what nationality you are. Dutch people take Australians and Americans flying around Europe; British staff look after American cruise clients in the Canaries, Germans look after Asian coach tourists in Italy, Australians and North Americans are highly prized as having the right attitude to look after trekking expeditions, etc. What matters is that you have the right kind of personality and what one tour operator calls 'stickability'.

The biggest change in recent years has been an increased demand for people with training. At one time tourism companies employed untrained people who sat at the elbow of an experienced guide or staff member until they were deemed ready to go it alone. European consumer legislation means that many companies will no long employ staff unless they have been trained (see chapter *Training*).

Standards are improving and today companies can afford to be more selective when hiring staff. Jobs for untrained people are still plentiful, but those who want to climb the career ladder should consider investing in one of the many tourism courses available that last from a few days to several years.

WHAT EMPLOYERS ARE LOOKING FOR

Anyone who enjoys looking after people, has stamina and the will to work hard under pressure has a good chance of finding work in tourism. Everyone involved with the travel industry agrees that personality is of paramount importance, and in many cases even more important than qualifications and experience. Although there are behind-the-scene roles, most travel industry employees deal with the public face-to-face, especially those who work overseas, and employers are looking for bright, enthusiastic and well-organised individuals to look after their clients. The literature from the Association of British Travel Agents (ABTA) addresses the issue of what skills and qualifications are needed and how to get them: 'It is vital that you have *or develop very quickly* a pleasant personality, presence and bearing, common sense and positive motivation' – quite a tall order in some cases.

Knowledge of a foreign language is becoming more valued, though a great many people employed in the industry are still monolingual. People who speak with a pronounced accent (regional, foreign, etc.) are not normally disadvantaged, provided they speak clearly and can be easily understood by other people.

Basic emergency first aid training, perhaps a health and hygiene certificate, plus any specialist qualifications will get you more interviews and will help you to give a better service to clients. For certain jobs a background in conservation, history, architecture or other professional qualification is more useful than general tourism training. Many attractions need local guides with specialised knowledge; for example, anyone with a background in marine biology has a good chance of being hired as a guide when they approach dive cruise firms from Queensland to Belize.

Returners (those returning to work after having children or for other reasons) and early retirers will find plenty of work. For example one firm (see entry in Directory of Travel Companies for *NSS Riviera Holidays*) runs a holiday village in the south of France staffed exclusively by mature couples. Mothers with young children can often find part-time opportunities in their local tourist organisation.

Recent years have seen a welcome and growing awareness of the damage that mass tourism can do. Groups which were once allowed to rampage through tourist destinations with no regard for the feelings of the locals or the preservation of the local environment (both natural and cultural) are being better controlled. Nowadays tourism bosses are beginning to realise that tourism has been destroying the very thing it seeks to promote, though there is still a great deal of scope for progress in this area. A more mature and sensible attitude prevails today, and applicants for many posts will be expected to show sensitivity to these issues. Anyone with a background in conservation or who can demonstrate an ability to interpret sympathetically the culture of foreign countries will have an advantage. The Association of Independent Tour Operators or AITO (www.aito.co.uk) has become active in promoting responsible tourism and the pressure group Tourism Concern is also a useful source of information on the subject (Stapleton House, 277-281 Holloway Road, London N7 8HN; 020-7133 3330; www.tourismconcern.org.uk).

Extensive travelling experience impresses prospective bosses, as in the case of Xuela Edwards who spent more than a year roaming around Europe filling temporary vacancies in hotels and other jobs. When she returned to England in the month of February, she got several interviews with tour operators, despite the lateness of her applications, on the strength of her work abroad. She ended up working as a rep for Olympic Holidays on Corfu. Carisa Fey from Germany wandered even further afield after leaving school: at eighteen she scraped a living in various catering and other jobs in London and Scotland before travelling to Mexico and South America for an extended period. She eventually returned to Stuttgart and found to her surprise that she was hired by a tour operator to work in their administrative department, a 'real' job she came to enjoy:

> *When I started out I didn't have much of an idea what I wanted to do afterwards... When I was 18 I was absolutely sure I'd never want to work in an office. But now I love my office and my computer. If I studied now it would not be music or history (dreams of the 18 year old) but business or economics (which I always thought extremely boring).*

One or two less publicised talents can come in very handy, including a talent for acting, which goes hand-in-hand with an ability to bluff. The last thing a punter wants is a dithering, angst-ridden leader. Although fluency in the language is not essential for directing holidaymakers to their accommodation, clients will expect you to speak some of the language.

REWARDS AND RISKS

The vast majority of people who turn to tourism as a career option want to meet and work with people. Many come from desk jobs and the variety and sociability of many jobs in tourism appeal strongly. Motivations for joining the industry vary from wanting simply to find a paid summer job (and tourism and hospitality are by far the greatest providers of this kind of seasonal employment), to wishing to gain experience or learn a language, to be paid to travel and work abroad, or to make a career in the world's most exciting industry, either at the beginning of their working lives or later on when a career change is called for or the stagnation of retirement needs to be avoided.

However reality doesn't always match dreams. It is necessary to think carefully about the drawbacks of the job you may be considering. Obviously the potential problems of becoming a ski guide in the Alps are completely different from those associated with leading overland trips through Africa. Yet there are some recurring issues. In the world of tourism, the client may have feet of clay, but he/she is still a god. The obligation to tolerate all sorts of obnoxious behaviour and the strain of non-stop smiling can become unendurable in some circumstances, whether coping with the incessant whinger on a cruise or the gang of lager louts in a resort. The firm of Thomas Cook runs an annual Round-the-World luxury tour and one might have expected the job of a tour manager on this month-long trip to be the kind to which any tour guide would aspire. But freelance tour director Valerie Forster expresses a different view:

Having to be sickeningly nice can take its toll very quickly

After two weeks people start to get tired and pick holes in the tour and each other. Having to look after the same group for 32 days is not my idea of fun. I really enjoy the 14 to 17 days trips when people are still expectant at the end of the tour.

Turn to the chapter on *Problems* for useful tips on how to anticipate and cope with specific problems which recur in the workaday world of tourism.

Some people do not realise to what extent the earnings of a guide or rep derive from tips and commissions. Often the non-stop smiling is not disinterested, and some people find this aspect of the job demeaning. Even worse is the pressure put on employees in certain jobs (especially reps) to sell excursions in order to boost company profits and incidentally increase their wages with commission.

Another potentially serious drawback to be taken into consideration is the discrepancy between the amount of responsibility most guides and reps must shoulder, often in very trying circumstances, and the low pay. The feeling of isolation when confronted with a problem can be daunting since, of course, you must maintain the fiction in front of the clients (whenever possible) that there are no problems. Long absences from home may sound romantic but almost always give rise to varying degrees of homesickness and can put a great deal of strain on any relationships you may have intended to preserve. On a more mundane level, the mechanics of collecting mail, doing your banking and laundry become more complicated.

Finally the insecurity of many jobs in tourism can come as a shock. Only a handful of the people taken on for the summer season (i.e. April to October) can be employed by the same company over the winter and, since summer wages are seldom enough to last for the rest of the year, an alternative has to be found. The majority of jobs in tourism, at least initially, are contract jobs, even in a year-round activity like cruising. This means that many employees in the field miss out on the benefits enjoyed by people in permanent jobs (and there is almost no union representation in the industry) and any downturn in business due to a war, hostage scare, transport strike, etc. inevitably means the overnight loss of jobs. In 2002 and 2003, Bali's tourist industry was decimated overnight after the bombing in Kuta Beach which killed more than 200 tourists. Similarly, a fever of hiring in a ski resort one year may be utterly absent the next if the snows don't fall on cue. Tourism is a fickle business.

It is not so long ago that reps working for tour operators that went bankrupt might have found themselves thrown into jail as security for debts. Today there is less chance of companies going bust, thanks to efforts by associations like ABTA in the UK and counterpart organisations in the US, Australia, etc. and their bonding scheme for members. The European Union Package Travel Directive has put the onus on tour operators to safeguard their clients' money. In the UK, it is worth enquiring about whether the employer for whom you may be considering working has an ATOL (Air Travel Organisers' Licensing) from the Civil Aviation Authority (CAA). A free leaflet about ATOL may be requested by phoning 020-7453 6488 or the information can be consulted online at www.caa.co.uk/cpg/atol/public/faq.asp; queries can be emailed to advice@cpg.org.uk.

On the other hand it is not unknown for staff in the field to be left in the lurch by dodgy tour operators. When Hannah Start spent a summer in France working for a major camping tour operator (since taken over), she was faced with a client with appendicitis and couldn't get any useful advice or support from the head office in England. Valerie Forster worked for such a company (since closed down) for 16 weeks:

I felt sorry for their clients and spent hours trying to sort out problems (and incidentally neglecting my health) because no one at head office had bothered. This was rather stupid of me, since my company had been offering cheap tours to people

who didn't care about the quality. At the end of the season, I had to threaten them
with solicitors' letters before I was paid the money owed me.

Try at all costs to avoid paying for expenses out of your own pocket, since there is no
guarantee you will be able to recoup the outlay.

The risk of outlining all the risks is that readers will be discouraged from pursuing
their idea, which is not the point at all. One of the unexpected pleasures of the job for
some people is the buzz they get from sorting out a difficult problem. Every day will be
different and in many respects you are your own boss. Although you have to work hard,
some of the clients always appreciate your efforts. One guide reports how gratifying it
was when an eight-year old on her coach tour would shush everyone up whenever she
picked up the mike and another remembers with great fondness the time she was taking
an old soldier around Europe. In the British War Cemetery near Assisi he burst into tears
when he found the grave of a comrade whom he had been told had no known grave.

Other pluses probably need no emphasis since it is the chance to travel the world, eat in
marvellous restaurants without paying, escape the drudgery of making your bed or doing
the washing up which prompted you to read this book in the first place. You can snatch
some off-duty time to swim or ski, to watch a superb sunset over the Aegean or sit in the
best seat for a performance of *Aida* at the Caracalla Baths. Even those who stay behind
in a tour operator's office or tourist board may have perks (e.g. meals in restaurants with

Clients often decide to buy their
rep a present rather than give
a tip

clients) but will also have to work long hours and weekends.

COMING HOME

Working in tourism is addictive, and once you are in, it is easy to find other jobs. However there comes a time when you may wake up in the middle of the night and not know which hotel or town or even country you are in, and furthermore not even care. Eventually people get burned out and go stale. If you find yourself agreeing with the Rev. Kilvert whose famous Victorian diary claims that 'of all noxious animals, the most noxious is the tourist', then it is time to head home, perhaps to work in the company's head office.

At some point most people in the field decide it is time to trade in the Mediterranean grapevine for the job-hunting grapevine at home which usually turns up some interesting offers. With a good CV, some administrative experience and possibly fluency in another language, you are in an excellent position to build a successful career. Tour operators, conference organisers and tourism companies need people with that kind of experience. Working back at base need not spell the end of travelling. But this time you will be in charge, fly business class instead of tourist, stay in hotels you choose and, within reason, plan where and when you want to go.

TYPES OF EMPLOYMENT

RESORT REPS

In an ideal work, working as a company rep in a foreign country gives you a unique chance to meet locals and become part of the local scene. That isn't the way it looked on the ITV fly-on-the-wall docu-soap *Club Reps* set in Playa Del Ingles in the Canaries, Europe's second largest resort. But the job is not always fuelled with drink and lust, and many have enjoyed the chance to spend a profitable season on the Med. The pay is not fantastic to put it mildly, but as your company often pays your salary into a bank account at home you are cushioned from currency fluctuations and can usually save.

The peak recruitment time starts the preceding September, though strong candidates can be interviewed as late as February. Most companies will not send anyone under the age of 21 abroad, since the responsibilities are just too great. Most employers want staff who will stay for the whole summer season April to October inclusive and normally hold back a range of bonuses and commissions to guarantee that you honour your contract.

Personality and maturity are what count most. As noted later in the relevant section, interviews can be fairly gruelling as they try to weed out the candidates who will crack under the pressure of holidaymakers' complaints and problems, or who may not cope well with the homesickness of being isolated for extended periods. It is estimated that only one in forty applicants gets a job.

The most important thing a company needs to know about new reps is whether or not they will fit in with the profile of a team. For many of the larger UK tour operators, the appropriate language comes very far down their list of priorities, even though knowledge of a European language is always requested. But even if the language requirements are not very rigorous, candidates should show that they are at least interested in learning about foreign cultures including the language. As you progress up the company ladder and are offered jobs as a senior rep or manager, then you will need to speak the local language. Reps from other European countries must be able to speak foreign languages, principally English.

A tour operator needs staff who can be flexible. Junior reps do not have any say in the resort to which they are posted, and six months in a place you hate is a very long time. Telling the tour operator you want to work in X in order to be near a partner will guarantee that you are sent to the opposite end of the Mediterranean, or not hired at all. No company wants their staff to have outside interests which might interfere with their work. Once trained in the company ways, e.g. to send in correct company paperwork, sell the company excursions and work the way the company wants, a rep can be transferred from one resort to another, sometimes one country to another, at short notice. Once you have a season or two of experience you should be given a say in where you go (a tip: try to choose a resort which does not have runway lights as this means that there will no night flights and therefore no sleepless nights). Note that it is normally necessary to work several seasons in Spanish and Greek resorts before having a chance of being sent to a long haul destination such as Florida, Thailand or India.

Reps are expected to work six or seven days a week between seven and fourteen hours every day depending on whether transfers, hotels check-ins, welcome meetings, excursions, client visits, hospital visits, etc. are scheduled. Time off is seldom enough to do much independent travelling. Most reps spend their day off catching up on sleep or flopping on a beach. The industry demands total dedication. If there is a strike and 40 clients are suddenly re-routed to another airport, you will just have to miss the party to which you had been looking forward. If there is a crisis, you could end up working up to 36 hours at a stretch, and are expected to be smiling at the end of it (even if it's your birthday).

Considering the rigours and pressures of the job of package tour company representative, wages are low, though of course accommodation, travel and some other perks are provided. The accommodation can be anything from a small dark room with only a bed and a shower to a room in a five-star hotel. Note that sometimes reps have to share accommodation with other reps. On more than one occasion male reps have been expected to share with females, but this is unusual. And the free travel may have its drawbacks too. Don't be surprised to be put on a flight that arrives in the capital at 2.30am with a connecting flight to the resort at 5.30am. Wages can be truly appalling, When Xuela Edwards was a rep on Corfu (admittedly a few years ago), a salary of £160 per month was paid into her UK bank account and was subject to deductions for National Insurance and income tax. Since your salary is usually paid in sterling into a bank account at home, be sure to take enough cash to see you through the first month and a supply of Eurocheques to give you access to your salary. Meagre wages will be supplemented with commissions from restaurants, shops and car hire as well as selling company excursions.

It is self-evident that reps looking after holidaymakers must remain aware of the consequences of giving bad advice. According to EU Package Travel regulations, the tour operator is responsible for the holidays they provide. Some companies have become so cautious in the face of possible litigation that they now prohibit their reps from recommending a local restaurant in case the punter gets food poisoning.

Obviously medical emergencies are among the most serious problems that reps may face, for instance if an elderly client has a heart attack or a young tearaway has a serious accident on a hired moped. Even worse occurred in the notorious resort of Faliraki in Rhodes in the summer of 2003 when a British teenager was murdered by a gang of other holidaymakers after a pub brawl. In emergencies the advice is normally to summon help as quickly as possible rather than to wade in, in case you make the wrong decision. Companies are much more worried about future litigation than they used to be. Yet in the opinion of at least one major insurance company, a rep who did nothing could be shown not to have offered a 'duty of care' as set out in EU regulations. For your own peace of mind, try to take a reputable lifesaving course before taking on a rep's responsibilities.

Another part of the rep's job is to look after the locals. If a small group of clients party noisily into the wee small hours, the rep is the one who has to placate the irate locals whose sleep has been disturbed. If those same troublemakers damage their apartment, the rep has to placate the villa owner and arrange compensation. In the words of journalist Sue Arnold who shadowed a company rep in Crete for a feature article, 'Amazing as it may seem, repping does not require commando training, a Berlitz language course, a St John Ambulance diploma and a background in the diplomatic service; all you need is guts... and a big smile.'

As must have become obvious by now, the life of a resort rep is not as glamorous as it may sound. An apt headline appearing in a European newspaper once read 'Fun-in-sun image belies hard graft of the tour rep.' When you're not sorting out some crisis or other, smoothing the ruffled feathers of some disappointed punter or irate local or struggling to achieve your sales target, you will be wading through your paperwork for the company. When your group implores you to join them in a tour of local night-clubs, you must have the discipline to wave them off and go upstairs to fill out the daily reports and plan for the next day. Even if you report to a resort manager, it is up to you to sort out your daily

You will need to employ all your powers of diplomacy when faced with a group of mixed ages and interests

routine.

Yet the job retains enough appeal to attract many more candidates than there are jobs. Charlotte Jakobsen, who has worked for a Danish tour operator as a rep and guide in Spain, Tenerife, Turkey and Thailand, concludes:

> *I can only recommend this job. You learn a lot, not only about the world and the people in it but also about yourself. Being a tour rep is never a holiday but very hard work, often for little pay. But also a great job. You get to travel a lot and you never do the same one day as the next.*

Like any job, it takes years of experience before most people are really good at being a rep.

New reps often have to work a one-month trial period, after which the contract can be terminated. Many tour operators provide a uniform, though there is normally a returnable deposit (say £60) for its return at the end of the season (so try not to spill red wine on it).

Commission rates for reps are very important, so pay close attention to the terms of your contract. Usually you earn a certain percentage 'on liquidation' (i.e. when the punters pay) and a bonus commission if you complete your contract. Anyone whose contract is terminated or who resigns before the end of the contract period forfeits all additional end-of-season commission payments. One rep explained the importance of being part of a good sales team:

> *At first I was embarrassed standing up to talk in front of clients, but now the other reps and I know enough to run a good double act together, with a lot of laughs. This is important. Our basic salary is very low so we need to earn commission from the sale of excursions. The team pools commission, so if I do badly, they won't be very pleased.*

Typically the rep might expect to receive 4% of income generated from excursions or local car hire plus a further 4% of sales beyond the set target, both paid at the time, plus a further 2% paid on successful completion of the contract. Do not be surprised if local taxes are deducted from these amounts. The most lucrative commission rate (say 10%) is paid for arranging local lets.

The two banes of every rep's life are sales targets and customer questionnaires. Often the questionnaires given out by tour companies to clients are crudely worded (e.g. was your rep's appearance excellent, good, adequate or poor?). The results are taken very seriously and can be soul destroying.

MEET-AND-GREET GUIDES

Meet-and-greet representatives stay in one place and accompany groups of tourists or conference-goers, often from an airport to a city-centre hotel. It is possible for temporary residents of a holiday resort, for example young people spending the summer season on a Greek island, to find this kind of transfer work with a tour operator by asking around at the local travel agencies which act as the headquarters for overseas reps. The work is intermittent and paid on a piece-work basis (which may not take into account whether the flight you are meant to meet and greet is delayed).

WORKING FOR GROUND HANDLERS

The company which looks after the clients on the ground is not normally based in the tour operator's own country but rather in the country where the holiday takes place. They service the incoming market, i.e. tours coming in to their area. The area may be defined rather broadly, and so the ground handler may be located in a third country. For example, an American group flies into Paris, tours France, Switzerland and Italy and flies home from Rome. The tour operator in the US will have contracted with a ground handler for all their European tours, who might well be based in the UK. This ground handler does not want the expense or bother of flying in tour guides from across Europe so draws their staff from people available for interview in Britain. The tour guide who is booked for the tour may well have to meet the group outside the UK, at the ground handler's expense. Therefore some of the best jobs in tourism are allocated in the ground handler's country.

Ground handling companies servicing American, Canadian, Australasian, Asian and Japanese markets are also based in the main European countries and some smaller ones like Luxembourg too. For the large segment of Scotland-only tours, ground handlers are based in Edinburgh and Glasgow. For the huge South American market, ground handlers are based in Spain and Portugal, and again they tend to interview and select local staff.

If you find yourself in a resort and would love to stay and work then it is worth approaching local ground handlers. They may be contracted by smaller operators, especially those with the more upmarket tours (which may mean the work is scarce or intermittent). Furthermore, ground handlers tend to employ locals. However if you have some experience and/or training and are persistent there is work. There may also be some last-minute work with ground handlers in resorts, usually only available to foreigners in the event of a sudden and unexpected vacancy. Therefore we have included the names and contact numbers of some ground handlers in the country-by-country guide. Note that ground handlers pay local wages that are unlikely to be less than a UK wage, however without all the attendant perks like free travel, accommodation, etc.

Ground handlers employ people on a permanent basis. Such companies need office staff who are good at administration and able to work on their own initiative. This can be extremely interesting as you have to visit the hotels and venues to find out whether they are suitable for your company's clients.

Tourism professionals working for big companies may not get to travel much as part of the job. However staff are often eligible for free or heavily subsidised trips when there is space on company flights.

TOUR PERSONNEL

The person who accompanies a group of holidaymakers on a packaged tour is variously known as tour manager, director or leader. The job title 'courier' has largely been superseded in the industry. The tour leader may be an employee of the tour operator, a freelancer or (less usually) someone who is operating (i.e. designing, marketing and leading) his or her own tour. Company employees are expected to project the company image, so someone who looks like they would win a wet T-shirt competition is unlikely to find work with Swan Hellenic and similarly an archaeological scholar need not apply to an 18-30s style tour operator like Contiki.

Officially the job of tour manager consists of representing the company, meeting and/or accompanying a group (usually on a coach), providing commentary, reconfirming accommodation and activity arrangements (which should have been put in place by the employing tour operator), helping with baggage, sorting out problems and generally creating an enjoyable atmosphere for the clients. This is quite a tall order and the scope for disaster is huge (see chapter on *Problems and How to Cope*).

The rewards are those which attract most people into the tourism business in the first place, the chance to travel, a desire to work with people and the chance to take responsibility. Many prominent members of the tourist industry started out as managers or reps as their first step on the career ladder. Recently, EU countries have tightened up on requirements and insist that personnel leading a tour have a recognised qualification. In some countries, staff have been hauled off coaches and taken to the local police station if they cannot produce a certificate. Make sure that you have an internationally recognised qualification (not just one issued by a local authority), and carry photocopies certified by the relevant Consul and translated into the language of the country you are visiting.

Although nationals of non-European countries do find work as tour managers, moving from one country to another with their groups, it is much more difficult to arrange to stay in one country because of the lack of a work permit. One possibility is to work with student groups based at a university campus.

Eventually when you have worked for one or more years as a tour manager, you can apply to become a member of the International Association of Tour Managers (IATM). Those who have completed a recognised tour manager training course may apply for Affiliate status (IATM, 397 Walworth Road, London, SE17 2AW; 020-7703 9154/fax 020-7703 0358; iatm@iatm.co.uk/ www.iatm.co.uk).

TOUR GUIDES

Someone who knows a great deal about a single town, building, museum, park or other attraction can become what is known as an on-site, local or (US only) step-on guide. This normally corresponds to the individual's field of particular interest. People passionate about anything from railways to butterflies can often find an outlet for their expertise in allying themselves to a tourist attraction. This is an excellent way to accrue experience which would be viewed favourably by any employer looking for local guides.

Guides accompany a group of people for a day or less and are normally found in big cities. (Note that it is illegal in Europe including the UK, for a coach driver to guide whilst a vehicle is moving, as is guiding whilst standing up on a vehicle.) Some countries require tour operators to book and pay for a local guide who is a national of the country. In the UK it is possible to become a Registered Guide by undertaking a rigorous training course monitored by one of the regional tourist boards (see chapter on UK). The director of any tourist information office would be able to offer advice on where to train as a local guide. Both clients and tour operators like including 'the local's inside view' and it may not be too difficult to persuade the people who design a tour that you can offer a personalised service.

Sometimes it is possible to do this on a more casual basis by making yourself known to the local excursion-organising tour operator and suggesting you could organise a specialist tour, e.g. birdwatching, local embroidery, etc. Although the official local guides won't want you to take away their work, they don't normally mind specialist walking tours, perhaps in the evening. You might also like to offer to pay commission to the local guides for suggesting your tour to their clients, which can result in a harmonious relationship with the official guides and their tour operators.

LONGER ITINERARIES

Most tour managers aspire to accompany groups on longer and more varied itineraries, at least those who don't mind the idea of staying in a different place each night and who do not suffer from motion sickness. Coach tour operators put together an itinerary, sell it through travel agencies or directly, and then employ someone to lead the tour. If you have had no training, there are companies that will take novices, but they may charge a training bond of between £200 and £400 which be non-refundable if you are considered unsuitable.

Most coach tour routes are along well-worn lines and the stop-overs, restaurant and hotel stops are long established ones. Still, the arrangements do often go wrong (the longer the tour, the more scope for hiccoughs) and it is essential that the tour manager continually check and confirm reservations. Sometimes the manager is with the same group from their point of origin; sometimes they join the group once abroad.

Much of the work for tour managers is freelance. A coach company will ask you to take a short two or three day tour. You make a success of it, and they ask you back. However, the amount of work (from Britain) is circumscribed by the coach industry's calendar. There tends to be bursts of between two and eight weeks of work with not much available between: Dutch bulb fields in April/May, Edinburgh Tattoo weekends in August, weekend shopping trips to Calais in November/December, etc., interspersed with longer tours to Austria, Italian Lakes, etc. in June/July.

The most lucrative trip is the complete European circuit (of the 'if it's Tuesday it must be Belgium' variety) when clients do not have time to organise their own excursions and are happy to sign up for those that are laid on. Experienced freelance tour guides have been known to make £400 for half a day's work in Rome or Paris, especially if they are not working with Britons (to whom it is difficult to sell anything) or Australians (who aren't in the habit of tipping).

Whatever the kind of tour you are leading, one of your main roles is as trouble-shooter. Inevitably at some point the hotel or restaurant on the itinerary will have lost the group reservation, the coach will break down, a tour member will go missing or (less drastically) his suitcase will, someone on the trip will get sick (perhaps you) and all of these problems must be dealt with efficiently and cheerfully. As we have seen in the case of resort reps, the scrapes into which holidaymakers can get are almost limitless, and may involve serious problems such as being robbed, offending local customs or even breaking local laws.

There is usually a chronic complainer whose complaints, in some cases, are justified if the itinerary has not been well worked out ahead of time. Very occasionally there is a know-it-all who makes it his or her business to catch the tour guide out on minor mistakes. There is always a bore. And on a long trip, there is no escape, unless the client is so disruptive that you undertake to remove him from the tour. Many problems can be avoided by taking a firm hand at the beginning. Lay down the rules for punctuality, seat rotation, etc. at the beginning and make sure everyone complies and understands that it is in everyone's best interests. Sometimes you must be uncharacteristically strict. For example the group may express an interest in going to see a venue which is not on the itinerary and if you agree, you will be made late for which you will (irrationally) be blamed. The only chance of surviving all this is to hear compliments from tour members who have had the time of their lives just because of you.

Your first coach commentary may not be an overwhelming success

CAMPING HOLIDAY TOUR OPERATORS

UK camping holiday operators hire very large numbers of people with language skills to remain on one family campsite on the Continent for several months. The Eurocamp Group alone recruits about 1,500 campsite couriers and children's couriers. These companies provide self-drive, self-catering holidaymakers with fully-equipped tents and mobile homes. The courier's job is to greet clients and deal with difficulties (particularly illness or car breakdowns), clean the tents and caravans between visitors and introduce clients to the attractions of the locality or even arrange and host social functions and amuse the children. All of this will be rewarded with on average £90-£100 a week in addition to free tent accommodation and travel to the site for those who complete their contracts). The season lasts from March to October, though some companies offer half-season contracts. Setting up and dismantling the campsites in March/April and September/October (*montage* and *démontage*) is often done by a separate team. This work is hard but the language requirements are nil.

CAMPSITE COURIERS

The advantages of the job of campsite courier are that you meet lots of people, are continually in a holiday atmosphere, get to know one area really well, improve your language skills and often manage to cultivate an enviable tan and a higher level of fitness into the bargain. Successful couriers make the job look easy, but it does demand a lot of hard work and patience. It can often be tedious and frustrating to have to clean out six family-sized tents in 90 degree weather or hang around all day waiting for just one family to arrive. Occasionally it is very hard to keep up the happy, smiling, never-ruffled courier look.

However most seem to end up enjoying the job and find their fellow couriers lively and congenial company. Alison Cooper described her job on a site in Corsica as immensely enjoyable, though it was not as easy as the clients thought:

Living on a campsite in high season had one or two drawbacks: the toilets and showers were dirty, with constant queues, the water was freezing cold, the campsite was very noisy and if you're unfortunate enough to have your tent in sunlight, it turns into a tropical greenhouse. Of course we did get difficult customers who complained for a variety of reasons: they wanted to be nearer to the beach, off the main road, in a cooler tent with more grass around it, etc. etc. But mostly our customers were friendly and we soon discovered that the friendlier we were to them, the cleaner they left their tents.

I found it difficult at first to get used to living, eating, working and socialising with the other two couriers 24 hours a day. But we all got on quite well and had a good time, unlike at a neighbouring campsite where the couriers hated each other. Our campsite had a swimming pool and direct beach access, though nightlife was limited. The one disco did get very repetitive.

Despite all this, she highly recommends that people who have never travelled or worked abroad before apply to a company like Eurocamp which provides accommodation, a guaranteed weekly wage (normally paid into a UK bank account) and the chance to work with like-minded people. Although the wages are not high, customers often leave food and drink behind and invite couriers to join them for meals.

Caroline Nicholls' problems at a campsite in Brittany included frequent power failures, blocked loos and leaking tents:

Every time there was a steady downpour, one of the tents developed a leak, and I would appear, mop in hand, with cries of 'I don't understand. This has never happened before.' Working as a courier would be a good grounding for an acting career.

She goes on to say that despite enjoying the company of the client families, she was glad to have the use of a camp bicycle to escape the insular life on the campsite every so often. Some companies guarantee one day off-site which is considered essential for maintaining sanity. The companies do vary in the conditions of work and some offer much better support than others. For example a company for which Hannah Start worked ignored her pleas for advice and assistance when one of her clients had appendicitis.

SUPERVISORS

All these couriers need area supervisors, which is a challenging role for which a week's training is arguably not enough. Area supervisors are sent out to their respective regions of Europe with a couple of 'squaddies' (who are drivers as well as tent erectors) to welcome couriers as they arrive. One supervisor is in charge of up to 30 couriers. Often it is a race against time as pre-season preparations can be hampered by bad weather, late

"I can't understand it; this has never happened before"

Campsite couriers have to contend with frequent floods in the tents, power cuts and 'blocked' loos

deliveries, temperamental campsite owners and general exhaustion.

Once all the sites are up and running, the supervisor visits each in turn every 10-14 days to sort out problems, deliver equipment (a never-ending chore), butter up the local campsite owners, etc. The closing down of the site at the end of the season is much more relaxed though harder work as there are usually fewer people left to help. Despite all the problems, Jayne Nash had a great season with Canvas:

> *Overall is was a great experience living and working the holiday spirit. At times things were dire but this was compensated for by the good times. I had an amazing summer living in a tent in the orchard of a chateau. It is definitely not a job for the faint-hearted: be prepared for accidents, deaths, robberies, floods and storms that whisk tents away. Have a solution to everything or at least be willing to try anything.*

Supervisors are paid a salary plus bonus, modest daily living allowance and given the use of a vehicle. Winter opportunities are few. The major campsite operators may be able to offer a job in the office, but probably at a lower salary.

APPLYING

Most of the major camping holiday and tour operators based in Britain begin recruitment in November and have finished most of their interviewing by the end of February or even January. But there is a very high dropout rate (over 50%) and vacancies are filled from a reserve list, so it is worth ringing around the companies as late as April for cancellations. Despite keen competition, anyone who has studied a European language and has an outgoing personality stands a good chance if he or she applies early and widely enough. Although the majority of couriers are aged 18 to 25, the big companies are keen to receive applications from mature applicants including couples. According to Carla Mitchell, not having too posh an accent helps when applying to companies based in the North; with her Surrey accent, she was given a job without too much 'client profile'.

Most companies provide a few days of training in the destination country before starting work.

DIRECTORY REFERENCES

For camping holiday tour operators based in the UK which operate in a range of European countries, see: Camping Life, Canvas Holidays, Club Cantabrica, Eurocamp, Haven Europe, Keycamp Holidays, Solaire Holidays and Venue Holidays.

Other companies operate in one country only (mainly France) and are listed in the relevant country chapter.

ACTIVITY HOLIDAYS

Many specialist tour companies employ leaders and reps to run their programmes of hiking (such as Ramblers Holidays, 2 Church Rd, Welwyn Garden City, Herts AL8 6PT; 01707 381133; www.ramblersholidays.co.uk), canoeing holidays (see *Headwater Holidays*), sailing flotillas (see *Sunsail*) or cycling holidays (see relevant entries in the Directory such as *Susi Madron's Cycling for Softies*).

Outdoor activity centres are another major employer of summer staff, both general domestic staff and sports instructors. One of the biggest is *PGL Travel* which recruit for about 2,500 seasonal vacancies at their holiday centres mainly in Britain and France, primarily for activity instructors, group leaders and support staff. The norm seems to be to pay low wages but to allow lots of free time and access to all the holiday facilities. The basic weekly rate of pay is £60, with higher rates being paid to those who hold certain qualifications.

CHILDREN'S CAMPS

The practice of sending children to summer camps used to be uniquely North American. However, the idea is catching on in Europe and large numbers of young people are needed to work on these camps, such as *Village Camps* which hire a range of staff for their camps in Switzerland, Austria and elsewhere. For detailed information about becoming a counsellor at an American summer camp, see the chapter on the USA. Anyone who has a connection with the YMCA-YWCA should enquire about international summer camp possibilities.

SPORTS INSTRUCTORS

Any competent sailor, canoeist, diver, climber, rider, etc. with relevant instructor's certificates should have no difficulty marketing his or her skills either at home or overseas. Do not apply for an instructor's job unless you have the proper qualifications and know what to do in the event of an emergency. Association initials are printed in brackets after the sport (and if you don't know what the initials stand for should you really be looking after kids taking part in these sports?)

Finding amusements which will appeal to children of all ages can be tricky

Many local colleges run courses in outdoor leisure including sports instruction, for example Bicton College (East Budleigh, Devon EX9 7BY; 01395 564200; www.bicton.ac.uk) which offers a range of courses such as the NVQ in Adventurous Activity Leadership, and Reaseheath College (Reaseheath, Nantwich, Cheshire CW5 6DF; 01270 625131; www.reaseheath.ac.uk). The Institute of Leisure and Amenity Management (01491 874800; www.ilam.co.uk) distributes information about the various qualifications and where to obtain them.

The Youth Hostels Association can advise on short courses around the country. For example, it is possible to train in Winter Hillwalking and Winter Mountaineering at weekend courses in the Lake District which costs £134; contact Summitreks, 14 Yewdale Road, Coniston, Cumbria LA21 8DU (www.summitreks.co.uk) for details.

Qualified divers and guide/leaders can find work in a range of exotic locations from the Philippines to Eilat in Israel, Queensland to Belize. The American PADI system of certification is more familiar than the one used by the British Sub-Aqua Club. Wages in developing countries would be subsistence levels, but the pleasures of the job for divers are enormous.

The following are the governing bodies of major sports which oversee qualifications in the UK: send an s.a.e. for more information.

Amateur Swimming Association, 41 Granby St, Loughborough LE11 3DU (01509 264357; www.britishswimming.org)

British Canoe Union, John Dudderidge House, Adbolton Lane, West Bridgford, Nottingham NG2 5AS (0115 982 1100; www.bcu.org.uk). The BCU Level 2 Coach Award is recognised by the Department of Education as the minimum standard for instructors.

British Horse Society, Stoneleigh Deer Park, Kenilworth, Warwickshire CV8 2XZ (08701 202244; www.bhs.org.uk).

British Mountaineering Council, 177-179 Burton Road, Manchester M20 2BB (0870 010 4878; www.thebmc.co.uk). The representative body for climbers can provide details of instructing courses. The basic qualification is the MLTB Single Pitch Supervisors Award.

British Association of Snowsport Instructors (BASI), Glenmore, Aviemore, Inverness-shire PH22 1QU (01479 861717; www.basi.org.uk). BASI runs training and grading courses for potential ski and snowboard instructors.

British Snowboard Association, First Floor, Hillend, Biggar Road, Midlothian EH10 7EF (0131-445 2428; www.thebsa.org). Snowboarding is the fastest growing sport in Europe.

British Sub-Aqua Club, Telford's Quay, South Pier Road, Ellesmere Port, Cheshire CH65 4FL (0151-350 6200; www.bsac.com).

Royal Yachting Association, Romsey Road, Eastleigh, Hants. SO50 9YA (0845 345 0400; www.rya.org.uk). Instructor qualifications available in sailing, windsurfing and motor cruising.

SAILING

Flotilla sailing refers to a fleet of yachts which set off together, usually sailed by the holidaymakers but under the guidance of a lead boat with skipper, engineer and hosts. The concept started in Europe but has now caught on in the Caribbean as well. Boats go out exploring the local area, meeting up in the evenings for barbecues and restaurant meals. Skippers need the RYA Yachtmaster qualification or equivalent experience. The engineer needs knowledge of diesel engines, electrics and pumps, ropes and rigging. Hostesses must be personable, good at organising and (often) able to cook.

The chartering business is booming in holiday resorts and many are owned by companies or individuals who need crew, hostesses and cooks. Pauline Power, an experienced sailor from Ireland, noticed a beautiful four-masted tall ship called *Sea Cloud* while she was in the Canaries. *Sea Cloud* is the world's largest private yacht with 3,000 square metres of sail which sails around the Mediterranean every summer and the Caribbean in the winter. When Pauline later applied to work for the charter ship, she was given one of the 80 contracts. Similarly Perry Morton from the States was so smitten by the vessel when he saw it moored in Livorno harbour that he asked to go aboard and was hired on the spot as a deck hand. Pay is negligible but tips can be good. (Perry stayed on to study for his Mate's ticket and is now Third Officer.)

Take copies of any sailing certificates when you go job-hunting or, if possible, a letter from a boat owner saying you are a useful crew member. Ask around when you are in a marina. Harbour masters can often tell you if there are yachts looking for crew.

SKI RESORTS

Skiing and all the employment it generates is by no means confined to the Alps. There are skiing centres from Geilo in Central Norway to Mount Hermon in Israel, from the Cairngorms of Scotland to dormant volcanoes of New Zealand. And there are many ski resorts in North America, in addition to the most famous ones such as Banff in the Canadian Rockies, or Aspen in Colorado. The standard ski season in Europe and North America is roughly Christmas until late April, whereas in the southern hemisphere (the Australian and New Zealand Alps, Chilean Andes), it lasts from late June until early October. Between Christmas and the New Year is a terrifically busy time in European ski resorts, as are the middle two weeks of February during half-term.

Reps working for ski tour operators tend to be skiers themselves though this is not a requirement. Often tact is more important than athletic skill, especially when snow conditions are less than ideal. The rep who tells a group of clients on the way from the airport that the resort has no snow, and ski cannon have been banned so there isn't any artificial snow either, is not doing their job well. It will be up to the rep to give a sympathetic explanation of the reasons for the ban, how the local farming community can't survive without alpine pastures, which won't develop properly if buried under artificial snow, and so on. And then to get the group enthused about all the other sports and activities they can indulge in instead.

Winter tourism offers some variations on the usual theme of reps and tour guides, hotels and catering. Staff are needed to operate the ski tows and lifts, to be in charge of chalets, to patrol the slopes, to file, wax and mend hired skis, to groom and shovel snow, and of course to instruct would-be skiers. If you are lucky you might get a kitchen or dining room job in an establishment which does not serve lunch (since all the guests are out on the slopes). This means that you might have up to six hours free in the middle of the day for skiing, though three to four hours is more usual. However the hours in some large ski resort hotels are the same as in any hotel, i.e. eight to ten hours split up inconveniently throughout the day, and you should be prepared to have only one day off per week for skiing. Because jobs in ski resorts are so popular, wages can be low, though you should get the statutory minimum in Switzerland (see chapter). Many employees are (or become) avid skiers and in their view it is recompense enough to have easy access to the slopes during their time off.

Snowboarding has become the fastest growing sport in the world, and anyone able to instruct this activity will find themselves in demand from the European Alps to New Zealand. Snowboard instructor courses are offered on dry ski slopes in the UK and on the Kaprun Glacier in Austria.

Either you can try to fix up a job with a British-based ski tour company before you leave (which has more security but lower wages and tends to isolate you in an English-speaking ghetto), or you can look for work on the spot.

SKI TOUR OPERATORS

In the spring preceding the winter season in which you want to work, ask all the ski tour companies whose addresses you can find for an application form. Their literature will describe the range of positions they wish to fill. These may vary slightly from company to company but will probably include resort representatives (who must be bilingual), chalet girls (described below), cleaners, qualified cooks, odd jobbers and ski guides/instructors. An increasing number of companies are offering nanny and crèche facilities, so this is a further possibility for women with a childcare background. Most staff have been hired by mid-June, though there are always last minute cancellations.

Among the many ski tour operators listed in the Directory of Tour Operators, the following are among the key players: Free Radicals, Ski Staff and Jobs in the Alps are all agencies working for a range of employers, plus companies such as Esprit Holidays, First Choice Ski Lakes & Mountains, Inghams, Neilson, Scott Dunn Ski, Ski World and Total Ski. There are dozens of others. Some have a limited number of vacancies which they can fill from a list of people who have worked for them during the summer season or have been personally recommended by former employees. So you should not be too disappointed if you are initially unsuccessful.

The new edition of *Working in Ski Resorts* (Vacation Work, £11.95) contains many other addresses of ski companies and details of the job hunt in individual European and North American resorts. In response to the thousands of enquiries about alpine jobs that the Ski Club of Great Britain receives, it distributes 'The Alpine Employment Fact Sheet'; send £3 and an s.a.e. to the Ski Club GB, 57-63 Church Rd, Wimbledon SW19 5SB; 0845 45 80783; www.skiclub.co.uk). The Club also takes on intermediate skiers over the age of 22 with extensive experience of on- and off-piste skiing to work as ski reps in 43 European and North American resorts. Ski reps work for between one and three months after doing a two-week training course in Tignes in December (which costs £1,000 including airfares).

You can meet representatives from many ski companies by attending the *Daily Mail* Ski & Snowboard Show held in late October at Olympia in London where some ski companies actually hand out job descriptions and applications. For a thorough list of ski resorts in Europe, consult the *Good Skiing Guide* in a bookshop. Some major ski resorts are listed in the chart below.

> **Rhona Stannage and her husband Stuart applied to all the companies they could find addresses for:**
>
> *Only one company (Skibound) gave us an interview. No one else would touch us because we were too old (i.e. 28), married and had no experience in the catering trade. Skibound gave us both jobs as chalet girls (yes, Stuart signed a 'chalet girl' contract) working in a four-person chalet with a manageress and a qualified chef. The wages were as expected (dire) but we got free ski passes, accommodation in our own apartment and food. Stuart was a bit worried about the uniform but it was only a purple T-shirt.*

CHALET STAFF

Many of the ski tour operators active in France and Switzerland accommodate their clients in chalets which are looked after by a chalet girl or boy (but usually the former).

"I don't eat meat and I'm allergic to vegetables"

Dietary restrictions must be given due consideration.

The chalet maid does everything (sometimes with an assistant) from cooking first-class meals for the ten or so guests, to clearing the snow from the footpath (or delegating that job). She is responsible for keeping the chalet clean, preparing breakfast, packed lunches, tea and dinner, providing ice and advice, and generally keeping everybody happy.

Although this sounds an impossible regimen, many chalet girls manage to fit in several hours of skiing in the middle of each day. The standards of cookery skills required vary from company to company depending on the degree of luxury (i.e. the price) of the holidays. Whereas some advertise good home cooking, others offer cordon bleu cookery every night of the week (except the one night which the chalet girl has off). In most cases, you will have to cook a trial meal for the tour company before being accepted for the job.

Pandora Balchin, who got a job as a chalet maid on the strength of her catering degree, described her job this way:

It was a fantastic experience though it was very hard work. Although I had never skied before I went, I have to admit that I am now completely hooked, as are all the others who worked there. The spirit of comradeship in the resort was amazing, and also typical of other resorts I'm told.

The pay will be from £75 per week, with lots of perks. Obviously your accommodation and food are free. Also you should get a season's ticket to the slopes and lifts (called an *abonnement* and worth several hundred pounds) and free ski hire. Recruitment of the 1,000+ chalet hosts needed in Europe gets underway in May so early application is essential.

SKI RESORTS WORLDWIDE

If you do end up in a resort looking for a job, try the ski equipment hire shops which may offer you very short term work on change-over days when lots of skis need prompt attention, or the ski-lift offices preferably in the autumn. You might even find that the tourist office in the big resorts like Zermatt and Val d'Isère may be able to help. Outside the EU you will encounter work permit difficulties (details in individual country chapters), though when there is a labour shortage, there is usually a way round the difficulties. Unfortunately the drifting population looking for jobs in ski resorts can be much greater in one area than the number of jobs available. You should therefore try as hard as you can to sign a contract ahead of time.

SKI RESORTS AROUND THE WORLD			
France	*Switzerland*	*Austria*	*Italy*
Chamonix	Davos	Kitzbühel	Cortina d'Ampezzo
Les Contamines	St.Moritz	Söll	Courmayeur
Val d'Isère	Zermatt	Lech	Sestriere
Courchevel	Gstaad	Badgastein	Bormio
Méribel	Klosters	St Anton	Campitello
St Christoph	Villars	Mayrhofen	Canazei
Flaine	Wengen & Mürren	Kaprun	Livigno
Avoriaz	Crans-Montana	Alpbach	Abetone
Les Arcs	Kandersteg	Brand	Corvara
La Plagne	Adelboden	Kirchberg	Selva
Tignes	Verbier	St Johann	Sauze d'Oulx
Montgenèvre	Grindelwald	Solden	Asiago
	Arosa	Obergurgl	S Stefano di Cadore

	Saas Fee	Zell am See	Alleghi
Spain	***Germany***	***Norway***	***Scotland***
Sol y Nieve	Garmisch-	Voss	Aviemore
Formigal	Partenkirchen	Geilo	Glenshee (Glenisla)
Cerler	Oberstdorf	Telemark	Carrbridge
	Berchtesgaden	Lillehammer	Glencoe
Andorra		Gausdal	
Arinsal		Synnfjell	***Finnish Lapland***
Soldeu			Levi
Pas de la Casa			Ylläs
New Zealand	***Australia***	***Canada***	***USA***
Queenstown	Falls Creek (VIC)	Banff	Aspen, Colorado
Coronet Peak	Mount Hotham	Lake Louise	Copper Mountain
Mount Hutt	Mount Buffalo	Waterton	Steamboat Springs
Mount Ruapehu	Baw Baw	Ottawa	Vail
	Mount Buller	Huntsville	Breckenridge
Bulgaria	Thredbo (NSW)	Collingwood	Alpine Meadows, CA
Borovets	Perisher	Barrie	Lake Tahoe
	Mount Field (Tas)		Mt Batchelor, OR
Romania	Ben Lomond		Mount Hood
Poiana Brasov			Aleyska, AK
			Park City, UT
			Sun Valley, ID
			Jackson Hole, WY
			Big Mountain, MO
			Waterville Valley, NH
			Stowe, VT
			Killington, VT
			Dore Mountain, NY

OVERLAND EXPEDITION LEADERS

While the participants on long-haul overland trips are paying at least £100 a week for the chance to visit safari parks, drive across sand dunes and shop for weird and wonderful vegetables in exotic markets, their leader/driver is being paid up to £150 for the same pleasures. The only difference is that he or she, along with one other crew member, will be responsible for keeping about 18 paying passengers as happy as possible.

Adventure travel companies which conduct small groups around the continents of Africa, Asia and the Americas require leader/drivers to escort these tours which last between three and 28 weeks. Most of the major overland companies are looking for experienced travellers with proven mechanical skills and of course good people skills. Other useful attributes include a knowledge of French (for Africa) or Spanish/Portuguese (for Latin America) and a first aid certificate. Most will consider only candidates who have a Passenger Carrying Vehicle (PCV) licence or a Heavy Goods Vehicle (HGV) licence. Most experienced drivers need five to seven days of tuition from a specialist driver training centre (at a cost of hundreds of pounds) before trying the PCV test. People without a specialist licence or knowledge of mechanics may be able to find a support position such as cook or tour leader.

Most companies use Mercedes or Bedford trucks which have been stripped and rebuilt to their specifications to withstand rugged transcontinental trips. The cooking is usually done communally and nights are spent in campsites or in modest rest houses, normally along a well worn overlanders' trail. Many of these trips are not as off the beaten track as the clients fondly imagine. If a vehicle breaks down in the Sahara, the head of an urchin usually pops up over a sand dune within 30 seconds.

There will be one or two crew members (often the second is a trainee) who have to contend with vehicle breakdowns, border crossings, attempted black market money exchanges and awkward social dynamics. One old hand, writing in the *Traveller* magazine published by WEXAS, claims that to be a good tour leader you have to be 'a cross between a Butlins redcoat and Scott of the Antarctic'. According to Brett Archer, who spent eight months in Africa as an expedition leader, one of the worst trials is coping with the chronic whinger (who in his experience, is usually a calculator-wielding female from New Zealand). Like all tour work, the job is unremitting but with the added challenges of dealing with sometimes frustrating bureaucracy in emergent Africa and difficult terrain over a much longer period of time. Most aspiring expedition leaders feel daunted to say the least at the prospect of being in charge of 20 adventure-seekers in the middle of the African bush or the Amazon rainforest.

Procedures vary for choosing and training leaders. Requirements vary but normally expedition leaders must be at least 23. After getting past the interview stage, the tour leader without extensive first-hand knowledge of the continent to be toured is usually invited to join a training trip of six to twelve weeks at their expense (at least several hundred pounds) with no guarantee of work at the end. If successful, however, this money is generally returned after completion of an agreed term of work.

Training for driver/mechanics usually includes time in the company's vehicle

There's always a whinger, usually a middle-aged woman with a calculator

workshop. Trainee leaders with some companies are paid a small weekly allowance in sterling though the pay is negligible considering how arduous the training can be. All incidental expenses such as visas, passports, air tickets, etc. are paid for as well as your contribution to the food kitty.

APPLYING

Competent expedition staff are greatly in demand by the many overland companies and youth travel specialists based in London and the southeast which advertise regularly in the London magazine for the Australasian community *TNT* published every Monday. (Distribution boxes can be found in selected locations thoughout London, e.g. outside travel agencies, tube stations, certain pubs around Earls Court, etc.). Specialist travel agencies such as Trailfinders (42-50 Earls Court Road, London W8 6EJ) act as agents for the major operators. Study the brochures carefully and attend the informal video evenings which many of them hold to get a feel for the company and the kind of back-up they are likely to offer to their staff (which varies significantly between companies).

Most of the main operators have entries in the Directory of Tour Operators: Dragoman/ Encounter, Exodus, Explore Worldwide, The Imaginative Traveller, Journey Latin America and Kumuka. Companies that specialise in Africa are listed in that chapter. Many smaller companies also need to employ tour leaders from time to time. For other companies, see the directory of tour operators maintained by Overland Expedition Resources (www.go-overland.com). It is worth checking their websites since some carry information on tour leader and/or driver recruitment. All UK employers are looking for staff who have the right to work in the UK/EU.

Note also that if you have the required skills, it is possible to fill a vacancy on-the-spot. While travelling the length of Africa, J. M. Rapp noticed that all the overland companies in East Africa were looking for mechanics to be drivers.

CRUISE SHIPS

Despite international unrest causing a downturn in tourism worldwide, the cruise line business continues to boom. It is estimated that the cruise industry will be hiring 35,000 new people over the next five years. More than 30 new cruise ships are under construction at the present time and at the beginning of 2004 it was the fastest growing sector within the worldwide tourist industry. Every cruise ship requires a full range of staff, just as a fancy hotel does. Most recruitment takes place through agencies or 'concessionaires', all of whom say that they are looking only for qualified and experienced staff. But in many cases it is sufficient to be over 21 and have an extrovert personality and plenty of stamina for the very long hours of work on board.

Job-seekers with no experience or specialised skills should be wary of agencies that invite them to pay a fee to circulate their CV on-line; this may well work for the highly qualified but there are probably far more people looking for work than there are employers looking for staff this way. Websites to try are: Sea Cruise Enterprises (www.seacruiseent.com), Blue Seas International Seafarers Exchange (www.jobxchange.com) which costs $39 to join and Ocean Crews Maritime Employment (www.maritimeemployment.com). The privately run site www.ucs.mun.ca/~rklein/cruise.html calls itself a no frills page of cruise lines and cruise links, and it is possible to find contact details of cruise lines and concessionaires here. Another useful list of links can be found in the Cruise Lines section of www.jobmonkey.com. Most cruise line websites feature an Employment icon which will set out how you should apply, e.g. Disney's site http://disney.go.com/disneycruise/ jobs/welcome.html advises phoning the dedicated Jobline 407-566-SHIP, and for

Radisson Seven Seas Cruises log on to www.rssc.com/employment/employment.cfm.

> **According to Jane Roberts, who crossed the Atlantic from Venezuela to Estonia as a cruise line croupier, not all employees are experienced professionals:**
> *I worked in the casino department of four different cruise ships and met many people doing jobs as waiters, bar tenders, stewards and stewardesses. These jobs are very easy to come by. In fact 80% of all crew members are people who have never done that particular job in their lives. The turn-over of staff is high, even when people sign year-long contracts, since few people complete them. It is difficult to live and work with the same people 24 hours a day. Crew don't get days off, perhaps just the odd breakfast or lunch off once a month. Patience levels have to be extremely high, since people who take holidays on cruise ships seem to think that they own the damn ship. Having to be sickeningly nice can take its toll very quickly.*

Contract lengths (some as short as four months) and conditions vary from ship to ship. Typically, crew are contracted for nine months and then get six weeks holiday. Wages are usually US$350-$500 a month but can be increased with tips or commission.

Some UK and European agencies that have advertised for cruise line staff in the past year include:

Crewships, V-Ships, Skypark, 8 Elliot Place, Glasgow G3 8EP (0141-243-2435; francoi se.reis@vships.com; www.vships.com).

Cruise Service Center Ltd, Palme & Associates, 2 Duke St, Northampton NN1 3BA (01295 701450; www.cruiseservicecenter.com). Recruits middle and senior hotel management and service staff year round.

CTI Group London, 207/209 Regent St, London W1R 7DD (020-7734 9412; www.cti-usa.com). Official recruiters of catering staff for Carnival, Celebrity, Crystal and Disney Cruise Lines. Head office is in Fort Lauderdale Florida: 3696 North Federal Highway, Suite 303, Fort Lauderdale, FL 33308-6262; ctigroup@cti-usa.com).

Grapevine International Cruiseline Recruitment, www.grapevine-int.co.uk. Specialist recruiter (andrea@grapevine-int.co.uk) based in Barcelona.

International Cruise Management Ag A/S, PO Box 95, (Jernbanetorget 4B), Sentrum, 0101 Oslo, Norway (+47 23 35 79 00; office@icma.no; www.icma.no). Recruits staff with 2-3 years experience for four luxury vessels (Crystal Cruises). More than 1,700 people hired each year out of 12,000 applicants.

Openwide International Ltd, 7 Westmoreland House, Cumberland Park, London NW10 6RE (020-8962 3400; www.openwideinternational.com). Recruits entertainers and performers to work on cruise ships in the Mediterranean and Caribbean.

Princess Cruises, UK recruitment via P&O Cruises Ltd., Richmond House, Terminus Terrace, Southampton SO14 3PN (recruitment@pocruises.com). North American recruitment via corporate office: Att. Employment, Building 5, Floor 2, 24844 Avenue Rockefeller, Santa Clarita, CA 91355 (careers@princesscruises.com). Information about seasonal jobs can be found at www.princessjobs.com.

Seefar Associates, 7 Berkeley Crescent, Gravesend, Kent DA12 2AH (01474 329990; seefarassociates@btclick.com). Hire casino and other staff for Disney Cruise Line, Festival Cruise Line, Royal Caribbean and Celebrity Cruise Lines.

Ads for professional hotel and catering staff for cruise lines appear in the specialist press like *The Caterer* and *Hotel Keeper.* Specialist catering agencies like VIP International (17 Charing Cross Road, London WC2H 0EP; 020-7930 0541; vip@vipinternational.co.uk) supply experienced catering, management and other personnel for various cruise lines.

A plethora of books and websites provide a starting point for anyone interested in working on a cruise ship, e.g. *Working on Cruise Ships* by Sandra Bow (Vacation-Work, £10.99). If you do not have time to explore the internet, you can ask for seven pages of hard information to be faxed to you by contacting the Cruise Ship Information Group in the UK; dial 09060 700701 from the handset of a fax machine and the information will be faxed by return which will cost about £3 on your phone bill.

Do not be misled by advertisements which read 'Cruise Ships are Hiring Now' or websites with names like shipjobs or cruiselinejobs. These are almost always placed by someone trying to sell a book about employment on cruise ships, and these are of varying quality. The *World Wide Cruise Ship and Yachting Career Guide* from Innovative Cruise Services (36 Midlothian Drive, Glasgow G41 3QU; 0141-649 8644/fax 0141-636 1016; i nfo@cruiseservices.co.uk/ www.cruiseservices.co.uk) costs £30/$55/€55 which includes two years' access to Newsletters containing vacancy lists.

RANGE OF JOBS

Musicians, medics and masseurs are all employed by cruise lines. However the largest number of personnel work in catering, dining room and bar services, as cabin stewards, assistant pursers and shop personnel. Croupiers and beauticians, nannies and entertainers are all in demand. In many cases it does not take long to acquire enough land-based experience in a casino, restaurant, hotel or shop to make your CV more attractive to hiring agents, particularly if you are free to travel at very short notice. It is not unusual for a long silence after an interview to be broken by a phone call asking whether you can meet a ship in the Caribbean in less than a week.

On the majority of ships there are three categories of employee and this hierarchy creates a marked class system: officer, staff and crew. Officers (from fourth pursers

To escape their minute cabins, cruise ship crew repair to the bar, where they unwisely over-indulge even in choppy seas

up) are free to make use of all ship facilities and enjoy superior living quarters. 'Staff' consist of shop staff, hairdressers, beauticians and casino staff. The lowest rung is 'crew' whose leisure activities are severely circumscribed and whose living quarters are often little better than grim, four sharing a small cabin in the noisiest dirtiest part of the ship. Often the only recourse is to the crew bar where the (duty-free) drink is very cheap and employees are tempted to overindulge, especially unwise when the seas are choppy.

Anyone who wants to become a croupier needs to be at least 18 years of age with no criminal record. It takes one or two months to train with a casino and obtain a licence from the Gaming Board of Britain, preferably for both blackjack and roulette. Casino companies normally offer in-house training.

Those who are interested in work as a deck engineer might make enquiries about the training available from Clyde Marine Training Ltd (209 Govan Road, Glasgow G51 1HJ; 0141-427 6655; www.clydemarine.com).

Because of the claustrophobic nature of on-board conditions for staff, the crew's social life is of critical importance, and most people (at least the types who get hired for the job) relish the party atmosphere. Kathleen Ager sums up the experience of working in the catering department of a clipper operated by Windjammer Barefoot Cruises in the Caribbean:

> *The ship, not being as stable as larger ones, was thrown about on long passages and on the first day nine-tenths of the passengers were extremely sick and it was impossible to set tables without things being thrown off again. I sometimes found I'd been working 16 hours non-stop. Our cruises were interrupted by strikes and riots on one island which had just become independent. But we had to keep the customers relaxed and happy despite the trouble. Altogether the work was very hard and poorly paid but I stuck it out for four months and have never been so miserable as I was when I left that ship. It really was a great experience and the mainly West Indian crew were all like my brothers.*

TRANSPORT PERSONNEL

AIRLINES

Scheduled airlines are constantly recruiting new staff from the thousands of unsolicited applications for the position of cabin crew that they receive. Every airport has a list of the airlines operating out of that airport, so contact the one to which you have easiest access. At one time, airlines hired only young people as cabin crew and compelled them to retire at an early age. That is no longer permitted, though older candidates will have more difficulty being hired in the first place. Most airlines have a career structure and it is possible to progress through the ranks to purser and flight supervisor, or join the ground administrative team that organises each flight. Passenger service agents to work at the airports and of course telephone sales agents are needed for the reservation office. All airlines undertake their own intensive cabin crew training programme which concentrates on onboard safety and covers first aid, health and hygiene as well as cabin service (see *Training: Airlines* section).

Charter airlines often need cabin crew on a seasonal basis, for example at the time of writing (2004) First Choice Airways (formerly Air 2000) was recruiting cabin staff to work out of its bases at London Gatwick, Manchester, Belfast, Birmingham, Bristol, Cardiff, Dublin, Glasgow, East Midlands and Stansted. The astonishing explosion in no frills airlines has created thousands of new jobs. For information about employment with

Luton-based easyjet, check their website www.easyjet.com/en/jobs. A brand new Luton-based airline that may need staff in the future is Now Airlines (jobs@now-airlines.com). Meanwhile the newly launched budget Polish carrier Wizz Air might be recruiting (www.wizzair.com/jobs/wizz).

Competition for jobs as flight crew (pilots) is intense. Some airlines will train you, but most entrants come already trained by the military or privately (flying courses are cheaper in the US than in Europe).

For a thoroughgoing examination of employment in this sector see the newly published book *Working in Aviation* from Vacation Work Publications (£10.99).

COACHES

There are more than 3,000 touring coach companies in the UK, over 6,000 in Germany and thousands more in France, Italy, the Netherlands, etc. To contact coach companies look in the Yellow Pages or the weekly *Coach and Bus Week* (01733 264666; www.cbwnet.co.uk) which also publishes *The Coach and Bus Guide* for £25 which lists all major UK companies. (Similar publications are available for other countries.)

A handful of coach companies train drivers but most accept only drivers who have had at least a year's bus or coach experience. EU qualifications are recognised in all countries, but there may be extra requirements, for example coach drivers working for German companies must have a first aid certificate. Some coach companies try to ask their drivers to work as driver/couriers, i.e. giving commentaries as they drive. As noted elsewhere this is illegal under the Conduct of Drivers Regulations which say 'a driver shall not, when a vehicle is in motion, speak to any person either directly or by means of a microphone'.

Since the tachograph was introduced (a clock which records how many hours a driver works) conditions have improved for drivers. There are still some cowboy companies around, but the better ones (particularly on the Continent) insist in their contracts with operators that the driver be given a single room with bath and, in the longer term, pension and other rights.

Part of the driver's job is to keep the coach clean, to wash down the outside and tidy the inside. If the coach has a loo, it is the driver's responsibility to clean and empty it, and therefore it is not unknown for drivers to hang up a sign 'Toilet out of use' to avoid this chore.

THE CHANNEL TUNNEL

The most glamorous jobs on European railways are with Eurostar which operates a rail service London (Waterloo) to Paris (Gare du Nord) in three hours and London to Brussels in a quarter of an hour longer. Eventually there are plans to run eight trains an hour (four in each direction) which will obviously generate many new jobs both on the trains and at the stations. Each train carries approximately 30 staff to look after up to 800 passengers. Train managers, catering staff and receptionists are needed at the arrival stations. The primary requirement is a good knowledge of a second language. Each train needs bilingual staff: a driver plus train managers and on-board service staff. They join a crew operating out of one of the three stations but can transfer to one of the others if they wish to change their base.

Train managers are on board to look after all passengers, especially disabled passengers, to help with connections and answer queries about onward travel. They must also be able to take over from the driver in an emergency. Their station-based counterparts in customer services work at Waterloo, the Gare du Nord and Brussels Midi marshalling and assisting passengers. Eurostar welcomes applications from anyone who can speak French, Japanese or another European language as well as English and who has experience of working with the public. Eurostar has its own language laboratory, but new recruits must be linguists. Their training programme includes courses on group travel psychology, emergency and first aid and cultural awareness.

Enquiries should be sent to the Human Resources Department (human.resources@e urostar.co.uk). Eurostar carry out much of their recruitment online through web-based recruiters like workthing.com.

FERRIES

Contrary to some predictions, the opening of the Channel Tunnel did not spell doom to the ferry companies that operate between England and France. Job opportunities exist on that route and also on ferries that ply the Irish Sea, the North Sea and around the Scottish islands. The expected range of service staff and, increasingly, child carers is needed by the ferry companies on a seasonal basis between April and September with a very much reduced staff over the winter.

> **According to Rhiannon Bryant, who spent a year working as a stewardess for P&O Ferries, the essential quality being sought at interview was a smile:**
> *Applying for a stewardess post on the ferries proved relatively easy. I sent my CV to a recruitment company in January and was invited to a group interview at Southampton. I was offered a place within a week, and was requested to attend various training sessions at my own expense, including basic sea survival in Poole and fire fighting in Portsmouth. This was followed by a day's on-board induction where behaviour is monitored. A couple of 'lads' who were confident that their jobs were secure were never seen again after larking around (possibly thrown overboard!)*

Rhiannon began her job on the last day of March and after a week of moving between jobs (main lounge, cafeteria, restaurant and cabins) was assigned her summer location, the shops. A further advantage was that few shoppers ventured to the shops when feeling seasick so (unlike the children's play areas) there was less cleaning to do. The abolition of duty-free advantage has dented the volume of retail business, however bored passengers still like to shop.

Depending on what company you work for, you may be working seven days or 14 days on, followed by seven days off. It is not unusual to work over 100 hours in those seven days on duty. The work is exhausting but it is reassuring to know that a full week's rest and relaxation is in the offing, which makes the experience completely different from working on a cruise ship. And the work is much more seasonal than cruise ship work. Even if you are kept on into October, your job may disappear at any time. Of the hundreds of temporary employees placed that year by the ferry recruitment specialist, Quest Marine Services, Rhiannon was only one of five who stayed on for the winter. Another difference which Rhiannon mentioned was that alcohol was forbidden by P&O.

As with all offshore work it is possible, though difficult, to reclaim tax. Permanent ferry staff can be given an official printout of sailing times by the purser's office, though it is wise to keep your own records for the purser to authorise. It is sensible to ask your local tax office what information and documents they will need.

When looking for a job, do not ignore the obvious of asking in Jobcentres in port towns. Here are the main operators between Britain and the Continent:

Eurotunnel, PO Box 302, Folkestone, Kent CT19 4QZ (01303 282175; www3.eurotunnel.com). See Recruitment icon on website.

Brittany Ferries UK Ltd, Brittany Centre, Wharf Road, Portsmouth PO2 8RU (www.brittany-ferries.com). Note that recruitment for onboard vacancies is in France or at least in French. The company has operations in Plymouth, Poole and Portsmouth and any vacancies are posted on the website. For example the Plymouth centre needs seasonal check-in staff (Training Manager, Millbay, Plymouth PL1 3EW).

Caledonian MacBrayne Ltd, The Ferry Terminal, Gourock, Renfrewshire PA19 1QP (01475 650100; www.calmac.co.uk)

Hoverspeed Ltd. Human Resources, International Hoverport, Dover, Kent CT17 9TG (0870 460 7474 for Recruitment Team; www.hoverspeed.com). See entry in Directory of Employers.

P&O Ferries, Richmond House, Terminus Terrace, Southampton, Hants. SO14 3PN (recruitment@pocruises.com; ww8.poferries.com)

Stena Sealink, 08704 006798 (www7.stenaline.co.uk)

HOTELS & CATERING

The hotel and catering industry is often treated separately from the tourist industry, and certainly the training for both is very distinct. Yet its primary function is to provide tourists with accommodation and (to a lesser degree) food, and so it is worth considering the range of employment available in what is often referred to (especially in North America) as the hospitality industry.

The marked hierarchy among hotel staff is most noticeable in large hotel complexes or resorts with the manager, administration, chef, maitre d'hotel and housekeeper at the top of their particular pecking order and the busboys, laundry staff and bell-hops at the bottom. Of course the majority of hotels are too small to support such a staff and you may find yourself hired as a 'general assistant' in a small family-run hotel which means doing everything from washing dishes to checking in guests.

OPPORTUNITIES FOR PEOPLE WITH QUALIFICATIONS

Qualified people in the field of hotels and catering have a great deal of mobility since good cooks and managers are needed throughout the world. Making contact with a range of hotels or restaurants from any appropriate directory or guidebook may well produce results, especially if the applicant can write in (and speak) the appropriate language. General guidance is available from the Hotel & Catering International Management Association (HCIMA, Trinity Court, 34 West St, Sutton, Surrey SM1 1SH; 020-8661 4900; www.hcima.org.uk). For some specialist recruitment agencies, see the chapter *Finding a Job: Recruitment Agencies.*

Although many luxury hotels belong to worldwide chains (Best Western, Hilton, Holiday Inn, Hyatt, Sheraton, etc.), most hiring is done independently by each hotel. The number of employees is staggering, for example the Hyatt Corporation (200 W Madison, Chicago, IL 60606) alone employs nearly 100,000 people worldwide. Some hotel groups operate management training programmes, especially in the US where trainees are recruited from universities.

Hotel and catering students may be able to take advantage of various exchanges which are run to provide training in other countries whether through EU-funded bodies or otherwise. For example, see the chapter on the US for details of the Hospitality Tourism Exchange Programme administered by CIEE (www.ciee.org). The Association for International Practical Training (10400 Little Patuxent Parkway, Suite 250, Columbia, Maryland 21044-3510, USA) runs a Hotel/Culinary Exchange programme with Australia, Austria, Germany, Finland, France, Ireland, Japan, Malaysia, Netherlands, Switzerland and the UK.

The American Hotel & Lodging Association's *Educational Institute* (see Directory of Training Courses) can send professional job-seekers a short list called 'Employment, Placement, Recruitment & Search Firms' which are primarily executive search firms operating at a very high level. For example the Yours in Travel Group with offices in several US cities is one of the largest travel and hospitality industry recruitment agencies for the US, placing directors and managers in all hotel departments across 50 states as well as 4 continents (www.yoursintravel.com).

OTHER TYPES OF EMPLOYMENT

CONFERENCES AND EVENTS

Full-time organisers known as PCOs (Professional Conference Organisers) are employed as well as freelance staff to manage congresses, seminars, exhibitions, outdoor events, etc. The PCO will promote the conference, take bookings from delegates, liaise with the venue, possibly organise accommodation and menus, book speakers, arrange a spouse programme, and look after many other aspects of the meeting. Information technology skills and a highly professional demeanour are essential. The Association for Conferences and Events (ACE, Riverside House, High St, Huntingdon PE29 3SG; www.martex.co.uk/ace) offers students a reduced membership fee which gives access to potentially useful job contacts.

TOURIST OFFICES

Tourist Information Centres normally employ local people who have a proven ability to communicate, preferably in more than one language. Experience in marketing, PR, administration, media work or advertising is useful. More than 500 TICs are scattered throughout the UK in places of visitor importance. Some are seasonal, some operate year round, and range in size from a small kiosk to high street shop frontage. Fired with enthusiasm, Mark waited for his first customer, only to be asked where the toilets were (apparently the most popular question). The other standard questions are where is the best place to eat or the best hotel, questions TIC staff are not permitted to answer, since they must not show favouritism. However there are lots of other problems that need solving, some of the most interesting of which come from locals. Otherwise the job consists primarily of replenishing the racks of literature (free leaflets always seem to walk out the door), selling books, booking beds and so on. Applications should be made to your local Regional Tourist Board's Personnel Department.

NATIONAL PARKS

With a growing awareness that the world's natural resources need better management, more people are being employed all the time to manage them and their visitors. Within this sector there are full-time jobs in management, plus the legal, planning, press and promotional departments, as well as jobs for wardens, trail guides, stewards, park attendants and shop staff. The basic requirement is a love of the outdoor life and a willingness to be outside in all weathers (more a consideration in the Peak District than Western Australia).

LEISURE CENTRES AND THEME PARKS

Theme parks, visitor attractions, museums and sports centres are normally considered part of the leisure business, though again distinctions are hard to draw. A day trip to a theme park is a leisure visit, whereas a visit by people who have rented accommodation on-site or in the neighbourhood is considered tourism. The great theme parks of the United States and Europe create a huge demand for labour which cannot be filled by local people. Some American amusement parks employ up to 3,000 staff, and *Disneyland Paris* employs 12,000 in total. For information on specific theme parks, see the country chapters.

Leisure centres are an expanding market, both individual sites and those developed in conjunction with a hotel. Sports qualifications are often necessary for advancement up the career path. The magazine and website of *Leisure Management* (Portmill House, Portmill Lane, Hitchin, Herts. SG5 1DJ; www.leisuremanagement.co.uk) contains a good selection of job ads; a student subscription costs £20 per year.

TRAVEL AGENCIES

In this era of on-line booking, you might have expected to see travel agencies closing left, right and centre. In fact they have been facing hard times of late, but still their trade paper *Travel Weekly* carries plenty of job and specialist recruitment ads. Many people are attracted to the idea of working in a travel agency to 'meet people' when what they really mean is that they would like to look after people on holiday, i.e. a rep's work. Most trainee positions in agencies are geared to school leavers who work on an apprenticeship scheme combining college and on-the-spot training (see *Training* chapter).

Business travel houses offer better pay, but of course competition for jobs is fiercer. Some business travel agents work in-house in big companies. A good knowledge of geography and professional approach are essential.

CASUAL WORK

Tourism creates a wealth of opportunities for casual work, both directly and indirectly. Your average tourist wants someone to sell him ice cream on the beach or croissants in his ski chalet, someone to mend the roof of his holiday villa before the season begins, someone to look after his children on a campsite, to sell him a souvenir sachet of Ardeche lavender or a Texan 10-gallon hat, to entertain him at the local disco or teach him to windsurf. His wife wants to keep up appearances so a freelance hairdresser's services are very welcome. And so it could continue. The point is that casual jobs usually proliferate in tourist centres.

The seasonal nature of tourism often discourages a stable working population, and so hotel and campsite proprietors, resort and hostel managers, etc. are often forced to employ people from outside the vicinity during the busy season. Also, many tourist destinations are in remote places where there is no local pool of labour. Travellers have ended up working in some of the most beautiful corners of the world from the South Island of New Zealand to Lapland.

Of course there are also many opportunities at the budget end of tourism, in travellers' hostels and so on. Dustie Hickey describes the way she went about getting a job in the Avignon Youth Hostel:

I checked out all the hostels in Avignon and found someone to help me write a letter in French. Then I telephoned because I did not get a reply. The hostel could not promise me any work till they met me. Before I left the farm in Brittany where I was working, I telephoned again to remind them I was on my way. When I arrived, the hostel was very busy. For free B & B, I just had to keep the dormitory clean, but I pitched in and helped with cleaning, laundry, breakfast, etc. The manager was pleased and gave me a little money. At the end of July the paid assistant left so I was given her job, and eventually I had a room to myself.

Many private travellers' hostels worldwide from the Greek islands to the Mexican mountains employ long-stay residents to act as PR reps at railway and bus stations, trying to persuade new arrivals to patronise their hostel. A free bed is always given and usually a small fee per successful 'convert'.

Even with the increasing value of a training qualification, the industry still respects somebody who has actually gone out into the world of work and experienced the trials and tribulations of tourism for themselves. Dealing with holiday-makers, solving unforseen problems, and working busy, unsociable hours, are all vital aspects of training in themselves. A summer doing a casual job can often benefit the CV of someone trying to break into a career in tourism.

PUBS AND CLUBS

Bars and night clubs should be included in any list of likely employers. Some globetrotters even carry a set of 'black and whites' (black trousers/skirt and white shirt) in case they pick up a job as a bartender or waiter. If you have no experience, it can be worthwhile volunteering to work at your local pub before you leave home for a week and then ask for a reference. Once you are abroad, ask at English style pubs which are found from the Costa del Sol to the Zamalek district of Cairo, from Santa Monica California to Austrian ski resorts and try to exploit the British connection. Irish people are at an even greater advantage since there is a Guinness pub around most corners of the world. In ordinary bars on the Continent you may be expected to be proficient in the prevailing language, although exceptions are made, particularly in the case of glamorous-looking applicants. Girls can find jobs from Amsterdam to Hong Kong, but should be sure that they can distinguish between bars and brothels.

Places like the Canaries, Ibiza, Corfu and the Caribbean islands are bursting at the seams with 'nite spots' of one kind or another. Not only is there a high turn-over of staff but there is a rapid turn-over of clubs too, and you may not have much job security. As long as you investigate the establishments in the place you want to work before accepting a job, you should not encounter too many unpleasant surprises. Handing out promotional leaflets for bars and discos is a job which travellers frequently do, especially in Spain.

SPECIAL EVENTS

Great bursts of tourist activity take place around annual festivals, major sporting events like the Grand Prix races, trade fairs and World Fairs. For example, the Oktoberfest in Munich takes place each year during the last two weeks of September and you should be able to get a few days or weeks of work either helping to set up the facilities or to dismantle them. It is not possible for an event to host over 6 million visitors without a great deal of extra labour being enlisted to prepare the 560,000 barbecued chickens, 346,000 pairs of sausages and to dispense the 1,000,000 gallons of beer consumed. Or you may be able to offer a peripheral service. At least one enterprising mechanic with tools and spare parts has made a killing in the car park at Oktoberfest, fixing and adjusting the thousands of travel-weary vans and cars which congregate annually. The main problem with this sort of work is that affordable accommodation will be very difficult to find.

CASUAL WORK IN HOTELS

Assuming you have not fixed up a season's work in a hotel or restaurant through the approved methods (see *Hotels and Catering*), it is very possible to find such work once you've arrived in a foreign country. All but the most desperate hoteliers are far more willing to consider a candidate who is standing there in the flesh than one who writes a letter out of the blue.

If you secure a hotel job without speaking the language of the country and lacking relevant experience, you will probably be placed at the bottom of the pecking order, e.g. in the laundry or washing dishes. Some hotels might confuse you by using fancy terms for menial jobs, for example 'valet runner' for collector-of-dirty-laundry or 'kitchen porter' for *plongeur*.

Reception and bar jobs are usually the most sought after and highly paid. However the lowly jobs have their saving graces. The usual hours of chamber staff (7am-2pm) allow plenty of free time. Some people prefer not to deal with guests (particularly if they are shaky in the language) and are happy to get on at their own speed with the job of room cleaning, laundering or vegetable chopping. The job of night porter can be excellently suited to an avid reader since there is often very little to do except let in the occasional late arrival.

Even the job of dish-washer, stereotyped as the most lowly of all jobs with visions of the down and out George Orwell as a *plongeur* washing dishes in a Paris café, should not be dismissed too easily. Nick Langley enjoyed life far more as a dish-washer in Munich than as a civil servant in Britain. Simon Canning saved enough money in five months of working as a dish-washer in an Amsterdam office block to fund a trip across Asia. Benjamin Fry spent a highly enjoyable two weeks washing dishes at the Land's End Hotel in Alaska and earned more per hour than he ever had in England.

When you are asking door-to-door at hotels, it is often a good idea to show up bright and early (about 8am) to impress prospective employers. Perseverance is necessary, especially midway through the season. It also might be necessary to return to the same hotel several times if you think there's a glimmer of hope. Kathryn Halliwell described her job hunt in Les Gets in the Haute Savoie of France:

I had to ask from hotel to hotel for three days before finding the job, and experienced what I have come to know through experience and others' reports is the normal way to hire a casual worker. The boss told me blankly that he had no work. As I was leaving he said, what sort of work? I told him anything. He said I could come back the next day in case something came up. I did and was told he was out, come again tomorrow. I eventually did get the job and realised he had just been testing my attitude as he had every other employee when they first applied.

When going door to door, you should start with the biggest hotels. Try to get past the receptionist to ask the manager personally. If you are offered a position (either in person or in writing) try to get a signed contract setting out clearly the hours, salary and conditions of work. If this is not possible, you should at least discuss these issues with the boss.

Another way to get a foothold in a resort is to cultivate the acquaintance of the reps from the big travel firms. Not only will they know of immediate openings, but they can establish your position with local hoteliers who normally know and respect the reps. This is a job-finding ploy which has to be used with care since reps are constantly being asked for favours. You might volunteer to help them, meeting a group or standing in for someone who is ill. Lisa Brophy from Australia got to know a British rep in an Austrian ski resort who soon introduced her to a restaurant manager with a staff vacancy.

Although Kathryn Halliwell was forced to share a windowless room which had an intermittently working light and water streaming down the roof beams into constantly overflowing buckets, she still enjoyed her time working at a hotel in Corsica, simply because of the conviviality of her 'fellow sufferers'.

Hotels represent just one aspect of the tourist trade, and there are many more interesting venues for cooking and serving, including luxury yachts, resorts, holiday ranches, safari camps and ski chalets. Railway stations and airports often have catering outlets which employ casual labour at busy times.

FAST FOOD RESTAURANTS

People with a background in catering often find it easier to transfer their skills to other countries than people with no relevant training or experience. Yet there are opportunities for the unskilled. You might find a job cooking hamburgers in a chain such as McDonalds or Burger King, which can be found from Tel Aviv to Toronto. Anyone who is not confident communicating in the language of the country can still hope for employment in a fast food kitchen. Pay is low, hours unreliable or inconvenient and the attitude to discipline more worthy of school children, however it is a good way of earning while you familiarise yourself with a new place and are in a position to move onto something better. When you are applying for jobs like this, which are not seasonal, you should stress that you intend to work for an indefinite period, make a career of fast food catering, etc. In fact staff turnover is usually very high. This will also aid your case when you are obliged to badger them to give you extra hours.

GLAMOROUS JOBS

The object of this book is to present a realistic picture of working in tourism. Therefore considerable space is devoted to puncturing illusions about the sun and fun image of working abroad in tourism. And yet cruising the world's oceans or crossing continents in a converted jeep are exciting and glamorous occupations, and a great many people would swap their office job any day for the unpredictability and variety of many jobs in the tourist industry.

People at a senior level, whether as chefs or conference organisers, may well get to move in glamorous circles; people working in incentive or upmarket tourism may have a chance to stay at some of the world's top hotels or go into some of the least visited corners of the world. Senior jobs in tour operations often involve familiarisation trips, familiarly called 'fam' trips, to inspect new destinations and work out the logistics. It may be hard work – assessing a dozen hotels in a day, checking the facilities thoroughly, dining with the agent, making notes about the restaurant, filling out reports, etc. – but it does make a change from working in the office. The new emphasis on responsible tourism has created new and interesting jobs like the one Rory has. He works as a conservation officer for a major tour operator, which involves monitoring the practices of the hotels used by his employer. Now the company uses recycled paper for its brochures, issues turtle watch leaflets to clients holidaying in Florida and is generally on the lookout for ways to help the environment.

The exciting and glamorous jobs do not come to the newcomer but to those who have made tourism their profession. A sample career structure is demonstrated by Bob Crossey who took a training course for tour guides. He speaks Norwegian, but at first found that this wasn't much help to him. His course finished in December, and he found work for two weekends before Christmas taking coach groups over the Channel on Christmas shopping trips. The Winter Olympics were due to take place in Norway, and he was provisionally booked by a British operator. A week before the job was due to start, Bob was told that due to lack of bookings his services would not be required after all. Meanwhile he had been making scores of phone calls and things suddenly looked up when coach companies began phoning him with offers of tours: OAPs to Bournemouth, weekends in Paris, London theatre weekends and so on. Bob found that he was getting regular work from three different companies. One paid well, but there was no opportunity to make commission on excursions; another paid badly but offered lots of lucrative excursions, and the third company had a short season to Norway which gave Bob the chance to use his Norwegian and show off the superb scenery to appreciative passengers.

At the end of the summer season Bob took out his diary and tried to make the companies book him up in advance so he knew what was happening. Although it was not possible to confirm bookings for the entire year, he was offered work month by month instead of day to day, so he began to see a pattern developing. Two years after completing his course, he is well satisfied. He has been all over Europe and one of his companies was so pleased that they offered him three coach tours through the Canadian Rockies. Bob loved these, but finds that long-haul trips take a lot out of you, and reckons to do no more than four a year, preferring to stay in the UK and Europe the rest of the time.

If you want to stay in one place there is glamorous work at the top level for registered guides. Kathleen is employed by the Foreign Office to meet guests of the British Government at the airport, take them around, look after them at lunch, introduce them to their hosts, interpret on official visits and be present at formal dinners. Eventually Kathleen was offered a promotion, to work in Brussels where she does a similar job with better pay and a small staff to help her. In jobs like these, you get to stay in lovely country house hotels, occupy the best seats at the opera or theatre (though one gets blasé about seeing the latest smash hit for the tenth time) and travel in chauffeur-driven limousines.

If you want to be a chalet girl with a difference try working as an assistant to the Chatelaine or *jeune fille* at the Chateau de Saran in France. Owned by Moet et Chandon Champagne, this is where important visitors from pop stars to politicians are entertained. You have to be able to speak impeccable French and talk about art, history or topics of the day, know how to arrange flowers and have an extensive smart wardrobe (something different for breakfast, lunch, tennis and dinner). The pay is about £120 a week for working from 9am-3am. As a past *jeune fille* says, 'it was a once-in-a-lifetime job, but you couldn't go on burning the candle at both ends for too long.'

Several small companies specialise in taking visitors to stay in castles and manor houses. The doyen of such companies is Take-a-Guide which has a team of personable staff who are good drivers and knowledgeable guides. They meet and look after clients, most of whom are wealthy and cultivated Americans, even ex-presidents and their families (whose visits are supposed to be secret, though there is little chance of this given how many secret servicemen come in their wake). The guides have to be experts at mugging up information, since each visitor's particular interests have to be catered for. One guide said, 'no sooner had I become an expert on Elizabethan embroidery than the next client had come to London to buy an Apostle spoon, so I had to make the acquaintance of silver dealers'.

Hotel booking/representation agencies in most major cities employ people to inspect hotels and look after the administration. Tired of being an interpreter at exhibitions and then a guide, Barbara Wenger de Po joined the company Leading Hotels of the World, an agency that represents exactly what its name suggests. After working briefly in their London office, Barbara was sent to France and Germany to visit the hotels which belonged to the consortium such as the Ritz Hotel and Le Bristol in Paris and Schloss Fuschl in Austria. She now runs the Spanish office and heads a team of staff who visit companies and travel agencies to promote their hotels. She is constantly on the go, flying to the States, organising smart dinners during exhibitions and speaking to the media, including doing the occasional television interview.

Smaller hotel marketing consortia such as Grand Heritage Hotels specialise in a specific style of upmarket hotel.

People at the top of their profession have to be able to take the high life in their stride. Chris has a company which looks after the top horse riders when they compete in international events, supplying everything from horse boxes to hotel rooms for the riders (who can be more temperamental than the horses). Drinking tea in the sumptuous Ritz Hotel in Paris, Chris broke off to phone his wife to ask her to take his dinner jacket to the cleaners since he would be needing it the next day when he and his group would be in Windsor and were invited to have dinner with Prince Philip.

Similarly Valerie, who started out by taking overnight coaches to Italy, has been to Buckingham Palace (and not just when it is open to the public), met French Presidents and maybe an American one too, though he was so surrounded by bodyguards she couldn't be sure whose hand she shook. She now organises VIP receptions for CIPs (Commercially Important Persons) who are guests of top manufacturers. During events like the Paris Air Show she may stay in a suite in the exclusive Crillon Hotel which has to be booked and kept in readiness for any unexpected clients. She is often involved in organising programmes for the spouses of conference delegates where she might organise a private lunch in a stately home with the owner taking the guests around afterwards or other themed lunches and visits, the most popular of which seems to be when she books a restaurant and gets the chef to give a demonstration cookery lesson.

Anyone with certain skills may have the chance to transfer them to exotic locations and glamorous settings. Just about any job in tourism has a glamorous side; even an over-stressed rep on a Greek island can take time out to admire a beautiful sunset or share a bottle of wine and a joke with friends on a taverna terrace, which beats a pizza in a rain-soaked town back home any day. Or as your coach climbs up into the Austrian Alps and your group sits back silent in admiration, you think how lucky you are to be paid to do this. There can be a tremendous amount of job satisfaction, from the game park warden who manages to get his group in exactly the right place to see wild animals at play to guiding children around little-known areas of London. There is satisfaction in nurturing a new hotel so that it becomes a favourite with clients, and helps the local economy by providing jobs. And if you like driving you can be paid to do this in some of the world's most beautiful scenery as a coach driver. There are always exciting moments in the tourist industry.

Even Saudi discos can go on into the wee small hours

DJS & ENTERTAINERS

The idea that Britons know their way round the music scene better than other nationalities is fairly widespread, and anyone who knows how to use a turntable has a chance of finding work abroad as a DJ. Experienced DJs who want to work abroad should request details from a specialist agency like Juliana's Leisure Services (15/17 Broadway, West Ealing, London W13 9DA; 020-8567 6765; www.julianas.com) which also has an office in Dubai. This company supplies entertainment packages to 5-star hotels and other clients especially in the Middle East and Asia.

Entertainers are also in demand abroad in a variety of roles for the tourist industry, from the actors who dress up in period costume at museums, like the London Museum of Transport to musicians in Spanish resorts. See the entries for *Resident Entertainers* and *Excellent Entertainment* in the Directory of Recruitment Agencies for information about the training courses they provide.

WORKING FOR YOURSELF/FREELANCE

As many as a third of tourism companies operate from home. Many famous companies, especially specialist tour operators, started out using the kitchen table. Until you have tested the market for an unusual tour from birdwatching to white water rafting, you don't know if it is going to work. If a recession hits small businesses, having a rent-free office makes sense, provided you are disciplined enough to settle down to a working day in your home. Loneliness is seldom a problem since in the tourism industry it is necessary to get out and about, visiting sites, venues and going on familiarisation trips.

Small companies that offer services for the tourist industry from meet and greet services at ports and airports, translations and brochure design, training courses, coach brokering, etc. are often home-based. Working from home has advantages for many people, including working mothers. Betty thought that if she worked from home (arranging homestays for visiting student groups) she could look after the 'unexpected' twins. Fat chance. She soon discovered that it did not make for a professional approach if a little voice could be heard in the background, 'Mummy, mummy, I need a wee' and the children were too major a distraction. So she sorted out childcare for four hours a day, and switched on the answering machine for the rest of the time.

Although most people who work for themselves do so in their home communities, it is also possible to work in an independent capacity abroad. Long-term residents who can speak authoritatively about the area and the local culture may well be preferred as guides to locals.

CONFERENCES

Conferences are held all over the world, at conference centres, hotels, universities, sports centres, etc. and many need people to supplement the programme for accompanying family members. If you want to find out about freelance work in the conference, meetings and events industry which includes exhibitions, outdoor events such as pop concerts and incentive travel, then the relevant source of information is ACE (Association for Conferences and Events, Riverside House, High St, Huntingdon PE29 3SG; 01480 457595; ace@martex.co.uk). Because they are inundated with enquiries about this 'glamorous' section of tourism, they only reply to queries from ACE members. The current student fee is £41. ACE publish a Suppliers' Directory in which you can be listed if your service is appropriate. Their *Buyer's Guide* costs £14.99.

Networking can be carried out at the World Travel Market in November in London (which in 2003 moved from Earl's Court to ExCel in Docklands). Another possibility for networking is the Meetings and Incentive Travel Show at Olympia in October. Those interested in working for an incentive company or at an exhibition should consult the *Hollis Directory* (see below).

RUNNING YOUR OWN TOURS

If you have money and/or time and/or expertise to invest there are plenty of opportunities in tourism, provided that you go about it in a sensible fashion. The fastest expanding tour market is for specialist tours from battlefield tours (which were started by ex-Army officer Tony Holt) to visits connected with hobbies such as gardens, railways, etc. To take one example, Jim had been in the Navy and travelled much of the world. He and his wife had frequently hosted visiting VIPs and their families. They had enjoyed organising tours for these visitors and thought they would like to do this professionally when he retired. His service gratuity set him up with a small office, paid for him and Betty to take a course in business admin skills and one in tour guiding, and also to join ACE. At their first ACE meeting they met a PCO who was organising a conference for 1,000 midwives in London, and wanted someone to set up a programme for the accompanying spouses. Jim and his wife produced a programme and asked a tour operator (a fellow member of the local tourist board) to advise on costings and details like coach parking. After a few hiccups, their first programme went well and now they run a small but successful business offering similar programmes for conferences in the UK and in places where they served in the Navy such as Malta, where they use a local agent as ground handler.

Anyone with a novel idea for a tour should try to interest the local tourism authorities or conference organisers with it. Judy is a registered guide who began to feel angry with the way visitors were thrust onto the same milk-run tours, all visiting the same places at the same time. Talking to a conference organiser at a Tourist Board function, she was asked to put up a proposal and three months later heard out of the blue that the conference organiser liked her idea (of a day out at a herb garden with a talk by the gardener and lunch with the owner) and wanted Judy to organise it for twelve people (conference spouses). The day was a big success and she now has a thriving business. She belongs to ACE and the Tourist Board, so uses both their logos on her headed paper to inspire confidence in enquirers.

To start your own small company, the basic tools of the trade are a telephone, computer and fax machine. Word processors and faxes are only as good as their helplines, so be sure to invest in one which offers a good back-up service on their PhD equipment (Push here, Dummy). Be careful about giving out your fax number. Junk fax mail has become a menace and you may find your machine blocked by useless 'special offers'. The same caution applies to E-mail.

While companies have advertising budgets, one-man companies cannot afford this luxury. Networking backed up by efficiency seems to be the recipe for success. Try to meet as many relevant people as possible often at official functions like promotion evenings, Association get-togethers, Tourist Board functions, etc.If you are organising a highly unusual tour, try approaching the editors of relevant publications to persuade them to print a feature story or small announcement. *Willings Press Guide* in any library contains the addresses of about 10,000 magazines and newspapers.

Magazines and trade journals can help by sparking off ideas. In particular look at *Group Travel Leisure* (from 9 Vermont Place, Tongwell, Milton Keynes MK15 8JA) which is aimed at the small tourism tour operator and is a mine of useful information. ACE has its own monthly magazine and also a *Job Spot* newsletter with information about functions (often free) where it is possible to make contacts. Subscribe to specialist magazines to find out well in advance about forthcoming sports matches, races and other events which might interest local clubs. Company directories can be very useful when trying to make relevant contacts or to market your services. In particular, look at the *Hollis Directory* which lists the PR contacts of thousands of companies. The cost is £145 but out-of-date copies are sometimes available for less (ring 020-8977 7711; www.hollis-pr.com).

As mentioned in the section on Tour Personnel, there can be lulls in the working year. Bob fills these by organising short trips through his local pub, e.g. a trip on Eurostar, a kid's day out at half term. The publican helps to promote about four of these trips a year. It was hard work at the beginning, with one trip making a loss but Bob decided to go ahead with it for the sake of publicity. Now pub regulars are confident in the arrangements and are happy to book well in advance, which helps with cash flow.

Apart from pubs, any clubs or societies are a good place to look for groups of clients, especially if you can tailor the tour to their interest whether it is art and antiques, history, flower arranging, beekeeping, tiddlywinks or any of a thousand others. If you are going to offer tours to sporting events, then membership of your local golf, tennis, football club is important. It doesn't matter if you don't play or take part. They will be especially keen to welcome you if you undertake to give back a portion of your profits.

If you are uncertain about what kind of coach to book for your tour, you can seek advice from the Coach Tourism Council (www.coachtourismcouncil.co.uk). On the whole, you get what you pay for, so beware an operator who undercuts. When choosing, visit the garage and see if it seems clean and efficient. Have seats been crammed in at the expense of legroom? Do the coaches have headrest covers and footrests? Do the drivers wear uniforms? Do they give commentaries? (This is against the law, but the driver may try to do this to get a tip; a giveaway is the position of the microphone.) Do you really need a toilet (which can get smelly) if there are going to be frequent stops?

INVESTING IN PROPERTY ABROAD

Mature people who, for whatever reason, want to change career or return to the workforce and have a substantial amount of money to invest might want to consider running a holiday villa or upmarket B & B. If thinking of investing in a villa, chalet or *gite*, you should do thorough market research (thinking of different seasonal possibilities, whether there is access to an annual festival, etc.), become a member of every tourist board and association that might be able to give information and go and stay at a similar property owned by expatriates to find out how it's done. Suitable training for such a business venture might include a health and hygiene certificate, a cookery course and a marketing and business administration course such as those run by tourist boards.

Today business people who are used to staying in hotels are looking for somewhere different when they go on holiday, and have taken enthusiastically to the chalet or villa holiday. However the accommodation has to meet very high standards of comfort and luxury, preferably with extra features like nannies and gourmet meals.

It is essential to start in an area that will welcome you. At present Bulgaria, Romania and Albania are all welcoming investment in small-scale tourist operations from campsites to luxury hotels. The cultural attractions of painted churches in Moldavia, wildlife attractions in the Danube Delta and the monastic heritage of Bulgaria are largely unknown, mostly because of the shortage of decent accommodation in these regions. Yet there are some beautiful old houses and farms which could be converted with skilled local labour (thereby providing much needed employment). The upmarket specialist tour operators are all keeping an eye on these countries but are waiting until there is enough accommodation of a high enough standard. Anyone with money to invest should consult the appropriate embassy.

The Savoie in France is an area in which foreigners have invested heavily (see chapter on *France*) and where the local *communes* are only too happy for foreigners to reclaim derelict farmers' cottages. Many of these take paying guests for winter sports, rent out their properties in the summer and welcome paying guests. One British couple say:

> *In these parts many houses still have outdoor loos and animals winter on the ground floor. But we have been pleased with the local services. The plumber and builders come at the time they say they will (we can't understand the problems Peter Mayle had with his Provencal builders). There are few local restrictions; you are simply expected not to do anything your neighbours won't like. There is nothing much that can't be sorted out over a glass or two.*

Once you settle on a property you have to place a deposit of 10% after which there is no backing out. It is essential to enlist the services of a good local accountant and solicitor.

People who own sizeable properties in the Alps can try to let them out to British chalet ski tour operators for the winter season. Nick Lunn does this and grosses £21,000 for the five-month season.

It helps to have a unique selling point. For example an exclusive hotel called the Sea Club (71-563310) integrates guests and English-speaking locals around a huge dining table. To publicise your property it is a good idea not only to become a member of the local tourist board but also to join ACE which makes networking with potential clients much easier.

TRAINING

THE VALUE OF QUALIFICATIONS

It is not essential to have a qualification to work in the tourism industry, but with today's consumer protection legislation, companies find that many of the jobs that used to be offered to students for the summer are better filled by people who have had training. There is a widespread recognition that the tourist industry would benefit from a better trained workforce. Training to become a representative, for example, can be as short as two weeks; but if the grounding is good, this training will help you to get a job and then to do it well. Fiona Groutage, Resourcing Manager for Tui UK in 2004, says 'we like people who have invested in themselves', i.e. shown their seriousness about the job by enrolling in a training course. A qualification is not a magic passport to a job, but it certainly makes it easier to obtain an interview, after which is it up to you and your personality. Remember that no training in the world can teach you how to get on with people. You must feel confident in yourself that this is what you want.

Traditionally, the ability to get on with people was much more important than academic credentials or specific tourism training. However, though it is still crucial to be able to get on with people, this is no longer enough to guarantee a job in the industry. Training and experience are what employers look for so if you take a gap year, take some time for training so that you improve your prospects in the long run. This 'investment' looks good on your CV and shows that you have an eagerness to learn. Of course, casual work is valuable because it shows you are a hard-working individual (see *Casual Work* section earlier) but today, many employers are not impressed with just stints as washers-up or 'bumming around'. If the applicant has not used her or his time wisely in trying to gain more specialised experience, it can look as if they have little career motivation. The training that tour operators do offer is usually in company procedures, not in the actual job.

The training period often gives the employer the chance to assess the suitability of the individual for the job and it is commonplace for trainees in these circumstances to be dropped before they even start the job.

Jayne Nash describes her experiences with Top Deck:
The lucky applicants were invited to take part on a training trip. This involves completing a 'dummy' tour of central Europe in around three weeks, along with 50 other hopefuls (potential couriers and drivers) aboard a convoy of double decker buses. The cost of this was £300 plus a lot of homework, swotting up on the history, geography and culture of the ten countries to be visited. The training trip alone was the experience of a lifetime. We had to take our turn at being courier under the critical eyes of our two trainers, which was at times a terrifying experience. Throughout the tour unsuccessful candidates were dropped off by the side of the road; we lost one in Barcelona. If you made it through without losing your driver, your fellow passengers or your head, you were taken back to London and eventually given a trip to lead on your own.

Hilary Sanger was excited to be offered training by a winter ski tour operator until she was told to go home half way through the course. Despondent she thought she should provide herself with a qualification that didn't depend on any one company, so she enrolled on a training course and, following up a lead from the course tutor, went on to become a senior rep in Greece with *Sunsail.*

Doing some training before applying boosts confidence and provides inside information about how the industry works, which will be invaluable during subsequent job searches. Course tutors may well have established contacts in the industry and can often help with job placement. Improving your marketability is not the only reason to take a training course. The assumption that just because you like dealing with people you can work in tourism is false. You must know the basics of administration, law and safety. A good course will give you confidence to handle all the problems that inevitably arise. (If there weren't any problems, there would be no need for your job.)

It often seems to be the case that a spell in charm school would be the best training for a job which will require becoming an intermediary between obnoxious or discontented holidaymakers and tetchy locals. Before proper training was widely available, a typical exchange between a new recruit and his employer might have resembled the one reported by Louis Weston:

My employer told me my first tour was to be to Italy. I told him I had never been to Italy, to which he replied there is no time like the present. When I pleaded that I knew nothing about Italy, he replied 'Now is the time to learn.'

Off Louis went and (luckily for him) he found his coach driver a mine of helpful information. But many of his colleagues were not so fortunate and gave up after their first tour.

But since then standards and expectations have risen. Despite the travel bargains around nowadays, a holiday is one of the most expensive items in anyone's annual budget and holidaymakers rely on holiday staff to ensure that their dreams come as near to reality as possible. Not only will you derive little job satisfaction from just muddling through, but you may feel guilt for having given a poor return for people's precious time and money.

Nowadays it is most unwise to subscribe to the old school which said 'In my day we just bumbled along' or 'the best training is to sit by Betty', i.e. shadow an experienced guide or rep. Competition for tourist jobs within Europe is much more intense than it was a generation ago. Quality control means that structured training is more important than formerly. EU Directives insist on good customer care and you must know what you are talking about. Furthermore, slipping standards of general education in the UK, especially in the study of modern languages and geography, mean that British nationals are often at a disadvantage when competing with their multilingual continental counterparts.

Tourism training seldom means a three-year degree course. Many courses do not need pre-entry qualifications. Fees vary enormously from one-day seminars for about £50 on how to become a resort rep to tens of thousands of pounds at prestigious schools of hotel administration in Switzerland. The vocational qualifications which the government has introduced in the past few years have a stronger reputation than they did in the beginning among employers. There have been complaints about the inadequacy of some of this training, so before signing up for any course, ask employers if they will tell you what qualifications they look for. You do not want to spend months on a course and then find out that no employer is interested.

GETTING A GRANT

If you need help funding a training course, you may be eligible for a Career Development

Loan. CDLs are bank loans covering up to 80% of the cost of a vocational course lasting less than two years. Payment can be deferred until three months after the course finishes, whereupon repayments have to be made. The participating banks are Barclays, the Co-operative, Royal Bank of Scotland and the Clydesdale. Write for details to Freepost, Career Development Loans; 0800 585505; www.lifelonglearning.co.uk/cdl). Note that long-term unemployed people may be eligible for a 100% loan. Ask your prospective course provider for details or the DfES's Training Loans Unit, Area 1A, Castle View House, Runcorn WA7 2GJ.

When choosing a course, it is worth asking certain questions which will indicate how useful the qualification will be at the end of it, such as, is there any external validation of the course? Also find out what size a class you will be in (10-12 is much better than 15-20) and what qualifications and experience the tutors have.

Americans can obtain details about financing their courses from the National Tour Association (NTA, 546 E. Main St, Lexington, KY 40508; 800-682-8886). Peterson's *Study Abroad* ($29.95) also offers valuable advice and information about financing a course overseas.

RANGE OF COURSES

As noted in the previous chapter, the tourist industry is so diverse that there is an enormous range of training possibilities for joining it. It is important to have a clear idea of the kind of work which interests you and for which you want to prepare yourself. For example, people often make the mistake of signing up for ticketing or travel agency courses, when they really want to train for a job that will enable them to get out and meet people, perhaps as a tour guide or representative. Those who want to go on to work for a tourist board, in tour operations or in incentive travel and conferences often find that a good business-oriented course covering marketing, promotion and sales is more useful than a basic travel and tourism course. Similarly a background in conservation, history, architecture, etc. can be more useful for jobs with some upmarket companies than general tourism training.

Many, if not most, colleges of further education and higher education offer courses in travel and tourism or leisure and hospitality at various levels. Unfortunately the structure and accreditation of these courses is confusing in the extreme with different award-making bodies using different systems. Furthermore additional courses are coming on-stream all the time. British readers should start by checking Appendix 1 of this book to find out whether a college in their vicinity offers any tourism-related course. Another useful starting point is the Travel Training Company, a subsidiary of ABTA, with an entry below (01483 727321; www.ttctraining.co.uk).

The Institute of Travel & Tourism (Mill Studio, Crane Mead, Ware, Herts. SG12 9PY; 0870 770 7960) distributes *ITT Careers Advice Brochures* (available for £5) providing useful advice for newcomers to the field. The ITT puts on specialist courses for people already in the industry, e.g. a one-day course on dealing with impossible clients; check their website (www.itt.co.uk). Springboard UK is an organisation that promotes careers in hospitality, leisure, tourism and travel through a network of centres across the UK. They have devised an educational programme to support the curriculum in schools and colleges, and co-ordinate the vocational Travel & Tourism Programme. The TTP is administered from the Cardiff office (Springboard UK, Enterprise House, Cardiff Bay, Cardiff CF10 5LE; 029 2043 5631; ttp@springboarduk.org.uk). Springboard can also provide details on training courses, CV advice and the qualifications needed for the various careers in the industry; check their website www.springboarduk.org.uk.

A useful introduction to working in the hospitality industry can be found in the free booklet *Target Hospitality* which is affiliated with Springboard, the British Hospitality Association and HCIMA. The specialist publisher GTI also maintains a useful website www.doctorjob.com/hospitality.

To become a registered guide in the UK, i.e. someone who works and is expert in a single city or region takes from 300 to 500 hours and will cost over £2,000.

There are also many short or long commercial courses which offer specific training in everything from how to apply to an airline to training in hotel administration. Many industry associations run useful short courses for their members, and will often allow non-members to join, though the fees may be higher. Not only do participants learn something on these courses, but they often have the chance to talk to prospective employers.

The current government is keen to disseminate information about training and education opportunities nationwide. The National Grid For Learning (www.ngfl.gov.uk) web portal brings together a vast and growing collection of sites that support education and lifelong learning including a large number of resources for parents and students assembled by the Department for Education & Skills. The National Organisation for Adult Learning (NIACE), Renaissance House, 20 Princes Road West, Leicester LE1 6TP (0116 204 4200; www.niace.org.uk) distributes information about vocational training courses throughout the UK, including courses in both private and public educational institutions. You should be able to consult this at your local careers office. Finally, Learndirect (0800 100 900; www.learndirect.co.uk) is a government-financed helpline that tries to provide advice and information about any aspect of training courses available in your area plus careers and funding. The helpline is open 9am to 9pm Monday to Friday and 9am to 12 noon on Saturday.

ABTA

The Association of British Travel Agents or ABTA is the industry lead body for travel agents and tour operators in Britain (68-71 Newman St., London W1T 3AH; www.abta.com); they operate a premium information and advice line on 0901 201 50 50 (50p per minute).

ABTA's training wing is the *Travel Training Company* (TTC) and it is responsible for designing courses and drawing up syllabuses. ABTA-accredited courses are run at more than 100 colleges and training centres throughout the country, and they also have a wide range of distance learning programmes. Contact them on 01483 727321 to obtain leaflets about the range of qualifications and courses on offer. From them you can get a complete list of the courses they operate, from one-day courses in booking UK rail tickets to a two-year Travel Training Programme.

The Travel Training Programme is one of the largest Modern Apprenticeship training schemes in the country. Each year they accept several thousand school leavers, or occasionally graduates, onto this training programme which in the majority of cases leads to full-time employment in the industry. Although no minimum standard is stipulated for acceptance, many have three or four GCSEs, preferably in English, Maths, a foreign language and geography. Note that a few companies like Tui UK, Thomas Cook and American Express offer a training programme specifically for graduates, though this is unusual.

Occasionally, TTC also provides a range of one-day or evening courses for people currently employed in the industry. This depends on demand by students and is usually advertised through colleges and trade magazines. Day courses on effective sales techniques, techniques of public speaking, etc. cost about £120 plus VAT and are held in major cities throughout Britain.

The standard ABTA qualification is for travel agents and is now offered in conjunction with City & Guilds; the Certificate in Travel (Travel Agency) is what used to be called

ABTAC and can be obtained after an examination at Level 2 (primary) or Level 3 (advanced). It is accepted by both travel conglomerates and independents as a good grounding for their agents. Many regional colleges and colleges of further education offer the course, often in combination with work placements and some distance learning. It is very flexible and can take between 6 months and a year to complete. TTC's website lists partner colleges that offer the course. Many impose no entry requirements. Level 2 covers basic air travel, car carrying services, travel geography and package holiday services, while Level 3 covers advanced air travel, cruising and shipping, independent and overseas holidays, etc. Prices are available from local providers.

Another mainstream offering from TTC is the Certificate in Travel (Tour Operators) formerly known as ABTOC, which is not as widely available as the Travel Agency Certificate. TTC also offers many other courses such as an Air Fares and Ticketing course for an IATA-approved qualification (often required to work in travel agents abroad). A Tour Guide course is also being established through partnership with companies like Tui UK.

ABTA's American counterpart, ASTA (American Society of Travel Agents) also runs training courses and can offer information on qualifications (ASTA, 1101 King Street, Suite 200, Alexandria, VA 22314; 703-739-2782; www.astanet.com).

GNVQs

General National Vocational Qualifications (GNVQs) are intended primarily for students aged 16-18 as a kind of vocational A-level and an introduction to various industries. Note that students aged 16, 17 or 18 on 31st August in the calendar year in which they commence their programme of study do not pay registration, tuition or administration fees since the government has made all courses for these young people free. The hundreds of colleges which offer the GNVQ in Leisure and Tourism offer two levels, Foundation and Intermediate, which can be completed in one or two years depending on the individual's background. The Advanced level is now called an AVCE (Advanced Vocational Certificate of Education) and is intended to be equivalent to an A level. It is widely offered though yet to establish itself as a well regarded qualification.

On successful completion of the course, participants receive a GNVQ awarded by Edexcel (www.edexcel.org.uk) or City & Guilds (www.city-and-guilds.co.uk). GNVQs have been described as 'a broad brush preparation for the world of work' though many people in the tourist industry have complained that their usefulness is limited.

Bowing to pressure, these qualifications are being updated and the old Leisure and Tourism GNVQ has been split into a Leisure & Recreation stream and a Travel & Tourism stream. If your local college offers GNVQs, ask if they include Travel Geography (the one unit the industry says is very useful) and whether or not and at what level the tutors have worked in the industry. Originally the Government required teachers on vocational qualification courses to have worked in the relevant industry. However, colleges sometimes can't recruit appropriate tutors and excuse themselves by saying the GNVQ is only 'foundational'. Hence, leaders in the industry are not yet convinced that GNVQs for tourism are of much use. Additionally, because registration for these qualifications is earlier in the year than academic counterparts, the apparent drop-out rate is much higher. This has seriously damaged its reputation in the industry. Yet the Government has poured so much money into developing these vocational qualifications, that they are here to stay.

People should find out about local courses and ask questions about the practical content of the course and relevant experience of the tutors before deciding. It might be worth having a look at a relevant GNVQ book such as the ones published by Oxford University Press or Pitman (see list on www.spinet.co.uk/careercompass) which would serve as an introduction to the industry and would help young people to ask the right questions about courses.

NVQs

NVQs tend to be more practical and less academic than GNVQs. They too are open to students aged 16-18 but also appeal to mature students and career changers. The NVQ in Travel Services prepares candidates for a variety of tourist-related jobs such as tour managers, travel consultants, resort reps and so on. NVQs are assessed in the workplace or in colleges where work situations are simulated.

There are no compulsory prerequisites. NVQs are available at Levels 1 to 4 in Travel Services (mainly for travel agency work), with options at Levels 2 and 3 in Field Operations (providing on-site services to tourists) and Guiding. NVQs are awarded at whatever level of achievement the candidate is assessed to have reached. For example for the NVQ Level 2, students have to demonstrate that they can book package holidays, whereas for Level 3 they have to be able to design a package holiday. After gaining relevant experience, candidates become eligible for NVQ Level 4.

When the government first announced National Vocational Qualifications and the Scottish equivalent (SVQs) in 1986, one of the most important criteria was that all students had to have some on-the-job training or, failing that, be taught by teachers and lecturers who had recognised and up-to-date industry experience. In some cases, that promise has been lost sight of in the drive to offer profitable courses, which means that vocational courses in the UK tend to be inferior to those offered in other European countries.

In 1995 the Government introduced the Modern Apprenticeship Scheme for school leavers with GNVQs or A-levels who do not wish to go to university but want to receive work-based training leading to an NVQ. The section about ABTA describes its co-ordination of the Modern Apprenticeship scheme in the tourism industry. More recently a Vocational Certificate of Education (VCE) was introduced which is meant to be equivalent to an A2 (A-level).

AWARD-GRANTING BODIES

The principal skill-testing and award-making bodies in the UK are City & Guilds, Edexcel and OCR.

Edexcel, Stewart House, 32 Russell Square, London WC1B 5DN. ☎ 0870 240 9800; www.edexcel.org.uk. Offer qualifications at various levels in Travel and Tourism. In England and Wales the normal entry requirement for the National Diploma is four GCSEs (Grade C or above), and for the Higher National Diploma (HND) one A level or equivalent. Travel & Tourism courses are run at more than 170 colleges. BTEC Edexcel also offer GNVQs at Foundation and Intermediate levels. At one time an Advanced level was available but this was so unpopular with employers and candidates that it has been dropped and in 2001 a vocational A level in tourism was introduced in a bid to raise the status of vocational subjects like tourism. The NVQ and BTEC Awards in Travel Services includes Tour Guiding, Tour Operations, Overseas Resort Operations, Children's Couriers and Worldwide Fares Training. Note that at the time of writing the specification for the BTEC Higher National Certificate and Diploma was under consideration and may be offered in the future.

City & Guilds, 1 Giltspur St, London EC1A 9DD. ☎ 020-7294 2800. Website: www.city-and-guilds.co.uk. Offers Vocational qualifications in various fields and at different levels, e.g. Level 2 in Business Travel, Level 4 in Travel & Tourism (High Professional Diploma) and the International Tourism qualifications at various levels. You can search their website for a suitable course within a 50 mile radius of your post code.

OCR (Oxford, Cambridge, RSA), 1 Regent St, Cambridge CB2 1GG. Tel: 024 76 851 509 (Information Bureau – Vocational). E-mail: cib@ocr.org.uk. OCR offers a range of qualifications in tourism and leisure studies including GNVQs, VCEs and the new Applied GCSE (Double Award).

NCFE, Citygate, St James' Boulevard, Newcastle upon Tyne NE1 4JE. ☎0191-239 8000. Website www.ncfe.org.uk. Awarding body accredited by the Qualifications & Curriculum Authority and with qualifications that form part of the National Qualifications Framework (NQF). Qualifications for resort representatives, tour managers, etc. offered by colleges such as Cavendish College (see entry below).

Note that there has been a move recently to make the HND and even degree courses in this field more vocational. In 2004/2005 many colleges are offering newly designed courses that should lead to global career opportunities.

UNIVERSITY COURSES

As well as the certificate and vocational courses available at colleges of further education throughout the United Kingdom (see entries below and Appendix 1), a large number of universities, many of them former polytechnics, offer degree programmes in leisure and tourism. Quite a number offer 'foundation degrees' which are courses of higher education that are shorter than full honours degrees, and have a high degree of work relevance. Their aim is to satisfy the practical requirements of key employers in the field and to create strong links between theory and practice. Most are two year courses that can lead on to the final year of a BA Honours programme.

The following UK universities and colleges offer degree courses in tourism studies: University of Abertay (Dundee), Bath Spa University College, Birmingham College of Food, Tourism & Creative Studies, Blackpool & the Fylde, Bournemouth University, Bournemouth & Poole College, University of Bradford, University of Brighton, Christchurch College (Canterbury), City College Norwich, Cornwall College Camborne, University of Derby, Fife College, Glasgow Caledonian, University of Gloucestershire, Grimsby College, University of Hertfordshire, Huddersfield University, Leeds Metropolitan, London Metropolitan University, University of Luton, Manchester Metropolitan, Mid-Kent College, Napier University, New College Nottingham, Newry & Kilkeel College Institute, North East Worcestershire College, North West Kent College, Oxford Brookes, University of Portsmouth, Queen Margaret University College (Edinburgh), University of Plymouth, Robert Gordon University (Aberdeen), University of Salford, Schiller International, Sheffield Hallam University, College of St Mark & St John (Plymouth), Somerset College of Arts, South Bank University, South Devon College, Suffolk College, University of Sunderland, University of Surrey, Thames Valley University, University of Ulster, University of Wales Institute (Cardiff), Westminster Kingsway College, University of Wolverhampton, Writtle College (Chelmsford) and York St John College.

The following British universities and colleges offer postgraduate courses in tourism: Birmingham College of Food, Tourism & Creative Studies, Bournemouth University, London Metropolitan University, University of Luton, Manchester Metropolitan University, Napier University, Oxford Brookes University, Sheffield Hallam, College of St Mark & St John (Plymouth), University of Surrey, Thames Valley University, University of Ulster (School of Hotel Leisure & Tourism), University of Wales Institute Cardiff and University of Wolverhampton.

DISTANCE LEARNING

Leisure Travel (54a Ifield Road, London SW10 9AD; 0906-553 2056 (premium rate line costing £1 a minute) have distance learning courses for holiday reps, conference and exhibition staff, tour managers and guides. These are theory courses on tape with programme books and lists of potential job contacts.

The Travel Training Company website lists 15 providers of distance learning courses, some of which have government contracts to carry out training courses for people who have been long-term unemployed.

USEFUL PREPARATORY COURSES

LANGUAGES

Although more than three-quarters of the world's tourism is handled in English, knowledge of a foreign language makes it much easier to advance along the path of a tourism career. German, Spanish, French, Italian, Japanese, Mandarin and Cantonese are probably the most important. Assuming you have not studied modern languages at school or college, evening language classes offered by local authorities usually follow the academic year and are aimed at hobby learners. Intensive courses offered privately are much more expensive.

Many people have been turning to the web to teach them a language; yet conventional teach-yourself courses are still on the market, for example from Berlitz (020-7518 8300), the BBC (08700 100222), Linguaphone (0800 282417; www.linguaphone.co.uk) and Audioforum (www.audioforum.com). All of them offer deluxe courses with refinements such as interactive videos and of course these cost much more (from £150). Linguaphone recommends half an hour of study a day for three months to master the basics of a language. A basic self-study programme with books and tapes will start at £30.

Try to learn the 'purest' version of the language, usually the kind spoken in the capital city. Dialects are understood only locally, while 'classical' pronunciation is generally understood by everyone. Some regional dialects can be incomprehensible to other speakers of the language, for example Swiss German, Quebecois French or Neopolitan Italian. Castillian Spanish is totally different from Mallorquine.

For those whose mother tongue is not English, there are special courses in most countries designed for the tourist or hotel industry. The Trinity College Exam Board (www.trinitycollege.co.uk) has developed a practical and efficient Oral Grade English Assessment, while the standard proof of competence in English is the Cambridge Proficiency and First Certificate. The other major assessor is the London Chamber of Commerce (LCCI) whose qualification is EFTI (English for the Tourism Industry).

COMPUTERS

Information Technology (IT) training is invaluable for many jobs within tourism. Of course it is absolutely essential for travel agents or for reservation clerks in any travel company. Most tour operator executives have a computer on their desks. Conference companies use computer programmes to run everything from the original enquiry through registration, badging and planning delegate kits, so if you can't use a computer, you are unlikely to find a job in a tourism office.

HEALTH AND SAFETY

Some tour operators are wary of allowing their reps or staff to attend to a medical emergency for fear of being sued later. That is why the NVQ for Reps does not include a requirement for Basic Emergency Aid. Other legal experts say that the rep who does nothing in a medical crisis might be accused of negligence. If something did go wrong, the rep should be covered by the company's public liability insurance. Whatever the legal niceties of the matter, any individual faced with a medical crisis would prefer to know the best action to take, so signing up for a first aid course is always a good idea.

A first aid certificate is valuable for many jobs in tourism. The St. John Ambulance (020-7324 4000) offers a range of Lifesaver and Lifesaver Plus courses. The standard one-day course costs £35-£50 (depending on region).

Alternatively, contact the Medical Indemnity Register (Training section), PO Box 44375, London SW19 8WA (020-8739 0066; info@medicalindemnity.com). One-day courses cost £300 and 4-day courses cost £1,200. All courses are adapted to the needs of the industry. A Basic Food Hygiene Certificate can be acquired in half a day or even on-line (course costs from £35) and could be a useful addition to your CV if you are going to look for a job that might involve catering.

A *Safety Training Video* has been produced by the Federation of Tour Operators mainly for use by tour operators' reps including emergency procedures in the case of fire, accidents at a swimming pool, plus general hygiene and safety issues. It clearly explains what you need to know and to check and costs £40 from FTO, 170 High St, Lewes, E Sussex BN7 1YE (www.fto.co.uk).

SPECIALISED TRAINING

Many areas of the tourist industry require staff to have specialised training and experience, for example museum tour guides, chefs, safari leaders and ski or other sports instructors. Many of these are discussed in the previous chapter which describes the many kinds of employment available in tourism.

TOUR MANAGERS AND GUIDES

Specialist guides are needed to look after visitors whose interests can range from engineering to embroidery. Contact the relevant association, museum or adult education centre for suitable courses leading to a qualification. Many tourist boards offer guide training courses and employ Registered Guides specifically for a region or city. In Britain these are known as 'Blue Badge' guides (due to their badge colour). Contact the Guild of Registered Tourist Guides for details of the training (52d Borough High St, London SE1 1XN; 020-7403 1115; guild@blue-badge.org.uk). The Institute of Tourist Guiding was launched in 2002 to set and maintain standards for the whole tourist guiding sector. A career structure will become clearer with recognised qualifications at each level. The Institute can be contacted at Lloyds Court, 1 Goodman's Yard, London E1 8AT (020-7953 1257; info@institute-of-tourist-guiding.org.uk).

Visit London (formerly the London Tourist Board) has passed the responsibility for training London guides to *Training Professional Guides Ltd* (see entry). Note that the City of London's Education Office (PO Box 270, London EC2P 2EJ) runs a three-term guiding course.

The IATM (International Association of Tour Managers) offers a Certificate of Tour Management (CTM). The first step is to acquire the IATM study manual for £20 from IATM Ltd, 397 Walworth Road, London SE17 2AW (020-7703 9154; iatm@iatm.co.uk) and start preparing for the examination which, if passed, will confer a recognised professional qualification as an experienced tour manager. The fee for sitting the exam is £180. Unfortunately this Certificate is not reliably recognised in Europe and indeed there is no qualification for Tour Managers that has official recognition abroad. In EU countries where Tour Managers have encountered hassles (primarily Italy) it might overcome some difficulties if you can present a certificate. In other European countries (notably Germany) foreign tour managers are rarely bothered by the authorities.

HOTELS & CATERING COURSES

The Hospitality Training Foundation (3rd Floor, International House, High St, Ealing, London W5 5DB; 020-8579 2400; info@htf.org.uk) is one of the lead bodies and training providers for the industry in the UK. In late 2001, HTF joined forces with the Travel, Tourism and Events National Training Organisation (TTENTO) to lay the foundations for a Sector Skills Council for Hospitality, Leisure, Travel and Tourism, a hugely powerful sector representing the interests of over 1.6 million employees.

Also look into the courses promoted by the Hotel and Catering Training Company

Ltd (26-28 Hammersmith Grove, London W6 7HT; 020-8735 9700; www.hctc2.co.uk). The free booklet mentioned above, *Target Hospitality,* explains qualifications and lists recognised colleges and training centres. It promotes apprenticeships as well as college-based training. For information about advanced qualifications contact the Hotel, Catering & International Management Association (HCIMA, Trinity Court, 34 West St, Sutton, Surrey SM1 1SH; 020-8661 4900; www.hcima.org.uk).

AIRLINES

The explosion in air traffic and launch of several new European airlines in the past couple of years has created thousands of new jobs. Advertisements for cabin crew have been seen across the travel press. They are looking for literacy, numeracy (for the arithmetic necessary to sell duty-frees) and geography. Although each airline runs its own training course for cabin crew, it might be worth signing up for a short course to prepare you for the interview (see entry for *Career In Travel*). Although Rosemary was rather sceptical about the possible benefit of enrolling in a commercial course, she soon realised that it could be helpful:

> *Andrew (the instructor) went round the classroom asking trainees general knowledge questions, like the ones they might be asked in their airline interview, e.g. what are the capital cities of European countries, what is the currency in various countries, how do you spell Edinburgh (only three correct answers, two of whom were from non-Britons), what is the name of the Chairman or Managing Director of the airline to which you want to apply, and so on. Well over three-quarters got answers wrong, but we were told how to revise. Hints such as 'in your numeracy test you may be asked to give equivalents for £2 not £1' were much appreciated.*

The best preparation for becoming check-in or ground staff is a representatives' course. Further training will be provided by whichever airline hires you, though this may be rather perfunctory if there is a staff shortage at the height of the season.

For a detailed look at employment in this sector, see the new title from Vacation Work Publications *Working in Aviation* (£10.99 from 9 Park End St, Oxford OX1 1HJ). The Aviation Training Association in High Wycombe ceased trading in 2003 when its various remits were divided among the new Skills Council, which are all explained on the website www.aviation-training.org.

CONFERENCE, INCENTIVE AND CORPORATE HOSPITALITY WORK

The forum for training and development in this sector is the Events Sector Industry Training Organisation (ESITO, Tetford House, Tetford, Lincs. LN9 6QQ; 01507 533491). This is the training wing of ACE (the Association for Conferences and Events) whose headquarters are at Riverside House, High St, Huntingdon PE29 3SG; 01480 457595; ace@martex.co.uk). In exchange for a large s.a.e. they will send a list of colleges and training centres, and can advise on whether the teachers and external verifier of an NVQ you are considering have industry experience.

For information outside the UK, it might be worth approaching the International Association of Professional Congress Organisers (IAPCO), 42 Canham Road, London W3 7SR; 020-8749 6171; info@iapco.org).

TRAVEL AGENCIES

In order to qualify to work in a travel agency, it will be necessary to complete an airfares and ticketing course. Global Distributions Systems (GDS) distribute reservation and other services to travel agents. The four main companies whose systems are in use are Amadeus, Galileo, Sabre and Worldspan, all of which are owned by airlines. Additional training for travel agents covers visas, foreign exchange, car hire, admin, etc. The courses are validated by IATA the International Air Transport Association (www.iata.org) and most reputable providers belong to the international body the UFTAA, the United Federation of Travel Agents' Association. The recruitment agency New Frontiers runs training courses on-line in airline reservations, fares and ticketing, hotel reservations and car hire; prices from £80 (0845 202 2222; www.train-in-travel.com).

Surfing the web will soon bring you to course providers. For example the website www.aviationjobsearch.com keeps an up-to-date list of courses on offer for example from T&T Recruitment & Resourcing (020-7426 9378; info@t-ttrainingsolutions.co.uk) who put on courses throughout the year in the different computerised reservation systems including Virgin Atlantic's Fares & Ticketing course at levels 2 and 3.

A new company entered the scene in late 2003 in Belfast. Global Travel Training Ltd. (77 Oakwood Avenue, Carryduff, Belfast BT8 8SW; 02890 817677; www.globaltravel training.com) markets flexible home-study training courses for the travel industry. This trend for self-study and distance learning is bound to increase with the rise in internet use among trainees. The specialist recruitment agency C&M (see Directory of Placement Agencies) has set up an online training facility at www.train4travel.com.

ABTA's course for trainee travel agents is mentioned earlier in this section and is widely available. Chameleon Training Ltd (PO Box 67, Virginia Water, Surrey GU25 4BF (tel/fax 01344 843344; www.chameleontraining.co.uk) is no longer owned by British Airways but continues as the sole provider of BA-endorsed Fares & Ticketing courses to the travel industry. Note that Virgin Atlantic is now the primary deliverer of Fares & Ticketing training and offers Levels 1 and 2.

For information about training in business travel agency work, contact the Guild of Business Travel Agents for advice (020-7222 2744; info@gbta-guild.com).

BUS & COACH COURSES

To work as a host or hostess on express or shuttle coaches, you will need a food and hygiene certificate. National Express Coaches (www.nationalexpress.com) publicise vacancies on the recruitment section of their website. Trainee PCV drivers are in demand in the Heathrow area (020-8990 6382). The overseeing body for drivers is Bus & Coach Training (43 High St, Rickmansworth WD3 1ET; 01923 896607). They advise that those interested in training as a driver should approach the coach companies directly. Most offer in-house training courses on a one-to-one basis in a coach. Course duration and cost depend on how much previous driving experience the candidate has.

THE LEISURE INDUSTRY

Theme parks, visitor attractions, museums, leisure and sports centres, etc. represent an expanding market which employs staff at all levels. The Institute of Leisure and Amenity Management (Lower Basildon, Reading RG8 9NE; 01491 874800; www.ilam.co.uk) can advise on qualifications and where to obtain them. They also publish the 168-page *Directory of UK Leisure Courses* free on the internet.

CHILDCARE

With the trend for tour operators to cater to families, people with a background in childcare are finding it increasingly easy to find attractive employment in summer and winter. The gold-plated qualification is the Diploma in Child Care and Education (DCE) formerly called the NNEB (National Nursery Examination Board) and still often referred to that way, although the NNEB was replaced by the Council for Awards in Children's Care (CACHE) some years ago. Whatever it's called it is the most widely recognised qualification and is taught as a two-year diploma course at 200 local authority colleges and several private ones throughout Britain. Write to CACHE (8 Chequer St, St. Albans,

Herts. AL1 3XZ; www.cache.org.uk) for a list of colleges. Various alternatives are available in the form of BTECs and NVQs and the tour operators who hire nannies will be familiar with the various levels.

CONSERVATION

Conservation is now an integral part of many tourism jobs. The Association of Independent Tour Operators (AITO), Tourism Concern and other organisations are doing a tremendous amount of work to encourage clients to think more carefully about the impact that their travels have on the environment and local cultures. Anyone who has done environmental studies at university might find themselves in demand for interpretative roles with more sensitive tour operators. One interesting course is run in Queensland to learn how to become an eco tour guide. The course provides a practical introduction to tour guiding with an environmental focus; contact Kingfisher Bay Resort on Fraser Island to find out if it is still running (+61 7-4042 2605; rangers@kingfisherbay.com).

For information about courses in museum conservation, send £4 to the UK Institute for Conservation (109 The Chandlery, 50 Westminster Bridge Road, London SE1 7QY; 020-7721 8721) for the publication *Training in Conservation*. Their website www.ukic.org.uk carries a list of full-time courses throughout the UK.

QUALIFICATIONS AND TRAINING IN EUROPE

For further information about whether certain qualifications will be recognised in the EU, request the free factsheets *Europe Direct: Routemap for Jobseekers in the EU* from the European Commission in the UK (Jean Monnet House, 8 Storey's Gate, London SW1P 3AT; 020-7973 1992). Recognition of experience and vocational training (as opposed to straight academic achievements) is especially important in tourist-related subjects. Progress has been made on improving the mutual recognition of professional and vocational qualifications though the dream of Europe-wide recognition is a long way from realisation. The Department of Trade & Industry has a special unit that can allocate Certificates of Experience to certain categories of worker such as construction workers (www.dti.gov.uk/europe/pagej.html). Currently, there is no official document stating the comparability of vocational qualifications concerning the tourism industry and it is easy to understand how difficult this would be to achieve.

The aim of the EU's Leonardo da Vinci programme is to improve the quality of vocational training systems and their capacity for innovation. The mobility measure offers opportunities for students and recent graduates to undertake work placements of between 3 and 12 months (for students) or between 2 and 12 months (recent graduates) in one of 30 European countries. It must be noted that applications for Leonardo funding must be submitted by organisations, not individuals. The programme is administered by the British Council (www.leonardo.org.uk) among others.

The Brussels-based Eurodyssey scheme gives young Europeans the opportunity of gaining work experience abroad. The programme is open to young Europeans between the ages of 18 and 30, unemployed or recently qualified, who fix up a work placement in one of the participating regions of Europe (see website). Application forms are available on the website www.eurodyssee.net. Sarah Skeet from Tiverton in Devon learned of the scheme only after settling down in a town in eastern France during her gap year. She discovered that the youth hostel could apply for people to work on this exchange and the participant would be paid by the EU, in order to help them develop language skills.

A few private organisations offer hospitality training in European countries, see entries for *Horizon HPL* in the Directory of Training and *Eurotoques* in the Directory of Placement Agencies.

In Europe there are excellent guiding courses, though most will be in the predominant language rather than English. Qualification for entry to the tourism industry in France is the BTS Tourisme, a course which takes two years after completion of the Baccalaureate and covers languages, law, administration and history, and includes *stages* (work placements) lasting between one and seven months. In the Netherlands the relevant association is called Guidor.

If you want to work in conferences, Trinity College London have developed a Certificate in Effective Communication for Conferences and Events. It is designed to encourage and evaluate oral communication skills in this sector.

US COURSES

Vocational schools, community colleges and proprietary travel schools throughout the US offer courses in travel and tourism including seminars on tour escorting, hospitality and recreation. After meeting with the course organisers, it is worth finding out if the State Post-Secondary Education Bureau or some other accreditation association has licensed the school. If in doubt, contact the state Department of Education. One of the best accredited schools for aspiring tour leaders is the *International Tour Management Institute* (www.ITMItourtraining.com).

For information about which universities and colleges offer degree courses in travel and tourism, see the annually updated *Peterson's Four Year Colleges* published by Thomson Peterson's Guides Inc. for $29.95 (1-609-896-1800; www.petersons.com).

The American Society of Travel Agents (ASTA, 1101 King St, Alexandria, VA 22314; 703-739-2782; www.astanet.com) has over 20,000 members worldwide. Because of anti-trust legislation, ASTA cannot play the same role as ABTA's training board. However the Education Department does publish a 20-page list of ASTA-affiliated travel schools in the US and worldwide, and a page of advice headed *Choosing a Travel School*.

The American Hotel and Lodging Association promote distance learning via their affiliated *Educational Institute* (see entry). They can also send a free list of colleges which offer hospitality degree programmes, as well as the addresses of useful organisations. Similarly, the International Council on Hotel, Restaurant and Institutional Education (CHRIE) produces *The Guide to Hospitality and Tourism Education*, a comprehensive directory of education programmes for hotel and restaurant management, food service management and culinary arts. The guide includes valuable information on career prospects, salaries, scholarships and grants. For more information, contact CHRIE (8040346-4800; info@chrie.org).

The American Hospitality Academy (AHA) provides year-round structured training programmes in resorts including Hilton Head Island and Myrtle Beach (South Carolina) and Orlando (Florida). Trainees from the US and abroad are placed in hotels, country clubs, holiday villages, etc. in order for them to gain a realistic hands-on introduction to working in the industry. Alongside the practical work, trainees participate in AHA's Certified Hospitality Professional education programme in conjunction with the Educational Institute of the American Hotel & Lodging Association (see entry). Details should be requested from the American Hospitality Academy Corporate Office (3 Pope Avenue, Executive Park Drive, Hilton Head Island, SC 29928; 843-785-4368; info@AmericanHospitalityAcademy.com). Their website www.AmericanHospitalityAc ademy.com also links to job vacancies. International students must pay a programme fee of $500 for an internship of less than five months, $1,000 for one lasting between five months and a year. All housing, transportation to and from the host property, a monthly stipend, classes and books are included. The AHA can assist applicants with the J-1 visa application (see chapter on the USA).

The Research & Education Department of the National Tour Association (800-682-8886; www.ntaonline.com) can advise on Certified Tour Professional training and various other courses.

The *Travel Institute* (formerly the Institute of Certified Travel Agents) offers a raft of courses, mainly by distance learning, for people who intend to make careers as travel agents.

CHOOSING A COURSE

In this popular field there is a plethora of choice. If you are going to invest some of your hard-earned cash in a training course, how do you choose the best course for your needs? One of the best ways to assess the value of a course is to talk to graduates and find out to what extent the course helped them in their job hunt. Another is to contact company recruitment departments directly and ask them what qualifications they prefer when hiring.

If you don't know anyone working in the industry, the telephone is one of the best introductory tools. Ask the relevant trade association which qualifications they recommend. Obtain a list of colleges or training centres (probably the ones near your residence) and phone for information, noting the following: the time it takes them to answer or to return your call if a message is left on an answering machine, whether or not you are put through to the right department or passed around the building because no one knows what anyone else is up to, and how promptly literature is sent. How your enquiry is handled can tell you something about a college or centre. After all, if their customer care is deficient, how can they teach it effectively? A request for a self-addressed envelope is probably a good sign, indicating that the course is popular and possibly oversubscribed.

Be prepared to ask questions about the course such as whether the qualification under consideration is recognised worldwide as well as in the UK. It is very important to ascertain whether the course tutors have extensive experience in the industry and, if so, how recent it is. Even if a college is on an approved list, the teacher who was teaching when the inspection was made may have moved on. These days colleges of further education and training institutes all have to make a profit, whereas in the past they could depend more on state funding. If one course is under-subscribed, teachers are regularly transferred from other departments. Tourism is such a popular subject that it is not unusual for colleges to have to scrounge for tutors. The course suffers if the teachers don't have first-hand experience of the industry.

When you visit the college or training centre, try to meet the lecturers. Some hold open days when you can inspect the place and ask questions. A good college will be very happy to tell you what industry experience the course tutors have. They may also be willing to put you in touch with past students or contacts in the industry who can comment on the quality and content of the courses. Naturally you will also be influenced by the general standard of the facilities. It is worth considering the health and safety standards. If you wouldn't want to use the loos, how can the college teach the fundamentals of the EU Directive on Package Travel?

As in most fields, there are some cowboy courses. These are set up by entrepreneurs who emphasise the glamour associated with the industry in order to attract students but do not offer much concrete training. There is of course more to working in tourism than talking about fun and sun, and some of the worst courses fold. But there are also some fairly useless courses which charge people to hear common sense advice such as the importance of smiling, dressing neatly and not taking complaints personally.

One hopeful young courier answered an ad in her local Midlands newspaper to take a training course:

After paying to join the company's excursion to Paris, I was told to sit in the back of the coach and take notes. Arriving in Paris exhausted after an overnight journey, I was told that my bedroom wasn't ready so I should 'go around Paris looking for tourist places.' No one offered any suggestions about where I should go. That evening I worked as an unpaid courier marshalling the group around on a night club tour. The next day we set off back to the UK. On the return ferry I was given 'an exam' but no one told me who would mark it or if I would be given the result. When we got home, it seemed as though they couldn't wait to get rid of me.

No one had answered her questions, given any training in admin procedures, in using a mike or anything else. And of course no one had helped her obtain a job.

Cost is no guarantee of quality. In the past, commercial courses available in London have charged up to £4,000 and yet offered virtually no practical training on a coach (which is both the most expensive and the most necessary part of any guiding course) and could not offer a recognised qualification. So it is wise to carry out thorough research before enrolling by asking senior industry employees familiar with the course.

Overseas students who wish to study tourism in the UK should contact their local office of the British Council for information on tourism courses. They can then send two international reply coupons to the colleges which are of interest for further details.

DIRECTORY OF TRAINING COURSES

The following colleges and private training centres offer various courses of possible interest to people wishing to join the tourism industry. This selection represents a fraction of what is on offer but conveys some idea of the variety available. See *Appendix 1* for a complete alphabetical list of Tourism Training Courses throughout the United Kingdom.

UK COURSES
ABTA - see Travel Training Company

BIRMINGHAM COLLEGE OF FOOD, TOURISM & CREATIVE STUDIES
Summer Row, Birmingham B3 1JB. ☎0121-604 1000. Fax 0121-608 7100. Website www.bcftcs.ac.uk.
Courses offered: BSc (Hons) Tourism Management, BA(Hons) Tourism Business Management, BA(Hons) Hospitality and Tourism Management, BA(Hons) Adventure Tourism, HND Leisure Management, HND Adventure Tourism, HND Business and Finance (Tourism), HND Leisure Management. Foundation courses as well.
Some courses provide opportunity for overseas cultural visits in second year. Application to be made through UCAS.

BLACKPOOL & THE FYLDE COLLEGE
Ashfield Road, Bispham, Blackpool, Lancs. FY2 0HB. ☎01253 504343. Fax 01253 356127. E-mail visitors@blackpool.ac.uk. Website www.blackpool.ac.uk.
Associate college of Lancaster University.
Courses offered: BA(Hons) in Hospitality Management with International Tourism component. HNDs in Travel & Tourism Management, Leisure Management, Hospitality Management and Culinary Arts.

BOURNEMOUTH AND POOLE COLLEGE
The Lansdowne, Bournemouth BH1 3JJ. ☎01202 205831/205205. Website www.thecollege.co.uk.
"Courses offered: GNVQ in Advanced Leisure & Tourism; various BTEC, City & Guilds and HCIMA courses; pre-university course for international students, in Leisure, Tourism and Hospitality management, certificate and Diploma in International Tourism. Mainly one year courses.

BOURNEMOUTH UNIVERSITY
School of Services Management, Talbot Campus, Fern Barrow, Poole, Dorset BH12 5BB. ☎01202 595110. Fax 01202 515707. Email smu@bournemouth.ac.uk. Website www.bournemouth.ac.uk/services-management.
Courses offered: degree, diploma and postgraduate courses in tourism, leisure, hospitality management and catering.

CAMBRIDGE INTERNATIONAL COLLEGE
College House, Leoville, Jersey JE3 2DB. Tel: 01534 485485. Fax: 01534 485071. E-mail learn@cambridgetraining.com. Website www.cambridgeco llege.co.uk.
Accredited by ASET (awarding body of QCA).
Courses offered: distance learning Diploma in Tourism & Travel Agency Management; Diploma in Hotel Operations & Management. Average completion time is 6-8 months.
Cost: £130 including final exam and marking.

CAREER IN TRAVEL
1a Fryen Arcade, Winchester Road, Chandlers Ford, Hampshire SO53 2DP. ☎0870 744 1701. E-mail course@careerintravel.co.uk. Website www.care erintravel.co.uk).
Founded in 1997.
Courses offered: one-day courses for Cabin Crew and Holiday Reps. Emphasis on maximising your chances at interview and also give concrete tips on job-hunting. Both courses are run at Gatwick and Manchester plus the holiday rep course can be attended in Arbroath (Scotland) and the cabin crew course in Glasgow, Bristol and Dublin.
Cost: £59 includes preparatory CD-Rom and recruitment assistance.

CAVENDISH COLLEGE
35-37 Alfred Place, London WC1E 7DP. ☎020-7580 6043. Fax 020-7255 1591. E-mail learn@cavendish.ac.uk. Website www.cavendish.ac.uk.
Private college established 1985 with large number of overseas students.
Courses offered: IATA/UFTAA Travel & Tourism Diplomas – Foundation and Consultant levels (both 6 months); Diploma in Travel & Hotel Operation Management (9 months), Diploma in Tour Guide Operations & Tourism (9 months), Diploma in Hotel & Catering Management (9 months) validated by the American Hotel & Lodging Association, BA(Hons) in Hospitality Management (3 years) validated by the University of Wales.
Cost: £3,000-£6,000 a year. Accommodation in host families costs about £120 a week.
Follow-up: assistance given to students who wish to apply for undergraduate and postgraduate university courses in the UK.

CORNWALL COLLEGE CAMBORNE
Trevenson Road, Camborne, Cornwall TR15 3RD. ☎01209 616161. Fax 01209

611612. E-mail enquiries@cornwall.ac.uk. Website www.cornwall.ac.uk.
Courses offered: huge range of courses from HNC in Heritage and Visitor Management (part-time over 2 years) to Advanced Vocational A-level double award (AVCE) in travel and tourism (2 years full-time). Also GNVQ (Intermediate) in Leisure and Tourism, IATA and ABTA ticketing courses, etc.

CORNWALL COLLEGE ST AUSTELL
Trevarthian Road, St. Austell, Cornwall PL25 4BU. ☎01726 226626. Fax 01726 226627. E-mail info@st-austell.ac.uk. Website www.st-austell.ac.uk.
Courses offered: NVQ in Travel Services, BTEC EdExcel, GNVQ Leisure & Tourism, Hospitality & Catering, Tourist Information and Guiding. Overseas Resort Representatives, Overseas Ski Chalet Hosts, Overseas Children's Couriers and many others.

EAST ANTRIM INSTITUTE OF FURTHER & HIGHER EDUCATION
Newtownabbey Campus, 400 Shore Road, Newtownabbey, Co. Antrim, Northern Ireland BT37 9RS. ☎01232 864331. Website www.eaifhe.ac.uk.
Courses offered: GNVQ Leisure & Tourism (Foundation), AVCE Travel & Tourism, BTEC GNVQ Travel and Tourism Management, HNC in Travel & Tourism Management (including Events Management).

GLASGOW CALEDONIAN UNIVERSITY
Department of Hospitality, Tourism & Leisure Management, 1 Park Drive, Glasgow G3 6LP. ☎0141-337 4254. Fax 0141-337 4141. Website www.caledonian.ac.uk.
Courses offered: degree courses in tourism management, international travel and information systems, hospitality management, leisure management.

HAMMERSMITH & WEST LONDON COLLEGE
Gliddon Road, Barons Court, London W14 9BL. ☎0800 980 2175 or 020-8741 1688. Fax 020-8741 2491. E-mail cic@wlc.ac.uk. Website www.wlc.ac.uk.
Courses offered: HND Travel & Tourism Management (2 years); Advanced AIRTAC (Airline & Travel Agents Certificates)(1 year); AVCE Travel & Tourism (2 years); Virgin Atlantic Air Fares & Ticketing Level 2 (10-week evening course from January or April). Other courses include Diploma in Tour Operations; GNVQ Foundation in Leisure and Tourism with ICT.
Cost: EU fee for HND £1,160 (£4,995 non-EU): for AVCE and Advanced AIRTAC £875 (£3,999 non-EU); £330 for Level 1 Ticketing course.
Follow-up: work placements can be found through college contacts. Travel agency on site allows students to get hands-on experience.

HIGHBURY COLLEGE
Dovercourt Road, Cosham, Portsmouth, Hants. PO6 2SA. ☎023 9238 3131. Fax 023 9232 5551. E-mail info@highbury.ac.uk. Website www.highbury.ac.uk.
Courses offered: GNVQ Travel & Tourism (Foundation and Intermediate), AS/A2 Travel & Tourism, BTEC HND plus 2-hour courses in Geography for Tourism.

KINGSWOOD INSTRUCTOR PROGRAMME
Operations HQ, Kingswood Centres, West Runton, Cromer, Norfolk NR27 9NF. ☎01263 835155. Fax 01263 835192.E-mail adventure@kingswood.co.uk. Website www.kingswood.co.uk.
Popular gap-year or leisure industry entry 'Earn-while-you-learn' instructor training programme. Kingswood has six residential Educational Activity Centres for school children where they participate in adventure activities, ICT and environmental studies. Over 200 Trainees (aged 18-24) obtain nationally recognised qualifications for the tourism and leisure industry, attainment levels in session delivery and work towards obtaining a Modern Apprenticeship in Activity Leadership.

LEEDS METROPOLITAN UNIVERSITY
School of Tourism & Hospitality Management, Calverley St, Leeds, LS1 3HE. ☎0113 283 2600. Fax 0113 283 3111. E-mail tourism@leedsmet.ac.uk. Website www.leedsmet.ac.uk.
HND/BA(Hons) International Tourism Management, HND/BA(Hons) Tourism Marketing Management, HND/BA(Hons) Tourist Destination Management, BA/BA(Hons) Managing International Tourism, Postgraduate Diploma/MA International Tourism Management. Top-up opportunities available for holders of an appropriate award, giving exemption from levels 1 & 2, resulting in the completion of a top-up course within 1 year.

NAPIER UNIVERSITY SCHOOL OF MARKETING & TOURISM
Craighouse Road, Edinburgh. Tel: 0131-455 6242. Fax 0131-455 6269. E-mail rmrobertson@napier.ac.uk. Website www.nubs.napier.ac.uk.
Courses offered: BA(Hons) in Tourism Management on its own or with Entrepreneurship, Languages, Human Resource Management or Marketing. MSc in International Tourism. Course incorporates 24 weeks employment in industry.

NATIONAL AIR TRAFFIC SERVICES LTD
College of Air Traffice Control, Bournemouth International Airport, Christchurch, Dorset BH23 6DF. ☎01202 472407. Fax 01202 472383. E-mail College@nats.co.uk. Website www.nats.co.uk.
Courses offered: in-house training for trainee air traffic controllers aged 18-30. Entry requirements are 5 GCSEs at C or above including Maths and English and 2 A-levels. **Applications procedure:** all year round. Duration of course 72 weeks.

OAKLANDS COLLEGE
St Albans Smallford Campus, Hatfield Road, St Albans, Hertfordshire AL4 0JA. ☎01727 737000/01727 737080. E-mail help.line@oaklands.ac.uk
Courses offered: Edexcel NVQ Levels 2 and 3 (part-time over a year).
Edexcel HND in Travel & Tourism Management, includes study of the travel and tourism environment, law, finance, marketing, operations and planning. Work experience of 50 days is a compulsory part of the course. Students may also study for IATA Levels 1 and 2 fares and ticketing qualifications. Airfares and ticketing can also be taken independently (one evening a week for 12 weeks). Also NCFE Certificate for Overseas Resort Reps (one evening a week for 20 weeks). Price of ticketing course is £125 and of NCFE course £175; concessions available. Access to college's own commercial travel agency (called Destinations) at Welwyn Garden City campus.

OPEN LEARNING CENTRE INTERNATIONAL
☎01267 235268. Fax 01267 238179. E-mail info@olcinternational.com. Website www.olci.info.
Courses offered: distance learning for ABTA, ABTOC, BA Fares & Ticketing Levels 1 & 2. 60-150 hours of self-study.
Cost: £290-£355.

OXFORD & CHERWELL COLLEGE
Oxpens Road, Oxford OX1 1SA. ☎01865 269215. Fax 01865 248871. E-mail fiona_laing@oxford.occ.ac.uk. Website www.occ.ac.uk.
Courses offered: AVCE Travel & Tourism, Intermediate Certificate for Resort Representative, Advanced Certificate for On-Tour Manager, IATA Airfares & Ticketing Levels 1 & 2 (17-week evening courses), ABTA Certificate in Travel (Travel Agency) plus various language courses.
Cost: IATA evening course £250; full-time courses for uner 19s are free; if over 19, registration and exam fees are about £220.

PARK LANE COLLEGE
Park Lane, Leeds LS3 1AA. ☎0113-216 2000. Fax 0113-16 2020. Website www.parklanecoll.ac.uk.
Courses offered: Edexcel GNVQ Foundation, Intermediate and Advance in Leisure and Tourism. At AVCE level (Advanced Vocational Certificate of Education), major options in Travel and Tourism, Animateur (those wanting to work as overseas representatives, entertainment officers, event organisers, etc.), Sport and Outdoor Recreation. BTEC NVQ in Travel Services and Foundation NVQ. A wide variety of full and part-time courses up to HNC level including air cabin crew and air ticketing training.
Duration of courses: various.
Follow-up: opportunities for overseas placements as part of many courses. Work placements locally can lead to employment for some students. College is often approached by local employers in the tourist industry when they need to hire.

ROEHAMPTON UNIVERSITY OF SURREY
Erasmus House, Roehampton Lane, London SW15 5PU. ☎020-8392 3000. Website www.roehampton.ac.uk.
Courses offered: MA/Postgraduate Diploma (awarded by University of Surrey) in Sociology and Anthropology of Travel and Tourism and in Tourism & Heritage.

SCHOOL OF FOOD, CONSUMER, TOURISM AND HOSPITALITY
Manchester Metropolitan University, Old Hall Lane, Manchester M14 6HR.

☎0161-247 2722. Fax 0161-247 6550. E-mail htm-admissions@mmu.ac.uk. Website www.mmu.ac.uk/hollings.
Courses offered: BA(Hons)/HND Tourism Management; BA(Hons)/HND Hospitality Management with Tourism. Available as a 4-year sandwich course, 3-year full-time degree or a 3-year sandwich or 2 year full-time HND. Year's paid industrial placement in UK or overseas is a key part of programme.

SCHOOL OF MANAGEMENT, UNIVERSITY OF SURREY
Guildford, Surrey GU2 7XH. Tel: 01483 689347. Fax 01483 689511. E-mail som@surrey.ac.uk. Website www.som.surrey.ac.uk.
Courses offered: BSc and MSc Management & Tourism; BSc International Hospitality & Tourism Management; MSc Tourism Development; MSc Tourism Marketing. All tourism programmes are accredited by the World Tourism Organization.

SCOTTISH HOTEL SCHOOL
University of Strathclyde, Curran Building, 94 Cathedral St, Glasgow G4 0LG. Website www.shs.strath.ac.uk.
Courses offered: postgraduate courses in tourism, and hotel and hospitality courses (approved by HCIMA and EuroCHRIE).

SHEFFIELD HALLAM UNIVERSITY
City Campus, Howard St, Sheffield S1 1WB. ☎0114 225 3506. Fax 0114 225 2881. E-mail l.j.merchant@shu.ac.uk. Website www.shu.ac.uk.
Courses offered: HND Hospitality Management and Tourism (full-time or part-time); BSc(Hons) Tourism & Hospitality Business Management or Tourism Management. BSc(Hons) International Tourism Business Management by distance learning. Similar range of MSc courses. Undergraduate courses either 3 years full-time or 4 years sandwich.
Cost: £2,400 distance learning; postgraduate £3,310.
Follow-up: designated placement officer assists students in finding vocational experience placements in UK or abroad in third year.

SOUTH TRAFFORD COLLEGE
Manchester Road, West Timperley, Altrincham, Cheshire WA14 5PQ. ☎0161-952 4600. Fax 0161-952 4672. E-mail enquiries@stcoll.ac.uk. Website www.stcoll.ac.uk.
Courses offered: Travel Services, GNVQ Leisure and Tourism (Foundation and Intermediate), AVCE Travel & Tourism, Airport Operations (recognised by Manchester Airport), cabin crew.
Duration of courses: part-time and full-time options.

STOKE ON TRENT COLLEGE
Cauldron Campus, Stoke Road, Shelton, Stoke on Trent, Staffs. ST4 2DG. ☎01782 208208. Fax 01782 603728. E-mail info@stokecoll.ac.uk. Website www.stokecoll.ac.uk.
Courses offered: AVCE Travel & Tourism (12 units).

STRATHCLYDE UNIVERSITY – see Scottish Hotel School.

T&T TRAINING SOLUTIONS
5-7 Folgate St, Bishopsgate, London E1 6BX. ☎020-7426 9378. Fax 08700 514980. E-mail info@t-ttrainingsolutions.co.uk. Website www.t-ttrainingso

lutions.co.uk.
Specialist recruitment agency T&T Recruitment & Resourcing Ltd offers in-house Virgin Atlantic Fare & Ticketing courses at level 1 & 2 and CRS training on Galileo, Worldspan, Sabre and Amadeus (IATA-accredited). Intensive and part-time courses offered.

THURROCK & BASILDON COLLEGE
Nethermayne Campus, Nethermayne, Basildon, Essex SS16 5NN. ☎01268 532015. E-mail info@tab.ac.uk. Website www.tab.ac.uk.
Courses offered: GNVQ (Intermediate) and AVCE Leisure & Tourism, Diploma and Certificate in Travel Agency Studies, Travel & Tourism with languages.

TOURISM TRAINING ORGANISATION
54a Ifield Road, London SW10 9AD. ☎0906 553 2056 (calls cost £1 a minute, refunded from cost of course if booked).
Courses offered: tour managers and guides, site guides, trail guides and walking tour guides. Courses cover tour managing and guideing, handling groups, transfers, check-ins, researching and delivering commentaries, basic emergency aid, selling excursions and how to find jobs. Recognised by British Council.
Also available by distance learning: covers theory for holiday reps, tour managers, guides, conference and exhibition staff, etc. Students choose the speed at which they want to work through tapes, programme books, project book, working manual and link book which can be assessed as a record of achievement.
Cost: £99-£200.

TRAINING PROFESSIONAL GUIDES LTD
31 Sterndale Rd, London W14 0HT. E-mail sallyempson@compuserve.com. Website www.guidetraining.co.uk.
Accredited to provide Blue Badge guide training for London.
Application procedure: pre-entry exam (for a fee of £25) followed by an interview in the autumn.
Duration of courses: one year part-time from January. 3 evenings a week plus Saturdays.
Cost: £2,465 plus VAT (2004).

TRAVEL TRAINING COMPANY
The Cornerstone, The Broadway, Woking, Surrey GU21 5AR. ☎01483 727321. Fax 01483 756698. E-mail info@ttctraining.co.uk. Website www.ttctraining.co.uk.
Subsidiary of ABTA (Association of British Travel Agents) which develops training courses for school leavers, travel agents, tour operators, transport operators and tourist boards, and also produces and manages examinations for the major travel industry qualifications.
Courses offered: wide range of qualifications for travel agents and others in the industry. The Travel Training Programme is a Modern Apprenticeship which offers an NVQ level 3 whilst gaining work experience. Also offer Certificate in Travel (Travel Agency), Certificate in Travel (Tour Operators) and airfare and ticketing course.
Duration of courses: self-study courses are at student's discretion.

UNIVERSITY OF WALES INSTITUTE (CARDIFF)
UWIC, PO Box 377, Western Avenue, Cardiff CF5 2YB. Tel: 029 2041 6070. Fax 029 2041 6286. E-mail uwicinfo@uwic.ac.uk. Website www.uwic.ac.uk.
Courses offered: BA and MA courses in Leisure & Tourism Management (including

with languages); MSc in Hospitality Management. Also HND in Tourism Management.

WEST LONDON COLLEGE
Parliament House, 35 North Row, Westminster, London W1R 2DB. ☎020-7491 1841. Email courses@w-l-c.co.uk. Website www.w-l-c.co.uk.
Courses offered: Confederation of Tourism, Hotels and Catering Managing Advanced Diploma in Tour Operation. Travel Agency Management. Virgin Atlantic Airways Levels 1 & 2 (Fares & Ticketing accredited by IATA) plus Galileo Computerised Flight Reservations.

COURSES ABROAD

Europe (countries in alphabetical order)

CLUB HABITAT
Kohlgrub 9, 6365 Kirchberg, Austria. ☎5357-2505.
Courses offered: annual pre-ski season course in job-hunting, German language and related issues. Future of course uncertain (see Austria chapter).

COLLEGE OF TOURISM & HOTEL MANAGEMENT
Larnaka Rd, Aglangia, POB 20281, Nicosia 2150, Cyprus. ☎+357 22-462846. Fax +357 22-336295. E-mail: cothm@spidernet.com.cy. Website www.cothm.ac.cy.
Courses offered: Travel & Tourism Administration (2-year Diploma); Hotel Administration (3-year Higher Diploma); Hospitality Management (4-year BA). Possibility of passing external exams such as IATA/UFTAA and AHLA.
Cost: undergraduate programmes cost about C£2,500 per year. Accommodation can be in Philoxenia Hostel or other.
Follow-up: possibility of summer internships in industry.

HORIZON HPL
Signet House, 49-51 Farringdon Road, London, EC1M 3JB. ☎020-7404 9192. Fax 020-7404 9194. E-mail Horizonhpl.London@btinternet.com. Website http://perso.club-internet.fr/horizon1.
Courses offered: Anglo-French training organisation offers package combining language tuition and live-in hotel work placements as well as company placements all over France. Wages are on a trainee scale, from £50 per week plus accommodation, while the package fee is £240. Horizon's office in France is at 22-26 rue du Sergent Bauchat, 75012 Paris (01-40 01 07 07/fax 01-40 01 07 28) while the Dublin office is at 3 Lower Abbey St, Dublin 1 (01-8745 002).

ANGELL ACADEMY FREIBURG
Mattenstrasse 1, 79100 Freiburg, Germany. ☎+49 761-70329-21. Fax +49 761-70329-40. E-mail m.bolte@angell.de. Website www.angell-akademie-freiburg.de.
Courses offered: Tourism Management and International Event Organisation. State-recognised diplomas as International Tourism Management Assistant (ITA), International Event Organiser (IEO), BA in International Hospitality & Tourism Management.
Duration of courses: ITA and IEO are 2 years including work placement of 3-6 months. Intake every September.
Cost: ITA €5,160 per year. IEO €5,760. BA €7,120 per year.

Follow-up: help with placements for internships and job placements.

FAILTE IRELAND
Irish Tourist Board, 88-95 Amiens St, Dublin 1, Ireland. ☎1-855 6555. E-mail training@failteireland.ie.
Government of Ireland tourism training agency, formerly known as CERT.
Courses offered: guide training and other vocational tourism courses. Qualification is granted only after an assessor has observed a candidate in action after the course. Candidates must demonstrate their ability to handle passengers and keep them interested.

CHN – UNIVERSITY OF PROFESSIONAL EDUCATION
Christelijke Hogeschool Nederland, Rengerslaan 8, PO Box 1298, 8900 CG Leeuwarden, The Netherlands. Tel: +31 58-233 0330. Fax +31 58-233 0505. E-mail info@chn.nl. Website www.chn.nl.
Courses offered: BA Tourism Management (4 years or less depending on prior education and experience); MA in International Leisure & Tourism (1 year). MA programmes accredited and validated by the London Metropolitan University.
Cost: €1,495 per year tuition for BA, €9,500 for MA.

GUIDOR
Postbox 261, 1110 AG Diemen-Zuid (Office address: Wildenborch 6, 1112 CB Diemen-Zuid), The Netherlands. ☎+31-20-624 6072. Fax +31-20-639 1378. E-mail info@guidor.nl. Website www.guidor.nl.
Courses offered: guide training in Amsterdam (in Dutch) during the winter season offered by Guidor, the Dutch professional guides' association.

HOGESCHOOL ZUYD
University of Professional Education, Department of Tourism Management, Brusselseweg 150, 6217 HB Maastricht, The Netherlands. ☎+31 43-3466250/ +31 6-53706854. Fax +31 43-3466619. E-mail hans.gijsbers@hszuyd.nl. Website www.hogeschoolzuyd.nl.
Courses offered: Bachelor of Business Administration & Tourism Management (4 years).
Cost: tuition fee €1,445 plus books (€450) and excursions (€400).

NETHERLANDS INSTITUTE OF TOURISM AND TRANSPORT STUDIES
International Office, PO Box 3917, 4800 DX Breda, The Netherlands. ☎+31 76-530 2203. Fax +31 76-530 2205. E-mail international.office@nhtv.nl. Website:www.nhtv.nl.
Courses offered: higher professional management courses in three areas: transport, logistics and planning studies; tourism and leisure studies (with which there is an English option), and tourism and recreation studies (which offers a respected course in tour management). Special option in studying sustainable tourism.
Duration of courses: 2-4 years.

NORWEGIAN GUIDE SERVICE
Guideservice AS, Akerhusstranda 353, 0150 Oslo, Norway. Terl +47 22-42 70 20. Fax +47 22-42 29 80. E-mail guideservice@online.no. Website www.guideservice.no.
Runs guiding courses through Treider College from September.
Cost 14,000 kroner. Can provide details of guiding courses in various regions of Norway.

LES ROCHES MARBELLA
Swiss Hotel Association School of Hotel Management, Urb. Las Lomas de Rio Verde, Ctra. De Istan km. 1, E-29600 Marbella Spain. ☎+34 952-764 437. Fax +34 952 764 438. E-mail admissions@lesroches.es. Website www.lesroches.es.

Prestigious private English-language hotel management school.

Courses offered: Swiss Hotel Association Hotel Management Diploma (3 years) taught in English or bilingual English/Spanish. Postgraduate degree in Hospitality Management (1 year). From 2004 Bachelor of Business Administration (Hospitality) Degree (1 year). Undergraduate distance leaning.

Cost: €14,000-€16,760 per year, including accommodation.

Follow-up: workplace training arranged in high end restaurants and hotels worldwide.

ALLIANCE INTERNATIONAL HOTEL & BUSINESS MANAGEMENT SCHOOL
IHTTI School of Hotel Management, Neuchâtel, Switzerland. ☎+41 61 312 30 94. E-mail headoffice@ihtti.ch.

Courses offered: 2 year course in hotel administration, taught in English. Guarantees jobs in Swiss hotel as part of course with opportunity to earn money to defray fees. Has links with hotels abroad, such as the Hilton Group in Britain.

GLION INSTITUTE OF HIGHER EDUCATION
Hotel School, 1823 Glion-sur-Montreux, Switzerland. ☎+41 21-966 35 35. Fax +41 21-966 35 09. E-mail glion@glion.ch. Website www.glion.ch.

Courses offered: prestigious training for hotel executive and management training. Bilingual French/English. Hospitality & Tourism Management and Hospitality Administration courses both cover food and beverage, kitchen and service, accommodation, marketing, financial management and human resources.

Cost: SFr25,000 per semester (BSc Programme comprises 4 paying semesters and 2 traineeships).

Follow-up: maintains contact with former students who have developed a networking system to help new graduates find good jobs.

'CÉSAR RITZ' COLLEGES, SWITZERLAND
Rte Cantonale 51, 1897 Le Bouveret, Switzerland. ☎+41 24-482 82 82. Fax +41 24-482 88 99. E-mail admissions@ritz.edu. Website www.ritz.edu.

Courses offered: Swiss Diploma in Hotel Management, Bachelor of International Business Degree in Hotel and Tourism Management, MBA in Hotel and Tourism Management; and MSc in International Hospitality Management Diploma is validated by New England Association of Schools and Colleges (NEASC) and degrees are offered in partnership with American Universities to European standards and consistent with the European Credit Transfer System (ECTS). MSc is awarded by Manchester Metropolitan University. Innovative programmes combining the art of Swiss hospitality with contemporary international business management education.

Duration of courses: Diploma: 2 years. Degree: 3 years. MBA: 15 months. MSc: 18-24 months. Start dates in January, April, July and October.

Cost: Diploma: Sfr.48,000. Degree: Sfr. 98,000. MBA: Sfr. 39,800. MSc: Sfr.48,200. Accommodation in double rooms and meals included.

Follow-up: intensive industry relations combined with annual career fairs, providing excellent career opportunities.

ÉCOLE HOTELIÈRE DE LAUSANNE
Le Chalet-à-Gobet, 1000 Lausanne 25, Switzerland. ☎+41 21-785 11 11. Fax +41 21-785 11 21. E-mail admissions@ehl.ch. Website www.ehl.ch.
Courses offered: prestigious hotel administration and hospitality management courses leading to a bachelor degree. Also MBA in International Hospitality Management.
Cost: €31,900 tuition.

HOSTA HOTEL & TOURISM SCHOOL
1854 Leysin, Switzerland. ☎+41 25-34 2611.
Courses offered: hotel operations and management, tourism management, leading to executive positions within tourism or hotel industry.
Duration of courses: 1, 2 and 3 year diplomas and Bachelor of Science Degree. Courses begin in August and January. Students are required to complete on-the-job training which is found by Hosta.
Cost: from £15,000 per year including tuition, board, lodging, books.
Follow-up: HOSTA is visited by companies such as Hyatt, Hilton, Intercontinental and Sheraton, who recruit students.

USA

CORNELL UNIVERSITY
School of Hotel Administration, G80 Statler Hall, Ithaca, NY 14853-6902, USA. ☎607-255-9393. Fax 607-255-8749.
Internationally recognised hotel training centre.
Courses offered: BSc, MSc, PhD and other advanced courses in hospitality management.

EDUCATIONAL INSTITUTE OF THE AMERICAN HOTEL & LODGING ASSOCIATION (EI)
2113 North High St, East Lansing, MI 48906, USA. ☎517-372-8800. Fax 517-372-5141. E-mail info@ei-ahla.org. Website www.ei-ahla.org.
Non-profit educational foundation of the American Hotel & Lodging Association. In operation since 1952.
Courses offered: 30+ hospitality management courses through its Distance Learning department. Students may pursue individual course certificates, or work toward a 5-course Certificate of Specialization, an 8-course Hospitality Operations Certificate, or a 12-course Hospitality Management Diploma or Food and Beverage Diploma. Certificates of Specialization are available in seven different subject areas: Rooms Division Management, Food and Beverage Management, Human Resources Management, Accounting and Financial Management, Marketing and Sales Management, Club Management, and International Hotel Management. Complete information on Distance Learning courses is available on the EI web site.
Duration of courses: students have up to four months to complete a course.
Cost: $250 per course; $200 for AHLA members.

INTERNATIONAL TOUR MANAGEMENT INSTITUTE
625 Market St, Suite 610, San Francisco, CA 94105, USA. ☎800-442-4864 or 415-957-9489. Fax 415-957-9474. E-mail itmitourdirector@aol.com. Website www.itmitourtraining.com.
Established in 1976, ITMI was the first US school with specialist courses in tour

management and directing. Accredited by California State Education Department.
Courses offered: group tour leading courses held in Los Angeles, San Francisco and Boston.
Duration of courses: 125 hours of instruction over 2 or 4 weeks.
Cost: $2,950 not including room and board.
Follow-up: ITMI offers help with résumés and job placement; many major tour companies interview graduates. ITMI has produced a 53-minute video 'An Introduction to Tour Management' which reviews full-time and part-time employment opportunities; cost $19.95.

THE TRAVEL INSTITUTE
148 Linden St, Suite 305, Wellesley, MA 02482, USA. ☎7821-237-2280/800-682-8886. Fax 781-237-3860. E-mail info@thetravelinstitute.com. Website www.thetravelinstitute.com.
Non-profit educational institute founded in 1964, formerly the Institute of Certified Travel Agents.
Courses offered: Certified Travel Associate (CTA) and Certified Travel Counselor (CTC) courses for career travel agents overseen by the Institute which can provide a list of institutes of education which offer the courses. Self-study with textbook *Travel Career Development* which provides basic foundation in the travel business. Further specialist programmes available via the Research & Education Department.
Duration of courses: CTP (Certified Tour Professional) programme requires more than 200 hours of study and testing over 18-36 months (in groups or independently) and at least 5 years travel industry experience.

VIRGINIA TECH UNIVERSITY
Department of Hospitality & Tourism Management, Pamplin College of Business, 362 Wallace Hall, Blacksburg, VA 24061-0429, USA. ☎540-231-5515. Fax 540-231-8313. E-mail bmihalik@vt.edu. Website www.cob.vt.edu/htm.
Courses offered: general hospitality and tourism courses, accredited by CHRIE. BSc, MSc and PhD degrees. MBA with concentration in hospitality management.
Cost: current fees posted on Virginia Tech home page www2.bursar.vt.edu/sp/tuition.shtml.
Follow-up: Virginia Tech has an on-campus placement office and Pamplin College has job fairs.

AUSTRALASIA

AUSTRALIAN FEDERATION OF TRAVEL AGENTS (AFTA)
Level 3, 309 Pitt St, Sydney, NSW 2000, Australia. Tel: +61 2-9264 3299. Fax +61 2-9264 1085. E-mail afta@afta.com.au. Website: www.afta.com.au.
Courses offered: Network of AFTA colleges in the main Australian cities delivers Certificate courses in Sales and Australian ticketing (Level II) and international ticketing, tour operations and other subjects (Level III). Also available by distance learning from the External Studies Department.
Duration of courses: full-time Certificate III course lasts 22 weeks; part-time course runs for 48 weeks.

BLUE MOUNTAINS HOTEL SCHOOL
1 Chambers Road, Leura, NSW 2780, Australia. ☎+61 2-4780 1659.

Fax +61 2-4784 3246. E-mail enquiry@bmihms.nsw.edu.au. Website www.hotelschool.com.au.
Founded in 1991, the Blue Mountains Hotel School in the small town of Leura provides international qualifications in hotel management. Affiliated to the Alliance of International Hotel & Business Schools in Switzerland (see entry).
Courses offered: Hospitality and Tourism courses from Certificate to Degree level. 6 months of study followed by a 6-month paid industry placement consisting of at least 800 hours each.

PERTH SCHOOL OF HOSPITALITY & TOURISM
14th Floor, Carillon City Office Tower, 207 Murray St, Perth 6000, WA, Australia. ☎+61 8-9322 1919. E-mail psht@bigpond.com. Website www.psht.com.au.
Courses offered: short, industry-based, nationally accredited hotel management and catering courses available full-time and part-time.

TOURISM TRAINING AUSTRALIA
GPO Box 2493, Sydney, NSW 200. ☎+61 2-9290 1055. Fax +61 2-9290 1001. Email reception@tourismtraining.com.au. Website www.tourismtraining.com.au.
Offices in all the states. National industry training body. Website links to all the state training authorities.

TRADE WINGS INSTITUTE OF MANAGEMENT
Rani Sati Temple Premises, Mahalaxmi Temple Lane, Mumbai 400026, India. ☎+91 22-2403776. Fax +91 22-2044334. Website www.tradewinginstitute.com.
About 60 affiliated training centres around India.
Courses offered: travel, tourism, cargo, hotel and in-flight management and personality development.
Duration of courses: 9-18 months, starting throughout the year.
Cost: Rs9,00-14,000.
Follow-up: assistance given with job placement.

MIDDLE EAST

TADMOR HOTEL SCHOOL
38 Bazel St, 46660 Hertzelia, Israel. ☎+972 9-952 5049. Fax +972 9-957 9622. E-mail orly@tadmor.co.il. Website www.tadmor.co.il (Hebrew only).
Courses offered: Advanced Hotel Management (2 years); Advanced Food & Beverage Management (2 years). Courses conducted in Hebrew. Accredited for continuation to a BA degree in Business Administration.
Cost: 18,400 New Israeli Shekels per year.

SKYLINE INSTITUTE
PO Box 5798, Safat, 13058 Kuwait. ☎+965 240 3776. Fax +965 242 7122. E-mail skyline@boodaiaviation.com. Website www.boodaiaviation.com.
Courses offered: aviation training, ticketing, etc.

EMIRATES ACADEMY OF HOSPITALITY MANAGEMENT
PO Box 11416, Dubai, United Arab Emirates. ☎+971 4-315 5555. Fax:

+971   4-315   5556.   E-mail   lars.eltvik@emiratesacademy.edu.   Website www.emiratesacademy.edu.
BSc (Hons) in International Hospitality Management and in International Travel & Tourism; also 2-year Associate degree in Hospitality Operations and in Business & Tourism. Provides good exposure to industry because of close affiliation with Jumeirah International, a group of luxury hotels and resorts in Dubai and London.

GETTING A JOB

Jobs in tourism are fixed up either from home or sought on location. Sometimes this corresponds to working for a tour operator in your home country or working for a ground handler in the destination country. In fact most people pursuing a tourism career abroad work for companies based in their home country. Others who may be more interested in seasonal or casual jobs in tourism abroad wait until they are in their destination to look for work. Both of these kinds of job hunt are covered in this chapter.

The best time to apply to the major tour operators is September for work during the following summer season, and the main interviewing season is December/January, with cancellations being filled after that, normally from a reserve list drawn up after the interview season.

Employment agencies such as *New Frontiers* register vacancies with tour operators at home and occasionally overseas. It may seem too obvious, but Jobcentres near airports, ferry ports and tourist resorts may have information about tourism vacancies, for instance the Jobcentre at Gatwick Airport bristles with airline vacancies. For information about the Europe-wide employment service EURES, see the chapter on Europe 'Job-Hunting in the EU'.

ADVERTISEMENTS

The vast majority of jobs in tourism are never advertised. Tui UK say that after receiving 50,000 job enquiries, they give up counting and most major tour operators receive scores or even hundreds of unsolicited applications for every vacancy they have. Still, it will do no harm to scour the classified pages of daily papers like the *Daily Telegraph, Times, Daily Mail* (Thursdays), *Daily Express* and London's *Evening Standard*, as well as major regional newspapers. The two mainstream travel journals are *Travel Weekly* and *Travel Trade Gazette* both of which carry advertisements on their websites. *Travel Weekly* (www.travelweeklyjobs.co.uk) lists masses of jobs exclusively in travel agencies and in the admin offices of travel companies. The number of vacancies posted on the *TTG* website is far fewer but covering more categories of employment from flight service staff for airlines like KLM and Qatar Airways to cruise line staff, but mainly sales and UK agency staff. Both journals are available in hard copy, though they are expensive, e.g. an annual subscription to *Travel Weekly* costs £105, half price for students, so try to consult a copy in a library or at the office of a friendly local travel agent.

One specialist online publication can be found at www.rollingpinjobs.com which seeks to post vacancies in international cruise lines, river cruise companies, ferry companies, event catering, airlines, casinos and entertainment, though when checked recently the selection was small. Its two bases are Miami and Basel.

As well as job adverts, the trade press contains news items which can indirectly help you to find a job. For example it might break the news that a major new holiday development or theme park is to be built so that you can make enquiries early about new jobs that are bound to be created. For example a past issue of a trade journal contained the news that the Rank Organisation was to build a major holiday village in Cumbria, that the former Irish Tourist Board director was about to launch a new car rental service, that Chester had been chosen to host the annual National Waterways Festival and that Stoke-on-Trent Tourist Office had launched a new visitor trail linked to the famous local author

Arnold Bennett. New ventures like these might well be recruiting new administrators, receptionists or guides, and people with initiative will follow them up.

INTERPRETING ADVERTS

Beware of ads with no company name or address. 'Golden opportunity to travel' can mean the travel takes the place of a salary. 'Opportunity to meet people' might mean working as a time share tout. To check the bona fides of a company, you might first check if it has an Air Travel Organisers' Licence or ATOL administered by the Civil Aviation Authority. Their easily searchable database of members , comprising both tour operators and travel agencies, can be found at www.caa.co.uk/cpg/atol; listings include head office addresses and telephone numbers but no email, web or fax details.

If in doubt about a travel agency, you can check its status with the Association of British Travel Agents. Formed more than 50 years ago, ABTA has 1,900 members which, among them, sell more than 90% of UK package holidays. Their website www.abta.com carries a great deal of potentially useful information for the job-seeker, including a new area of up-to-date job vacancies. The ABTA office is at 68-71 Newman Street, London W1T 3AH; member checks can be requested on 020-7307 1907 or by e-mail on information@abta.co.uk.

Another source of reputable independent tour operators is AITO (Association of Independent Tour Operators, 133A St Margaret's Road, Twickenham, Middlesex TW1 1RG; www.aito.co.uk) which publishes a free handy directory of its 150 members indexed according to special interest and destination. To check the credentials of companies offering tours in Britain, contact the British Incoming Tour Operators' Association, (BITOA, 14 Leicester Place, London WC2H 7BZ; www.bitoa.co.uk). If a company has membership of one of these associations they have to abide by rules, and have responsibilities when employing staff. If the company is not a member, you need to find out why. It may be because it is highly specialised and doesn't fit into an Association's criteria. Or it could be a fly-by-night operation.

In the States, the best known national trade journal is *Travel Trade* (www.traveltrade.com) distributed to 230,000 travel agents, which is of limited use to the job-seeker.

RECRUITMENT AGENCIES

Specialist recruitment agencies for the travel and tourism industry tend to place people with relevant training or experience in jobs in the UK, though they may also be able to advise on training placements as well. Some specialise even further in placing candidates in, say, travel agencies, airlines, etc. *T&T Travel Recruitment and Resourcing Ltd* was established in 1983 and employs 10 consultants working to place suitable candidates in travel-related employment. It is also the only agency to offer in-house Virgin Atlantic Fares & Ticketing plus Galileo (Levels 1 and 2).

Other key recruiters have entries in the Directory of Placement Agencies near the end of the book. *New Frontiers* is a major consultancy for the travel industry and is planning to add a Newcastle office in the near future. It registers temporary and permanent vacancies in the entire UK travel industry, including retail travel, business travel, tour operations, airlines and hotels. It also offers both careers guidance and ABTA/IATA approved training courses. The recruitment service is free and the careers training and advice is at a reasonable cost. Also recommended are C&M with a massive on-line presence and Changing Places.

Mediating agencies are also involved to a small extent with job placement abroad in the hotels and catering industry. Specialist consultancies with client hotels and restaurants around the world undertake to place qualified chefs and other personnel, mostly in senior positions. In very few cases agencies and leisure groups can place people without any expertise in foreign hotels; however wages in these cases are normally negligible. Even more specialised agencies recruit personnel for cruise ships (see chapter) or for particular jobs such as disc jockeys and entertainers (see *Glamorous Jobs*).

People with a background in hotels and catering may be able to fix up overseas contracts while still in the UK. The Overseas Placing Unit of JobCentre Plus registers quite a few foreign vacancies in the tourist industry (particularly in France and Italy) with Jobcentres. Specialist agencies will be of interest to qualified hotel staff including chefs, hotel receptionists and restaurant staff, such as *Quest Elite* which has some international as well as British vacancies and *VIP International*. The Recruitment and Employment Confederation (020-7323 4300; www.rec.org.uk) has a special listing of recruitment agencies for the hospitality industry. Contact details for these and other recruitment agencies are listed in the Directory of Placement & Recruitment Agencies at the back of this book.

One of the most useful websites for job-seekers in the hospitality and catering industry is www.caterer.com which now has a special section of international jobs.

INTERNET RECRUITMENT

A host of websites promise to provide free on-line recruitment services for job-seekers. These include specialist hospitality websites like voovs.com, doctorjob.com and travelrecruit.co.uk. Also check the relevant sections of the more general recruitment sites like workthing.com and jobsite.co.uk. For non-professional openings abroad, check out the non-commercial free Jobs Abroad Bulletin (www.payaway.co.uk), www.summerjobseeker.com (for jobs in the tourist industry), www.gapwork.com, www.anyworkanywhere.com, www.jobsmonkey.com (especially for North America), http://jobs.escapeartist.com and www.hotrecruit.co.uk, among many others.

In the infancy of web-based recruitment, many sites seemed to promise more than they could deliver, e.g. great search engines but very few decent vacancies. The dotcoms that have survived have developed their client base and now serve a useful function for job-seekers. For links to many relevant sites, check the British web portal toxiclemon.co.uk.

It seems that everywhere you look on the internet potentially useful links can be found. A surprising number of tour operators and other travel company home pages feature a Recruitment or Human Resources icon you can click on to find out about jobs with that operator.

SPECULATIVE APPLICATIONS

If you are trying to break into the tourism industry, you will have to resign yourself to doing a great deal of leg work or at least a lot of letting your fingers do the walking. The majority of companies are small owner-operated firms with occasional vacancies which are often filled through their network of contacts or with people who contact them on the off-chance of a job. That is why a good training course is worth its weight in gold. If the teachers know the industry they know where to find jobs, which companies are hiring locally, and will have their own list of companies worth applying to. Companies often contact good courses with job vacancies.

When you go it alone, try to improve your marketability as much as you can before actually approaching prospective employers (see chapter on Training). Without formal training, get as much exposure to the industry as possible, though tour operators are inundated with requests for work experience. Find out as much as possible about the business in general and the firms to which you might apply in particular. One possible source of advice is your local travel agent who may know which companies employ reps (but try to establish some rapport with the agent before asking such questions and choose a quiet time to make such enquiries).

As a preliminary to conducting a job search, it may be worth wandering round the lobbies of major tourist hotels looking for tour operators' notices, complete with their addresses. Try coach parks and ask the drivers if they know of any jobs going. Keep your eyes peeled at the charter arrivals section of airports and see which reps are meeting groups. Find out from porters which coffee bar the reps use when waiting for flights, and then offer to buy them a coffee and ask a few questions.

The earlier you decide to apply for seasonal hotel work the better are your chances. Hotels in a country such as Switzerland recruit months before the summer season, and it is advisable to write to as many hotel addresses as possible by March, preferably in their own language and enclosing international reply coupons. A knowledge of more than one language is an immense asset for work in a European hotel or restaurant. If you have an interest in working in a particular country, get a list of hotels from their tourist office in London and write to the largest ones (e.g. the ones with over 100 rooms). If you know someone going to your chosen country, ask them to bring back local newspapers and check adverts.

The Directory at the back of this book provides a starting point for speculative applications to companies around the world. For more addresses of major American tour companies, you can also contact the National Tour Association (546 East Main Street, Lexington, KY 40508; 859-682-4444; www.ntaonline.com).

TOUR OPERATORS

Tour operators vary in size from the local coach company selling a dozen short tours a year, up to the giants such as the German company TUI and the Swiss company Kuoni which send millions of clients to all corners of the world. Many jobs exist in the Outgoing Tour market, e.g. a British tour operator sells tours to British people who fly off to holiday in Greece, Spain, Italy or a hundred other countries. For the general market they will employ staff selected in Britain principally because package tourists often prefer to be looked after by a compatriot and also the selection process is so long and involved that it is just not practicable to employ nationals of the destination countries. There are exceptions, for example the adventure tour operator Guerba with offices in Wiltshire wrote in 2004 to say that they have achieved their long term policy aim of employing and training leaders and drivers locally, so no longer hire expedition staff in the UK. And tour operators to the US normally hire Americans since there is no language or visa barrier.

Most tour operators interview in their country (Britain, Germany, Netherlands, etc.) and send the selected staff out at the beginning of the season to stay in the resort for the duration of the season. Although this means that the majority of staff do not speak the language fluently, most tour operators do not consider this a priority. As one major operator says, perhaps a trifle optimistically, 'Anyone who speaks one foreign language will find it easy to learn another; and anyway most locals in a resort speak English'.

A further advantage for the tour operator of employing expat staff is that if there is a crisis elsewhere in their empire, they can transfer a staff member at a moment's notice from Spain to Greece say, which is not possible if the employee is a local with local commitments. Nevertheless a few European operators do contract with a local ground handler who employs staff on location in the resort, but this is not common.

Because of price wars, the mass-market operators make little or no money on selling holidays. Instead their profits derive from selling excursions (and before 2000 on duty-free sales). If you don't feel comfortable with this emphasis on selling or know that you can't sell for toffee, you will have to try to find work with a more upmarket operator who does not rely on excursion sales.

Some tour operators advertise a training course for which you have to pay. This is more likely to be the case with companies like *Contiki* and *Topdeck* and also with overland expedition operators (see introductory section) which are well known 'fun' employers and therefore very popular. To ensure that applicants are serious about the work, these companies insist that they put their money where their mouths are. Before signing on, find out exactly what ratio of trainees are taken on from the course, and what your realistic chances are of numbering yourself among them. Normally this training fee will be refunded after you have worked for the company for a certain length of time. Three other youth-oriented European tour operators to try are Busabout (258 Vauxhall Bridge Rd, London SW1V 1BS; 020-7950 1661) which posts full recruitment information on its website (www.busabout.com); *Tracks Travel* which advertise for road crew in the autumn; and Stray Travel Network (171 Earls Court Road, London SW5 9RF: 020-7373 7737; www.straytravel.com) which runs month-long training trips around Europe for which the 30 candidates are charged £500, £350 of which is refunded to those who go on to work for the company.

In many cases the recruiting departments of tour operators are open only during the recruitment period. Once they have chosen the required number of staff, the department is closed down and the permanent staff redeployed to the reservations department or wherever needed. Large companies like *Tui UK* and *MyTravel* employ so many people to service their estimated three million customers that they publish their recruitment requirements on their websites or in a large-format brochure which can be requested from the Overseas Personnel Office (for Tui UK ring 020-7420 2917). As is the case with the mass-market operators, MyTravel (trading as Airtours, among others) employs reps, children's reps, entertainers and ski resort staff. Their reps must have all the usual qualities (flexibility, diplomacy, etc.) and preferably knowledge of French, Spanish, Italian, Greek, Portuguese or German (in order of numbers needed). There may be an assumption that you have a commitment to make tourism a career, though this is not essential.

A number of companies specialise in tours for school children, both British and American. For example the London office of *ACIS*, the American Council for International Studies hires 100 clever linguists each year to accompany groups of American high school students around Europe. *Casterbridge Tours* employ guides to escort groups between March and July. Successful applicants must attend one of their weekend training courses for tour guides in the winter.

SPECIAL INTEREST TOURS

The vast majority of tour companies (particularly those offering 'the unspoiled Europe that only we know how to find') stick to the well trodden paths, herding their customers along the 'Milk Runs' whether that is around the Ring of Kerry in Ireland or to the castles along the Rhine. If you despair at the prospect of travelling in a coach along the same route taken by hundreds of others, it is worth considering trying to find work with a more specialised travel firm.

The variety and choice of what enterprising companies offer are increasing all the time. It seems that whatever hobbies people have, there is a tour company that specialises in providing holidays for this market, from battlefield tours to stamp collecting, and there is work for someone with a deep knowledge of just about any hobby. There are gourmet tours of Japan, garden tours of Italy, jungle bird tours of Peru, photo holidays to Lapland and so on. These tend to appeal to a more upmarket clientele, and the sharper focus of these tours often engage the interest of the rep or guide in charge to a much higher degree than ordinary tours. Judy Wilson was asked to take a group from America around East Anglia, searching for their families' roots:

That was fascinating, just like a living treasure hunt, and I got just as much
satisfaction out of finding a grave or an item in a local library as they did.

First check the AITO Directory mentioned above (send a large s.a.e and two first-class stamps.) For example people with experience of hill-walking can find a range of companies looking for trek leaders, though there are plenty of others which are not members of AITO. Anyone with an avid interest in a specific activity from orchid-hunting to wine-tasting should concentrate on the handful of firms which cover these specialities. In the US the *Specialty Travel Index* (305 San Anselmo Ave, Suite 309, San Anselmo, CA 94960; www.specialtytravel.com) is published every spring and autumn for $10 ($22 if it has to be sent overseas). The substantial A4 booklet lists more than 500 tour operators worldwide, the majority American, including hiking, biking, golfing, winery, cookery, cruising and a host of others.

A great many orchestras and choirs tour other countries. Specialist firms like *Specialised Travel Ltd* employ guides for the summer season, who need not be musical but they should speak languages and have experience of leading groups. Touring musical groups, particularly from the US, cause special problems. On arriving in Europe, the band or choir master suddenly feels that their reputation is at stake and will try to fit in extra rehearsals, which usually necessitate the use of the coach. While the company will not have costed in the extra kilometres and won't pay, your driver will baulk at the extra work. The solution is to point to the tachograph and explain that the driver's hours are very strictly controlled and, much as you would both like the driver to work extra hours, the law won't allow this.

If you have experience with horses, you might look in magazines like *Horse and Hound* especially in May to look for announcements of tours to Europe, or further afield to Australia and Argentina. Alternatively contact your local Polo Club and look in their programmes for companies that advertise. Tours go from Germany, the USA, Spain, etc. as well as from the UK.

Many attractions need guides with specialised knowledge. For example anyone with a background in marine biology has a good chance of being hired as a guide when they approach dive cruise firms from Queensland to Eilat.

INTERVIEWS

When tour companies come to choose their reps and guides, their priority is usually to find someone with the right kind of personality. Therefore the interview is even more crucial than it is in other fields of employment where experience and background may be of equal or more importance.

At one extreme is the 30-second interview for a job as a rep or guide in which the employer (usually an upmarket agency) is interested only in assessing a candidate's manner of dressing and speaking, claiming that the rest can be taught on-the-job. At the other extreme (and much more usual) is the gruelling one-day assessment interview as offered by the big tour operators like *Tui UK* and *Olympic Holidays.*

Study the company's brochures thoroughly beforehand, especially the fine print of the Terms and Conditions. If you know a friendly travel agent, ask them informally to assess that company's strengths and what their target market is. Make a preliminary list of questions about the content of the job or the policies of the company.

Arrive well in advance of the starting time, bringing pen and paper and a copy of the brochure to demonstrate your keenness. Be friendly and polite to the receptionist. In smaller companies it is not unknown for the boss to slip out at the end of a tiring day, unable to differentiate one candidate from another, and ask the receptionist for her opinion.

One of the keys to success is to keep smiling, no matter how stressed or undermined you feel at times. They are looking for a capacity to remain calm and cheerful under pressure so a smile should be glued to your lips from the moment you step through the door. It is also important to look presentable and immaculately groomed at any interview and especially for jobs in tourism which require a great deal of client contact. People in personnel departments (sometimes called Human Resources) say that first impressions are crucial, and often admit that they make up their minds in those first important seconds. Wear smart business-like clothes. Women may wear trousers if these are well tailored, but skirts are preferable. Bear in mind that most package tourists are conservative so wear what makes your mother happy, not your mates. Men should wear a tie and should refrain from wearing earrings. Women should avoid jangly jewellery, nose studs, heavily bleached hair, heavy make-up or too-short skirts and low-cut tops. Take spare tights and, if you wear nail polish, a carefully capped bottle for touch-ups. Dirty fingernails will certainly be noticed as will scuffed shoes and over-casual items of clothing like jeans or trainers, except possibly for sports jobs.

Although the various companies use different interview approaches, it may be helpful to give an example of how one might be structured. The day progresses from group interviews to individual ones, as people are weeded out. In the first place, all candidates are assembled in a room for a briefing on the company by a (charming) Senior Representative who tries to make everyone relax. But do not relax too much because you may later be quizzed on what you have been told. Basic working conditions should be set out. If this is the first time you have been told the proposed wage, try not to gasp at the lowness of the figure. It can normally be supplemented by the commissions you earn on the excursions, etc. that you sell.

You then have coffee and wait to be called for individual interviews in front of a panel. This is where you will be asked to demonstrate your suitability for the job; take along any relevant certificates you have earned. You then have lunch which is not normally laid on. Further in-depth interviews are held in the afternoon, individually or in small groups, when it will be appropriate to mention any relevant training or knowledge of languages (take your certificates). Sample tasks may be to sell an excursion so be prepared to design a poster, keeping your presentation simple but striking. You will have a chance to ask questions such as what are the prospects of work at the end of an initial season; what insurance the company offers; to which resort/s you would be most likely sent if selected; whether accommodation is shared, or a uniform provided, etc.

Xuela Edwards was told that she was one of 30 applicants selected from a pool of 2,000 to be interviewed by a major tour operator, an experience she found intimidating. She didn't get through to a one-to-one interview:

Some other rejects and I went over the session afterwards and could find no common trait or logic at work, but then we didn't know who was successful. I have heard that other companies ask bizarre questions such as 'Which would you rather be – a bishop or a colonel?' Most companies require you to give a strictly timed presentation on your favourite holiday or hobby for which you are supposed to bring visual aids (I had 24 hours' notice). I can honestly say that I see no connection between the intimidating standards at interview and the general level of most reps. Although the operators all say they require a minimum of two languages, this is not necessary. Very few applicants bring genuine language skills to the job.

Some companies use psychometric testing (to measure mental ability) at their interviews, which can be daunting and in some cases humiliating. Do not be downcast if you do not excel; the tests are normally bought in from outside consultancies and may be inexpertly administered and interpreted. One favourite test is to seat applicants in a circle and ask them who they would throw out from a sinking balloon. (Avoid choosing the interrogator unless you have decided you do not want the job after all.) A competent interviewer can find out what someone is like without having to demean him or her, so if the company does employ these tactics, you are probably better off not working for them. A good employer will explain what is expected of you in the interview, treat the candidates with dignity and inform the ones who have not been given jobs as discreetly as possible.

If, after the interview, you decide that you like the company, it is a good idea to write to thank the chief interviewer for a most interesting day, mentioning how much you enjoyed meeting everyone and, even if you are not suitable on this occasion, you would like to be considered for any future jobs.

Sometimes acceptance at this stage is still no guarantee of a job. It may be that you will now be invited to join an in-house training course, which gives the company more leisure to weed out weaker candidates. UK tour operators provide only local training, whereas some European tour companies send their successful candidates abroad, as Charlotte Jakobsen from Denmark describes:

After doing various jobs in the travel industry (air hostess, hotel work, etc.) I decided that becoming a tour rep would be great and therefore applied to one of Denmark's biggest companies, Tjaereborg. Thousands apply every year so I was lucky to be accepted for an interview and written personality tests. After the first meeting I was sent with 45 others on a three-week training course in Costa del Sol (for an all-inclusive price of £400). After three brilliant but extremely hard weeks in which we learned a lot about doing guided tours, giving good service to clients, first aid, etc., only half of the group were offered jobs.

PREPARATION

The preceding chapters on how to find a job and on training set out ways in which you can make yourself more attractive to potential employers. One of the best ways in which to prepare for a stint of working in tourism abroad is to work with groups of people locally whether tourists or locals. Relevant experience for guides and reps can be gained by volunteering to lead groups around a museum, factory, nature reserve or whatever interests you. Even organising a day-trip advertised in your local library, school, church, club or community centre will stand you in good stead. It could have some charitable value, such as taking a group of senior citizens on an outing or disabled children to the zoo. Contact the Volunteers Organiser of the County Council for ideas. If you are more interested in the catering side, it should not be too difficult to get experience waiting on tables or assisting in a kitchen in a local establishment.

More prolonged exposure to the world of tourism can best be gained by getting a summer job in a resort or campsite in your home country. The skills of serving the needs of tourists are the same wherever you work and a summer spent organising activities at a language camp for European teenagers, operating a ride at a local theme park or chambermaiding in a 4-star resort hotel can be invaluable. This will not only provide a chance to find out whether you will enjoy the working world of tourism and enhance your CV, but it may put you in touch with people who are well-informed on other possibilities in the field.

WHILE YOU'RE WAITING

After you have secured a job, there may be enough time to organise the practicalities of moving abroad and to prepare yourself in other ways. If you are going to a country that requires immigration procedures, you can start the visa procedures. In addition to deciding what to take and how to get to your destination, you should think about your tax position and health insurance, plus find out as much as you can about the situation in which you will find yourself.

RED TAPE

Since most tourism staff are employed by a company in their home country, they do not generally require a work permit. For example a resort rep working a summer season with a giant tour operator like Tui UK does not need a permit to work in Turkey, whereas someone who works for a local employer does need to consider the legality of his or her situation. If you do need a permit, your employer should help you to obtain one. Try to ensure that the company that has employed you fulfils its legal obligations. For further information about the red tape necessary for EU nationals working in another member state, see the beginning of the chapter *Europe*.

Outside the EU, legislation varies from country to country. Most governments want to encourage tourism and therefore give more latitude to tour operators than in other industries. Normally tour guides travelling with a group do not need work authorisation for the various countries they pass through. However there may be restrictions on them taking their party around local sights. Problems have arisen, especially in Italy, when a Tour Manager is deemed to be 'guiding' which is illegal in those countries where guiding is licensed.

In these countries tour operators are required to book and pay for a local guide who is a national of the country, but this does not mean that the accompanying tour manager cannot remain with the group.

For passport information ring the Passport Agency on 08705 210410 (www.passports.gov.uk). If you are working in tourism and lose your passport, the Passport Office in Globe House, Eccleston Square, London will make special arrangements for you to get a replacement speedily.

RESEARCH FOR GOING ABROAD

After you have studied all the relevant literature from the tourist office and in the library, the best way to prepare yourself is to buy reliable guidebooks, maps and phrase book or dictionary. Good English language books about the history and culture of a country are almost never for sale in souvenir shops, and good bookshops are seldom a feature of resorts.

Browsing in the travel section of any bookshop will introduce you to the range of travel guides. If in London, try to visit the recently revamped map and travel bookshop Stanford's Ltd in Covent Garden (12-14 Long Acre, WC2E 9LP) or explore their on-line catalogue (www.stanfords.co.uk). They carry a breathtaking range of maps and guides. Swiss Hallwag maps are known as the 'tour guide's friend' as they are very detailed for the scale and helpful for tour planning.

There are dozens of travel specialists throughout North America, including the Complete Traveller Bookstore (199 Madison Ave, New York, NY 10016; 212-685-9007) which also issues a free mail-order catalogue and, in Canada, Wanderlust (1929 West 4th Avenue, Kitsilano, Vancouver, BC, V6J 1M7; 604-739-2182).

Blue Guides and Michelin green guides can seldom be faulted for historical accuracy and comprehensiveness. Some of the worst guidebooks are those spawned by a TV travel series. The celebrity presenter thinks he or she knows it all, even though they have been cosseted from reality by the local tourist board. One of the best examples of this kind of book was a guide to Turkey written by an American who had spent a total of 36 hours in the country. Guidebooks written for the independent backpacker are seldom much use to your average package tourist. Sometimes the dullest looking guidebooks are the best choice since they deliver the facts and you can supply the interesting gloss.

Local adult education institutes often run short courses on history, history of art, social history, archaeology, etc. which are worthwhile investments if you know which country you intend to work in. However no investment in learning is ever a waste. At the least you will learn how to do research quickly, and what to look for. Any course on European history can provide background information for talks from Moscow to Madrid and all places in between. The Habsburgs went everywhere, as did the Medici, the Frescobaldi, the Hanseatic League – and the British. It can all be woven together into a fascinating pattern.

After you have done some homework, try to make contact with a previous employee of the tour operator which has hired you. Your employer should be willing to pass on a couple of addresses. Past guides/reps will be in a position to pass on priceless minutiae like how to handle a prickly hotel owner on the route or recommending pubs, cafés, etc. which the punters seem to prefer. If you have an acquaintance who has visited or lived in the resort you are heading for, pump them for all the memories they can muster.

Tour managers will be given a list by their company of contacts along the route: managers of hotels, restaurants, sites of interest, etc. One useful preparatory exercise is to call these people even before the tour begins. Although confirmation should have been sought by the tour operator, a friendly call can only serve to improve relations with the service-providers and, on a first trip, help to lessen the feeling of casting yourself into the great unknown.

Study very carefully all the literature the company has sent you. Try to imagine problems which could arise which have not been covered in their training or briefings. What is your emergency fund and for what uses is it authorised? Find out if there is a budget for inessential extras, such as prizes for little competitions you might hold or stationery for making posters.

Don't forget to reread the brochure from the client's point of view, and be prepared to do your best to deliver whatever is promised. If it says 'all our staff have an in-depth knowledge of local amenities', this is what the clients have every right to expect, even if you have never been on that route or to that beach resort before.

CONTRACTS

This is the point at which a formal contract or at least a memorandum of agreement should be drawn up. Any employer who is reluctant to provide something in writing is definitely suspect. The following items should be covered in most contracts or at least given some consideration.:

O company name and address of employer
O details of the duties
O how much time off you will receive, provided there are no emergencies
O amount of pay and how it will be paid (i.e. into bank account in home country or as expense allowance in local currency). Is any held back against the return of the uniform or the completion of your contract?
O length of the contract and whether it is renewable
O type of accommodation. Will you have to share with another staff member? Are utilities included?
O tax liability
O provisions for health care and sick pay. What are you insured for under the company policy?
O payment of pension or national insurance contributions
O bonus and commission rates, if applicable
O details of the travel arrangements to and from your destination
O any probationary period and length of notice on either side
O penalties for breaking the contract and circumstances under which the penalties would be waived (e.g. extreme family illness, etc.)

Other issues have particular relevance to guides and reps. In addition to the routine points covered in most contracts, you can expect to see the following:

O emergency contact number/s. These are vitally important and you should try to insist on having them at the time the contract is signed. Any employer who does not provide an emergency contact will not be a good employer
O to whom are you expected to report
O return travel. Make sure you do not find yourself stranded at the end of the season (when aircraft are usually full) with no return ticket.
O commission rates (usually paid on a sliding scale, explained in the Reps section in the Introductory chapter).
O luggage allowance to/from resort (which is usually not a problem if you are flying on a company charter)
O float or advance payment for materials you will be told to buy
O conditions under which a company can move you from one resort or country to another
O the company insurance (may not cover individual items of high value).

Freelancers who lead a succession of tours quite often do not have a contract. It is more usual to be sent a letter asking which dates and tours you would like to take, and this is often on a gentleman's agreement. But even if you are working only for a few days at a time, you should try to have in writing the routine points covered in most contracts (although freelance guides are usually expected to carry their own health insurance) plus the following:

O emergency contact number/s
O detailed itinerary including list of pick-up points and name of coach company (if applicable)
O positioning fee/wage (if you are expected to arrive at departure point the night before)
O return travel
O details of accommodation (it is important that both guide and driver have a private bath)
O what (if anything) you are insured for under the company policy
O float for expenses and what this covers.

INSURANCE

No matter what country you are heading for, you should obtain the Department of Health leaflet T6 *Health Advice for Travellers Anywhere in the World*. This leaflet should be available from any post office or you can request a free copy on the Health Literature Line 0800 555777.

If you are a national of the European Economic Area (most of Europe except Switzerland), and will be working in another EEA country, you will be covered by the European Community Social Security Regulations. Advice and the leaflet SA29 *Your Social Security Insurance, Benefits and Health Care Rights in the European Community and in Iceland, Liechtenstein and Norway* may be obtained free of charge from the Inland Revenue National Insurance Contributions Office, International Services, Benton Park View, Newcastle-upon-Tyne NE98 1ZZ (08459 154811, local rate call; www.inlandrevenue.gov.uk/nic).

The leaflet T6 contains an application form to obtain form E-111 (called the 'E-one-eleven') which is a certificate of entitlement to medical treatment within Europe. The E-111 is not issued to EEA nationals who are going to work in another member country for less than 12 months and who continue to pay UK National Insurance contributions. Form E128 is now issued which gives entitlement to a full range of health care. If you will be working for a foreign employer, you should seek advice from the Contributions Office, International Services. Note that from 2005, Brussels plans to abolish the E-111 form and replace it with a standardised EU-wide health card.

But the E-111 covers only the basics and does not necessarily extend to non-emergency treatment, dental treatment, prescription drugs, etc. Furthermore it is not always treated as a sacred document by health officials. Resorts clinics in Greece and Spain often do not recognise it, and if they did, their fees would be considerably higher than what can be recouped on an E-111. It usually doesn't cover extras such as ambulance transport. One rep was very relieved he happened to be carrying his credit card when a stroppy Greek ambulance driver refused to convey an injured client until it was made clear how payment would be made.

Reputable employers will obtain health insurance for you. Read the fine print to find out whether you are covered both on and off the job. Most tourism professionals top up the company policy, making sure that they are covered for loss of personal effects, loss of earnings, public liability and repatriation insurance. One broker that has been recommended is Coaching Insurance Consultants (11 Harvest Bank, Hyde Heath, Amersham, Bucks. HP6 5RD; 01494 783595). Specialist expatriate policies might be worth investigating.

A firm that specialises in providing insurance for Americans living overseas is Wallach & Company (107 West Federal St, PO Box 480, Middleburg, VA 20118-0480; 1-800-237-6615; www.wallach.com).

HEALTH

A standard first aid kit should suffice for working round Europe. If your destination is tropical, it is worth looking at a general guide to travel medicine such as *Bugs, Bites and Bowels* by Dr. Jane Wilson Howarth (Cadogan, 2002, £9.99) or *Traveller's Health: How to Stay Healthy Abroad* by Richard Dawood. These books emphasise the necessity of avoiding tap water and recommend ways to purify your drinking water by filtering, boiling or chemical additives (i.e. iodine is more reliable than chlorine).

Malaria is continuing to make a serious comeback in many parts of the world, due to the resistance of certain strains of mosquito to the pesticides and preventative medications which have been so extensively relied upon in the past. You must be particularly careful if travelling to a place where there is falciparum malaria which is potentially fatal. Out of 2,000+ British travellers who return home to the UK with malaria each year, up to 20 will die. Your employer should pay for any necessary medical expenses for you and also give you plenty of guidance on how to help protect clients by preventing mosquito bites and on prophylactic drugs. Increasingly, detailed health advice is available on the internet so if you have anxieties your tour operator hasn't addressed, check www.fitfortravel.scot.n hs.uk; www.tripprep.com; www.tmb.ie or www.travelhealth.co.uk.

For advice on protecting sexual health, Marie Stopes International (0845 300 8090; www.mariestopes.org.uk) is helpful. The government's free booklet 'Drugs Abroad' has sound advice. The National Drugs Helpline (0800 776600 or +44 151 706 7324 from abroad) can give information on drugs laws abroad. Some countries such as Russia have introduced HIV antibody testing for long-stay foreigners and the certificate may be required to obtain a work or residence visa.

If you are going to be spending a lot of time in countries where blood screening is not reliable you should consider carrying a sterile medical kit. These are sold by MASTA (Medical Advisory Service for Travellers Abroad; www.masta.org) at the London School of Hygiene and Tropical Medicine, Keppel St, London WC1E 7HT. MASTA (www.masta.org) maintains an up-to-date database on travellers' diseases and their prevention.

Americans seeking general travel health advice should ring the Center for Disease Control & Prevention Hotline in Atlanta on 404-332-4559; www.cdc.gov/travel/destinat.htm.

NATIONAL CONTRIBUTIONS AND SOCIAL SECURITY

If you fail to make National Insurance contributions while you are abroad, you will forfeit entitlement to benefits on your return. You can decide to pay voluntary contributions at regular intervals or in a lump sum in order to retain your rights to certain benefits. Unfortunately this entitles you only to a retirement/widow's pension, not to incapacity benefit or Jobseekers' Allowance. Since tourism employees abroad are seldom in a pension scheme, it is usually worth maintaining your right to a state pension.

TAX

Some companies may tell you that your earnings are not high enough to be of interest to the Inland Revenue. Nonsense. Tax computers talk to each other all over the world and, sooner or later, any wages will have to be declared. Calculating your liability to tax when working outside your home country is notoriously complicated so, if possible, check your position with an accountant. Also consult the Inland Revenue information leaflets IR20 'Residents and Non-Residents: Liability to Tax in the UK'. Everything depends on whether you fall into the category of 'resident', 'ordinarily resident' or 'domiciled'. Most people working in tourism count as domiciled in the UK since it is assumed that they will ultimately return. If you are out of the country for a complete tax year, you will be entitled to the exemption, provided no more than 62 days (i.e. one-sixth of a year) have been spent in the UK. Don't make the mistake of thinking that because no one looks at your passport Inland Revenue won't know if you have stayed longer than the permitted number of days in Britain. Declan had to return to England when his mother was taken ill and nearly made the mistake of disrupting his tax status. Instead he beat a hasty retreat across the Channel.

Note that people working offshore for cruise lines and even ferry companies may be eligible for claiming tax rebates. Keep detailed records of sailing times, and have these authenticated by the purser.

Don't forget that if you have a car, you can get a rebate on your Road Tax for every calendar month it is off the road. You have to submit a Statutory Off Road Notification (SORN) declaration instead of renewing your tax disc. However you must retax your car before taking it back on the road.

TRAVEL

Anyone who is hired by a tour operator in their own country should have the travel to their place of work arranged and paid for by the company. But for those who are heading off to conduct a speculative job hunt, the following advice may be of use.

London is the cheap airfare capital of the world and the number of agencies offering discount flights to all corners of the world is seemingly endless. Consult specialist travel magazines such as *TNT* (which is free in London) plus *Time Out* and the Saturday edition of the *Independent*. By ringing a few of the agencies with advertisements you will soon discover which airlines offer the cheapest service. The student/youth travel agency STA is always worth consulting, though their popularity often means that there are queues both in their offices and on their phone lines.

In North America, the best newspapers to scour for cheap flights are the *New York Times* (the Sunday edition has a section devoted to travel with cut-price flights advertised), the *LA Times, San Francisco Chronicle-Examiner, Miami Herald, Dallas Morning News, Chicago Sun Times,* the *Boston Globe* and the Canadian *Globe & Mail.* If your dates and even your destinations are flexible, contact Air-Tech at 588 Broadway, Suite 204, New York, NY 10012 (212-219-7000; www.airtech.com) and Airhitch (1-800-326-2009; www.airhitch.org).

Throughout North America, many churches run tours for their congregations to Europe, usually led by the pastor or priest. It might be worthwhile offering your services for free to help with the tour in return for an open air ticket to Europe. Robert from Vancouver contacted his local church to see if they needed anyone to assist the pastor in the church's annual tour of religious sites in Europe. They did, and in return for a promise to work as an unpaid tour leader assisting the thoroughly competent pastor, he received a free air ticket. Robert said he worked a very long day during the tour but valued the experience.

Airlines offer generous group discounts which can work out to one free ticket in every 20 sold, though it may not be as easy to benefit from this as it sounds, as Matt Tomlinson discovered:

We thought we had found an interesting angle on getting a free airfare. We were hoping to sell a cheapie flight of £690 to like-minded souls who wanted to join us in New Zealand for the ski season. It didn't really work. Airlines force you to commit

really early and as well our marketing sucked. If anything had gone wrong, we
would have been severely in the legal mire. However I can still recommend it if you
have a solid group who want to go.

WHAT TO TAKE

Consider taking a language course with you, since tapes and books (including a good
dictionary) may not be available locally and your enthusiasm to learn may be rekindled
once you are on location. Of course it is much easier to learn the language once you are
on-site.

Take some currency for your personal use to see you through the first few weeks.
Having your own credit card can also be reassuring. Even those who know enough not
to expect any expatriate perks are sometimes shocked by the expenses they incur living
abroad, especially before they ascertain the cheapest places to shop.

The research you do on your destination will no doubt include its climate, which will
help you choose an appropriate range of clothing to take. It is worthwhile taking warm
clothing for the beginning and end of the season, including a raincoat. It is essential that
the clothes that you take are simple to maintain, colour co-ordinated and reasonably
smart. Take comfortable shoes to go with your uniform (e.g. dark-coloured court shoes
for women) plus another casual pair (e.g. espadrilles, deck shoes). You may be walking
over cobblestones, across all sorts of uncomfortable surfaces and standing for hours.
Shoes should be well broken into without looking broken down.

Looking neat, and in some cases smart, is important in most jobs so you must choose
your clothing with this in mind. Blue jeans are rarely acceptable, apart from on wild and
woolly overland trips. Several smart outfits are a great morale booster and also impress
the local restaurateurs and other service providers whose hearts sink when confronted
with a sea of T-shirts and flip flops. Bear in mind that resort reps do not really earn a
high enough salary to go out and buy expensive new jackets or shoes after arrival, so it is
necessary to take these with you. Be sure to take lightweight long-sleeved garments and
a sun hat to guard against both sunburn and mosquitoes. If you are working in a Moslem
country like Turkey or Tunisia, modest dress is essential. You also want to be able to
set a good example to your clients who must be encouraged not to offend against local
sensibilities.

To keep your clothes neat, it may be worth taking a travel iron (making sure you
have any appropriate adapters). On the other hand, many reps find that time is too short
for this chore and prefer to use the 'courier's iron' (even if it does ride roughshod over
considerations of conservation), i.e. by hanging clothes up in the bathroom, turning the
shower to scalding, and shutting the door for ten minutes (making sure there is time for
the clothes to dry). Skirts in particular get very creased so it is an idea to take a tip from
models and ask for one size too large since it won't crease as easily.

It is also not a bad idea to take any favourite toiletries to avoid having to pay inflated
resort prices, though this is more worthwhile in some countries (like Portugal) than
others (like Greece). If possible find out from recent company employees or anyone else
what items, such as certain items of clothing or toiletries, are in short supply or very
expensive, or perhaps if you would need a torch if lighting is unreliable. If you can't live
without marmite or a special brand of tea, take a supply, though it is more fun to explore
the cuisine of your new country.

Here is a list of items to consider packing which most often crop up in the recommendations of experienced workers in the tourism industry. Some may seem more relevant for certain areas of work but all are useful to consider taking. Keep receipts in case you are entitled to reimbursement from your company at a later date:

- passport photos for permits are essential.
- for reps, the employer will provide you with a reps' handbook and ancillary supplies (bag, clipboard, extra copies of the company brochure, possibly a uniform) which will have to be collected from the company offices.
- calculator
- laptop(if you happen to have one already). Reps will normally have access to a computer in the resort office, but it can be much more convenient to do your paperwork in your own room. You keep your report in the machine and tap out the day's events on your return each evening, emailing it at the end of the week.
- travel alarm clock for those times when you have to meet a group at the airport at 5am
- emergency rations (e.g. muesli bars) in case you have to miss a meal sorting out a problem
- guide books, maps, dictionaries (see above)
- large notebook for jotting down tips for subsequent trips, noting client requests to which you will have to return and generally keeping track
- supply of greeting cards for when you find out that a client's birthday or anniversary is coming up
- ideas for games and quizzes to fill the hours you may have to spend on a coach, plus perhaps a few novelties to be given away as prizes
- one optional idea is a set of song sheets
- coloured pens and markers, cardboard, and assorted stationery like Blutak, stick-on labels, stapler, ruler, scissors and even Letraset if your handwriting is execrable. These should be covered by a float from the company
- basic medications like aspirin, sunscreen and lip salve for your personal use only
- pre-moistened towels (like the ones given out by airlines) to refresh you when you're feeling hot and sticky

---

STAYING IN TOUCH

News junkies should consider taking out a subscription to the *Guardian Weekly* (164 Deansgate, Manchester M3 3GG; 0870-066 0510; www.guardianweekly.com); a one-year subscription costs £73 in Europe and North America, £79 elsewhere. You might prefer to wait until you arrive at your destination to see what newspapers are available. Newsagents in major resorts usually sell a couple of British dailies, albeit a couple of days late and at a premium price. One resort rep (Sandie) offers a tip: make friends with the incoming flight crew who can save the passengers' newspapers, including the Sunday supplements.

Hotel radios never seem to pick up the stations you want to hear. Access to the World Service can be a godsend. You will need a good short-wave radio with several bands powerful enough to pick up the BBC. 'Dedicated' short-wave receivers which are about the size of a paperback start at £65.

BIBLIOGRAPHY

Career guides and travel books of possible interest include the following:

The AA Truckers Atlas of Britain, (AA Publishing; 2002, £13.99). For all those minor roads where you do not know if bridges are high enough for a coach.

Airline Passenger's Guerrilla Handbook, by George Albert Brown (Blakes, US). Out of print but available via amazon. Inside information about what goes on and how to get better treatment for groups. Also an amusing read.

Blue Guides (A & C Black). Available to most European countries (60+ titles in series). All are written to a very high standard with accurate and helpful information, and heavily relied on by tour managers.

Careers in Travel and Tourism, (Trotman, £7.99). Overview of the main career opportunities in hotels and catering, travel agencies, and as tour managers, guides, representatives or on board cruise liners.

The Traveller's Handbook (WEXAS; www.wexas.com; £14.99 or £7.50 to WEXAS club members). 900-page reference book written by many expert contributors with useful appendices.

Work Your Way Around the World and *Directory of Summer Jobs Abroad* (Vacation-Work Publications). Contact addresses and practical advice for people wanting holiday jobs or casual work in the tourist industry (among many others).

Inside Secrets to Finding a Career in Travel, by Karin Rubin (JIST Publishing, 2001; $14.95/£7.35 on amazon). Especially useful for Americans.

Punters get robbed, get bitten by snakes, get sick, some even die.

PROBLEMS

Travel advertising shows a glowing picture of attractive people walking on deserted moonlit beaches and sipping cocktails in a pavement café. But in the real world, delays, traffic jams, crowds and jet lag mar the happy picture. If travel was easy, no one would book a package holiday nor would tour companies employ a battalion of people to sort out problems.

As we saw in the introductory section about Rewards and Risks, the scope for disaster when trying to co-ordinate the requirements of groups of people on holiday and service providers wanting to make a profit is enormous. This chapter takes a closer look not just at the array of problems that can arise, but in concrete ways to avoid or solve them.

It may be unfair, but in many jobs you are the one who will have to solve problems, sometimes serious problems, on your own. The client who has been mauled by a wild animal on safari or who has had her passport stolen while wandering around Rome cannot wait for the rep to ask for instructions from head office. Action must be speedy and decisive. Often what is mainly required is a confident front and reassurance. Remember that many problems have more than one solution. What is needed is someone in authority to start solving them in a confident manner. If people trust you, they will leave you to get on with the work, relieved that it is no longer their own responsibility.

Most reps are given a one-week induction in their resort before the season gets underway, in which the standard procedures for dealing with illness are covered, including a visit to the nearest clinic or hospital. You will always have telephone access to a helpline, for example the one operated by the insurance company Europ-Assistance. Rob Williams worked for them as a controller and reports that some of his time was spent trying to calm down a badly shaken rep in charge of a sick or injured client by talking him or her through the necessary steps. In more than one case he had to remind the rep where the nearest hospital was.

PROBLEMS AT WORK

Make sure your company allows you adequate time off. Undoubtedly tour companies and hotels have a tendency to exploit staff, especially if they are deemed to be working illegally in a resort. Knowing that you have no rights and therefore can't complain about working long hours for slave wages, they will have you working a 16-hour day seven days a week and your health and spirits will suffer. Most people working in tourism spend so much time looking after customers that they tend to neglect themselves. Try to avoid this at all costs.

Accommodation is at a premium in resorts, and often staff are assigned to fairly undesirable rooms, often shared. Accommodation provided for staff on cruise liners probably hits an all-time low: cramped, noisy and airless. Anyone who thinks it is pedantic to worry about accommodation if the group are staying in hostels, etc. hasn't tried to find a telephone on a university campus in an emergency, or joined the early morning bathroom queue when in a hurry to supervise the loading of luggage. And your driver certainly can't do a good job if he has had to share a room with people who keep him awake.

LOST LUGGAGE

Luggage is usually lost (or 'misrouted') by an airline and their ground staff will handle the PIR (Property Incident Report). It is the airline's responsibility to return the luggage to their passenger, and this almost always happens within 48 hours. In the meantime they may offer a necessities bag or compensation in cash. It is very rare for luggage to go missing for good.

On tour it is the tour manager's responsibility to ensure that all luggage is accounted for and loaded into the coach each day. Some lazy tour managers leave this to the driver, but if anything goes wrong it is up to you, as John Boon recounts. He had to represent his company in court when they were sued by one of their tour managers. One day a suitcase had been left behind and the tour manager had had to hire a taxi to pick up and deliver the luggage to the next stop many miles away. The company refused to pay, claiming that it was the tour manager's responsibility, and she took out a court summons claiming for the cost. After allowing both sides to put their cases, the judge concluded that tour managers are responsible for luggage throughout a tour and that this particular tour manager had not shown due care and attention, so the case was dismissed. The moral is to count, count and count luggage again and again.

There is always a chance that the tour manager's own luggage will go astray. It is a good idea to carry two small suitcases rather than one large one, so that you can have back-up clothes and toiletries in both. Smart suitcases are much more likely to be picked on by corrupt baggage handlers. Hard suitcases have the advantage that they cannot so easily be slit open but are of course heavier.

DELAYS

Aircraft delays are an every day occurrence, especially in high season. Until passengers are checked in they are your company's (i.e. your) responsibility. After check-in it is up to the airline to pay for meals, overnight accommodation, etc. So pray when you arrive at the airport that the airline checks your group in before they realise there is going to be a problem. If your group is going to be late for a connecting flight or ferry, phone the carrier, explain the situation and they will tell you whether they will be able to hold the flight or ferry for you. It happens more often than you think. If you have to fly with your group, you are officially off-duty, so always ask for a seat away from the group.

Coaches cost up to a quarter of a million pounds new, and a coach operator must keep the wheels turning to make a profit. This means that they work to tight schedules, and any delay can have a domino effect. If the promised transfer coach has not turned up on time, encourage the clients to do their banking which will happily waste some time. If the driver is surly, he has probably been up since dawn, had to clean the coach before taking it out and may not have had breakfast. Like babies, most drivers work better after something to eat and drink. If a coach breaks down, it is the coach company's responsibility to provide a replacement, although you obviously do what you can to help the driver, which includes making phone calls if they don't speak the language. In alpine countries, snow can fall unexpectedly at any time of the year and if the NO COACHES sign is up, it means exactly what it says. Any driver who ignores the sign is subject to an automatic fine.

PROBLEMS WITH CLIENTS

Everyone worries about the 'three losses': lost passport, lost luggage and lost passengers. If someone loses their passport you take them to their nearest consulate where a duplicate will be issued. Sometimes this is very easy and the whole process takes no more than an hour. Sometimes it can involve a journey from one end of a country to another. The rule is that you are as helpful as possible, but must remember that your first priority is to the

Persuading a large group to keep to the schedule may be problematic.

majority of your group, even if it means you have to leave clients behind to sort things out for themselves.

The European Union was supposed to make travel simpler but in some ways it has become more complicated, for example with respect to visa requirements for non-EU nationals; check your passenger list and make the appropriate enquiries. Then when the passengers join, check their passports. If the necessary visa is missing, your company will probably refuse to accept them. Now that most internal borders in Europe have disappeared, this is less of a worry.

Often someone in your care has an accident or gets sick; and even if they are not actually ill they think they are. One tip is to ban oranges on coaches since they commonly react badly with stomach acid and make some travellers sick. Drink cans are another problem. A coach driver was killed when a can rolled down the coach and stuck under the brake pedal. If people bring cans onto the coach, ask them to ensure that they put them into a rubbish bin. Clients often make the excuse of a gammy leg to lay claim to a front seat. They should be seated in the second row because, if the driver has to slam on the brakes, their gammy leg won't allow them to brace themselves and they will end up through the windscreen.

If you have any disabled clients, contact the police before arriving at each major stop and request permission to drop passengers off in the centre of town rather than the coach park.

Apart from health problems, the most common aggravation for tourists (and therefore reps, etc.) usually involves robbery. You must not only offer practical advice about what documents the victim will need to fill out, but you must offer constant reassurance that the loss of their camera or money is not the end of the world.

As noted in the section on Tour Personnel, certain kinds of punter can be a thorn in the sides of their manager, guide or even waiter. There is always a dizzy tour member who lingers too long in the souvenir shop or the rest stop toilet and cannot be found when the coach is ready to depart. Or perhaps they repeatedly leave their spectacles behind in the café and their passport under the pillow in their hotel room.

There is usually a compulsive whinger who complains about every little delay or deviation from the printed brochure. Fussy eaters are a real nuisance. Tom, who worked for Fourways, claims that Australians can be even more unadventurous eaters than Britons:

Italian cooking really seemed to set off the grumbles. I personally like Italian food so I got fed up with all the complaints about 'greasy' meals. Taking the mike one day, I proceeded to talk about how beautiful Italian women are, all because the olive oil in their diet gives them beautiful skin. As a result, all the women lapped up the food and told their husbands not to complain.

What pleases one group will not work with another. Sandra Miller of Wholesale Tours tells the story of an American group in London who asked her why she didn't wear miniskirts. Promising to wear one on their last day, she went to the airport wearing boots, short skirt and lots of make-up, and was the focus of so many photos they almost missed the plane:

Then there was a tannoy announcement for me to phone my office. My boss asked me to bring a group back to London because their own tour manager was ill. The group leader's name was the Reverend Brown, and his religious group from the Bible Belt took one look at me in my gear and wanted to return home on the next plane. Giving my introduction on the way from Heathrow, the only time I captured their attention was passing Earls Court where I pointed out that this was where the Evangelist Billy Graham had recently preached. Dark mutterings along the line of 'Pity he didn't save her' were heard.

There is usually a know-it-all who makes it his or her business to catch the tour guide out on minor mistakes. Trainee guides are always worried when they see a client arriving on the coach with their own guidebook. Seeing someone flick though a guidebook while you are delivering your speil can be nerve-wracking. One trick is to stroll over and say something like, 'I see you have guidebook X. They have some interesting ideas on dates, and I find most of their information is accurate'. After a chat about differences in guidebook facts, you hope that they leave their book behind for the next excursion. Then there are the guidebooks that mention the delightful little hotels that are so much cheaper than the ones your group uses. Try to drive past some of the uglier examples, pointing them out in a friendly manner 'and that hotel is mentioned in X's guidebook' to stop comparisons.

Personality clashes are almost inevitable either between you and a client or among members of the group. When Mike Whitby was an Oxford undergraduate, he was taken on as a volunteer guide by a rather eccentric but charming classics professor who ran educational summer cruises around the Aegean on a somewhat downtrodden but adequate vessel. One of the paying clients (from Texas) was obviously not used to the prevailing standards of comfort and complained rudely and vociferously. With a temper inclined to the fiery and a zeal for defending his boss, our rugby-playing student picked up Sam the Texan and forcibly removed him from the boat. Professor Winspeare decided the only course was to leave both of them on the nearest island and the tour continued without either of them.

A high degree of tact, patience and charm is necessary when dealing with awkward customers who may be (wittingly or otherwise) offending against local customs or even breaking local laws. Drunkenness is a perennial problem. Lager louts can often be sensible when sober so that is the time to explain to him and his mates that although the local men drink copious amounts, they never become incapacitated with alcohol and they should try to follow local custom. Then just hope that the troublemaker's mates whisk him away before things get out of hand; it's worth a try.

Disagreeable and boring clients must be gently but effectively controlled so that there is no danger of their spoiling other clients' holidays. A windbag can be thanked for his contribution and told to share his anecdotes with his fellow passengers later at lunch. One way to win complainers over is by joining them and showing (feigning?) an interest in their experiences. On a long trip, there is no escape. The only chance of surviving all this is to hear the occasional compliment from a tour member who has had the time of their life just because of you. Experienced tour managers learn how to minimise negative behaviour, though very occasionally the individual is so disruptive or even violent that the police have to become involved, which is very stressful. However situations seldom deteriorate to such a level, and your anxiety focusrd more on whether or not your jokes are getting a little stale on the umpteenth retelling.

PROBLEMS WITH COLLEAGUES

Colleagues can be extremely helpful. The network of people doing the same job as you will pass on information, warn of changes, etc. Do not try to buck the system until you know what you are doing. There is a pecking order, and you will almost always benefit by asking advice from more experienced people in the field. Generally they will go out of their way to be helpful. Just remember this when it is your turn to help out a newcomer.

Occasionally you will come across someone who is unhelpful, probably because they are insecure in their job. There was a new tour manager on a tour of Ireland who thought she knew it all, so didn't need to ask advice. She proceeded to cause chaos by putting her people into the glass factory before they visited the coffee shop, and later when she arrived at the lunch stop at the same time as several other coaches. A driver kindly tried to tell her the form but she decided to ignore him. His revenge was sweet: he joined her group of Americans at lunch (something drivers almost never do) and casually mentioned how useful air-conditioning was in this spell of hot weather. He left an angry mob demanding to know from the troublesome tour manager why their coach lacked the up-to-date equipment the others had. The bumptious tour manager was never seen again.

Most drivers are stalwart rocks with broad shoulders, an ability to see the funny side of the worst problems and a colleague who supports you through thick and thin. Meals are eaten with the driver, not the group (to avoid jealousy). In the unlikely event of guides and drivers not getting on, never row in front of the passengers. Both end up with egg on their faces... and no tips.

PROBLEMS WITH EMPLOYERS

With the EU Directive and increasing recognition of associations such as ABTA, the tourist industry is better regulated than it was, though standards of performance are still very uneven. There is nothing much in the way of employee associations or unions to protect workers' rights. So it is important to have a detailed contract, to protect yourself against exploitation.

Although a tour company should have ironed out any problems in the itinerary ahead of time, the arrangements do often go wrong (the longer the tour, the more scope for hiccoughs) and it is essential that the tour manager continually check and confirm reservations. Herding a group of holidaymakers into a roadside restaurant which is not expecting you or waiting for a coach which does not show up are unpleasantly commonplace experiences for many managers. You must have access to some alternatives in these cases, and make sure they don't happen the next time round.

Freelance guides should insist on being paid for one tour before starting another. Cowboy tour companies have been known to weasel out of giving their reps and guides an adequate float before they set off with their groups. Inadequate supervision or a muddled line of command are frequently cited as problems. You must know ahead of time to whom you report and how often. It is not unknown for a rep to arrive in a resort and find that the ground handler's girlfriend has put herself in charge and you don't know where you stand.

Some countries require tour operators to book and pay for a local guide who is a national of the country. In some ways, this may make the job of the accompanying manager easier. But if the local person does not grasp what your group wants or expects, problems can occur. Officially you must defer to the local guide; unofficially you have to act as mediator.

STUDENT TRIPS

Problems crop up when unofficial tour leaders, for example teachers accompanying a school trip, shift the burden of responsibility onto the tour manager. For example Marie Bayliss was booked to work as a tour manager for a group of teenage students going to Belgium for an Easter holiday. After a day of hard work guiding the group around Bruges, Marie booked them into their hotel in Ostend and went to bed. At 3am she was awakened by one of the students who had a stomach ache and couldn't find a teacher. Nor could Marie. After calling the doctor and then making sure the girl was asleep, Marie waited up for the teacher-chaperones who came in at 5am from a disco crawl. She told them in no uncertain terms that they had been sent by the parents to look after their children and were getting a free trip on this understanding. It was her job to look after tour planning, theirs to be *in loco parentis* and around to attend to the children's needs.

Valerie, another experienced tour manager, had a different problem. She found her group of American students delightful but typically naïve. In Rome one night she was woken at midnight by a frantic teacher knocking at her door. Calming the teacher down, she discovered that three girls had decided to live it up by ordering a bottle of whisky from room service. When the room waiter arrived, the girls were dressed in short nighties and naturally the red-blooded Italian waiter thought all his fantasies had come true. As soon as he made his first overture, the girls panicked and screamed for their chaperone. Valerie deflected the teacher from her determination to see the waiter sacked, explaining that he might have been a tiny bit justified in making certain assumptions. She told the hotel manager to give the waiter time off to reflect until the girls had left the hotel. 'Phew. Did I earn my money that night. Being an agony aunt on one hand, telling the waiter not to be so stupid again and reassuring the manager that the girls were OK.' Sometimes the company manual is no use at all and you will have to rely on common sense.

WORKING IN HOTELS

If your only experience of hotels is as a guest, you may be in for a surprise when you go backstage. Even the most luxurious hotels have been known to have dirty, disorganised kitchens, inadequate laundering facilities and lousy (literally) staff quarters. It is quite possible that the waitress who smilingly emerges from the kitchen bearing your food has just been threatened and abused by the chef for not working quickly enough. It may have something to do with the heat generated by the ovens in large kitchens, the pride they take in their creations, or the pressures under which they work, but chefs have a terrible reputation for having volatile tempers. S. C. Firn describes the working atmosphere in a 'rather classy restaurant and bar' in Oberstdorf in Southern Germany near the Austrian border:

I had to peel vegetables, wash dishes, prepare food, clean the kitchen and sometimes serve food. Everything was done at a very fast pace, and was expected to be very professional. One German cook, aged 16, who didn't come up to standard, was punched in the face three times by the owner. On another occasion the assistant

chef had a container of hot carrots tipped over his head for having food sent back.
During my three months there, all the other British workers left, apart from the chef,
but were always replaced by more.

So if you consider yourself to be the sensitive fragile type, perhaps you should avoid
hotel kitchens altogether.

On the other hand many people thrive on the animated atmosphere and on kitchen
conviviality. Nick Langley, who also worked in a German kitchen loved the atmosphere.
He maintains that once you're established you'll gain more respect by shouting back if
unreasonable demands are made, but adds the proviso, 'but not at the powerful head cook,
please!'. Heated tempers usually cool down after a couple of beers at the end of a shift.

The same complaints crop up again and again among people who have worked in
hotels: long and unsociable hours (often 8am-10pm with a few hours off in the afternoon
plus lots of weekend work), exploitative wages, inadequate accommodation and food,
and unbearably hot working conditions exacerbated by having to wear a nylon uniform.
A great deal depends on whether or not you are the type to rough it. The working
atmosphere can vary a lot from hotel to hotel. If you are lucky enough to get a job in a
small friendly family hotel, you will probably enjoy the work more than if you are just
one in a large anonymous group of workers in a sterile and impersonal institution where
you have little job security.

It can be very aggravating to be asked to do extra duties beyond the ones specified in
your contract. It seems to be a common occurrence that hotel proprietors take for granted
that you will do unpaid overtime, without time off in lieu at a later date. If a contract is
being breached in this way, you should try your best to sort it out with the employer.
If this fails don't hesitate to go to the appropriate employment authorities to lodge an
official complaint. This has far more chance of success if you have a written contract to
show the authorities.

Not all hotels are like this and many people emphasise the benefits which they have
found in the experience of working in a hotel: excellent camaraderie and team spirit, the
opportunity to learn a foreign language, and the ease with which wages can be saved,
including the possibility of an end-of-season bonus. Although Kathryn Halliwell was
forced to share a windowless room which had an intermittently working light and water
streaming down the roof beams into constantly overflowing buckets, she still enjoyed
her time working at a hotel in Corsica, simply because of the conviviality of her 'fellow
sufferers'.

PROBLEMS OUTSIDE WORK

CULTURE SHOCK

Enjoying yourself won't be at all easy if you are suffering from culture shock. Shock
implies something which happens suddenly, but cultural disorientation more often creeps
up on you. Adrenaline usually sees you through the first few weeks as you find the novelty
exhilarating and challenging. You will be amazed and charmed by the odd gestures the
people use or the antiquated way that things work. As time goes on, practical irritations
intrude and the constant misunderstanding caused by those charming gestures – such as a
nod in Greece meaning 'no' or in Japan meaning 'yes, I understand, but don't agree' – and
the inconvenience of those antiquated phone boxes and buses will begin to get on your
nerves. Even if you are feeling depressed and disappointed, do not broadcast your feelings
randomly, certainly not to the holidaymakers nor to the locals. Try to find a colleague or
someone outside work – perhaps an understanding expat who has long passed through the
phase of feeling hostility for the host country – with whom to let off steam.

The best way to avoid disappointment is to be well briefed beforehand. Gathering general information about the country and specific information about the job before arrival will obviate many of the negative feelings some tourism employees feel. If you are the type to build up high hopes and expectations of new situations, it is wise to try to dismantle these before leaving home. Have a realistic idea of the difficulties you might face and be open-minded about cultural differences. It may take time to settle into your surroundings but the local mannerisms which once caused frustration, might become charming and even make you feel at home.

LONELINESS

When you are in resort miles away from home you can feel very lonely. Large tour operators try to place first-timers in major resorts where they will be working as part of a team. The job in the small resort on the other hand is given to someone who knows the country and will have enough friends to visit when they want to talk to someone other than a client. If you are really homesick, some companies have concessions for relatives to visit after a certain time, so take advantage of these. On tour you can be in the thick of a group, but alone. Here your coach driver is a friend, colleague, someone to joke and laugh with, who understands when you are tired and dispirited.

Creating a social life from scratch is difficult enough at any time, and so is even more difficult in an alien tongue and culture. However, you will probably find that many of your fellow reps and guides are lots of fun and able to offer practical help in your first few weeks (especially any who are bilingual). There may be a local support network most tourism workers never think of: the local English-speaking priest or vicar, the Consul, British Council (their library can be useful) and even English teachers. When you arrive in a resort make a point of searching them out and making friends before you need them. Bernadette Hayden from Holidayrama says she always makes a point of going to church on the first Sunday after she arrives to meet with the local community.

Whatever your hobby there will probably be one individual or even group locally who will welcome another enthusiast. Bridge breaks down barriers, bird watching, jazz or any number of sports can give you social contact and take you away from work when you feel like screaming. Often the local bookshop or post office can help. Or try the police who often know who does what locally.

Even if you don't have a hobby, an enquiry along the lines of 'I want to know about local stamps/flowers/history so I can tell my group' will find you instant friends longing to show off their knowledge. However much you feel frightened to leave the security of your working environment, make an effort to get out of your patch on your day off. Too much of the same place can make you very stale and this is a recipe for frustration and eventually disaster. It might even turn out that the idyllic village you discover on your day off has a rundown house which eventually you can convert to become a holiday villa. It happens.

HEALTH AND HYGIENE

People in travel jobs that require frequent flying will develop their own ways to combat jet lag either by drinking gallons of water during the flight to avoid dehydration or using aromatherapy products. Frequent flying and exposure to the sun is very hard on skin and many tourism personnel devote a great deal of time and money on skin protection. Some of the most often recommended products are Clarins' after-sun products (which contain an anti-mosquito preparation), moisturisers and fake tans. Hand cream is vital for men as well as women especially in the more rugged kinds of tour. Boots make a range of non-perfumed products though Kanebo and Christian Dior make much more expensive ones.

PART II

Country by Country Guide

EUROPE

As of May 2004, the European Union consists of 25 member states: Austria, Belgium, Denmark, Finland, France, Germany, Greece, Ireland, Italy, Luxembourg, the Netherlands, Portugal, Spain, Sweden and the United Kingdom, Hungary, Poland, the Czech Republic, Slovakia, Slovenia, Estonia, Latvia, Lithuania, Malta and Cyprus. The only outsiders in Western Europe are Norway and Iceland (which belong to the European Economic Area or EEA) and Switzerland. Eventually there will be free movement of labour across all these borders but it will take several years for the new members to be fully welcomed into the employment club.

Europe encompasses scores of the world's most beautiful tourist destinations. According to the statisticians in Brussels, Europe is still the most popular tourist destination. With over 60 million arrivals, France is first, though in 2003 it was pipped to the post by Spain in the number of incoming tourists from the UK and, more worrying for the French tourist authorities, China is predicted to overtake it in the coming years. Spain is the second most visited country of Europe, Italy third, followed by Hungary and the UK.

The abolition of duty free goods within Europe and the inexorable rise of cheap flights has changed the patterns of tourism in Europe, but only up to a point. The main Mediterranean resorts continue to heave with holidaymakers in the season, who need a lot of looking after by people who are employed in the tourist industry.

RED TAPE

Legislation has existed for some years guaranteeing the rights of all nationals of the European Union to compete for jobs in any member country. According to Article 8a of the Maastricht Treaty, every citizen of the European Union has the right to travel, reside and work in any member state. The only reason for refusing entry is on grounds of public security and public health. This will not immediately apply to the countries acceding in 2004 when most EU countries (but not Britain) have negotiated a delay of up to seven years. But even in those countries which have been EU members for a long time, the red tape and attendant hassles have by no means been done away with. Talk of the Single Europe should not lull Euro-jobseekers into thinking that the job hunt will be easy and that they need not worry about the formalities. Tourism jobs are often seen as the best jobs and perhaps the only jobs available to locals and many measures are in place to protect local employment. Nationalism still plays a large part in most employment situations. If you arrive to work as a rep and do not know how to do your job, the hotelier who thinks his sister could do the job better has the power to make your working life unbearable. EU rulings notwithstanding, barriers to the free movement of labour do remain.

The EU Directive on Mutual Recognition of Qualifications requires tour managers and tour guides to provide proof of qualifications to work in many EU countries, Spot checks have taken staff off coaches and into police stations, sometimes resulting in a fine. Contracts or letters of appointment from your boss are not sufficient forms of proof. The IATM (International Association of Tour Managers) has introduced a Certificate of Tour Management (CTM) which they claim is accepted throughout Europe. Possessing a professional qualification as an experienced tour manager will at least give you some credibility if challenged.

The standard situation among all EU countries is that nationals of any EU state have the right to work for up to three months. At the end of that period they should apply to the police or the local authority for a residence permit, showing their passport and job contract. Even if your employer is well versed in the regulations, none can guarantee that these procedures will be easy. It has been known for EU nationals working in France to wait, say, eight months for their *carte de séjour* to come through or for a Greek residence permit to arrive on the last day of a seasonal contract. On his year out from university, Matt from Manchester worked in ski resorts in both France and Germany. In theory he should have had no problem regularising his status. In practice, he encountered many difficulties. The social security number for which he applied in France took 12 months to come through. In Germany he fared even worse, trapped in a vicious circle of 'no job – no papers – no accommodation'. Without papers he was turned away by the federal employment service, which all EU nationals are entitled to use. But resistance was useless.

Residents of Commonwealth countries may need visas for a short term of work; contact the relevant High Commission or Embassy for advice. Nationals of non-European countries who want to work longer than the three months standard for tourist visas in European countries normally find it virtually impossible to obtain work permits. Typically, they leave the country every three months, perhaps leaving with one group and returning with another, in order for their visitor status to be renewed on re-entry. In many cases the authorities know what is happening but turn a blind eye, since tourism is seen as such a big earner. Yet such a worker is in the unenviable position of having no employment protection.

WORKING IN EUROPE FOR A UK EMPLOYER

A large proportion of Britons working in European resorts, ski resorts, campsites, holiday centres, etc. are working for British tour operators who do not have to conform to local employment regulations (minimum wage, protection from dismissal, etc.). Attempts have been made to force them to comply, most famously in the ski resorts of France, but they have found ways around it, i.e. to pay a sterling wage – often more like pocket money – directly into a bank account and to provide a package of benefits (e.g. free travel, free ski pass) in lieu of the national minimum wage.

JOB-HUNTING IN THE EU

Every EU country possesses a network of employment offices similar to UK Jobcentres, details of which are given in the individual country chapters if relevant. Although EU legislation requires national employment services to treat applicants from other member states in exactly the same way as their own citizens, it is impossible to prevent a certain amount of bias from entering the system. For obvious reasons, an employer is allowed to turn down an applicant who does not speak enough of the language to perform his or her job adequately.

Average unemployment across Europe is holding at a steady 8%, lower than it was five years ago, but still significant. No amount of positive legislation will force employment office officials to treat locals and foreigners equally. If there are two equally qualified job applicants of different nationalities, most employers will choose their fellow countryman/woman. In the words of Paul Winter from Cumbria who has worked several seasons in the German tourist industry:

All this talk of one Europe and a Europe without borders doesn't mean that jobs are easy and simple to get abroad. It's not easy. Plan ahead, try to learn a language and

take as much money as you can. That being said, the chances of working around
Europe are still there to be enjoyed, just use a little common sense.

Every EU country possesses a network of employment offices similar to British
Jobcentres. A Europe-wide employment service called EURES (EURopean Employment
Service) operates as a network of more than 400 EuroAdvisers who can access a database
of jobs within Europe. These vacancies are usually for six months or longer, and for
skilled, semi-skilled and managerial jobs, many in the hospitality field. Language skills
are almost always a requirement. Ask at your local Jobcentre how to contact your nearest
EuroAdviser. In the UK most of the expertise is concentrated in the headquarters of the
national Employment Service. Details on the EURES service can be obtained from the
Overseas Placing Unit (Level 4, Skills House, 3-7 Holy Green, Off the Moor, Sheffield S1
4AQ; 0114 259 6051, or from the EURES website: http://europa.eu.int/eures/index.jsp.

Euroguidance Centres covering European careers have been set up in all EU member
states to provide information on training, education and employment in Europe, mostly
to help careers services and their clients. Careers Europe, Onward House, Baptist
Place, Bradford BD1 2PS (01274 829600/fax 01274 829610; europe@careersb.co.uk/
www.careerseurope.co.uk) produce the Eurofacts and Globalfacts series of International
Careers Information, and Exodus, the Careers Europe database of international careers
information, all of which can be consulted at local Connexions careers offices. Another
source of information on European programmes is Eurodesk (Community Learning
Scotland, Rosebery House, 9 Haymarket Terrace, Edinburgh EH12 5EZ; 0131-313 2488)
which has an on-line database (www.eurodesk.org.uk).

US STUDENT WORK EXCHANGE PROGRAMMES

The two most important work exchange organisations in the US are CIEE (3 Copley
Place, 2nd Floor, Boston, MA 02116; 1-888-268-6245; www.ciee.org) and InterExchange
Inc. (161 Sixth Avenue, New York, NY 10013; 212-924-0446; www.interexchange.org).
In CIEE's work abroad programmes for students in France, Germany, Ireland and other
countries, participants are given visas which allow them to work at any job for the time
allowed. CIEE has offices in Paris, Berlin and other cities which will help with the job
hunt. InterExchange can fix up internships or short-term work in selected countries.

United Kingdom

The World Travel and Tourism Council estimates that in 2003 the travel and tourism
industry of the United Kingdom provided jobs for just over 1,000,000 people directly and
nearly 3,000,000 indirectly. This is despite the fact that the UK share of world tourism is
continuing to fall – from 6.7% in 1980 to 4.2% in 1995 to 3.6% at present). The levels of
tourism employment have remained similar over the past few years; predicted increases
have not taken place. The foot-and-mouth crisis of 2001 had a devastating impact not
just on rural tourism but more generally, as has the perceived fear of rising risks from
terrorism.

Traditional trips to the seaside and family holiday camps have been the staple diet
of British tourists for more than a century. One of the pioneers of British tourism was
Billy Butlin, who realised that visitors to his showgrounds would like to stay for a week.
Hence, he started his popular holiday camps, of which famous institutions as disparate as
the French Club Med and Dutch Center Parcs are permutations.

The British tourism scene has also widened its offerings with more glamorous locations discovered through television and film. The picturesque Yorkshire village of Kettlewell has seen a huge increase of tourist traffic since the release of the hit film *Calendar Girls* which was partly filmed there. Americans flock to Oxford not only to see the dreaming spires but for a tour of Inspector Morse locations. The blockbuster film *Braveheart* about one of Scotland's most celebrated heroes has helped to lure as many as two million extra tourists to Ben Nevis. Meanwhile Thirsk in North Yorkshire attracts a steady stream of fans of the famous vet James Herriot.

The United Kingdom is split into the four national areas of England, Northern Ireland, Scotland and Wales, each with its own tourist board to promote their interests at home and abroad (addresses below). Under each National Tourist Board come Regional Tourist Boards. The Boards have to rely on government funding and members' fees so, in typically British fashion, they operate on a shoestring. That is why the response to requests for information is often disappointing; budgets do not allow for the printing and distribution of masses of free leaflets. Recently resources have been poured into developing their websites so that information can be disseminated through cyberspace. Either way there is very little chance that the tourist boards will be able to assist job-seekers.

The four principal tourist boards in the UK are:

English Tourist Board, Thames Tower, Black's Road, London W6 9EL (020-8846 9000; www.visitbritain.com)

Visit Scotland, Fairways Business Park, Deer Park Road, Livingston, Edinburgh EH54 8HF (www.visitscotland.com)

Wales Tourist Board, Brunel House, 2 Fitzalan Road, Cardiff CF24 0UY (029 20 499909; www.visitwales.com)

Northern Ireland Tourist Board, 59 North St, Belfast BT1 1NB (028 90 231221; www.d iscovernorthernireland.com)

FINDING A JOB

The British airport and transport industries create a vast number of jobs. For tourists using this transport, meet and greet staff, local guides and local reps all have a role to play. Attractions such as theme parks, nature reserves, national parks, etc. need local guides with specialised knowledge, as do stately homes and museums.

Members of the British Incoming Tour Operators' Association can be searched online, ranging from companies that bring students into the UK to take English language courses to companies that operate coach tours; contact BITOA at Victory House, 14 Leicester Place, London WC2H 7BZ (020-7734 9569; www.bitoa.co.uk). Anyone who speaks a language fluently should look through the BITOA list and approach companies that handle visitors from the relevant country.

You have to be prepared to work hard at finding a job, for example be willing to make over a hundred phone calls to get a few leads. But first carry out some preliminary research. If you want to work locally, visit your local Tourist Information Centre (TIC) of which there are more than 500 in the country, and find out what types of visitor come to the area: backpacking students? families? older people with grown-up children who have more money to spend on leisure? If you are interested in working in the region, investigate the visitor attractions, stately homes, hotels, etc. If you want to work nationally and therefore away from home for extended periods, there are plenty of tours visiting every corner of the British Isles.

Although it is possible to find a job without any training, it is much more difficult. It is now incumbent on tour companies to abide by EU legislation which covers anyone on a package holiday or tour consisting of two of the three elements of accommodation, transport and services for an overnight trip or more. Every company in the tourism industry has become very conscious of customer care, and of their duty to look after visitors. Trained applicants will find it much easier to convince employers that they are conversant with things like health and safety requirements and able to carry them out.

Even more than in other industries, many jobs are found by networking. Those that are advertised will have thousands of applicants. Most people find jobs from contacts met on their training course or by joining the appropriate industry association. To keep abreast of developments in the tourism industry of Britain and Northern Ireland, it is a good idea to read the industry newspaper *Travel GBI* (3rd Floor, Foundation House, Perseverance Works, 38 Kingsland Road, London E2 8DD; 020-7729 4337; travelgbi@talk21.com).

GUIDES

In the UK it is possible to become a Registered Guide by undertaking a rigorous training course monitored by one of the regional tourist boards. For general information contact the Guild of Registered Tourist Guides (52d Borough High St, London SE1 1XN; 020-7403 1115; guild@blue-badge.org.uk) or the new Institute of Tourist Guiding (Lloyds Court, 1 Goodman's Yard, London E1 8AT; 020-7953 1257; info@institute-of-tourist-guiding.org.uk).

In excess of 800 official guides offer tours of London in nearly 40 languages. They have taken the two-year part-time course and obtained the coveted blue badge. To work for a prestige organisation like English Heritage (PO Box 569, Swindon SN2 2YP; www.english-heritage.org.uk) or the National Trust (36 Queen Anne's Gate, London SW1H 9AS; www.nationaltrust.org), it will be necessary to be persistent in knocking on the doors of their human resources department. The National Trust runs in-house training for house guides, most of which are for volunteers though there are a few paid jobs.

Among other things, guiding courses will steer you towards the most dependable books and guides. One large British tour company used to hold a competition among its trainee guides to find the worst guidebook errors; the only London guide books that no one could fault were the *Blue Guide* and the *Penguin Guide*. According to Simon Calder, travel editor of the *Independent,* there is even a mistake in the *A-Z* for London, an intentional one to be able to detect pirate publishers.

For touring round Britain one of the best resources is the AA's *Great Britain Road Atlas* which contains clear maps and useful information for tour planning; the 2004 edition retails for £20 (AA Publishing, 0870 240 0804) or can be purchased for £14 through the website (www.theaa.com). Publications from Group Leisure online (www.groupleisure.com) may provide some leads, for example *Who's Who in the Bus & Coach Industry* (£29.99) and *Who's Who in Group Leisure* (£42.50).

Of course incoming groups always prefer to employ someone who speaks the group language fluently or is a national of the country from which the tour group comes. For example the huge incoming Scandinavian market will often employ locally (mostly London) based Scandinavian staff. The major Scandinavian tour operators can do this because they maintain offices in the UK and can therefore interview staff *in situ*.

English language schools and centres often need guides to take their students out on sightseeing trips either as recreation or part of their studies of the British way of life. Other possibilities include universities and residential schools which run special courses during the holidays or let their accommodation to tour operators who may need local guides. One way of becoming known is to join the local Tourist Board as an individual member and offer to provide free guiding for familiarisation trips for tour operators coming into the area.

Guides in the London area should be aware that, officially, groups are not permitted in Westminster Abbey on Sundays, the Tower of London or Windsor Castle, but are admissible everywhere else. All guides in Britain must be prepared to cope with bad weather. Not only does a wet and rainy day make everyone feel gloomy but many sights and excursions will have to be hastily rearranged if it rains, for example the Changing of the Guard is cancelled when it's wet.

TOUR MANAGERS

There are over 3,000 touring coach companies in the UK. To contact local coach companies look in the Yellow Pages. The weekly *Coach and Bus Week* (01733 264666; www.cbwnet.co.uk) also publish *The Coach and Bus Guide* (£25) which lists all the major UK coach companies. Some of these companies will need tour managers to look after their tours as they travel around the UK (and continent). Many seasonal jobs are available with the companies which handle incoming groups. Major companies like EF Language Travel (EF House, 36-38 St Aubyn's, Hove, Sussex BN3 2PD; 01273 822777) host groups of young people from around the world and need as many as 650 guides, leaders and activity organisers throughout the UK for short periods of time in the summer.

Eventually when you have worked for one or more years as a tour manager, you can apply to become a member of the International Association of Tour Managers (IATM). Those who have completed a recognised tour manager training course may apply for Affiliate status to IATM (397 Walworth Road, London, SE17 2AW; 020-7703 9154/fax 020-7703 0358; iatm@iatm.co.uk/ www.iatm.co.uk). This association is very active on behalf of its members and represents them in the Brussels bureaucratic jungle. It also has regular contact with tour operators looking to hire tour managers. As a tour manager, bear in mind that student groups often arrive in Britain with a collection of tapes to play on the coach's sound system. Unless your coach has a blue PRS declaration that the company has paid a licence fee to the Performing Rights Society, you will be breaking the law, and fines can be stiff.

FREELANCE WORK

Once you have gained experience working for an employer, you may want to explore the possibility of setting up your own business or filling some niche in the market (see introductory section 'Working for Yourself'). In fact there is very little regulation and plenty of scope for entrepreneurs. Any guide with a convincing presentation can find it surprisingly easy to persuade companies to send foreign clients their way, especially during the busy conference season when business executives are looking for ways to keep their visiting contacts entertained. Become a member of ACE (Association for Conferences and Events; www.martex.co.uk/ace) for job leads.

ADMINISTRATION WORK

The National Trust has career courses for gardeners and countryside managers training for horticulture and environmental conservation. English Heritage, which administers such sites as Stonehenge, sometimes needs stewards and wardens.

If you are considering developing your own tours in the UK, bear in mind national preferences, as identified by the *Sunday Telegraph*: 'the Japanese are fond of woollen mills and clean restaurants, Arabs like halal picnics and casinos, Malaysians love gardens' and all nationalities seem to like tours which revolve around murder and ghosts. A Russian group once complained that it had been shown banks and financial institutions but no factories and wanted to know where all the wealth comes from. Meanwhile a Korean group was thrilled to go round the British Museum taking notes to give to their children at home. One expanding section of the market is short breaks in southern England for Belgians and French coming through the Tunnel; apparently while Britons go to French ports to buy wine, French people cross the Channel to buy McVities biscuits and Mother's Pride bread.

Some of the following specialist organisations may be of interest:

Association of Independent Museums (AIM), London Transport Museum, 39 Wellington Street, London WC2E 7BB (www.museums.org.uk). They produce bulletins highlighting new museums, and may offer suggestions for special days out.

British Arts Festival Association (020-7247 4667; www.artsfestivals.co.uk) provides an information service.

British Horse Society, Stoneleigh Deer Park, Kenilworth, Warwickshire CV8 2XZ (01926 202224; www.bhs.org.uk). Offer horse riding opportunities all over the UK at inspected and approved centres.

Heritage Railway Association (01707 643568) can advise on trips on steam railways.

Racecourse Association, Ascot (01344 625912) publish a list of major race days at all their 59 member racecourses in the UK.

Royal Collection Enterprises (www.royal.gov.uk) handle enquiries for the opening of Buckingham Palace and also the special exhibitions in the Queen's Gallery, which are popular for day trips.

Society of London Theatre (020-7557 6700; www.officiallondontheatre.co.uk) represents 50 theatres in the West End of London and provides an information service.

Sport England (020-7273 1500; www.sportengland.org) holds information about where sports championships are being held, addresses of clubs, events, etc.

Venue Masters, The Workstation, Paternoster Row, Sheffield S1 2BX (0114 249 3090; www.venuemasters.co.uk). Has taken over the British Universities Accommodation Consortium to help groups find academic accommodation.

In every corner of Britain there is scope for walking tours, whether to discover where famous people lived and died, or to see architectural oddities. This is a boom industry: who would have thought twenty years ago that we would want to visit old prisons, lead mines and pencil-making factories? After retiring from the Metropolitan Police, Allen Evershed took a guiding course and started a company called Diplomatic Guide Services which runs walking and taxi tours around the back streets of Southwark (where he had worked as a policeman). His fellow guides are all ex-Scotland Yard or police service. Although he doesn't talk about his police work, he can tell many interesting stories about the area.

Apart from the mainstream opportunities for freelance guides, there are other tourism-related openings for self-employed people. For example anyone who has some experience in the field of press and PR can set up on his or her own. Stately homes, visitor attractions and other tourism venues might want a short campaign to advertise an opening, a new feature, etc. Large companies don't want these one-off jobs, so turn to freelancers instead.

FARM TOURISM AND NATIONAL PARKS

After the devastation of 2001, people involved in rural tourism (those at least who survived the foot and mouth catastrophe) have been benefitting from some government compensation and have miraculously picked themselves up. As more visitors seek to escape the urban grind, visits to working farms and related businesses have begun to increase again. Often these days farmers' wives make more money offering bed and breakfast than their husbands working on the farm. Even farms which do not offer accommodation often run open days and need reception staff to help out. Farms also turn their outbuildings into self-catering units, and need cleaners, carpenters and maintenance staff. Tourist Information Centres can tell you which farms are open to the public. The organisation Farm Stay UK (www.farmstayuk.co.uk) based at the National Agriculture Centre, Stoneleigh Park, Warks CV8 2LG (024 7669 6909) also update annually a guide *Stay on a Farm* listing farms open to the public and farm accommodation.

National park authorities try to maintain the tricky balance between conservation with visitor management, which means more people are needed to do the managing. Britain has 13 national parks which require wardens, trail guides, stewards, park attendants and shop staff as well as managers, legal advisors, planners and press staff. Obviously many of these people are distinguished by their love of the outdoor life and their commitment to interpreting the environment to the general public.

Further information may be obtainable from the Association of National Park Authorities (126 Bute St, Cardiff CF10 5LE; 029 2049 9966; www.anpa.gov.uk).

HOTELS & CATERING

The best starting place for finding out about career prospects in the hotels and catering industry is the website of the Hotel & Catering Training Company (www.hctc2.co.uk). Thousands of vacancies at all levels have to be filled in hotels and restaurants every week and there are definite skills and labour shortages in certain areas. As a result many hotels, particularly in London, could not survive without a huge foreign workforce. Seaside and countryside hotels normally provide staff accommodation and food, though the standard will be considerably lower than that enjoyed by the paying guests at the hotel. Live-in positions are not easy to find in London where accommodation is at such a premium.

The introduction of the national minimum wage in 1999 has gone a long way to reducing the exploitation that was once common. The rate is currently £4.20 per hour for workers over 21, £3.60 for 18-21 year olds. For details contact the NMW information line 0845 845 0360 or check the DTI website www.tiger.gov.uk. Hotel staff with silver service or other specialist experience can expect to earn above the minimum wage as can restaurant staff in London who should also receive free food. Waiting staff can supplement their wages with tips, however chamber and bar staff will generally have to be content with their hourly wage.

People who are available for the whole season, say April to October will find it much easier to land a job than those available only for the peak months of July and August. Most hotels prefer to receive a formal written application in the early part of the year, complete with photos and references; however it can never hurt to telephone (especially later in the spring) to find out what the situation is. You can work systematically through a hotel guide such as those published by the Automobile Association, the Royal Automobile Club or the Tourist Boards. The more bedrooms listed in the hotel's entry, the better the chances of a vacancy.

It is worth contacting large hotel chains for up-to-date vacancy information only if you are going for senior positions like chef or manager. For example Hilton National & Associate Hotels (Maple Court, Central Park, Reeds Court, Watford WD2 4QQ; 020-7850 4000) can give advice on which of their three dozen UK hotels have current vacancies, although these should be applied to individually for employment. Similarly C.H.E. Group Plc (Choice Hotels Europe) can give advice on the opportunities they are offering in over 120 units in the UK and Ireland. For information on applying, contact the Group HR Department by post (112 Station Road, Edgware, Middlesex HA8 7BJ), fax 020-8233 2080 or email HR@ChoiceHotelsEurope.com. Applicants must have hotel qualifications/experience, a reasonable to good level of English, be available for a minimum of a year and be EU nationals or already in possession of valid working papers. Another promising chain of hotels is Travel Inn with 100 properties in England, Scotland and Wales (Oakley House, Oakley Road, Luton LU4 9QH; 01582 499297; www.travelinn.co.uk).

Anyone who can acquaint themselves with EU hygiene regulations before being interviewed would have the edge or, even better, the Basic Food Hygiene Certificate which can be obtained after a day's training course. Many employment agencies specialise in placing seasonal staff in the UK hospitality industry, for example:
Aspire Recruitment, 31 Carvosa Road, Truro, Cornwall TR1 UBA (01872 241485;

info@aspirerecruitment.co.uk). Chefs, managers, reception, bar, waiting, and other staff mainly for Southwest England and the Channel Islands.

EuroCom, Suite 45, Surbiton Business Centre, 46 Victoria Road, Surbiton, Surrey KT6 4JL (020-8390 4512; post@europeancommunications.com). Provide staff to 4 and 5 star hotels; minimum contract 6 months year round.

European Work Experience Programme – 020-8572 2993; www.ewep.com. Places Europeans in the UK.

Adria Recruitment, 24 Stourvale Gardens, Chandlers Ford, Hants. SO53 3NE (02380 254287; info@adriarecruitment.com; www.adriarecruitment.com). Live-in hotel and catering staff for minimum of six months. Can be arranged in conjunction with English classes.

Lucy Locketts & Vanessa Bancroft Agency, 400 Beacon Road, Wibsey, Bradford, West Yorks. BD6 3DJ; tel/fax 01274 402822. Placement of European waiters, porters, chambermaids, etc.

Montpelier Employment Agency, 34 Montpelier Road, Brighton, Sussex BN1 2LQ (01273 778686/ www.themontpelieremploymentagency.co.uk).

Southern Work Experience, 12 Eversfield Road, Eastbourne, East Sussex BN21 2AS (01323 638523). Hotel and industry work experience placements for 2-3 months.

Scores of online recruitment agencies have sprung up to publicise and fill UK vacancies online. An evening of surfing should show you the range of assistance that may be on offer, normally free of charge to job-seekers. Try for example www.acornjobs.co.uk (for hotels and catering jobs); www.actionrecruitment.co.uk (for hospitality professionals); www.barzone.co.uk for employment at all levels in the licensed trade and the excellent www.doctorjob.com which keeps its vacancy lists up-to-date.

PUBS

Live-in pub work is not hard to come by. You usually have to work throughout pub opening hours six days a week, but you should be rewarded with about £5 an hour. The introduction of the minimum wage affected many pubs which traditionally offered live-in work, since they are now allowed to deduct only £20 a week for accommodation, which is good news especially for the army of foreign young people who come to work in the UK for a season or two, while improving their English. However it has increased costs for the brewery chains like Fullers and Youngs. Waiting for an ad to appear is usually less productive than going pub to pub. Americans may need to be reminded that pub staff do not get tips in a British pub though they may be bought a drink now and then.

REGIONAL TOURIST BOARDS

For a job in most national and regional Tourist Board offices, a minimum of two languages is a requirement. Visit Britain has its own recruitment website (www.visitbritaincareer s.com) though actual vacancies are seldom posted. The Human Resources Department telephone number is 020-8563 3083/3066. Experience in marketing, PR, administration, media, publications or advertising would be useful. There are ten regional tourist boards in England:

Cumbria Tourist Board, Ashleigh, Holly Road, Windermere, Cumbria LA23 2AQ (01539 444444; www.cumbria-the-lake-district.co.uk)

East of England Tourist Board, Toppesfield Hall, Hadleigh, Suffolk IP7 5DN (0870 225 4800; www.eastofenglandtouristboard.com)

Heart of England Tourist Board, Woodside, Larkhill Road, Worcester WR5 2EZ (01905 761100; www.hetb.co.uk)

Visit London, 1 Warwick Row, Victoria, London SW1E 5ER (020-7932 2000; www.visitlondon.com)

North West Tourist Board, Swan House, Swan Meadow Road, Wigan Pier, Wigan Lancs.

WN3 5BB (01942 821222; www.visitnorthwest.com)
Northumbria Tourist Board, www.visitnorthumbria.com or www.tourismnortheast.co.uk
Tourism South East, The Old Brew House, Warwick Park, Tunbridge Wells, Kent TN2 5TU (01892 540766; enquiries@tourismse.com/ www.seetb.org.uk)
Tourism South East, 40 Chamberlayne Road, Eastleigh, Hants. SO50 5JH (023 8062 5400; www.tourismsoutheast.com). Information about possible funded training initiatives in the region.
South West Tourism Ltd, Woodwater Park, Exeter EX2 5WT (01392 360050; post@swtourism.co.uk)
Yorkshire Tourist Board, 312 Tadcaster Road, York YO24 1GS (01904 707961; www.ytb.org.uk)
There are over 500 Tourist Information Centres in the UK, some open on a seasonal basis, others open year round. Whereas most of the time is spent replenishing stocks of leaflets and answering questions about the location of toilets, there is plenty of variety in the questions which tourists ask (e.g. why didn't the Queen choose a quieter location to build Windsor Castle instead of under the flight path for Heathrow?) Winter is obviously quieter but weekend break holidaymakers still fill up the TICs.

HOLIDAY CAMPS AND ACTIVITY CENTRES

Anyone with a qualification in canoeing, yachting, riding, climbing, etc. should be able to find summer work as a children's leader or instructor. If you don't know what the governing body initials stand for, you should seek further qualifications before trying for a job in which the safety of others will be in your hands: horse riding (BHS), sailing/ windsurfing (RYA), canoeing and kayaking (BCU), rowing (ARA Instructor), swimming (ASA), lifesaving (RLSS), fencing (AFA Club Leader), judo (brown belt), cricket (NCA leader), climbing (MLTB Single Pitch Sup. Award), orienteering (BOF Level 1 Instructor), and archery (GNAS Leader). See the introductory section *Sports & Activity Instructors*.

There are also plenty of jobs as general assistants for sports-minded young people, especially at children's multi activity centres. In these jobs, character and personality are more important than qualifications. The trouble is that the pay is not usually very much for this kind of work, perhaps about £50-£60 per week in addition to food and accommodation costs, though this will be supplemented by an end-of-season bonus at some centres. Applicants are normally asked to provide police clearance forms for any job working with children. For some of the main operators in this field, see entries for *Kingswood Group* and *King's Camps* in the Directory of employers.

Seasonal staff who work for language holiday operators tend to be better paid; try for example EF Language Travel (mentioned above), Embassy CES (Lorna House, 103 Lorna Road, Hove, E Sussex BN3 3EL; 01273 322353; www.embassyces.com) which hires about 200 activity leaders each summer) and *Ardmore Language School* (see Directory of Employers).

One of the largest employers is *PGL Travel*, with a staggering 2,500 vacancies during the season March to October. The Youth Hostels Association's Adventure Holidays programme (Trevelyan House, Dimple Road, Matlock, Derbyshire DE4 3YH; 0870 770 8868; www.yha.org.uk) employs a large number of sports leaders, offering only free board and lodging, rail fares and sometimes pocket money.

Once you have the appropriate qualifications, try the travel ads in the quality papers, ask Regional Tourist Boards which companies are in membership or contact the British Activity Holidays Association (01932 252994) whose members submit to regular safety inspections. To find out whether a centre is licensed, contact the Adventure Activities Licensing Authority (17 Lambourne Crescent, Cardiff Business Park, Llanishen, Cardiff CF14 5GF; 029 20 755715; www.aala.org). With some high profile tragedies occurring since the Lyme Bay canoeing tragedy of 1993 in which several young people were drowned at an activity centre on the south coast, directors are trying to maintain the highest possible standards in their staff.

Here are some other activity centres which may require domestic as well as leadership staff:

3D Education & Adventure, Osmington Bay, Shortlake Lane, Weymouth, Dorset DT3 6EG (01305 836226; www.3d.co.uk/jobs). 750 staff for multi-activity and educational courses.

Barracudas Summer Activity Camps, Bridge House, Bridge Street, St Ives, Cambs. PE27 5EH (01480 497533; jobs@barracudas.co.uk). Various day camps for 5-15 year olds in southern England.

EAC Activity Camps, 1st Floor, 59 George St, Edinburgh EH2 2LQ (0131-477 7574; www.activitycamps.com). 100 activity staff for July/August camps in Scotland and England.

EF Language Travel, EF House 36-38 St Aubyn's, Hove, Sussex BN3 2PD (01273 201406; ltrecruitment@ef.com). Language programmes for international students throughout Britain. Up to 1,000 group leaders and EFL teachers are hired.

Kids Klub, The Lodge, The Hall, Great Finborough, Stowmarket, Suffolk IP14 3EF (01449 742700; www.kidsklub.co.uk).

Family holiday centres proliferate around the British Isles and employ a large range of people to do catering, entertainment and managerial work. As well as the usual scivvying jobs, they may also require entertainers for both children and adults, lifeguards, DJs, shop assistants, etc. The main disadvantage is that accommodation is generally unavailable. Try the following:

Butlins Skyline, Roman Bank, Skegness, Lincolnshire PE25 1NJ (01754 761502) require receptionists, lifeguards, car park attendants, entertainers, shop assistants for Family Entertainment resorts. Application form and information pack available from regional hotlines: Bognor Regis 01243 841190; Minehead 01643 709638; Skegness 01754 761502.

HF Holidays – see Directory entry

Pontin's Ltd, Sagar House, Eccleston, Nr. Chorley, Lancs. PR7 5PH; 01257 452452; www.pontins.com. Hiring takes place for eight family holiday centres.

THEME PARKS AND LEISURE CENTRES

American-style theme parks have very large seasonal staff requirements. Major theme parks (including Alton Towers) run their own training programmes; apply to their Personnel Officers for information. As well as the usual skivvying jobs, they may also require ride operators, entertainers for both children and adults, lifeguards, DJs, shop assistants, etc. The main disadvantage is that accommodation is generally not provided. Among the largest are:

Alton Towers, Alton, North Staffordshire ST10 4DB (01538 704039). Approximately 1,000 vacancies between March and November.

American Adventure Theme Park, Pit Lane, Ilkeston, Derby DE7 5SX (01773 531521). 150 ride operators, 70 retail staff, 120 catering assistants, etc.

Bourne Leisure Ltd, Park Lane, Hemel Hempstead, Herts. HP2 4YL. Staff needed at 40 holiday parks throughout Britain.

Chessington World of Adventures, Human Resources Department, PO Box 125, Chessington, Surrey KT9 2WL (0870 444 4678). Employs between 500 and 1,000 people each year.

Frontierland Western Theme Park, The Promenade, Morecambe, Lancs. LA4 4DG (01524 410024). 40+ ride operators and general assistants in all departments.

Legoland Windsor, Winkfield Road, Windsor, Berks. SL4 4AY (01753 626150). Over

300 seasonal workers needed in total.
Pleasureland Amusement Park, Marine Drive, Southport, Lancs. PR8 1RX (01704 532717).
Thorpe Park, Human Resources Department, PO Box 125, Chessington KT9 2WL (0870 444 4678). Limited accommodation provided for the 400+ ancillary staff.
Leisure centres are an expanding market, both individual sites and those developed in conjunction with hotels. Often they require their staff to maintain meticulous standards of hygiene. For example it may be necessary to check the water in a swimming pool three times a day to satisfy Health & Safety requirements. Swimming pool staff will need first aid and a lifesaving qualification. Jobs are often advertised in *Leisure Management Magazine* (Portmill House, Portmill Lane, Hitchin, Herts. SG5 1DJ; 01462 431385; www.leisuremanagement.co.uk); a student subscription costs £18 per year.

YOUTH HOSTELS

From February to October, the Youth Hostels Association (YHA) recruits 400 Seasonal Assistant Wardens to work in Youth Hostels throughout England and Wales. Duties include general domestic work, cooking, manning the hostel shop and the reception desk. Food and accommodation are provided plus a basic monthly salary of £370. You must be over 18 years old, have experience of dealing with the general public, an appreciation of good customer service and a pleasant personality. A proven ability to cater for numbers and perform clerical tasks would be an advantage. For further information, send a SAE to The National Recruitment Department, PO Box 11, Matlock, Derbyshire DE4 2XA (01426 939216; recruitment@yha.org.uk). The YHA encourages employees to undertake nationally recognised occupational qualifications while working in a hostel.

SPECIAL EVENTS

Conferences, seminars, exhibitions, outdoor events and pop concerts all need freelance staff as well as full-time organisers known as Professional Conference Organisers or PCOs. Established members of ACE (Association for Conferences and Events, Riverside House, High St, Huntingdon PE18 6SG; 01480 45759) receive lists of upcoming events and attend ACE functions at which they put out the word that they are looking for work, and jobs are fixed up accordingly.

Events such as the Henley Regatta in June, Test Matches at Headingley in Leeds, the Edinburgh Festival in August/September and a host of golf tournaments and county shows need temporary staff to work as car park attendants, ticket sellers and in catering. This could be a useful way of gaining experience of the world of event management. Sporting events like the British Open and Wimbledon employ a myriad of casual workers. Ask the local tourist office for a list of upcoming events and contact the organisers. Outside catering and other companies which hold the contracts for staffing special events include:

Afar Exhibition Services, 34 Craighall Rd, Edinburgh, Lothian EH6 4SA (0131 552 9988; www.eventservicenet.co.uk).
Events Staff, 25 York Road, Northampton NN1 5QA(01604 627775). 1000+ stewards, programme sellers, car park and security staff for racing fixtures, etc.
FMC, All England Lawn Tennis and Croquet Club, Church Road, Wimbledon, London SW19 5AE (020-8947 7430; resourcing@fmccatering.co.uk). One of the largest outdoor caterers in Europe.
Leapfrog International, Riding Court Farm, Datchet, Berks. SL3 9JU (01753 589300; emt@leapfrog-int.co.uk). Up to 100 event crew for family fun days, etc.

THE CHANNEL ISLANDS

In general, the Channel Islands are a favourite destination for seasonal workers in the hotel/ hospitality industry. For a list of 100+ establishments, many offering accommodation in Guernsey, write to the States Tourist Board, PO Box 23, St. Peter Port, Guernsey GY1 3AN (01481 723552; enquiries@guernseytouristboard.com; www.guernseytouristboard .com). Several agencies specialise in recruiting catering and other staff for the Channel Islands, e.g. Jersey Recruitment (La Rue le Masurier, St Helier, Jersey JE2 4YE; 01534 617373) and Towngate Personnel (3 Alum, Chine Road, Westbourne, Bournemouth BH4 8DT; 01202 752955; enquiries@towngate-personnel.co.uk). Towngate supply staff for permanent live-in vacancies in the Channel Islands and in the UK.

The tax status of the Channel Islands works to the advantage of employees (just as it does to offshore millionaires). The exemption limit for a single person is in the region of £11,000 per calendar year; further details are available from the CI Tax Department (01534 603000). The lovely island of Sark is also a magnet for itinerant workers.

Niamh Cordon is one of the many people who regularly returns to Jersey to work the season:

Despite the untrained horses, they loved driving the horse-drawn carriages on Sark

After returning home to Ireland from working on the Greek islands, I still had itchy feet. I had heard from friends that Jersey was a great place to go to pick up work easily. There is a job centre but more importantly a recruitment agency that deals with the catering trade and also has jobs for bar staff, waiting staff and receptionists. Accommodation is very expensive in Jersey but most hotels have live-in positions. You need to get over in early May before the hordes of students arrive. I spent two summer seasons as a receptionist and then signed up with the temping agencies and began clearing £300 working as a typist.

One unusual seasonal opportunity on Sark is driving the horse-drawn carriages, a job which Lyn and Dave Howard saw advertised in the *Horse and Hound*. Despite working very long hours with untrained horses for £40 a week, they loved the job and the island.

RED TAPE

Nationals of the European Union (plus Norway and Iceland) are not subject to immigration control and are therefore entitled to enter Britain to look for work, including citizens of the new EU member states (unless the government loses its nerve and reverses its decision to welcome them on equal terms from May 2004). Many find the job hunt easier than the natives do, simply because they can speak more than one language.

Because of chronic labour shortages in the Southeast of England, it is now possible for non-EU/EEA citizens to be granted work permits for hospitality work, particularly for well qualified applicants. Agencies like *Worldnet* for example (see Directory entry) can assist with permit applications. If employers who have advertised their vacancies for a specified period are unable to fill them, they may be granted permission to employ foreign workers. It is much easier of course if you can offer a sought-after skill such as a knowledge of Japanese and are applying for a high-level permanent position.

The Training & Work Experience Scheme (TWES) is a special arrangement within the Work Permit scheme which allows foreign nationals to do work-based training for a professional or specialist qualification, a graduate training programme or work experience. TWES permits are issued on the understanding that the individual will return overseas at the end of the agreed period and put the skills learned to use for at least two years. Normally, they will not be allowed to transfer to work permit employment. Applications for permits can only be made by employers based in the UK on behalf of the person they wish to employ. Details are available on the IND website www.workpermits.gov.uk.

Students who are not nationals of a European Economic Area (EEA) country who are studying in the UK, and who have in their passports a stamp stating that they cannot work 'without the consent of the Secretary of State' are no longer required to obtain permission to take spare time and vacation work, or to undertake work or internship placements. Only students on courses lasting more than six months are eligible. They are allowed to work up to 20 hours a week during term-time and they should not fill a permanent full-time vacancy in pursuit of their career.

The British Hospitality Association (Queen's House, 55-56 Lincoln Inn Fields, London WC2A 3BH; 020-7404 7744; www.bha-online.org.uk) which is the trade association of the hotel and catering industry in the UK refers work permit queries to a specialist agency: Work Permit Experts Ltd, 92 New Crane Wharf, New Crane Place, London E1W 3TU (020-7709 7886; immex@btclick.com).

SPECIAL EXCHANGE SCHEMES

American students who wish to work in Britain may participate in the Work in Britain Program, which allows about 3,750 full-time college students over the age of 18 to look for work before or after arriving in Britain. They must obtain a Blue Card (work permit) for a fee of about $240, which is authorised by the British Home Office. Participants may arrive at any time of the year and work for up to six months. Candidates must be US citizens enrolled at an accredited US or Canadian university or college or no more than one semester away from the most recent full-time semester. They must prove that they have access to at least $800. For further information contact BUNAC USA, PO Box 430, Southbury, CT 06488 (1-800-GO-BUNAC or 203-264-0901; enquiries@bunacusa.org). The *Work in Britain Participants' Handbook* contains the addresses of scores of potential employers. The BUNAC offices in London (16 Bowling Green Lane, EC1R 0QH) and

Edinburgh have files of possible UK employers as well as current vacancy lists of cheap accommodation and job offers.

US citizens who have been offered a full-time position in their field of study or experience in the UK may apply for a work permit through the Association for International Practical Training (Career Development Exchanges, 10400 Little Patuxent Pkwy, Suite 250, Columbia, MD 21044-3510; www.aipt.org). They have a special Career Development programme devoted to Hospitality and Tourism. The cost of the working visa to the candidate is $250 plus £295 to the employer and the processing time is 8-10 weeks.

Members of the Commonwealth, mainly Australians, New Zealanders and Canadians, may obtain 'Working holiday-maker' status if they are between the ages of 17 and 30 (recently raised from 27) with no dependants over the age of five. The permit entitles the holder to work in Britain with the primary intention of funding a holiday, for up to two years, though there is now a mechanism for turning this into a permanent work permit. You will have to prove that you have enough money to support yourself and fund a return airfare; around £2,000.

TAX AND NATIONAL INSURANCE

Most new employees are put onto the emergency tax code (denoted by 'X' at the end of your tax code) and immediately begin to forfeit roughly a quarter of their wages. UK and Commonwealth nationals are entitled to the single person's personal allowance (currently £4,615 per year). Foreign nationals can claim personal allowances if they have been in the UK for at least 183 days in any tax year (which starts on April 6th). Eligible candidates who have earned less than the personal allowance, such as those who have done a seasonal job, may be entitled to apply for a rebate of the overpaid tax. When they finish work, they should send both parts of the P45 given to them by the employer to their employer's tax office. When they are ready to leave Britain, they must complete and submit form P85, a leaving certificate which asks your intentions with respect to returning to the UK to work. Inland Revenue operates a telephone information service for the public on 020-7667 4001 and an informative website www.inlandrevenue.gov.uk.

Many companies, such as those who hire freelance guides, pay cash. Do not think that this will enable you to avoid paying income tax. Every company has an accounting department which will insist that all money paid out be accounted for, so your name and address will figure in the accounts sent to Inland Revenue at the end of the year. Inland Revenue has tried to make tour operators deduct tax at source (PAYE/Pay as you Earn) but without success in most cases. If you are paid gross, you can claim against tax for training courses, taxis, books, even some clothes expenses in some circumstances.

In addition to income tax, you must also pay National Insurance Contributions. If you earn over £64 you must pay 11% on taxable earnings above £89 a week. Companies may tell you that you don't have to pay National Insurance contributions but unless you keep up voluntary payments, you may land yourself in trouble in years to come. You can make things easier for yourself by having an accountant. All freelance workers or people employed on seasonal contracts must make their own arrangements for pensions and (sometimes) insurance.

UK TOUR COMPANIES

The following operate tours or provide travel services in the UK. Some of the biggest are members of the British Association of Wholesale Tour Agents (www.bawta.co.uk) and others are members of the British Incoming Tour Operators Association, referred to earlier. Check with BITOA for other companies to approach.

Albatross Travel Group, Tour Operations, Albatross House, 14 New Hythe Lane, Larkfield, Kent ME20 6AB (01732 879195; www.albatross-tours.com). Guides who can speak German, Dutch, Scandinavian languages or Italian needed.

APA Travel Services, 138 Eversholt St, London NW1 1BL (020-7388 1732; www.apatraveluk.com). Incoming operator for groups from Spain, Italy and Portugal.

Axis & Globe, 15 King's Terrace, London NW1 0JP (020-7388 3838; www.axisglobe.co.uk)

Barton Hill, 30 Parkstone Road, Poole BH15 2PG (01202 665500; www.bartonhill.com). UK tours, conference work.

Botel Ltd, 50 Morthen Road, Wickersley, S. Yorks. S60 1EN (01709 703535; www.botel.co.uk)

British Tours, 49 Conduit St, London W1S 2YS (020-7734 8734; www.britishtours.com)

Destination Great Britain, Voyages Systems Service, Sterling House, 150 High St, Tonbridge, Kent TN9 1BB (01732 369090; www.voyagesystems.co.uk)

DFDS Seaways, Scandinavia House, Parkestone Quay, Harwich, Essex CO12 4QG (01206 271788; www.dfds.co.uk). Shuttle work for good linguists between London and Harwich to meet incoming groups of Germans, Dutch and Scandinavians.

Discover Travel & Tours, International House, Pierpoint St, Worcester WR1 1YD (0870 225 8000; www.discovertravelandtours.com)

EuroWales, Prince's Square Montgomery, Powys SY15 6PZ (01686 668030; www.eurowales.co.uk)

Greatdays Travel Group, Travel House, 2 Stamford Park Road. Altrincham, Cheshire WA15 9EN (0161-928 9966; www.greatdays.co.uk)

IGS, Norman House, 105-109 Strand, London WC1R 0AA (020-7212 9880; www.igs-london.com)

Independent Coach Travel Ltd (ICT), Studios 20/21, Colmans Wharf, 45 Morris Road, London E14 6PA (020-7538 4627; www.ictsqt.co.uk)

Interopa, 21-23 Chilworth St, London W2 3HA (020-7258 0009; www.interopa.co.uk). UK tours for Italian speaking clients.

Miki Travel, 18-20 Cannon St, London EC4M 6XD (020-7398 5098). UK tours for Japanese people.

Norman Allen Group Travel Ltd, Portfield House, Daws Road, Hereford HRI 2JJ (01432 277 666; www.group-travel.com)

Sovereign Tourism, 6 Weighhouse St, London W1K 5LT (020-7491 2323; www.sovereigntourism.com). European, American and Asian clients, including religious groups.

Success Tours Ltd, Level 4, The Mill, Court Street, Trowbridge, Wiltshire BA14 8BR (01225 764205; www.success-tours.co.uk)

T4 Travel Ltd, Suite 10a, Newton House, 147 St Neots Road, Hardwick, Cambridge CB3 7QJ (01954 213 121; www.t4travel.co.uk)

Tourwise of London, 177-179 Hammersmith Road, London W6 8BS (020-8741 8666; www.globusandcosmos.co.uk). Meet and greet staff for Americans arriving at Heathrow. Uniform provided.

Trina Tours, Isis House, 74 New Oxford St, London WC1A 1EU (020-7462 1558; www.trinatours.com). Destination management. Website invites people who are interested in working to make contact.

Wedgewood Britain, 7 Prescot St, London E1 8AY (020-7265 7000; www.wedgewood.co.uk)

Austria

Although Austria is only about the size of Scotland or the state of Maine, it is one of the most important tourist destinations in the world. With more Alps than Switzerland, a multitude of both winter and summer resorts, cultural, historical and sporting attractions and well-developed conference venues, Austria offers tremendous employment opportunities.

Even before Roman times, Austria attracted travellers who used the Brenner Pass to cross between northern and southern Europe. When the Romans arrived they built the Via Salaria (traces of which remain) to convey the precious salt from the mines near Salzburg to Rome to be used as payment for their soldiers (hence the English word salary). In later centuries, the great Austro-Hungarian Empire exerted its influence from Paris (Napoleon married a member of the Habsburg family) to Mexico (where the haloes on images of saints are still composed of stars in the Austrian style).

But during the 19th century the Habsburg empire began to crumble and when the heir to the throne was assassinated at Sarajevo, Europe went to war. The empire collapsed entirely at the end of World War I, taking with it Austria's industrial might. No sooner had the country started to rebuild than it was invaded again. In the aftermath of the Second World War, the Austrian government realised that snow and mountains were its principal resources, and so helped towns, villages and hamlets to build the infrastructure needed for winter tourism. Later it gave grants to hotels and pensions, which would be otherwise empty in the summer, to build swimming pools, etc., so that today the country has a year-round tourist industry.

PROSPECTS FOR WORK

For many years Austria has offered seasonal employment in its summer and winter tourist industries. Even though the rate of unemployment has been slowly climbing (about 6% at present), more than a quarter of people employed in tourism are not Austrian citizens. A good knowledge of German will be necessary for most jobs apart from those with UK tour operators. In winter, jobs proliferate for resort managers, ski reps, children's reps and chalet staff in addition to all the usual jobs. Austria is popular among ramblers, birdwatchers, opera and music lovers, etc. and a number of mostly upmarket tour operators offer Danube cruises. Many British coach companies run ten-day holidays to the lakes and mountains.

While the Austrian tourist industry creates a huge number of jobs, competition for those jobs comes from the thousands of economic migrants who have poured into Austria from neighbouring states to the east, especially the former Yugoslavia. From May 2004, four of Austria's neighbours - Hungary, Slovenia, Slovakia and the Czech Republic - will join the EU, intensifying that competition. All of these countries provide a pool of both skilled and unskilled labour, so that it will become harder for aspiring job-seekers to show up and find a congenial job. However possibilities are still plentiful for trained staff who can communicate in German, not just because that is the language of Austria but because the majority of tourists come from neighbouring Germany.

Vienna is a favourite destination for British incentive conferences, though there are also conference centres in Graz, Innsbruck, Salzburg, Villach, etc. Speakers of German and English (and preferably one other language) who want to enquire about temporary work as stewards, etc. should contact the centres (see below) for a list of local conference organisers.

FINDING A JOB

Tour operators that are active in Austria are included in the sections that follow. Once you are in Austria, you should visit the state-run regional employment office AMS (Arbeitsmarktservice) though it would be virtually essential to speak German before they could assist. The AMS web pages might be of assistance to German speakers (www.ams.or.at) and the links to EURES Advisers could be followed up.

Private employment agencies exist in Austria, mostly registering professional vacancies for chefs, restaurant managers, etc. For example L.S.C. (Land Sea Career) Personalvermittlung (Kohldorferstrasse 98, A-9020 Klagenfurt; 0463-509837; fax 0463-509837/4; office@l-s-career.com; www.l-s-career.com) is an agency that places suitable candidates in hotels throughout Austria plus on international river and sea cruises. The websites of recruitment agencies like Oscar's Agency and GastroHelp, both based in Liechtenstein, may also be of assistance to international jobseekers (www.oscars.li and www.gastrohelp.com) for hotel and other vacancies throughout Austria.

There is no shortage of hotels to which you can apply independently either for the summer or the winter season. The prestigious hotel group Austria Hotels International belongs to the International Association of Tour Managers; its website www.austria-hotels.at provides contact details for the managers of the 16 hotels in the group. Otherwise any hotel guide or local tourist offices can provide details of other potential employers.

Outside the cities, the largest concentration of hotels is in the Tyrol though there are also many in the Vorarlberg region in western Austria. One possibility for the summer season is *Travelbound* which hires a large number of people to work in resorts, chalets and hotels in Austria through First Choice Holidays recruitment.

WINTER RESORTS

The majority of British ski holidays are based in the resorts of the Tyrol. The main winter resorts are St Anton (the most popular with British holidaymakers), Kitzbühel, Mayrhofen, Brand, Klösterle, St. Johann-im-Pongau, St. Johann in Tirol, Lech, Söll and Zell-am-See. The Innsbruck region normally offers more reliable snow conditions from early December until the end of April due to the proximity of the Stubai Glacier, though due to global warming only resorts above 1800m are reliable.

British tour operators which are active in the Austrian Alps include *Crystal Holidays* (now part of the Specialised Holiday Group), *Inghams, Equity Ski, Thomson* and *Total Ski. Headwater* runs cross country skiing holidays.

Most *Saisonstellen im Hotel und Gastewerbe* (seasonal hotel jobs) for the winter season are notified in November for the start of the season at the end of November. At one time Club Habitat in the Tyrol (Kohlgrub 9, A-6365 Kirchberg) employed alpine staff in winter and summer and also hosted a pre-season training course for prospective workers every December, allowing them to brush up their German and find out about employment regulations and opportunities. At the time of writing there was a possibility that the hostel would be sold and it was not known whether this would survive the sale; ring Chris Bullinger in Austria (0664 912 0469) for information.

In fact Kirchberg is such a popular tourist destination that it might be worth job-hunting there. For example an adventure holiday company Fankhauser Rafting has been seen advertising for rafting, cycling, and hiking guides as well as support staff (Dorfstrasse 17, A-6832 Kirchdorf; www.tirolrafting.com/index.html).

James Nibloe worked as a chalet host for Thomson Ski and Snowboard in Zell-am-See in 2003/4. Aged 26, James was a trainee chef with Best Western Hotels and did an advanced Hospitality and Catering GNVQ. He then had a change of direction, went to university and gained a degree in English and Business Studies. Using the book *Work Your Way Around the World* as a starting point he contacted several ski companies and preferred Thomsons as they allow their cooks more flexibility with menus than some others.

James Nibloe explains the recruitment procedure and how Thomson gave him their only chalet in Zell-am-See to run on his own:
We had to attend an assessment day for which we had to take with us a cake we had made. During the morning we were given basic literacy and numeracy tests and a kind of theoretical 'Ready Steady Cook' test. At midday the interviewers conducted a cake tasting, and then summoned for interview the best cake makers. I was interviewed and five days later was told I had a job. Two days after than I was in Austria for the ten-day induction in Ellmau.

During the induction they were trying to work out who got on best with each other and who would work well together. Obviously I didn't get on with anyone because I was given a chalet for 12 to run on my own. However, I was told that this was a compliment.

I really enjoyed the season. I felt that the chalet was my home and that it was like welcoming guests to my own house. Most of the time guests got on well, but occasionally there were hitches: two burly macho men found that an Austrian twin bed is actually two beds in one frame and spent the whole week terrified of possible misunderstandings and prefacing their remarks to other guests with 'I'm not gay, but...'

In positively romantic contrast, there were two pairs of British sisters who shared the chalet with a bunch of New Zealand guys who demonstrated the haka (Maori ceremonial war dance accompanied by chanting) which must have impressed at least one of the girls who is going on holiday with one of the New Zealanders this year.

The highlights were being out in the mountains every day in a beautiful place, affordable mountain restaurants, and the companionship of the guests. I went out drinking with the guests and this level of commitment really impressed them, and also meant that after a hard night they would make their own breakfast while I lay in bed, although I had to put up with being ribbed endlessly for a couple of days afterwards.

James is planning another season in a ski resort working for a private chalet company in Les Arcs, France. After that he hopes to lease his own chalet and run it for himself.

SUMMER CAMPS

Village Camps (see entry in Directory) needs monitors and EFL teachers for its summer camp at Zell-am-See. Room and board, insurance and a weekly allowance of approximately £75 and £200 respectively are offered.

Two organisations that run summer language camps are the similarly named English for Children (Salzachstrasse 15/38, 1220 Vienna; 01-958 1972; www.englishforchildre n.cc) and English for Kids (A. Baumgartnerstr. 44/A 7042, 1230 Vienna; 01-667 45 79; www.e4kids.co.at) both of which are looking for young monitors and English teachers with experience of working with children and preferably some TEFL background.

TOUR OPERATORS

The best starting place for a list of UK-based carriers and tour operators featuring Austria is the website of the Association of National Tourist Offices in the United Kingdom: www.tourist-offices.org.uk/Austria/uktourops.html. If you patiently follow the links, many of the websites of the 150 tour operators listed give details of their recruitment needs.

For example Equity Travel (01273 886901; www.equity.co.uk/employment) recruit chefs, housekeeping and waiting staff, handymen, night porters, plongeurs and bar staff (EU nationality essential) for its sizeable operation in the Austrian Alps. Lotus Supertravel (Sandpiper House, 39 Queen Elizabeth St, London SE1 2BT; 020-7962 1369) takes on winter staff for Austria, primarily chalet hosts with excellent cooking skills, reps fluent in German, qualified masseurs, nannies and handymen. All applicants must hold an EU passport and be over 21. *PGL Ski Europe* hires a small number of ski staff for winter as well as sports instructors for their summer programme and *Tall Stories* require resort staff in Austria, among other countries. Another possibility for both seasons is *First Choice/Skibound* (London Road, Crawley, West Sussex RH10 2GX; 01293 588585; overseas.recruitment@firstchoice.co.uk) which hires hundreds of people to work in hotels and resorts in Austria; no qualifications are required because staff are given in-house training, but you must be available to stay for the whole season from May to September.

UK companies often arrange sightseeing and cultural tours, many with a musical or opera bias, such as Martin Randall Travel (10 Barley Mow Passage, London W4 4GF; info@martinrandall.co.uk). Those who look after music or opera groups are always given free tickets to concerts and may get the chance to meet international performers.

If working for a budget operator, make sure that your accommodation has heating in the winter and access to bath or shower. 'Getting away from it all' is popular in the Alps, which can sometimes mean getting away from what are normally considered basic necessities.

If working on a campsite or for activity holiday operators where your job will involve being out of doors for long periods, make sure you are vaccinated against Tick Encephalitis. Eighty-four percent of the Austrian population has been vaccinated and newcomers can receive the protection at local clinics on arrival. Subsequent doses should be administered after 14-90 days and again after 10 months.

CONFERENCES

For details and addresses of conference centres, check the website of the Austrian Convention Bureau (www.acb.at) which has links to them all or contact the ACB at Faulmanngasse 4, 1040 Vienna (1-581 1611). The major hotels that offer conference facilities are worth contacting to ask if their organising clients need staff. Most belong to Round Table Konferenzhotels (1-505-5349; konferenzhotels@rtk.at). The major conference centres in Austria are the Austria Centre Vienna (1-26069 2302) which is one of 22 members of ACB in Vienna, Grazer Congress (316-80-490), Congress Innsbruck (512-59-36120) and Salzburg Congress (662-889-870).

GROUND HANDLERS

Fluent speakers of German or tourism professionals may find it worthwhile approaching one of the following ground handlers: Dr. Degener Reisen, Intropa, Lüftner, Reisebüro Mondial (www.mondial.at), Ökista Reisen and Raffeisen Reisebüro.

CASUAL WORK

Despite the competition for work mentioned above, opportunities can be found especially at the height of both winter and summer seasons by those who persevere. Once you are in a resort like St Anton or Brand which accommodates and services thousands of holidaymakers from December to April, it should be possible to find an opening. Try putting an ad in the *Tiroler Tageszeitung* newspaper. Camilla Lambert found a live-in job this way with a family whose father coached the Austrian ski team. Several years before this, she had pre-arranged a job in a hotel in Brand, and concluded that there are plenty of on-the-spot opportunities:

> *It is easy to find out about jobs in hotels, shops, as an au pair, in specialist areas like the 'skiverleih' (ski hire) as a technician or just working on the drag-lifts. If you arrive without a job, it would probably be best to target one or two villages where there are a lot of guesthouses and hotels. Ask in the Tourist Information first, but I found the bus driver who whizzed up and down the valley every day a good source of info, as were most of the bar staff in the various cafés and the 'British' pub. I was offered several positions for the coming winter.*

There is a department in the Kitzbühel employment office whose sole function is to cater for foreigners seeking work. Arbeitsamt Kitzbühel (Wagnerstrasse 17, 6370 Kitzbühel; 05356-62422) updates its comprehensive list of local vacancies daily. A personal visit to this office is much more likely to achieve a result than a written or telephone enquiry.

Offices that specialise in seasonal work are called BerufsInfoZentren or BIZ. There are 59 in the country including six in Vienna, eight in the Tyrol and so on (addresses on the AMS website). For example many hotel and catering vacancies in the South Tyrol are registered with the Euro BIZ Jobcentre at Schöpfstrasse 5, 6020 Innsbruck (eurobiz.inn sbruck@702.ams.or.at). The Ufficio di Lavoro is responsible for job information in the Italian-speaking region of South Tyrol.

Pubs, clubs and discos should not be overlooked since many of them regularly hire foreigners. Karin Huber, a native of Zell-am-See, reckons there are plenty of openings for foreigners, especially in the winter, since she found herself the only Austrian working in a club. The best time to arrive is late November.

Asking door to door is the most effective way though it is by no means guaranteed to succeed as Carolyn Edwards discovered in January:

> *We arrived in Söll on a Sunday and things looked very quiet. They were. It took me only two days to try everywhere in Söll with no luck. So I started on day trips to other resorts with no luck. The reps told me that the tour companies had brought very few people because of the bad snow conditions that year.*

Ordinary wages in hotels and restaurants are lower than those in Switzerland, but then the cost of living is much lower (and also lower than in the UK). So many foreigners work on a casual basis that exploitation is rife in this sector and many stories circulate of people being treated shabbily, for example being fired after an injury.

One of the more unusual casual jobs in Austria was described on a post card from Fionna Rutledge:
I spent two months working for a classical music concert company (Strauss) in Vienna. There are loads of these in Vienna and most of them employ students without working permits. I was paid on commission and spent the day dressed up in Mozart costume in the main Vienna tourist spots. Hard work, but a great opportunity to meet people. You have to sell the concert to complete strangers. And I earned about £1,300 in six weeks. All you need to do is approach the 'Mozarts' on the street and ask them to introduce you to their boss.

REGULATIONS

The Austrian Embassy in Britain (18 Belgrave Mews West, London SW1X 8HU) publishes *Living and Working in Austria* on its website (www.austria.org.uk) which gives information about immigration and social security procedures.

As noted above, the accession of ten additional countries to the EU in 2004, including several that share borders with Austria, will put more pressure on the job market. The arrival in recent years of many refugees and others from Eastern Europe had already increased competition in the job hunt in Austria.

People working officially for an Austrian employer can expect to have between 15% and 30% of their gross wage deducted for contributions to the compulsory Health and Social Security Scheme.

DIRECTORY REFERENCES

For companies which operate in Austria, see the following entries in the Directory section: Grapevine International, Airtours/MyTravel, Alpine Tracks, Astons Holidays, Canvas, Esprit, Eurocamp, FirstChoice/Skibound, Freewheel Holidays, Headwater, Inghams, Keycamp, Lotus Supertravel, Mark Warner, NBV Leisure, Neilson, Shearings, Ski Miquel, Skiworld, Specialist Holidays Group, Tall Stories, Total Holidays, Travelsphere, Village Camps.

Belgium

Among the first of the numerous invading armies that have trampled over Belgium were the Romans, who left behind a massive problem that is still around today. When Rome withdrew from the region, many legionnaires stayed on and settled in the south of the country, eventually merging with the neighbouring French to form the nucleus of the French-speaking Walloons. Meanwhile the north was swept by invading Germanic tribes who spoke a language which eventually became Flemish, a dialect of Dutch. The country is still divided linguistically: French is spoken in Wallonia (south) while Flemish is spoken in Flanders (north) which is now much more prosperous and bitterly resented by the Walloons who represent just over 40% of the population. In 1971 Brussels was declared bilingual, although a large majority in the city are French-speaking.

PROSPECTS FOR WORK

UK coach companies looking to expand their weekend breaks programmes are understandably keen on Belgium. The excellent rates being offered by the ferry companies (thanks to competition from Eurotunnel) together with relatively inexpensive hotels and superb food makes Belgium a highly attractive destination for short breaks. Small coach companies have plenty of work, particularly during September (for the Belgian Beer Festival at Wieze) and October to May for weekend breaks. Ostend has a mini-season in February/March during its annual Carnival.

Look for opportunities as a seasonal guide with one of the coach tour companies which run tours of scenic and historic Belgium. Venture Abroad (Rayburn House, Parcel Terrace, Derby DE1 1LY; www.ventureabroad.co.uk) employs reps, including students with a background in scouting or guiding, for its programme in Belgium.

A list of tour operators and coach companies with a Belgium programme can be found on the website www.tourist-offices.org.uk/Belgium/brussels-ardennes/uktourops.html. Because of its ease of access, Belgium attracts a large number of British school groups and musical tours. Many American universities have student tour programmes which are handled out of Brussels and Luxembourg. The number of Belgian coach companies which run tours of scenic and historic Belgium far exceeds what one might expect for such a small country (population ten million). The majority are based in Flanders and may have vacancies for English-speaking personnel prepared to work hard. Coach drivers, tour guides and shuttle staff are taken on in March/April for the season which lasts until September. Openings may also be available on barges.

Although such Belgian seaside resorts as Knokke-Heist, Blankenberge and De Panne, and other holidays centres like Bouillon in the Ardennes are hardly household names, there is a sizeable tourist industry in Belgium where seasonal work is available. The more mainstream tourist centre of Bruges is very busy in the summer, with holidaymakers and with incentive tours arriving via the Eurostar service to Lille in northern France. According to Brett Archer, who worked several seasons at the Bauhaus International Youth Hostel at Langestraat 135 in Bruges, there are never enough people around to work in restaurants and bars during the summer.

FINDING A JOB

The best way of finding short-term work, apart from contacting possible employers directly, is to visit a branch of the Belgian employment service in any town. A special division called T-Interim (in the Flemish part) or Trace (in French-speaking Belgium) specialises in placing people in temporary jobs. Most jobs obtained through T-Interim or Trace offices will be unskilled though they may also be able to advise on more professional posts for candidates you can speak French or Flemish. As the headquarters of the European Union, Brussels hosts many international conferences for which bilingual reception and other staff are needed.

People who live in the south-east of England can make use of EURES Crossborder HNFK based at South Kent College (Maison Dieu Road, Dover CT16 1DH; 01304 244356) which assists people looking for jobs in Belgium, especially in West-Vlaanderen and Hainaut (western Belgium). Two bilingual Euro-Advisers can put job-seekers in touch with network partners on the continent and can also give advice and information about living and working conditions.

Private employment agencies in Belgium are licensed either to make temporary or permanent placements but not both. One of the most important is Randstad (www.randstad.be) which operates an English-speaking personnel department at its office in central Brussels (Hoofdkantoor, Muntplein, Prinsenstraat 8-10; 02-209 12 11) and has dozens of branches throughout the country. Randstad is particularly strong on placing catering personnel. For many years the agency has organised specialised training for waiters and 'hygiene in the kitchen' courses for personnel in the catering and food industries. In co-operation with a number of companies in the industry, Randstad has written a manual for temporary personnel in this sector.

Another specialist recruitment agency for candidates looking for hotel and catering jobs in Belgium belongs to the Adecco Group: Hospitality Solutions is at rue du Fossé-aux-Loups 33, B-1000 Brussels (www.horeca-jobs.com).

Americans can apply through Interexchange in New York (161 Sixth Avenue, New York, NY 10013; 212-924-0446) to be placed in a summer job, or internship in Belgium. Applicants over 18 with a working knowledge of French (or Dutch) can be placed in companies or organisations for between one and three months. The programme fee is $700 and the application deadline is late April; full details on the website (www.interexchange.org). Some companies advertise in the *Herald Tribune* and receive thousands of applications. It might be better to approach companies directly. One way to make contact with Belgian coach companies is to follow Sam's example. Sam had grown up speaking basic Flemish (because his father had worked for an American company in Antwerp) and decided that he wanted to work in tourism. One Saturday he went to London and walked down the row of coaches parked in Park Lane. Several had Flemish names and, when he approached the drivers, was willingly given names and telephone numbers of the company offices. Armed with these, he went off to stay with friends in Antwerp and landed a job as a shuttle host from the second company he contacted. Belgians love a joke, and Sam came in for some teasing over his accent, but he didn't mind, especially when he found out what generous tippers Belgians can be.

If military history is your forte, there are many UK-based companies like Holts' Battlefield Tours (www.battletours.co.uk) which offer tours to the battlefields of the First World War, Mons, Waterloo, etc. Just as the local French-speaking Walloons did little to help the Duke of Wellington to victory at Waterloo, so today most of the souvenirs sold at the site of the battlefield are devoted to the famous loser.

LUXEMBOURG

If Belgium is sometimes neglected, Luxembourg is completely by-passed. Yet it is an independent country with an unemployment rate of less than 2%, the lowest in the EU, and a number of useful facilities for foreigners. The national employment service (Administration de l'Emploi or ADEM) at 10 rue Bender, L-1229 Luxembourg (352-478 53 00; www.etat.lu/ADEM/adem.htm) operates a *Service Vacances* for students looking for summer jobs in hotels, restaurants, campsites, etc. To find out about possibilities, you must visit this office in person, although EU nationals looking for long-term jobs may receive some assistance from EURES counsellors. Paul Newcombe found the service very helpful and was delighted to be given details of a job vacancy at an American bar in the capital. While cycling through the country, Mary Hall was struck by the number of foreign young people working on campsites and in restaurants in Luxembourg City.

The main recruitment search engines may be helpful, for example there is a Luxembourg-specific monster site at http://english.monster.lu. A frequent advertiser is the hotel and restaurant group Groupe Goeres (111 ave du X Septembre, L-2551 Luxembourg; +351 44 23 32 2215).

The Centre Information Jeunes (CIJ), 26 Place de la Gare/Galerie Kons, 1616 Luxembourg (26 29 32 00; www.cij.lu) runs a holiday job service between January and August for students from the EU.

With a population of less than 400,000, job opportunities are understandably limited, but they do exist in the tourist industry. Even the Embassy in London at 27 Wilton Crescent, London SW1X 8SD (020-7235 6961) maintains that 'seasonal jobs are often to be found in the hotels of the Grand Duchy of Luxembourg' and will send a list of the 250+ hotels in exchange for an A4 envelope with a 50p stamp. Wages are fairly good in this sector, often above £500 per month after room and board.

Work exists with the large Luxembourg-based coach companies, working as a tour guide for groups of Americans and Australasians, and as shuttle staff for Benelux nationals going to Spain. Ask the Luxembourg Tourist Office (same address in London as the Embassy) for an up-to-date list of companies.

Cyprus

The Cypriot economy, like the Greek economy, relies heavily on tourism: in 2003, 2.3 million tourists visited Greek Cyprus plus a further half million entered Turkish Cyprus for holidays. However this represents a decline of nearly 5% over the previous year, primarily because of the Iraq war and continuing instability in the Middle East (Syria is only 100km to the east).

For many years one of the great stumbling blocks for foreign people who wanted to work in the tourist industry of Cyprus was the difficulty of obtaining work permits. However Cyprus has negotiated an invitation to join the European Union from May 2004 and this should in time make it much easier. Without reunification with the Turkish-controlled north, only the internationally recognised Greek Cypriot part of the island will gain membership.

Cyprus is a divided island with the northern third inhabited by Turkish-Cypriots and the southern two-thirds by Greek Cypriots. The Green Line dividing the two runs through the capital Nicosia and has been patrolled by United Nations Troop since the Turks invaded in 1974. With the acceptance of Greek Cyprus into the EU combined with Turkey's hope of doing likewise, 2003 saw some easing of the restrictions and in fact hundreds of thousands of Cypriots crossed between the Turkish Republic of Northern Cyprus (Kibris) and the Greek part.

Job opportunities exist in both the Greek and the Turkish parts, though mass tourism is much more established in the Greek-dominated south. For the present, Turkish Cyprus must be entered via a Turkish airport as there are no direct flights from the UK, which is a serious impediment to expanding the tourist industry. (Turkish Cyprus is considered separately at the end of this section.)

PROSPECTS FOR WORK

Most big tour operators consider placement in Cyprus as a perk to be offered to staff who have worked well for the company elsewhere, especially if they have worked in Greece and picked up some of the language. Cyprus has the advantage of offering work during the winter as well as the summer, though it has special short seasonal attractions when it is especially busy, such as for the spring flowers.

For a list of tour operators to Cyprus, see the listing on www.tourist-offices.org.uk/Cyprus/uktouops.html and also on www.visitcyprus.org.cy. Specialists include Cyplon Holidays (561-563 Green Lanes, London N8 0RL; www.cyplon.com), Cyprus Elite (www.travelmania.ltd.uk) and Amathus Holidays (2 Leather Lane, London EC1N 7RA; 020-7611 0900). Cyprus features in most Winter Sun brochures such as that of Mastersun (63-67 Kingston Road, New Malden, Surrey KT3 3PB; 020 8942 9442) whose website describes its job vacancies (www.mastersun.co.uk/jobs.asp).

Self-catering is a major part of most tour operators' work, so villa reps are hired by some of the main companies like Golden Sun Holidays (Masons House, 1-3 Valley Drive, Kingsbury, London NW9 9NG; 020-8206 4731; www.goldensun.co.uk, which features a Recruitment icon), Manos Holidays (01273 427 777) and Sunvil Holidays Cyprus (see Directory entry). The British and Germans in particular like to see well-kept gardens surrounding their rented villas, so there is work for gardeners.

SPECIAL INTEREST TOURS

Walking holidays in the beautiful Troodos mountains are organised by a number of companies including Naturetrek who occasionally hire tour leaders and guides and invite suitable candidates to submit their CVs to the Personnel Department, Naturetrek

& Wildlife Worldwide, Cheriton Mill, Cheriton, Alresford, Hants. SO24 0NG (01962 733051; www.naturetrek.co.uk).

The Mediterranean waters that surround the island of Cyprus are perfectly suited to cruising, and both the international liners and local companies berth in the harbour at Limassol, etc. The three main indigenous cruise companies are Louis, Salamis and Paradise (details on www.cruisecyprus.com) which hire mostly Cypriot crew though they may occasionally hire entertainers through foreign or local agents. The only cruise line recruitment agent in Cyprus is Columbia Ship Management in Limassol whose website (www.columbia.com.cy/career.htm) carries information about shore-based jobs and jobs at sea.

The long-established diving holiday operator Cydive invites anyone interested in job or training opportunities in diving to contact them at the Cydive Diving Centre, 1 Poseidonos Avenue, Myrra Complex, 8042 Paphos (cydive@spidernet.com.cy). They offer advanced instruction to divers who want to qualify as instructors and seek employment locally.

CASUAL WORK

As in Greece, women are at a great advantage when looking for work in cafés, bars and restaurants, but they should exercise caution according to Karen Holman:

> *In my two years there I heard stories about Cypriot employers expecting more of their barmaids than just bar work. I worked in two pubs and I would say that both bosses employed me with an ulterior motive. I was lucky – both of them were shy. By the time they realised I wasn't going to be their girlfriend, they had found me to be a good worker and were used to me being around. Many employers will sack the girls, or threaten to report them for stealing. If you're legal, your work permit is valid for that job only, so if you leave the job, you have to leave the country.*

Just such a serious case of exploitation and harassment was reported in the British press. A 23 year old trainee lawyer who had met her employer on a previous holiday found herself working 15 hours a day without a day off in temperatures of over 100°. The final straw came when the manager made advances which she declined which prompted her employer to hit her. She instantly quit and was paid a pittance for 15 days work. She had no recourse because she had no work permit.

Rhona Stannage was much luckier: her boss (whom she met in a novel way) was gay. In the supermarket in Protaras she and her husband Stuart introduced themselves to a man whose trolley was so full of bottles, they reckoned he must run a restaurant. He practically offered Rhona a job on the spot as waitress and cleaner, and offered Stuart a cooking job two days later.

Tom Parker arrived in Limassol in April and started the search along the seafront, with little success:

> *The same evening we headed for the tourist area and were soon told that we would stand a better chance if we bought a drink for the manager before asking about jobs. The only concrete result was that we got very drunk. No job opportunities (they told us we were too early). The next day we concentrated on the small cafés in the back streets of the old town. Here my two companions (both girls) were offered jobs in separate cafés. The kitchen job paid £13 a day and the waiting job £16, both plus tips. They both also worked in a bar in the evening, sitting round talking to the mainly local customers and being bought drinks for which the customer was charged*

"They introduced themselves to a man in a supermarket whose trolley was so full of bottles they reckoned he must run a restaurant"

£6.50 whether it was water or vodka and they earned a commission of £1 per drink, in addition to the evening fee of £13.

REGULATIONS

The free movement of labour to Cyprus is unlikely to take place immediately after May 2004 when Cyprus joins the EU. Restrictions are likely to operate for at least several years to a maximum of seven. Until that happens, foreigners must obtain an employment permit, although the authorities are likely to become more lenient towards applications from other EU countries. The prospective employer must apply on behalf of the foreign employee to the Migration Officer at the Ministry of the Interior in Nicosia (D. Severis Avenue, 1457 Nicosia; 02-804410/fax 676944).

Employers who want to hire English-speaking staff often maintain that work permits are not needed for temporary work and many foreigners accept work on this basis. However it should be stressed that in the recent past strict penalties have been imposed: a fine of up to £500 and a five or ten-year ban from the country.

TURKISH CYPRUS

Although the scope for employment is much smaller in the TRNC or Kibris than in Greek Cyprus, many people do find work in the country's tourist industry, mainly in bars, restaurants and hotels. Most of the tour operations are managed by local companies, though some British tour operators do employ some staff in the UK, such as *Tapestry Holidays* (www.tapestryholidays.com/contact/jobsoverseas) who start interviewing in December for the following season. Other jobs may be found in holiday villages and on cruise boats.

There is a sizeable English-speaking community with British churches and a British Residents Society (behind the Post Office). A number of restaurants and bars are owned by expats, many of whom employ at least one foreigner to communicate with the tourists. It may be worth making contact with one or other association located in the main town of Kyrenia (Girne in Turkish) e.g. the North Cyprus Hoteliers Association (392-815 8758; www.northcyprus.net), the Tourism Workers' Association (392-228 7831) or the Cyprus Turkish Restaurants' Association (392-815 5727). The Cyprus Turkish Tourism & Travel Agents' Association is in Nicosia (392-228 2443) as is the Tourist Guide Association (392-231 4647). Kibris Travel Service (392-815 7555/815 7730), the ground handling agent for ten UK tour operators, might also be of use.

Northern Cyprus is not a cheap package holiday destination and tends to attract a more discerning clientele, who are interested in visiting the sites as well as enjoying the marvellous climate. It is a popular destination for Germans, so an ability to speak some German would improve your marketability. After making friends with several residents, Theresa Thomas (a trained teacher) accepted a job with a local tour operator. Typically, the interview took place in a café:

My job was to take out daily coach tours (the clients were mostly professionals from the UK) six days a week, explain the history of the island and communicate with bus drivers, restaurateurs, etc. (in Turkish). The good features were that I was able to see so much of this beautiful island and mix with interesting people. The bad features were poor pay for long working hours sometimes in extreme heat, having no workers' rights and always having to deal with sexual harassment.

With a population of just 170,000, job vacancies become known as soon as they exist. Most opportunities lie in the catering trade and are open to men and women. The wages are poor by British standards, but most include food and accommodation, and can usually be supplemented with tips. The cost of living is low and life is relaxed, like Greece was a generation ago.

> **Eric Mackness, who spent more than two years working in a resort near the capital Kyrenia, reiterates his enthusiasm for Northern Cyprus as a destination for job-seekers:**
> *I can't praise Northern Cyprus enough, for its wonderful scenery, excellent climate and friendly people. There are mountains, fairytale castles, Roman ruins, all virtually tourist-free. I'm sorry if I sound like a holiday brochure but it's all true and at the moment 99% unspoilt.*
> *I think that Turkish Cyprus is quite a unique location work-wise. I don't want to make light of my undoubted charm and my ability to chop a tomato into four pieces, but I think anyone with a little common sense can always find a job here. I hear of job vacancies literally every day. Of course it is early in the year and as the season progresses the vacancies won't be quite so numerous. But if you work*

> *hard, prove yourself to be honest and reliable, there are always vacancies here in the North. Quite a few new restaurants have opened since I was last here, all looking for chefs and bar and waiting staff.*

Eric arranged his restaurant job before he left Coventry by writing directly after seeing it mentioned briefly on a BBC travel programme.

RED TAPE

To date, the authorities have seemed relatively unconcerned about the red tape, whatever your nationality, though with political changes afoot, the authorities may become a little more efficient in checking paperwork. It is possible to obtain a work permit after you have been offered a job, which involves a trip to the Hospital in Nicosia for medical tests costing £100+. Because of the expense, some seasonal workers prefer to renew their tourist status every three months by leaving the country; this entails a two-hour catamaran trip to mainland Turkey. Long-stay travellers may be able to persuade an employer to obtain a work permit on their behalf.

DIRECTORY REFERENCES

The following companies which employ staff in Cyprus are listed in the Directory: Openwide International, Cosmos, MyTravel, Olympic Holidays, Style Holidays, Sunvil, Tapestry.

France

Ideally placed between the two great travelling nations of Germany and Britain, France has always been one of the most popular countries for tourists in the world, welcoming over 60 million a year. However at the end of 2003 it was announced that Spain had overtaken France as the most popular destination for British holidaymakers. In fact 2003 was a bad year all round for the French industry with a severe decrease in numbers coming from the US (due to the rift over the Iraq War) and further problems caused by forest fires in the Riviera and oil contamination of beaches in the southwest.

All the same, 11.7 million Britons visited France in 2003, along with millions from the rest of Europe and elsewhere. The four main areas to which tourists head are of course Paris (including Disneyland), the Côte d'Azur, the Alps and the vineyards and cultural highlights of the interior. The French kings built mediaeval visitor attractions which today bring visitors to see the chateaux and palaces of the Loire Valley and environs of Paris.

Britain helped develop the Riviera in the last century, when the Côte d'Azur was a favourite winter destination for the British leisured class. When the lemon crop of Menton failed one year, the British set up a fund to pay for unemployed farm workers to construct the Promenade des Anglais in Nice. Today the Riviera is packed in summer, mostly with people staying in the campsites behind the hills. The quieter times of spring and autumn are when the high-spending conference delegates take over the casinos and shops.

PROSPECTS FOR WORK

In an industry which employs 1.5 million people directly and indirectly, and accounts for more than 11% of the country's GNP, employment prospects are good in all the areas mentioned above. With impeccable French and an immaculate presentation, there is work at the elite end of the market in conference, cruise and incentive travel. Opportunities are less exclusive with ordinary tour operators. A great many UK companies which run activity holiday centres, campsite or ski tour operations, etc. in France employ Britons on British contracts. This is primarily to avoid having to comply with French employment legislation which is the most generous to workers in Europe. Several years ago, the French government cut the length of the working week from 39 to 35 for anyone working in a firm with more than 20 employees. Also the minimum wage is rigorously enforced: the basic *SMIC (salaire minimum interprofessionel de croissance)* is at present €6.83 per hour gross or €1,154.27 per month. Naturally this degree of employment regulation frightened the large number of UK tour operators who do not offer their campsite couriers, chalet girls, etc. SMIC-level wages nor statutory perks. Obviously the wage of a typical British seasonal worker, i.e. £50 (in addition to free travel, board and lodging, insurance, etc.) for working a 50-hour week does not come close to *le SMIC*. It has now been decided that because of the short-term nature of the contracts, they are exempt. Their workers are paid in sterling into British bank accounts. This has not prevented a lot of resentment from French employers trying to compete in the same resorts (summer and winter) where Britons are seen to be taking jobs away from locals.

Hotels throughout France absorb many foreign workers, both at the skilled and unskilled level. Children's activity centres, canal holidays, escorted cycling tours and every imaginable themed holiday operate in France, all of which are potential employers of your skills.

Coach holidays leave from most parts of the UK throughout the season. The best way to find the jobs is to look in the local UK press for companies advertising 'Bargain Breaks' or 'Fun Weekends in Paris.' If the company wants shuttle staff, often for overnight trips to the Riviera or on to Barcelona, they don't usually ask for languages; the ability to work for 36 hours with only cat-naps on the front seat of the coach is more important. On the other hand coach tour guides accompanying trips to Paris which operate year-round should be able to speak French fluently (though many don't). The better your French, the better the jobs open to you. Freelance reps in Paris can do very well on commissions, especially on a 'Paris by Night' tour; for example competition among cabarets is so fierce that they have been known to pay large commissions per head.

Campsites are the big success story of French tourism. (See the introductory section *Campsite Reps* for further information.) This end of the market is still expanding, and large numbers of reps, children's reps, maintenance officers and activity instructors are needed each season. Theoretically the companies want you to speak French but many say that they were hired without being tested.

Paris is the most popular destination for short breaks from the UK. Eurostar has hundreds of job opportunities though its catering operations have recently gone to an Italian company. As the service has expanded with trains connecting with the TGV network (the high speed French trains that operate from Paris to Dijon, Marseille, Montpelier, Bordeaux, Brest, etc.), more jobs have come on-stream. Many continental tours start from Paris, as this is one of the major European gateway airports. For example, the many tours that fly in to Charles de Gaulle airport from Quebec need tour managers who speak French (or, better, Québecois).

Outside Paris there is scope for people with a background in architecture or history of art. Many special interest tour operators combine the chateaux of the Loire with vineyard tours, cycling, walking or even hot air balloons.

Anyone who is looking to invest in a tourism project will find plenty of opportunity in France, particularly in the field of upmarket B&Bs *(Chateaux Acceuil)*. Hosts that can offer 'English spoken here' have an added advantage. One recommended area for purchasing affordable alpine chalets is in the Savoie, where farmers who once practised transhumance (moving herds to high pastures in the summer) owned several large huts at different altitudes. British families who have bought these abandoned buildings are normally welcomed into the valleys. Once these properties have been converted they can be rented out as *gites* or run as B&Bs. For example see entry for *Savoy Chalet Holidays*.

FINDING A JOB

EURES, the European Employment service which can be accessed through Jobcentres, always knows of vacancies for EU nationals in France, most of them in the tourist industry. It has a regional branch in south-eastern England (EURES Crossborder HNFK, South Kent College, Maison Dieu Road, Dover CT16 1DH; 01304 244356) which assists people looking for jobs in the northern French region of Nord-Pas-de-Calais (as well as West Flanders in Belgium). Two bilingual Euro-Advisers can put job-seekers in touch with network partners on the continent and can also give advice and information about living and working conditions, though it does not hold current vacancy specifications.

THE FRENCH EMPLOYMENT SERVICE

The *Agence National pour l'Emploi* or ANPE is the national employment service of France, with dozens of offices in Paris and 600 others throughout the country. The headquarters are at 4 rue Galilée, 93198 Noisy-le-Grand (1-49 31 74 00/49 31 77 11) and their website lists all the branches by region or postcode (www.anpe.fr/contacts), providing addresses, telephone and fax numbers. For example the ANPE in Narbonne (ANPE, BP 802, 29 rue Mazzini, 11108 Narbonne Cedex) has seasonal hotel vacancies from May to September. Although EU nationals are supposed to have equal access to the employment facilities in other member states, this is not always the case in France unless the job-seeker speaks good French and has a stable local address. If possible foreign job-seekers should work with a EURES Adviser.

Seasonal offices are set up in key regions to deal with seasonal demands like the *Antennes Saisonnières* set up in ski resorts. These may be more likely to assist working travellers than the permanent offices which deal primarily in full-time jobs for French/EU citizens. The addresses of ANPE offices recommended as offering seasonal work are listed in the relevant sections later in this chapter.

Anyone with access to a private telephone should be aware of the widely used French Telecom subscriber service *Minitel* similar to Ceefax. With it, ordinary people can access a variety of databases including one for job vacancies or even to advertise their own availability for work. Dustie Hickey used the system to make contact with hostels in Avignon where she wanted to fix up work for the festival (prior to 2003, the year the Festival was cancelled due to a strike by performers).

CIJ

There are 32 *Centres d'Information Jeunesse* or CIJ in France which may be of use to the job-seeker. The main Paris branch is CIDJ *(Centre d'Information et de Documentation Jeunesse,* 101 Quai Branly, 75740 Paris Cedex 15; 1-44 49 12 00; www.cidj.asso.fr) whose foyer notice board is a useful starting place for the job-hunter in Paris. Employers notify centres of their temporary vacancies; some offices just display the details on notice boards, while others operate a more formal system in co-operation with the local ANPE.

You will find *Centres d'Information Jeunesse* in the following towns: Amiens, Bastia (Corsica), Besancon, Bordeaux, Caen, Cergy Pontoise, Claremont-Ferrand, Dijon, Evry, Grenoble, Lille, Limoges, Lyon, Marseille, Melun, Montpellier, Nancy, Nantes, Nice, Orleans, Poitiers, Reims, Rennes, Rouen, Strasbourg, Toulouse and Versailles. The CIJ in Marseille at 96 rue La Canebière (4-91 24 33 50) mainly holds details of jobs at holiday centres, especially as *animateurs*. Needless to say it is necessary to visit the Centre in person in order to find out about these.

HOTELS AND RESTAURANTS

People with enough time to make long term plans can write directly to the hotels in the region which interests them, listed in any tourist hotel guide. Remember that the vast majority of restaurants are staffed by waiters rather than waitresses.

Hotels often employ non-French staff provided they speak the language. It is regarded as *très chic* to have foreign reception staff. Since the French (like the British) are not noted linguists, there is less competition for such jobs than there would be in Holland or Germany. If you want to make a career in the hotel industry, a stint in a French hotel is obligatory. Superb country hotels are listed in the Relais et Chateau brochure, many of which attract incentive groups from Britain and the US. People with professional training in hotels and catering may well find suitable adverts to which they can reply in the weekly publication *L'Hôtellerie* (5 rue Antoine Bourdelle, 75737 Paris cedex 15). Newspapers in holiday towns (e.g. *Nice Matin*) also carry adverts. The major French hotel chains are Hotel Mercure in northwest France with 500 hotels and Novotel and Sofitel, all part of the Accor group, whose recruitment needs are posted online at http: //jobs.accor.com/frm_ihomepage.asp.

Horizon HPL (Signet House, 49/51 Farringdon Road, London EC1M 3JP; 020-7404 9192/fax 020-7404 9194; horizonhpl.london@btinternet.com) is an Anglo-French training organisation which offers packages lasting between three and 12 months combining language tuition and live-in hotel work placements (among other kinds) all over France. The wages are on a trainee scale, from £50 per week plus accommodation, while the package fee is £240. Candidates can choose to prepare for Sorbonne University language exams. Horizon's office in France is at 22-26 rue du Sergent Bauchat, 75012 Paris (1-40 01 07 07; horizon1@club-internet.fr) while the Dublin office is at 3 Lower Abbey St, Dublin 1 (1-8745 002; horizonhpl@eircom.net).

Sodistour Touristra, 126 rue La Fayette (BP 112), 75463 Paris cedex 10; 1-44 83 43 16; recrutement@touristra.com) which is a tour operator which runs 15 holiday villages along the Mediterranean and Brittany coasts and in the Alps. Vacancies exist for *animateurs* (for children and adults) plus for bar, kitchen and waiting staff.

BARGES

Holiday barges that ply the rivers and canals of France hire cooks, hostesses, deckhands and captains. It is better to apply to the companies in the new year; addresses may be found in the travel advertisement sections of English Sunday papers. All will want to employ only people who feel comfortable functioning in French.

European Waterways employs staff for its 12 hotel barges. If you land a job before the season begins, you may be flown to Amsterdam to join the barge on which you will spend April to October as a steward/stewardess earning £500 a month (which can be substantially increased with tips). The UK address is European Waterways Ltd, 35 Wharf Road, Wraysbury, Staines, Middlesex TW19 5JQ; fax 01784 483072; www.GoBarging.com). Vacancies also exist throughout the year for chefs, housekeepers, deck hands, tour guides and barge pilots for the luxury barge fleet. All applicants must have an EU passport (or have the right to work in the UK), be at least 21 and possess a current driving licence. A knowledge of French is useful.

Continental Waterways (PO Box 31, Godalming, Surrey GU8 6JH; 01252 703577: cr ew@continentalwaterways.co.uk) take on seasonal crew including chefs, driver/guides, stewardesses and deckhands in five regions of France to work with a mainly American clientele. Long hours are rewarded with from £600 a month. Interviews of EU nationals are held in London in January. The French office is in Dijon: Continentale de Croisières SA, 1 Promenade du Rhin, B.P. 41748, 21017 Dijon (fax 03-80 41 67 73).

Another possibility is Canals of France, which operates luxury barges between Toulouse and Sete. For jobs ring their Carcassonne office 04-90 15 42 60 (www.canals offrance.com).

After being hired over the phone in Ireland by European Waterways, Pauline Power was flown to Amsterdam to meet her vessel and spent April to October as a hostess (even though she had previous seagoing experience as a deckhand) earning £100-120 a week plus tips of up to a further £100 a week.

CAMPSITES

A number of British-based travel companies offer holidaymakers a complete package providing pre-assembled tents and a campsite courier to look after any problems which arise. Since this kind of holiday appeals to families, people who can organise children's activities are especially in demand. In addition to the Europe-wide companies like *Eurocamp* and *Canvas*, the following companies listed in the Directory all take on site reps and other seasonal staff: *Carisma Holidays, Club Cantabrica, Fleur Holidays, French Life Holidays (see entry for Camping Life), Haven Europe, Keycamp Holidays, Ian Mearns Holidays, Matthews Holidays, Sandpiper Holidays, Select France* and *Venue Holidays*.

The best time to start looking for summer season jobs with UK operators is between November and January/February. In most cases candidates are expected to have at least A-level standard French, though some companies claim that a knowledge of French is merely 'preferred'. It is amazing how far a good dictionary can get you.

There are at least 7,000 campsites in France, some of them small family-run operations which need one or two assistants, others on an industrial scale. You can write directly to the individual campsite addresses listed in any guide to French campsites (e.g. the annually updated Michelin *Camping and Caravanning Guide @* £8.99), or you can simply show up (see *Casual Work* below).

ACTIVITY HOLIDAYS

Outdoor activity centres are another major employer of summer staff, both general domestic staff and sports instructors. Try the companies listed in the Directory which cater for children such as *Acorn Venture Ltd* and *PGL*, or the ones for adults like *Mark Warner, Headwater* and *Discover Ltd*. You might also be able to find work with a French firm like one of the numerous canoe hire centres in the Ardèche.

Keen cyclists could try to get a job with a cycling holiday company active in France such as *Belle France* or *Susi Madron's Cycling for Softies*. Mountain walking guides over the age of 24 are needed to work in the Pyrenees and Corsica by the French company Itinéraires (Avenue de Fontestorbes, Belesta 09300).

For work in a more unusual activity holiday, contact *France Montgolfières Balloon Flights* (see entry) or Bombard Balloon Adventures, Chateau de LaBorde, 21200 Beaune (3-80 26 63 30; www.bombardsociety.com/jobs) who hire hot-air balloon ground crew for their summer season May to October. The job requires excellent physical fitness and strength, a cheerful personality, clean-cut appearance and year-old clean driving licence.

Interesting and varied opportunities are offered by the specialist independent company French Encounters (63 Fordhouse Road, Bromsgrove, Worcestershire B60 2LU; www.fr

enchencounters.com). They hire tourism and other students with a knowledge of French for the period February to May. Staff work with groups of British children on field study holidays based at chateaux in rural Normandy, after undergoing a fortnight's intensive training in presentation skills, first aid and the French language.

> **Eighteen-year-old Juliette Radford summarised her experiences with French Encounters with enthusiasm:**
> *By the end of the season, you will not only have gained the patience of a saint (and a warped sense of humour) and lost all traces of self-consciousness and shame, but you will also have acquired an extensive repertoire of French folk songs. I'm more independent, more confident and can cope in crises. I found I could manage and supervise all sorts of different people and I've practised tact and patience. I've been given the opportunity to use my initiative in lots of ways. Thanks to the people I have been working with, I have had one of the best times of my life, despite how hard we have had to work.*

Those with fluent French who want to work in a theme park or resort centre can find links to the major holiday parks that belong to SNELAC (Syndicat Espaces de Loisirs, d'Attractions et Culturels) on www.snelac.com.

Well over 20,000 *centres de vacances* employ an army of *animateurs/animatrices* (counsellors and instructors) to look after the mostly French children who spend part of their school holidays there. People who look after children at French holiday centres need to acquire the *Brevet d'Aptitude aux fonctions d'animateur* (BAFA) certificate (www.sports.gouv.fr/formations/bafa.asp). The training consists of eight days in the classroom, 14 days spent on the job and six or eight days on a specialist activity. The cost of this course is roughly equivalent to one's monthly wage as a monitor. The following organisations are three of a number that arrange the BAFA training and can also refer trainees to prospective employers:

CPCV - Organisme Protestant de Formation, 47 rue de Clichy, 75311 Paris Cedex (1-42 80 06 99).

Association pour la Formation des Cadres de Loisirs des Jeunes (AFOCAL), 29/31 rue Michel Ange 75016 Paris (1- 40 71 46 46; www.afocal.asso.fr).

Union Française des Centres de Vacances Loisirs (UFCV), 10 quai des la Charente, 75019 Paris (1-44 72 14 14).

According to French law (aimed primarily at unregistered ski instructors), the teaching or supervision 'in any sport, whether as a principal, secondary, seasonal or occasional occupation' is prohibited without a recognised diploma. However those employed on British contracts are not subject to this regulation.

Christine Pennington describes the way she was hired by one major tour operator:

After studying the brochure to make sure I'd like living in 'rural, unspoilt France', I filled out the lengthy application form and sent it off from France where I was working in a ski resort. I was then contacted by telephone by the owner herself, inviting me for an interview in England. All was well until I thought we were subject to a crossed line. After three 'excuse mes,' it occurred to me that she had suddenly switched to French to test my knowledge of the language. In shock and with a low muffled voice, I told her (in French) what my ski resort was like and that yes I do enjoy cycling and walking. To this day I don't know if that is what she had asked me. I must have done something right, because I was eventually given the job of senior rep, though I was expecting to go as an ordinary rep.

At Headwater's informal training weekend in England, the new reps learn some bicycle

The reps have to know their Baguettes from their Boules

mechanics and practise reversing minibuses with canoe trailers around corners. One of the major parts of the job is doing the 'bag runs' which involves transferring clients' baggage (and in some cases, the clients themselves) from place to place. At the height of the season with 50 bicycles, 20 canoes, and lots of clients and their luggage to keep track of, bag-moving becomes a complicated business and requires keeping to a tight schedule. Many of Headwater's clients come year after year so the reps have to know their baguettes from their boules.

DISNEYLAND PARIS

'Cast members' (Disneyspeak for workers) are needed to staff the scores of hotels, restaurants, shops and attractions. The majority of jobs are in food and beverage, housekeeping and custodial departments, though one of the best jobs is as a character like Mickey Mouse. Contracts are from three to eight months between March and October. Further details are available from Service du Recruitement-Casting, Euro Disney SCA, BP 110, 77777 Marne-la-Vallée Cedex 4, France (1-64 74 61 47).

Keith Leishman from Dundee found the process of getting his job for the summer of 2003 initially quite frustrating:

I first sent a letter to the company around November. After another couple of letters and emails without reply, I was just about giving up hope. Finally around March I received notification of an interview in Edinburgh (my nearest venue). A good standard of French is required for most of the jobs at the resort with the exception of those in the parades or dressing up as characters, where the emphasis is on dancing ability. Most of the jobs are dealing with the public, however it might be possible to get away with only basic French in the more menial jobs.

Once you obtain the job you are pretty much left to your own devices until you show up on the first day of your contract. This was rather a shock to me after working for Eurocamp the year before who provided transport to France and some preparatory material. Disney do reimburse travel costs to the tune of €76 each way.

I was employed in the ticketing side of operations. Wearing a Prince Charming costume, my job was to supervise the entrance of guests to the Park and stamp their hands. This meant standing for the whole shift in what were often scorching conditions. This was very beneficial for my French as people would ask a whole range of weird and wonderful questions. Another advantage was the mixture of nationalities with whom you work: Poles, Canadians, a Colombian and a boy from Tanzania as well as Europeans.

Free time at Disney is good. The sheer number of young people in the same place means that there are always lots of parties and barbecues in the residences. And of course the Disney Village complex offers a wide range of bars and a night-club. On days off I usually went to Paris which is only 40 minutes away on the train. I stayed for two months which was about right since it can be quite hard to keep up the Disney smile when it's hot and you are tired. The job is demanding because you are creating an illusion.

For all jobs a professional look is required, and of course they are looking for the usual friendly, cheerful and outgoing personalities. The monthly gross wage is €1,138-€1,154 (approximately £785) based on a 35-hour week, from which substantial deductions will be made for social security and shared apartments in their comfortable purpose-built complex accessible by bus. Employees who arrive after the accommodation is allocated may have to live in student accommodation scattered around the suburbs. All summer employees are offered a chance to do a 15-month tourism diploma (*Hôte d'Acceuil Touristique*).

A secondary theme park is Parc Astérix, also within easy range of Paris, which operates its own training programme. There are also aqua parks in France which need lifeguards.

SKI RESORTS

France is the best of all countries in Europe for British and Irish people to find jobs in ski resorts, mainly because it is the number one country for British skiers, 200,000 of whom go there every year. Most of the resorts are high enough to create reliable snow conditions throughout the season. The main problem is the shortage of worker accommodation; unless you find a live-in job you will have to pay nearly holiday prices or find a friend willing to rent out his or her sofa. Since many top French resorts are purpose-built, a high proportion of the holiday accommodation is in self-catering flats or designed for chalet parties. This means that not only is there a shortage of rental accommodation, but there are fewer jobs as waiters, bar and chamber staff for those who arrive in the resorts to look for work.

If you are employed by a British tour operator, be aware that you will not be paid according to French employment law, something that has been causing major problems to the big operators like Mark Warner. The French authorities have estimated that 10,000 staff are employed to work for ski chalet companies and all of them are being paid much less than the SMIC, typically between £50 and £65 plus living expenses and lift pass. If trying to fix up a job from Britain, there are one or two agencies that arrange for young people with a very good knowledge of French to work in ski resorts. Check out Free Radicals (www.freeradicals.co.uk), Natives (www.natives.co.uk) and Jobs in the Alps (www.jobs-in-the-alps.co.uk) all of which match job-seekers with alpine vacancies. Qualified/experienced nannies are especially sought after. For example the agency Kids Etcetera (8 Arolaz 1, 73550 Méribel Les Allues, Savoie; tel/fax 4-79 00 71 39; shirls@kidsetc.co.uk) specialises in placing qualified or experienced nannies in the

Méribel Valley for the ski season.

An agency to contact for work in French resorts is UK Overseas Handling (UKOH, PO Box 2791, London W1A 5JU; 020-7629 3064; cv@ukoh.co.uk or candidatures@eurogroup-vacances.com) which recruits young people for Eurogroup, a French tourism and property management company that owns and operates hotels and restaurants in the French Alps, on the Atlantic and Mediterranean coasts and in Paris and Montpellier. For students, Eurogroup offers a work placement scheme either in resort or in the head office in Chambéry (BP 429, 73004 Chambéry Cedex; 4-79 65 07 79). Places are available all year round, and accommodation is always provided. Applicants should have a good level of French and be EU-passport holders.

As many as 30 British tour companies are present in Méribel alone, so there are plenty of jobs in French resorts with UK ski holiday operators. Resorts like Méribel are flooded with British workers and British skiers, many of them on school trips. Since the infrastructure work was done for the Olympics, British chalet operators have established a strong presence in Courchevel; Neilson and Simply Ski have their main French offices in the picturesque village of Le Praz, one of the five villages that comprise the resort of Courchevel. If you are not already familiar with the resorts, try to do some research beforehand which Susan Beney regretted failing to do:

We took pot luck with the resort and on reflection would have done a bit more homework on resorts we might have preferred. La Tania was very limited; La Plagne would have been one hundred percent better.

Most jobs with British companies pay low wages but allow workers to ski or snowboard between 10am and 4pm. Wages are typically just £65 a week plus bed, board and a ski pass, which is what French employers who are subject to French employment legislation are up in arms about. One of the excuses given for the low pay is that staff can supplement their wages with tips, something that made Susan Beney and her husband uncomfortable when they worked for Le Ski in 2002/3:

We did make good tips which became our spending money, so no tips, no treats. Being Aussies (with joint UK nationality), it goes against the grain to expect tips. And then you find yourself judging guests by how much they tip you – horrible way to be. We worked long hours six days a week, and were probably a bit too conscientious due to our age (we have just become grandparents). It's still a good way to experience a season in the Alps, but just be prepared to be overworked and underpaid. Listen to the young folk who have got the work down to a fine art and really know how to cut corners since they are there to ski and socialise.

UK operators which recruit staff for Méribel and France generally include the following:

Belvedere Chalets, jane@blounts.force9.co.uk. Couples employed to manage chalets in Méribel.

Family Ski Company, Bank Chambers, Walwyn Road, Colwall, Malvern WR13 6QG (01684 541444; www.familyski.co.uk). Offer many jobs in the French Alps.

Le Ski, 25 Holly Terrace, Huddersfield, HD1 6JW (0870 754 4444; www.leski.com). Jobs in Courchevel, La Tania and Val d'Isère.

Lotus Supertravel, Sandpiper House, 39 Queen Elizabeth St, London SE1 2BT (020-7962 1369; alice@lotusgroup.co.uk). Takes on winter staff for France, primarily chalet hosts with excellent cooking skills, reps fluent in French, qualified masseurs, nannies and handymen. All applicants must hold an EU passport and be over 21.

Meriski, 1st Floor, Carpenters Buildings, Carpenters Lane, Cirencester, Gloucestershire GL7 1EE UK (01285 648518; www.meriski.co.uk). Chalet cooks and nannies in greatest demand.

Scott Dunn Ski, Fovant Mews, 12 Noyna Road, London SW17 7PH (recruitment@scot tdunn.com).

Simon Butler Skiing, 159 Boundary Rd, Woking, Surrey GU21 5BT; 0870 728706; info @simonbutlerskiing.co.uk. Jobs for nannies, chalet people, cooks and ski instructors in Megève.

Ski Armadillo, 07801 570040 or 07781 411820; www.skiarmadillo.com. For chalets in Verbier.

Ski Beat, Metro House, Northgate, Chichester, Sussex PO19 1BE (01243 780405; www.skibeat.co.uk). Jobs in La Plagne, Tignes, Val d'Isère and La Tania.

Ski Esprit, 185 Fleet Road, Fleet, Hants. GU51 3BL (01252 618318; www.esprit-holidays.co.uk).

Ski Olympic, PO Box 396, Doncaster DN5 7YS (01709 579999; www.skiolympic.co.uk).

SkiPlan Travel, Lees House, Brighton BN1 3GD (01273 774778).

Nannying is a very promising area of employment in ski resorts. Matt Tomlinson spent the winter season in Courchevel:

I'm not sure if I just luck out getting work or whether it is a question of having done most jobs, being presentable and enthusiastic. There certainly doesn't seem to be any shortage of employment opportunities in Courchevel and Le Praz during the busy periods. My first job was as a private nanny: easy work, £100 for the week plus another £70 for extra babysitting. I moved on to doing Children's Club with Simply Ski and then Snow Club with Ski Esprit. Not everyone was NNEB qualified though all had substantial childcare experience and most were hired in England. I would recommend anyone thinking of doing a nanny job in the Alps to think seriously before taking it on. The days were very long and tiring, especially when you have to keep track of 18 sets of ski gear.

In Tignes, Harri's Bar (Evolution 2 Hotel, Le Lavachet, 73320 Tignes, 04-79 06 48 11; info@skibarjobs.com; www.skibarjobs.com) encourages applications from ski enthusiasts to work in a hotel/bar complex. Another promising resort is Chamonix.

The ANPE mount a concerted campaign every winter called A3 (ANPE Alpes Action) to attract qualified resort staff. Temporary job centres *(Antennes A3 ANPE Saisonnières)* are set up in most resorts and are co-ordinated by the permanent ANPE offices in Albertville, Annecy, Cluses and so on. For example the Albertville ANPE in the Savoie (45 ave Jean Jaurès, BP96, 73203 Albertville Cedex; 04-79 32 20 03) has a centralised placement service for vacancies in a range of resorts including Tignes, Val d'Isère and Méribel.

Some other relevant offices open year-round include:

Annecy ANPE, 8 bis Rue de Rumilly, 74000 Annecy (04-50 51 00 42).

Cluses ANPE, Immeuble l'Armorial, 14 rue du 8 Mai 1945, 74300 Cluses (04-50 98 92 88).

St Jean-de-Maurienne ANPE, 100 rue du Grand Coin, 73301 St Jean de Maurienne (04-79 64 17 88).

Chambery ANPE, 32 rue Paulette Besson, 73000 Chambery (04-79 60 24 70).

Thonon les Bains ANPE, 5 place de la Gare, 74207 Thonon les Bains Cedex (04-50 71 31 73).

Success is far from guaranteed in any ski resort job hunt and competition for work is increasing. Val d'Isère attracts as many as 500 ski bums every November/December, many of whom hang around bars like G-Jays or the ANPE for days in the vain hope that work will come their way. With such an inexhaustible supply of willing sometimes desperate workers, some employers are ready to hire people for Christmas, work them non-stop over the high season, pay them far less than the *SMIC* and fire them if they complain. If looking for work in Val, try Radio Val, which broadcasts from next door to the tourist office.

A problem that recurs every winter is the dispute between British tour operators and French ski schools. The rules state that only qualified instructors and guides can accompany holidaymakers which means that English-speaking ski guides or ski-hosts (part rep, part guide) hired by UK tour companies face arrest on the slopes. But for the past three years, the French have at least accepted (under pressure from the European Commission) that BASI-qualified British ski instructors have an equal right to work in the Alps. Top tour operators pay for official ski guides to take their clients around while some other companies claim to offer 'guiding' by their chalet staff. If challenged they may claim that guiding is merely showing clients around, i.e. pointing out where to find the lifts, the bars, etc.

Official ski guides in any alpine country have to take a stringent training course which includes very important lessons on reading and understanding local weather conditions. Although British staff can take a BASI course (British Association of Snowsport Instructors; www.basi.org.uk), this will not include this valuable training. When the avalanche season comes it is important that a ski guide can read weather signs to help steer clients away from danger.

At La Rosière, high in the Savoie Alps, they welcome trainee British ski guides who go through the ESF (École du Ski France; : info@esflarosiere.com) training course. Your French must be good and you must be dedicated, in exchange for excellent training. In Britain, BASI offer training and have made significant progress in getting their qualifications recognised on the continent.

In resorts, ski guides, local weather forecasters and avalanche specialists work closely together. Yet every year at least a dozen people die in alpine avalanches. The rescue services warn that it is essential to be properly trained if you are going to be responsible for people's lives.

CORSICA

The tourist industry of Corsica is concentrated in a small number of towns: Ajaccio the capital, Bastia, Bonifacio, Calvi, Ile Rousse and Propriano. Fortunately these have not been targeted by separatists' bombs in recent years. Anyone with a knowledge of German would be at an advantage since the level of German tourism in Corsica is very high. Kathryn Halliwell found her job in the hotel Grand Sofitel at Portticio, a resort about 12km down the coast from Ajaccio, by the time-honoured method of asking from door to door. She worked as a chambermaid on a hotel staff of 150, and mentioned that the worst problem faced by the female members of staff was the level of unwelcome attention from local men.

Alison Cooper found the heat to be a more serious impediment to her enjoyment of the summer as a Eurocamp courier in Corsica, but managed to have a great season:

I enjoyed this job immensely even if it did get unbearably hot when it's 40°C and you're trying to clean a tent in direct sunlight and with a hangover. We had one and a half days off a week on average with a fantastic beach to go and chill out on, or a quick dip in the campsite pool after cleaning. On the whole it was a good summer.

British tour operators with programmes in Corsica include *Mark Warner* and *Tall Stories*.

SPECIAL EVENTS

Many famous events in the French calendar may employ people as guides and interpreters as well as general dogsbodies. The Monte Carlo Rally is in late January while the Monaco Grand Prix is in late May and *Les 24 Heures du Mans* is in mid-June. Although the latter race is 24 hours long, the event stretches over a week; for information about the race and possible job opportunities for French-speakers, contact Automobile Club de l'Ouest, 72019 Le Mans (2-43 40 24 20).

One of the biggest summer festivals is in Avignon in August, though there are jazz festivals in Antibes, Nice and Nimes as well.

CASUAL WORK

Those without any training or experience in the tourist industry will probably end up in a low-expectation job like that of *plongeur*. At least such jobs will allow you to improve your standard of spoken French and give you a glimpse into French working practices. Most people succeed in finding casual work by turning up at a resort and asking door to door. In the opinion of veteran British traveller Jason Davies, 'door-to-door' should be just that:

Before I was down to my last few coins, I had been choosy about which establishments to ask at. 'That doesn't look very nice' or 'that's too posh' or 'that's probably closed' were all thoughts which ensured that I walked past at least three in five. But in Nice I discovered that the only way to do it is to pick a main street (like the pedestrianised area in Nice with its high density of restaurants) and ask at EVERY SINGLE place. I visited 30-40 one morning and I would say that at least 20 of those needed more employees. But only one was satisfied with my standard of French, and I got the job of commis waiter.

Speaking French to a reasonable standard greatly improves chances of finding a job, though fluency is by no means a requirement. Kimberly Ladone from the American east coast spent a summer working as a receptionist/chambermaid, also in Nice, though her job hunt did not require the same dogged determination as Jason Davies' did:

I found the job in April, at the first hotel I approached, and promised to return at the start of the season in June. While there, I met many English-speaking working travellers employed in various hotels. My advice to anyone seeking a job on the French Riviera would be to go as early in the season as possible and ask at hotels featured in English guidebooks such as Let's Go: France, since these tend to need English-speaking staff. My boss hired me primarily because I could handle the summer influx of clueless tourists who need help with everything from making a phone call to reading a train schedule.

CÔTE D'AZUR

Beach restaurants are another hopeful possibility. Julian Peachey put on his one white shirt and pair of smart trousers and began visiting the restaurants along the beach by Avenue Montredon in the eastern part of Marseille. After the third request for work he was handed a tea towel, and proceeded to work 14-16 hours a day, seven days a week. Only the thought of the money kept him sane. The wage was severely cut on days when it rained or the mistral blew and no one came to the beach.

Campsite jobs proliferate along the Mediterranean coast, especially in August when almost everyone in France takes their annual holiday. There is a point in the summer at which workers who have been there since the beginning of the season are getting bored and restless, which creates a demand for emergency substitution to cover the last two months of the season. Jobs include cleaning the loos, manning the bar or snack bar, doing some maintenance, etc. Some will be especially interested in people with musical ability; all will want you to speak French and also German if possible.

Many people think the Riviera has lost its glamour and is hardly worth job-hunting. In the opinion of Andrew Giles the best time to look for work on the Côte d'Azur is the end of February when campsites well known to working travellers, such as Prairies de la Mer and La Plage at Port Grimaud near St Tropez host representatives from camping holiday companies trying to get organised in time for Easter. If you are on the spot you can often wangle free accommodation in exchange for three or four hours of work a day. If you can't be there then, try the middle of May at the beginning of the peak season. Bars recommended by Andrew where you can meet local workers and residents include Marilyns (Prairies de la Mer), Mulligans (Holiday Marina), Finnigans (Port Grimaud) and L'Utopée (Marines Cogolin). Emiliano Giovannoni found the McMahon's Pub in central Nice was a meeting place for Brits, Americans and Aussies. Also, try to listen to the English station Radio Riviera based in Nice which at 9.30am and 4.30pm broadcasts job vacancies along the coast and will also announce your request for a job free of charge. When Peter Goldman couldn't find work on boats as he had hoped (because of rainy September weather) he tuned in to Radio Riviera and got a job stripping wallpaper from luxury apartments in Monte Carlo.

YACHTS

Kevin Gorringe headed for the south of France in June with the intention of finding work on a private yacht. His destination was Antibes, where so many British congregate, and began frequenting likely meeting places like the Gaffe Bar and the Irish bar as well as the agencies like Adrian Fisher and Blue Water. He recommends using the services of The Office (La Galerie du Port, 8 Blvd d'Aguillon, 06600 Antibes; 04-93 34 09 96; theoffice@wanadoo.fr) which for a small fee can be used as a contact point for potential employers. Frequenting the yachties' bars and listening to Radio Riviera can also pay off.

Bill Garfield describes his job hunt in Antibes:

Boats frequently take on people as day workers first and then employ them as crew for the charter season if they like them. I had no previous experience of this work, which turned out to be to my advantage because the captain wished the work to be done his way.

I lived on board with plenty of food provided and the pay was quite good, though some boats were paying much more.

Look tidy and neat, be polite and when you get a job work hard. The first job is the hardest to get, but once you get in with this integrated community, captains will help you find other jobs after the refitting is finished. Of course many continue through the summer as deckhands on charter yachts and are paid £100 a week plus tips (which sometimes match the wage). The charter season ends in late September when many yachts begin organising their crew for the trip to the Caribbean.

PARIS

This city is the most popular destination on the continent for British short breaks. Each year thousands of coaches cross over by ferry creating plenty of work for people to look after these groups, even in winter. However the French authorities have been known to stop coaches and demand to see a tour guide's 'equivalence', i.e. a certificate of qualification under the EC 75/368 Directive on Mutual Recognition of Qualifications. To get one, take a nationally recognised course in leisure and tourism that covers tour guiding such as that offered by OCR. Ideally, the certificate should be translated into French and carried at all times, so that any *agent de police* can see that you possess an appropriate qualification.

The hunt for a casual job in Paris doesn't get any easier, as Mark Davies describes:

Although it has taken me five and a half weeks to find paid employment (as a plongeur in a creperie) I console myself with the fact that there is high unemployment here at the moment. To give you an example, I turned up as stated on the job notice at 5pm for a dishwashing job, and there were eight other people doing the same, and they were by no means all poor-looking immigrants. The pay for the job I'm doing now is lousy but it pays the rent while I look for something better. But as long as I'm in the Jardin du Luxembourg and the sun is shining I can't complain.

Stephen Psallidas went around all the Greek restaurants in the Quartier Huchette in the Latin Quarter and found a job in half an hour (though the pay was appalling). Sarit Moas from Israel doggedly enquired at all the restaurants and street food stalls until she got a job selling crepes and taffy in the Tuilleries amusement parks.

One of the easiest places to find work is at fast food establishments; Americana is still trendy in France and English-speaking staff fit well with the image. There are many American-style fast food restaurants like the Quick chain and Chicago Pizza Pie Factory which employ non-French staff. If there is a vacancy (as there often is) you could be offered a 45-hour-a-week job at SMIC rates plus tips and one meal a day.

HOSTELS

Hostels are always worth trying. The Youth Hostels Association of France (FUAJ) employs young people for short periods at various hostels to work in the kitchen, reception and as sports leaders. The headquarters of the Fédération Unie des Auberges de Jeunesse (27 rue Pajol, 75018 Paris; www.fuaj.org) distributes a guide to the 185 French hostels to which interested workers must apply directly.

REGULATIONS

A powerful political lobby wants to clamp down on black work, and the authorities are committed to enforcing French employment legislation. Tax inspectors and immigration officers carry out spot checks in tourist resorts, and employers in even the most out-of-the-way places have refused to hire anyone who lacks the right documents, whether or not they are EU nationals.

As in all member states, EU nationals are permitted to stay in France for up to three months without obtaining a residence permit *(carte de séjour)*. Once you have a job and know you are going to stay longer than three months, you should apply for a *carte de séjour* at the local police station *(préfecture)* or town hall *(mairie)*. Take your passport, four photos, some proof of your local address (e.g. rental contract, receipt for rent) and a job contract or, failing that, proof of funds and credit cards (with recent receipts to prove their validity). The *carte* can take some time to come through – eight months to be precise in Stephen Psallidas's case – but in the meantime a *récépissé* for a *carte de séjour* should satisfy most employers. Having a residence permit improves your chances of being hired; for example Vicky Nakis is fairly sure that she missed out on a short-term job at Disneyland Paris the first time round because she lacked one.

Confusingly, some employers and job centres have insisted that prospective employees obtain a *fiche d'état civil* from the *mairie* (town hall). For this you will need the same documents as for the *carte de séjour* apart from the job contract.

When you start work, you or your employer should apply for a social security number (usually referred to as a *sécu*) from the relevant local office who should issue you with an emergency number straightaway. Social security deductions amount to approximately 18% of your wages, and these can be counted towards National Insurance in Britain, if you subsequently need to claim benefit. It can save a lot of hassle if you arrive with your birth certificate translated into French so that you can register more easily for social security and receive wages from a French employer.

NON-EU FORMALITIES

Non-EU nationals must obtain work documents before they leave their home country in order to work legally and this is fiendishly difficult since it depends on finding an employer who can argue that no French or EU national could do the job. A more manageable approach is to turn yourself into a student. After an initial year of study, people on a student visa are permitted to work 10-20 hours a week in term-time and up to 39 hours in vacations. In order to obtain a student visa, you will have to have good French language skills, two years of higher education and proof of financial support in the form of a notarised statement from a bank or benefactor that you can access at least $500 a month. With a student visa and stable accommodation, you can apply for a *carte de séjour* and after that for jobs, preferably jobs that French people can't do like guiding groups of foreign students, etc.

There is a special scheme by which American students with a working knowledge of French (normally a minimum of two years' study at university) are allowed to hold a job in France at any time of the year and work for up to three months with an *authorisation provisoire de travail*. This scheme is organised by the Council on International Educational Exchange (3 Copley Place, 2nd Floor, Boston, MA 02116; 1-888-268-6245; www.ciee.org). Eligible Americans already in France may apply to the CIEE office in Paris (112 ter rue Cardinet, 75017 Paris; 1-58 57 20 50; info@councilexchanges-fr.org; www.councilexchanges-fr.org) which provides a lot of support to programme participants. For example it produces a list of potential employers who have hired American students in the past. According to CIEE's most recent statistics, 95% of participants work in Paris and suburbs.

The Cultural Service of the French Embassy (4101 Reservoir Road NW, Washington, DC 20007; www.frenchculture.org) collates information of use to Americans who wish to study or intern in France with information about teaching assistantships. Americans who are interested in arranging a hospitality internship in France should contact AIPT (see *UK* chapter) who co-operate with Espace Emploi International (48 Boulevard de la Bastille, 75012 Paris; 1 53 02 25 54). Further information is available on the website of the Office des Migrations Internationales (www.omi.social.fr).

US nationals can also benefit by contacting the French American Chamber of Commerce which oversees an International Career Development Program for candidates aged 18-25 (6th Floor, 1350 Avenue of the Americas, New York, NY 10019; 212-765-4460; www.faccnyc.org). Internships in companies are normally open to graduates with relevant professional experience. The Chamber can assist suitable candidates arrange a six-month visa that can be renewed twice.

DIRECTORY REFERENCES

The following companies which employ staff in France are listed in the Directory: Acorn Venture, Alpine Tracks, Alpotels, Camping Life, Canvas, Carisma, Casterbridge, Club Cantabrica, Continental Waterways, Discover Adventure, Discover Ltd., Disneyland Paris, Duvine Adventures, Equity, Esprit Holidays, Eurocamp, European Waterways, Family Ski Company, Fleur Holidays, France Montgolfières Balloon Flights, Freewheel Holidays, Handmade Holidays, Harry Shaw, Haven Europe, Headwater, Ian Mearns Holidays, King's Camps, Lotus Supertravel, Mark Warner, Matthews Holidays, Meriski, MyTravel, NBV Leisure, Neilson, NSS Riviera, NST, PGL, Purple Ski, Sandpiper, Sarl Star Hotels, Savoy Chalet Holidays, Scott Dunn, Select France, Shearings, Ski Activity, Ski Amis, Ski Miquel, Ski Olympic, Skiworld, Susi Madron's Cycling, Tall Stories, TJM Travel, Total Holidays, UK Overseas Handling, Venue Holidays, Village Camps.

Germany

The most important tourist magnets in Germany for foreign tourists are the River Rhine and Bavaria. The most popular coach tour to Germany from the UK is the three or four day tour of the Rhine Valley including Rüdesheim where many thousands of day-trippers crowd into the Drosselgasse and similarly overcrowded streets.

According to the most recent figures, the number of people employed in the German tourist industry has declined due to the international downturn in tourism, i.e. nearly 5% fewer people were employed in the first half of 2003 than in the corresponding period a year earlier. Yet the industry in Germany still employs well over one million people. The best job opportunities in cities like Bremen, Hamburg, Hannover, Frankfurt and Stuttgart are at conferences and exhibitions, and in hotels, as all major (west) German cities have excellent venues for international events. Berlin, which replaced Bonn as the capital of the united Germany in 1999, is enjoying a huge resurgence in popularity among tourists, as are some less known cities to which no-frills airlines like Ryanair are flying, e.g. Friedrickshafen on Lake Constance and Erfurt and Leipzig in the former East Germany.

Famous towns like Heidelberg (the oldest university in Germany) and the spa town of Baden Baden (also a Ryanair destination) now is visited mainly for its casinos, attract other groups. Extensive tourist developments elsewhere, such as along the Baltic coast and inland lakes near Munich, attract mainly German tourists, and the Bavarian Alps (along the border with Austria), the shores of Lake Constance, the Bohmer Wald (along the Czech border) and the Black Forest (in south-west Germany) all have flourishing tourist seasons. Employment opportunities in the old east Germany are fewer unless you can find a UK operator which is too small to tap into the East German workforce, or which wants the same person to look after their group from departure from the UK.

PROSPECTS FOR WORK

It is difficult for foreigners to obtain skilled work in the indigenous tourist industry, though work is sometimes available with German ground handling and conference organising companies. Competition to work in a tour operator's office in Germany is fierce, unless you are fluent in German and are already employed by a major British or American tour operator who is able to transfer you to work for their German ground handler. The two giant operators in Germany are TUI (which has bought up major UK operators like Thomson and Crystal) and the Frankfurt-based Dertour.

At the unskilled level, the German tourist industry depends heavily on immigrants and students during the busy summer months. EU nationals have an advantage over the many job-seekers from the former Yugoslavia, especially those who speak German. Prospects exist for German-speakers to become tour managers taking UK groups to Germany and for tour managers working for American companies using Frankfurt as their European gateway city. People looking for rep work should apply to the big camping tour operators like *Eurocamp* and *Keycamp Holidays* (see their entries in the Directory).

In summer the deluxe German coach operators sometimes hire English-speaking drivers with a PCV licence and valid First Aid certificate for American groups. (German coach drivers take a compulsory first aid course before they can obtain a licence.) An endorsement for driving double deckers is useful, and also an ability to translate the sign *Umleitung* (which is not a place on a map but the German word for 'Diversion'). Coach driver/guides are obliged to point out the emergency exits to passengers. The police can board a coach and ask a randomly chosen passenger to point out their nearest exit; if they can't, the guide is fined.

Interest in 'green' tourism is very strong in Germany, so rambling and cycling holidays offer possibilities. The old hearty hiking holidays are giving way to tours that include cultural visits as well. These are often run by enthusiasts who organise and lead the tours themselves; anyone who has the ability, training and a good prospective client list may be tempted to do likewise.

FINDING A JOB

The best chance for finding work in Germany is with a UK company which sends clients to Germany. Otherwise, it may be worth consulting a German Jobcentre or *Arbeitsamt*.

GERMAN NATIONAL EMPLOYMENT SERVICE

The whole of Germany is covered by the network of employment offices run by the state *Bundesanstalt für Arbeit* (Regenburgerstr. 104, 90237 Nürnberg; www.arbeitsamt.de). There are 181 principal *Arbeitsamter* (job centres) and a further 660 branch offices. These are all connected by a number of co-ordinating offices that handle both applications and vacancies that cannot be filled locally.

Arbeitsamter are entitled to refuse to help you if you do not have residence papers though the self-service system (SIS) means that anyone can inspect job vacancy information updated daily on SIS computer terminals. Even before this computerised system was introduced, many praised the efficiency of the *Arbeitsamt*:

Amongst them was Nick Langley who used the Arbeitsamt in Munich near the U-bahn station Goetheplatz:
Germany has one of the most efficient National Employment Services in the world. In Munich there is a massive modern complex which is organised on the basis of different departments handling job vacancies for different work categories such as building and construction, engineering, restaurant work, hotel work, etc. It may be necessary to visit several departments to maximise your chances of a job. Each department has counsellors to handle enquiries, tell you what's on offer and arrange interviews. There is also a microfiche reader listing hundreds of vacancies in the area. I was immediately offered a job at a new Burger King restaurant about to open in the main station.

The full address is Kapuzinerstrasse 26, 80337 Munich (muenchen@arbeitsamt.de; www.arbeitsamt.de/muenchen).

It is possible to use the Federal Employment Service from outside Germany. The Zentralstelle für Arbeitsvermittlung (Central Placement Office) has an international department *(Auslandsabteilung)* for dealing with applications from German-speaking people abroad. Details and application forms are available from ZAV, Villemombler Str. 76, 53123 Bonn (0228-713-0; fax 0228-713 1111; Bonn-ZAV@arbeitsamt.de; www.arbeitsamt.de/zav). All applications from abroad are handled by this office. Although people of any nationality can apply through the Zentralstelle, only citizens of EU countries who have German language skills are entitled to expect the same treatment as a German. People of other nationalities are accepted only within the framework of special exchange programmes and government-approved schemes such as the one administered by CDS International mentioned below.

There is one exception to this rule. The Zentralstelle has a special department which finds summer jobs for students of any nationality, because this is felt to be mutually beneficial to employers and employees alike. Students who wish to participate in this scheme should contact ZAV before March. Students must be at least 18 years old, have a good command of German and be available to work for at least two months. ZAV places students in all kinds of jobs, but mainly in hotels and restaurants. Those with fluent German may be found service jobs while those without will be given jobs such as chambermaiding and dishwashing. If you decline the first job offered by the Zentralstelle, you may not be offered another.

RHINE CRUISES

For general touring inside Germany, the average tourist thinks exclusively of the Rhine and its valleys. At a minimum, they take the obligatory hour-long trip from Cologne (Köln) past the Loreley Rock and stay overnight in Heidelberg. If you are guiding a group on the short trip down the Rhine or who will be spending several days in one of the boats of the Köln-Düsseldorf Line (www.k-d.com) founded in 1826, you will probably embark with them in or near Köln. (Passengers should be warned that the ships stop just long enough to allow disembarkation and then move across to the other side of the river.) For other cruise operators to contact, check www.mainz.de/english/tourist/engl066.htm. Some like the K-D Line sometimes hire English-speaking waiters, chambermaids, etc. to staff their vessels, as Lyn Bayley relates:

After answering a newspaper advert in England and having a short interview, I was employed as a cabin girl on a Rhine cruiser. The boat trip began in Amsterdam, but the rest of the season was spent in Germany. We travelled the same section of the Rhine every week, which I enjoyed because I came to know each place really well. We five cabin girls seemed to have the best deal, mostly working 8.30am-5pm, compared to the catering staff whose hours extended from 7.30am to 10.30pm. I stayed on the boat for four months and made lots of great friends. I also managed to save £300 which subsidised further travels.

Lyn was paid a modest monthly wage in addition to free food, accommodation and travel to and from Britain.

BAVARIA

Bavarians like to think that they inhabit a separate country. Throughout the country you see the blue and white chequered flag of the Wittelsbachs (a royal family installed in the 12th century) and people wearing the traditional costume of lederhosen and dirndl.

Both Amersee and Starnbergersee can be reached by S-Bahn from Munich. These two lakes are ringed by towns and villages which all have hotels and restaurants, popular mainly with German tourists. But recession has hit this region hard in recent years and it has become more difficult to find work here than it was when Paul Winter worked several seasons on the lakes near Munich:

I found that it is best to apply around April/May in person if possible. What they usually do is to tell you to come back at the beginning of June and work for a couple of days to see how you get on. As long as you are not a complete idiot they will keep you on until September. Even as late as July I knew of places looking for extra staff but as a rule most places are full by the end of May. I worked for the summer as a barman/waiter and usually managed to double my wages with tips.

WINTER RESORTS

Not many UK tour companies operate skiing holidays in Germany, and yet people do find work in the resorts. The UK agency Alpotels carries out aptitude tests on behalf of German hoteliers looking for about 50 English-speaking staff (with EU nationality) for the summer and winter seasons (see entry).

Three resorts to consider are Garmisch-Partenkirchen (which also has hotels and services for the American Army) on the Austrian border 80km southeast of Munich, the spa resort of Oberstdorf in the mountains south of Kempten and Berchtesgaden in a portion of Germany which juts into Austria, south of Salzburg.

At one time the US Forces Recreation Camp in Garmisch generated a lot of employment. However the strict labour laws which protect German employees (and by extension EU nationals) mean that the base has stopped hiring local nationals and only hires Americans since they are not subject to the same regulations and are therefore much cheaper to employ.

SPECIAL INTEREST TOURS

Opera tours are a possible avenue to explore, with companies like Travel for the Arts which is affiliated to Specialised Travel (see entry) and which occasionally recruits new staff (enquiries to ablair@stlon.com) or Brompton Travel (020-8398 3672; opera@bromp tontravel.co.uk) who organise opera tours to Berlin, Munich and Stuttgart. If you need to learn more about the legends and myths which inspired Wagner's *Parsifal, Lohengrin,* etc. before approaching music tour operators, go to the children's section of the public library.

Tourism professionals may wish to approach tour operators specialising in Germany, such as Moswin's Germany (Moswin House, 21 Church St, Oadby, Leicester LE2 5DB; 0116 271 4982; germany@moswin.com) who run a large range of tours from basic escorted tours of the Moselle region to wine, painting, walking and language study tours. Another company with a Germany-only brochure is Taber Holidays (30A Bingley Road, Saltaire, Shipley, W. Yorks BD18 4RD; www.taberhols.co.uk).

Predictably, the major language tour operators for students such as Euro Academy (020-8297 0505; www.euroacademy.co.uk) have extensive programmes in Germany. Like some other members of the Association of Language Tour Operators, they can also place young people in unpaid internships, sometimes in a requested field such as tourism, provided the candidate is willing to sign up for a four or eight-week German language course before taking up the placement. Theresa worked for an American company offering holidays with language tuition:

I was booked for the whole summer, and they expected me to work from my bedroom which had no telephone. Trying to contact the company from a public phone meant I would lose out on lunch and any other free time. It's not good for discipline if you

"I was booked for the whole Summer, and they expected me to work from my bedroom which had no telephone"

have impressed on your students that they must always be on time for excursions, and then you are late because you are in a queue to wash in the morning.

A few 'failed' attempts to return urgent phone calls from her company soon convinced them that if they needed to contact her they would have to provide her with a room in the local hotel with a telephone and an en-suite bathroom as well.

HOTELS & CATERING

As usual, international hotel groups may allow staff to move between countries. If you want to work in Germany, try to get a job at a hotel which is a member of one of the marketing chains focused on the German market.

The German Hotels Association is DEHOGA and its website in English has links to all the German hotel chains such as Steigenberger Hotels AG (Personnel Development, Lyoner Strasse 40, 60528 Frankfurt) whose website – www.company.steigenberger.com – carries lots of information in English about careers. The same applies to the Romantik Hotels group also based in Frankfurt (www.romantikhotels.com).

An organisation which finds jobs for German-speaking foreign young people in German hotels is the *Bloomsbury Bureau* (see entry) which recruits up to 40 general assistants for hotels mainly in Bavaria. Applicants must be EU citizens and have a knowledge of German. A net wage of £360 on top of free room and board is promised in exchange for working a 45-hour week.

DEHOGA's official publication is *Allgemeine Hotel und Gaststättenzeitung* (www.ahgz.de) which has a digital employment portal to which German-speaking job-seekers can subscribe (http://ahgz.job-klick.de). The specialist publisher Matthaes Verlag (www.matthaes.de) publishes many books for the hotel and catering industry including *Etage Exclusive* covering training placements throughout Germany (cost €26).

Eurotoques is a scheme by which German-speaking trainees are assigned to work for at least three months as kitchen assistants and waiting staff in German hotels in exchange for room and board but no wage (Winnender Str 12, D-73667 Ebnisee/Schwäbischer Wald; 07184-91055/ fax 07184-91053; office@eurotoques.de/ www.Eurotoques.de).

Be prepared for hard work. In hotels, it is not unusual to work 10 or 12 hours a day and to have only a day or two off a month. The punitive hygiene laws do not help matters. Once you realise that restaurants and hotels are frequently visited by the health department you will appreciate why it is that the head cook insists that the floors be scrubbed, the fat filters cleaned regularly, etc. But the high wages make it worthwhile.

CONFERENCES AND EXHIBITIONS

Some of the largest fairs and exhibitions in the world are held in Germany. For example the international tourism congress (ITB or International Tourismus Börse) held every March in Berlin's massive *Messe* (exhibition hall) is attended by nearly 10,000 exhibiting companies (more than twice as many as exhibited at London's World Travel Market in November 2003) and visited by a staggering 130,000 people.

British companies exhibiting at German fairs, especially the Hannover Fair, often need interpreters. Contact the British Chamber of Commerce, Severingstrasse 60, 50678 Köln; www.bddg.de which accepts paying advertisements for their website.

Destination management is big business in Germany and the UK company Travel Contacts Ltd. (PO Box 173, Camberley, Surrey GU16 5GD; 01252 681093) maintains an up-to-date list on its website of important companies and organisations all working with English-speaking groups; see www.travelcontacts.com for information about the following:

Conference & Touring Berlin, Kaiserdamm 110, 14057 Berlin (030-301 280; www.dmcgermany.de)

Conference & Touring Hamburg, Bogenstrasse 5.4A, 20144 Hamburg (040-4291 8130; www.dmcgermany.de)

Conference & Touring Munich, Preysingstr. 5, 81667 Munich (089 61 46 930)

Saxonia Touristik International GmbH, Alaunstrasse 14, 01099 Dresden (0351-810509-0; dresden@saxonia-touristik.de). Branch offices in Leipzig and Berlin (www.saxonia-touristik.de)

Life Tours, Obertorstrasse 2, D-63454 Hanau (06181-74 05 77; www.lifetours.de)

Major German cities usually have an association of operators geared up for handling conferences and these may give contact details of their members on their website. For example in Hamburg, the Verband der Incoming-Agenturen e.V. provides this information on www.via-hamburg.de and the following The following companies may need bilingual staff for incoming groups:

HSG Hanseatische Service GmbH, Bismarckstr. 117, 20253 Hamburg (www.event-hamburg.de)

CPO Hanser Service, Hanser & Co. GmbH, Zum Ehrenhain 34, 22885 Hamburg-Barsbüttel (040-6708820; www.cpo-hanser.de)

Hamburger Führungsdienst, Uschi Scholz GmbH, Budapester Straße 20, 20359 Hamburg (040-31999601)

"Whenever I wanted a bath, the landlady's tights were dripping down my neck"

Harries Solution GmbH, Bismarckstr. 117, 20253 Hamburg (040-4293880; www.harries-solution.de)

Vista Tours Reisedienst GmbH, Raboisen 38-40, 20095 Hamburg (040-3097980; www.vista-tours.de)

Accommodation is always a problem at Fair times, and company offers should be carefully checked. One interpreter found herself in a B&B 60 miles from Hannover, which meant four hours of commuting a day and 'whenever I wanted a bath, the landlady's tights were dripping down my neck'. If you are doing some freelance work, from translating to stall dismantling, it is better if you can arrange accommodation independently, preferably with local friends.

Oktoberfest starts each year on the last Saturday in September and lasts a fortnight. They begin to erect the giant tents for the festival about three months ahead so you can begin your enquiries any time in the summer. Some of the hiring is done directly by the breweries, so it is worth contacting the Hofbräuhaus and Löwenbräu for work, as well as pubs, restaurants and hotels. There is also work after it finishes as Brad Allemand from Australia discovered:

On the Monday after Oktoberfest finished I went around to all of the Beer Halls which were being taken down asking for some work. The first one I went to was

Spatenbräu and the boss obliged. Even though my German was almost non-existent, I managed to understand what was needed of me. Many other foreigners were also on the site – English, Australian, Yugoslav, etc.

In Hamburg they hold a fair *(Dom)* three times a year, for a month after Christmas, Easter and late summer. 'Worker Wanted' signs are often posted on the stalls.

Special events that need large numbers of people to set up stands and deal with the maintenance, catering, etc.:

March	Frankfurt Trade Fair
April	Hannover Trade Fair
August	International Frankfurt Trade Fair
August	Mainz Wine Festival
August	Wiesbaden Wine Week
August	Rüdesheim Wine Festival
late Sept/early Oct	German Wine Harvest Festival (Neustadt)
late Sept/early Oct	Wiesbaden-Rheingau Wine Festival
late Sept/early Oct	Cannstadt Folk and Beer Festival (Stuttgart)
late Sept/early Oct	October Beer Festival (Munich)
mid October	Frankfurt Book Fair

Many high-profile trade fairs are held at the huge Frankfurt Exhibition Hall *(Messe)* in addition to the Frankfurt Book Fair in mid-October. Applications for work at one of the numerous fairs held in Frankfurt can be addressed to Messe Frankfurt GmbH, Ludwig-Erhard-Anlage 1, 60327 Frankfurt (069-75750; bewerbung@messefrankfurt.com). Only people with a stable base in Frankfurt and a good command of languages (for example for running messages) can be considered.

INCENTIVE TOURS

UK incentive tour companies often organise programmes to Germany, since the standard of deluxe hotels is excellent. These companies normally take German-speaking freelance staff from the UK, but sometimes there is work from their ground handlers. American and Canadian companies often organise incentives to Germany, especially from Texas and other states with large German communities. Contacting incentive multinationals such as Maritz in St Louis can produce job offers if you speak German; they maintain a German office in Düsseldorf (www.maritz-germany.com).

GROUND HANDLERS

One of the best sources of incoming tour operators and ground handlers is the website of the German National Tourist Office www.visits-to-germany.com. The page www.visits-to-germany.com/pages_trade/623.htm lists incoming leisure operators for English speakers, including the selection listed here. Fluent speakers of German or tourism professionals may find it worthwhile approaching one of the following companies:
Autobus Oberbayern GmbH, Heidemannstrasse 220, 80939 Munich (089-323 040; www.autobusoberbayern.de)
Beer Travel & Tours, Dr.Böcale-Str. 7, 92331 Parsberg (09492-90 20 01; www.beer-bus.de)
Compact Tours, Prenzlauer Allee 180, 10405 Berlin (030-446 739 30; berlin@compact-tours.com)
Compass Tours Incoming Dr. Kater GmbH, Lindemannstrasse 30, 40237 Düsseldorf (0211-407 021; info@compasstours.de)

Deutsche Touring GmbH, Am Römerhof 17, 60486 Frankfurt (069-790 326; www.touring-germany.com)
Events & Touring AG, Dessauer Strasse 38, 06886 Wittenberg (03491-660 195; www.event-touring.com)
Top Tours Travel, Hochbrueckenstrasse 10, 80331 Munich (089-228 3143; www.ttt-munich.de)
Weichlein Tours & Incentives, Neuhauser Strasse 33, 80331 Munich (089- 85 636 630; info@weichlein.de)

GERMAN COACH COMPANIES

This is a selective list of German companies which run coach tours. The busweb.com website gives further leads:
Busreisen Ettenhuber GmbH (Munich) Am Hochrain 2, 85625 Glonn-Schlacht (089-21 63 36 0; www.ettenhuber.com/html/kontakt/jobs.html)
Binder-Reisen (Stuttgart) – 0711-13 96 50 (www.binder-reisen.de)
Schielein Reisen (Nuremburg) – 0911-64 20 60 (info@schielein.de)
Taeter (Aachen) – www.taeter.de
Starship Coaches (Berlin) – 030-55 77 91-0 (www.starship-berlin.de)

CASUAL WORK

If your German isn't up to scratch, taking a job at a basic level is the best way of learning quickly. But beware, it is no use taking a job if all your fellow workers are non-German speaking.

Seasonal jobs for summer or winter can be fixed up by sending off speculative applications. Alternatively, look for adverts in the local press, especially *Abendzeitung* in Munich (www.abendzeitung.de). Key words to look for on notices and in adverts are *Notkoch und Küchelhilfe gesucht* (relief and kitchen assistant required), *Spüler* (dishwasher), *Kellner, Bedienigung* (waiters/waitresses), *Schenkekellner* (pub type barman); *Büffetier* (barman in a restaurant), *Büffetkräfte* (fast food server), or simply *Services.*

Munich is estimated to have 2,000 pubs and restaurants (concentrated in the fashionable suburb of Schwabing) and Berlin is similarly well endowed with eateries (try the Kurfürstendamm area). The Munich beer gardens, especially the massive Chinese Tower Biergarten, pay glass collectors and washers-up (most of whom would have lined their jobs up at the beginning of the season) €45 a day tax free at the height of the season, when people work 14-hour days.

The Happy Hands working holiday scheme places language and gap year students from the UK and the rest of Europe in the field of rural tourism. Participants are given weekly pocket money of €51 and full board and lodging with families on farms or in country hotels. In return they look after children and/or horses and farm animals. The preferred stay is three to six months though a two-month commitment is also allowed; details available from Happy Hands, Römerberg 8, 60311 Frankfurt; 069-293733; Anne.Gleichen@t-online.de; www.workingholidays.de. An agency registration fee from €230 is charged.

One employer on the Baltic coast hires a number of general assistants, food and beverage staff, child carers and sports instructors at a coastal campsite/golf and holiday park. The hours are long and you must be able to speak German but the wages are good. Apply in the spring to Camping Wulfener Hals, Riechey Freizeitanlagan GmbH, 23769 Wulfen/Fehmarn (04371 8628-0; www.wulfenerhals.de).

REGULATIONS

EU nationals who are employed by a German employer should benefit from the good working conditions and high wages standard throughout regulated industries in Germany but will have to contend with the labyrinthine bureaucracy. Procedures are supposed to be standard throughout the country, but they can still be confusing. Assuming your UK employer (if you have one) has not registered you, the first step is to register with the local authority *(Einwohnermeldeamt)* at the town hall *(Ortsamt* or *Rathaus)*. After the form *(Anmeldung)* has been signed by your landlord and employer, it should be taken back to the *Ortsamt* in order to pick up a tax card *(Lohnsteuerkarte)*, after which you will be fully legal. Legal workers can expect to lose between 33% and 40% of their gross wages in tax and social security contributions, including a church tax *(Kirchensteuer)* which accounts for 8-9% of income tax, unless you claim an exemption due to atheism (and thereby forego the possibility of ever being married or buried in a German church).

Many jobs in catering require a *Gesundheitszeugnis* (health certificate) and it can help if you have taken a course in basic kitchen hygiene. Anyone who has acquired the Foundation Certificate in Food Hygiene from a local college or training organisation before leaving home will have the edge; this can be earned after a one day course costing £40-£60. You may also have to acquire a *Gesundheitszeugnis* (health certificate) from the local *Gesundheitsamt* (health department). Restaurants will be heavily fined if they are caught employing anyone without it.

CIEE in the US administer two programmes in Germany. American students who have studied German for at least two years at college can work for up to three months between mid-May and mid-October or students who can fix up a career-related internship can work for up to six months at any time of year. CIEE's office in Germany can be found at Oranienburger Str. 13-14, 10178 Berlin (030-28 48 59-0; InfoGermany@councilexchan ges.de; www.councilexchanges.de).

InterExchange in New York (161 Sixth Avenue, New York, NY 10013; www.interexchange.org) can place full-time students in German resorts during the summer provided they have intermediate German. Applications must be in by the middle of February.

Non-EU nationals who land a job independently must obtain a residence permit *(Aufenthaltserlaubnis)* if they intend to stay longer than three months. The minimum requirements for this are a certificate of good conduct notarised by your embassy or consulate, a *Gesundheitszeugnis* (as above), proof of health insurance, a stable address and means of support. If you intend to work and to apply for a work permit *(Arbeitserlaubnis)* from the *Arbeitsamt,* your *Aufenthaltserlaubnis* must bear the appropriate stamp.

DIRECTORY REFERENCES

For companies which operate in Germany, see the following entries in the Directory section: Alpotels, Bloomsbury Bureau, Canvas, Equity, Eurocamp, European Waterways, Eurotoques, Travelsphere.

Greece

Since the days of the Grand Tour when privileged young Englishmen (and a handful of women) braved the journey to Greece to explore the ruins of ancient civilisation, Greece has attracted culture vultures. But it also hosts a huge number of sun-seekers as well. The range of resorts and tourist destinations varies enormously from glamorous yacht marinas frequented by wealthy Athenians (such as Aegina) to young people's 'party islands' like Ios.

After the last war, Greece was in turmoil, and tourism was seen as a saviour for the poor economy. Eventually so many visitors poured over the land frontiers that the Greeks had to rethink their tourism strategy. For the 2004 Olympics in Athens they hope to be better prepared, though at the time of writing, they seemed to be behind schedule. Greece has benefited enormously from EU funding which has improved the tourist infrastructure helping it to become one of the most popular tourist destination countries in the Mediterranean. However, Greece remains one of the poorest of the original 15 EU countries and facilities are not always luxurious. Indeed some tour operators have withdrawn from certain resorts and properties because of complaints about the low standards of bathroom amenities.

Obviously there are still many employment opportunities at both ends of the spectrum, both casual and professional, in a country whose tourist industry employs a third of a million people and welcomes ten million tourists annually. Unemployment has been decreasing from a high of 11% in 2000 to a current rate of about 9%, which is only slightly higher than the Eurozone average. The huge influx of economic migrants from Albania and the Balkans of the 1990s seems to have partially been brought under control and preparations for the Olympics has created a great deal of new employment.

PROSPECTS FOR WORK

In recent years the name Faliraki (the Rhodes resort) has become synonymous with drunken tourists behaving badly. That has prompted a new emphasis on promoting conference delegates and families who rent villas or stay in hotels. At this end of the market, the main areas for employment are as villa company reps and, to a lesser extent, tour managers and conference staff. Athens is the main venue for conferences, particularly connected with shipping and the oil industry.

Many tourist establishments around Greece are family businesses where the concept of 'marketing' is alien and the cooking is done by a female relative, not by someone who has been to catering college. This is all part of the charm. Yet there is also a growing demand for a more professional and sophisticated brand of tourism, and an acknowledged shortage of people with experience and qualifications to work in these.

Corfu, Crete, Rhodes, Ios and Paros seem to offer the most job openings in tourism, though Naxos, Santorini, Mykonos and more recently Kefalonia (in the wake of *Captain Corelli's Mandolin*) are also recommended. The vast majority of reps working in Greece are hired by the large tour operators in their home country. However anyone who takes a holiday in Greece or has an extended stay and falls in love with the country can sometimes fix up a repping job, by meeting and making a good impression on the reps and their supervisor.

Apart from conference work, there is almost no work to be had in the winter. Once the autumn storms come, the villages and resorts fade into ghost towns. However many operators run programmes to Cyprus during the winter, and may employ those staff who have worked well for them in the summer (especially if they speak some Greek).

FINDING A JOB

The hundreds of tour operators that feature Greece want reps, kiddies' reps, resort office staff and transfer staff, most of whom are hired in the tour operator's country of origin. Opportunities for advancement from junior rep to manager in charge of reps on one or more islands are good. People who are on self-catering holidays in villas or apartments are looked after by company reps who will be in charge of several locally-owned villas/apartments. In addition to *Olympic Holidays, Sunvil* and the *Greek Islands Club* (see Directory entries) Kosmar Holidays specialise in package holidays in Greek resorts and employ many overseas reps and admin staff over the age of 21; details from Kosmar, The Grange, 100 High St, Southgate, London N14 6FS; www.kosmar.co.uk (follow the Careers link).

Seasonal jobs can be arranged from the UK. *Mark Warner* (020-7761 7300) run several beachclub hotels in Greece which require British staff who are paid anything from £50 per week depending on the position, in addition to full board and accommodation, use of watersport facilities and flights.

Other possibilities include:

The Best of Greece, Suite 114-118, 125 High Holborn, London WC1V 6QA (0870 442 2442; info@bestofgreece.co.uk)

Golden Sun Holidays, Mason's Drive, 1-3 Valley Drive, Kingsbury, London NW9 9NG (020-8206 4733; www.goldensun.co.uk). Employs 150 overseas representatives to work in Greece or Cyprus for three months or more between April 1st and October 31st.

Pavilion Tours, Lynnem House, 1 Victoria Way, Burgess Hill, West Sussex RH15 9NF (0870 241 0425; www.paviliontours.com). Hire watersports instructors for children.

Hillwood Holidays, Lavender Lodge, Dunny Lane, Chipperfield, WD4 9DD (01923 290700; www.hillwood-holidays.co.uk). Family tour operator employs children's reps and sailing instructors at Crete resort of Bali.

Laskarina Holidays, St. Marys Gate, Wirksworth, Derbyshire DE4 4DQ (01629 822203; info@laskarina.co.uk). Specialise in unspoilt Greek islands; have been seen advertising for representatives aged 30-50 for March-October season.

Debbie Harrison discovered that tour operators seem to be more interested in attitude than experience:
Last summer I worked as a holiday rep on the island of Kos. I was introduced to my employers by an English friend who had worked for them before. Despite the fact that I had no qualifications or relevant experience, had never been to Greece and had never even been on a package holiday, I was offered a job on the island I wanted immediately at the end of my interview. Perhaps this had something to do with the fact that it was mid-March, less than a month before training began and they obviously still had positions to fill. However tour operators do hire reps as late as May or June to help out with the extra workload of high season. Six or seven months is a long time to stay in one place. One of the reasons I stuck it out to the end was so I'd get my £100 deposit refunded. As a rep my wages were about £300 per month on top of accommodation. The youngest full-time rep was an 18 year old who had just finished a college course in Tourism, and at the other end of the scale, one of my colleagues was 28 and had resigned from her position at an advertising agency to work in the sun for a bit.

The season is usually a long one, from Easter until October. Most major tour companies do not seriously expect applicants to speak Greek, though a smattering certainly helps when wanting to explain to a Greek villa owner that the plumbing needs repairing. You can also avoid the mistake Rhiannon Bryant made in a Cretan resort, of greeting everyone 'psari' which means fish during the first week of her job. At the least, job-seekers should familiarise themselves with the Greek alphabet.

Many members of the Association of Independent Tour Operators specialise in Greece. Various indexes indicate to which islands each company sends clients, from Crete to 'very small remote islands'. However these companies may need to take only a couple of seasonal staff, and so can afford to be choosy and in some cases insist on a knowledge of Greek. One source of information about tour operators that support the sustainable development of the areas to which they send holidaymakers is Friends of the Ionian (www.foi.org.uk) an organisation sponsored by British tour operators worried about the impact of tourism on the Ionian islands of Levkas, Zakinthos, Kefalonia, etc.

Up-market tour operators often look for guides with a good classical education. Although these tours will pick up excellent local Greek guides for visits to classical sites, the tour manager will be expected to discuss everything from Homer's *Iliad* to Byron's poetry (since Byron went to Greece to fight the Turks) to the controversy currently raging about whether or not the Parthenon Marbles removed by Lord Elgin in the 19th century should be returned by the British Museum. Many American student and college tours visit Greece, though the level of sophistication may not be so high on these, as one guide points out:

All I needed to know was where to find ice cold Coca Cola especially as our tour was a cheapie and the coach didn't have air-conditioning.

High-season transfer reps are recruited locally in resorts where the number of arrivals is too high for full-time reps to accompany each coachful. Most transfer reps meet night flights. At the beginning of the season, companies are quite selective but as the drop-out rate is high, they sometimes become desperate, perhaps desperate enough to offer a free end-of-season flight. Initially, you must present yourself as someone who is well-groomed, sober and reliable. The pay is usually equivalent to about £20 per night, and you might get two or three per week.

According to Nicky Brown who did this for a UK tour operator on Rhodes:
In theory the job of seeing a coachload of passengers into their accommodation sounded easy. But sometimes it was a nightmare if the self-catering apartments had been wrongly numbered, double booked, occupied by passing drunks, locked and the key lost, not cleaned, trashed, unlit, not what the customer expected or any combination of the above. The driver will certainly not have had enough sleep and may be a danger on the road, rude, unco-operative, lecherous, violent, stupid or any combination of the above. (Your customers may be likewise.) I tried without success to find out whether I was insured to be driven at high speed without a seat belt in clapped-out coaches full of beer monsters driven by bug-eyed xenophobic misogynists around narrow mountain roads in the middle of the night. I suspect the answer was no.

GREEK EMPLOYERS

Working for a Greek company can be a hazardous enterprise because the contract you sign before the job starts may be worth very little once you arrive at the site. Cases have been reported of reps travelling all the way to Athens, only to be disappointed with the hours and wages they were expected to accept. With this in mind, if you are considering working for a local company, make sure the contract is legitimate and, if possible, try to talk to previous employees for reassurance.

It is sometimes worth checking the Situations Vacant column of the English daily *Athens News* (9 Christou Lada, 102 37 Athens; 210-333 3404/8; an-classified@dolnet.gr). You can check the classified ads on the internet (www.athensnews.gr). Travel agencies in Athens may be willing to take on an assistant even if they do not know Greek. Ana Güemes from Mexico always carries her diploma from the tourism course she had completed at home and on the strength of that was offered a summer job in the travel agency attached to the Athens hostel in which she was staying (Hostel Lozanni, 54 Kapodistriu Str., Vathis Square). Without tourism training, Rhiannon Bryant spent the season working in a Cretan resort travel agency, on the strength of having spent several previous seasons there doing less elevated jobs (see section on Casual Work below).

Largely because of his ability to speak some Greek, Jerry Graham was hired several years ago by a Greek tour operator as an excursion guide in Aghia Galini (southern Crete). In a typical week he did three excursions, one of which was an overnight trip to the Samaria Gorge, and one or two days in the office. Although he didn't receive commissions (which was what kept guides working for British tour operators solvent), he did earn generous tips. The experience did not leave him with a very favourable impression of Greek tour operator bosses:

> *Without wanting to get into racist stereotypes it is important to be flexible, since your average Greek tour operator runs on an emotional rollercoaster which, depending on the state of business, means you can be treated anywhere from the best thing since sliced bread to something you would scrape off the underside of a shoe.*

Jerry went on to say that his boss asked him not to point out defects (apart from life-threatening ones) in cars that were being hired, hotels or restaurants on excursion routes, etc., all of which has been made illegal under EU-wide regulations. The money was generally poor, though Jerry did receive lots of perks including free food and drink, reduced car hire on days off and free Greek lessons.

JOBS AT SEA

Flotilla sailing companies like *Sunsail* cater for Germans, Swiss, Austrians, and Scandinavians as well as Britons, so European languages are an advantage. Hostesses, cooks and other crew are sometimes taken on by skippering brokers and yacht agencies around Piraeus. The specialist tour operator *Setsail Holidays* recruits a similar range of staff for the full seven-month season in the eastern Med. Sailing Holidays Ltd (105 Mount Pleasant Road, London NW10 3EH; 020-8459 8787; www.sailingholidays.com) hire flotilla skippers and hostesses, boat builders and marine engineers for their upmarket holiday programme in the Greek and Dalmatian islands. On a more homely level, a couple of marine guides are employed in the summer for boat excursions run by an English-speaking couple who run Unique Excursions (Nidri Travel, P.O. Box 6710, Levkas 31100; 26450-93116; enquiries@uniqueexcursions.com).

English companies such as Camper & Nicholson prefer to hire English speakers, as do many local firms. One large brokerage firm to try is Yachting Greece Ltd (12 Lekka Street, Athens 10562; 210-3233057; info@yachtingreece.gr). This can also be fixed up in any island marina after meeting the right people.

The numerous cruise ships that ply the Aegean Sea are occasionally looking for personnel to replace people who have left their jobs. Phone numbers of the relevant companies can be obtained from travel agents or in the Yellow Pages under *Krouazieres*. A number of cruise lines have shipping offices along the docks in Piraeus on Akti Miaouli e.g. Epirotiki at number 87 (www.epirotiki.gr), Dolphin Hellas at 71 (www.dolphin-hellas.gr), Festival at 99 (www.festivalcruises.com) and Fantasy Cruises at number 95.

FREELANCE WORK

Foreigners (especially women) may also be hired on-the-spot in tourist resorts to deliver cars for car rental firms or to act as transfer couriers. Xuela Edwards and her companion Nicky Brown went to the package resort of Lindos on Rhodes in April and were offered several jobs on the first day. They worked as tour guides on day-trips from the village and also did airport transfers for British tour companies. They found this work by asking around at those local travel agencies which acted as the headquarters for overseas reps. According to Xuela this work requires that you be 'presentable, reliable, able to work all night and get up very early in the morning'. When Debbie Harrison was repping on Kos, they were so desperate for more transfer reps that they attempted to recruit their customers.

Bear in mind that guides who take responsibility for a group must have the correct insurance cover.

CASUAL WORK

Casual work in bars and tavernas is available almost exclusively to women for the wrong reasons. Word of mouth and the direct approach are the only effective ways to find work in Greece. Anyone who looks for work at the beginning of the season (from early May) should be able to find an opening somewhere. A good time to look is just before the Orthodox Easter when the locals are beginning to gear up for the season. If you do fix up a job that early, you will have to be prepared to support yourself until the job starts. There is very little work outside the May to September period although, in a few cases, a bar or restaurant may let you stay on a commission-only basis.

Most foreigners are employed in American/European style cocktail bars and other places frequented by a tourist clientele, though jobs in cafés patronised by locals are not

" *Late each night the Saloon doors would Swing open and the local cowboys would step in, twirling their moustaches and shooting up the toilet* "

an impossibility as Rhiannon Bryant discovered in Crete:

> *I was the only bar girl in Paleohóra who enjoyed working at the Jam Bar; all the others had left within a month. The only customers were Greek men, no English-speaking modern types, just local 'cowboys'. Late each night, the cowboy saloon doors would swing open and in they'd step, always in a group with synchronised movements. The right foot, a twiddle of their moustaches, then the left foot, followed by a flick of their worry beads, their pockets bulging with pistols and bullets. I was fascinated. The Cretan music would drive them to a frenzy, smashing bottles, glasses and on one occasion, a guy was so excited he shot the toilet. The atmosphere was explosive. If I wasn't dodging bullets and glass, I'd stare mesmerised. Actually one of them became my boyfriend. Beneath their macho exteriors they are very kind-hearted, gentle guys.*

Women travellers will find it much easier than men to land a casual job in a bar or restaurant. As one disgruntled male traveller wrote to us:

> *In general I would say that if you're a girl you have a 50% better chance of finding work in the tourist industry abroad. In Greece I would say women have a 500% better chance. Every pub I went into on Corfu seemed to have an English barmaid.*

Alison Cooper describes the transience she experienced working in the tourist industry:

> *I spent the summer on the island of Ios doing the typical touristy work: waitressing, touting, dishwashing, etc. It was very common to have worked at four different places in a week due to being sacked for not flirting with your boss, but I had a great time partying all night and sunbathing all day long.*

If men are finding it difficult to find a service job, they may find taverna-owners willing to hire them as washers-up or roof menders. Some men are needed to build, paint or clean villas and hotels. In populous resorts, men are hired to unload trucks of supplies (crates of soft drinks, Retsina, etc.) for the cafés.

EMPLOYMENT AGENCIES

Athens agencies which place young people in tourism jobs do not generally enjoy a good reputation. Jane McNally visited the agencies in search of work and offers the following warnings:

> *I've come across some very dodgy agencies which ask for applicants' passports and hold them as security while they go off on a wild goose chase for a job. They have also been known to promise the same job on an island to more than one person. Never pay an agency fee before you leave for the job. If they are unwilling to negotiate taking the money out of your first month's salary, do a vanishing act. Instead of leaving your passport, leave some less important document like an old student card. Women should never accept a job outside Athens unless they have enough money to flee if they have to. Agencies sometimes send girls to seemingly safe waitressing jobs which turn out to be as 'company girls' in sleazy bars.*

HOSTELS

The competition for business among hostels and cheap pensions is so intense that many hostel owners employ travellers to persuade new arrivals to stay at their hostel. In exchange for meeting the relevant boat, train or bus, 'runners' receive a bed and a small commission for every 'catch.' The work is tough and people don't usually stick at it for long. Well established hostel runners can also earn kickbacks for giving tourists advice, i.e. recommending certain bars, nightclubs and restaurants. Apparently some employers reward good runners with island-hopping passes or even free plane tickets when the season finishes.

A great many hostels offer a free bed, pocket money and in some cases meals to people who will spend a few hours a day cleaning. Many enjoy the hostel atmosphere and the camaraderie among hostel workers, and they regard the job as a useful stop-gap while travel plans are formulated, often based on the advice of fellow travellers. Those who stick at it for any length of time may find themselves 'promoted' to reception; in this business a fortnight might qualify you for the honour of being a long-term employee.

WORKING CONDITIONS

Anyone working in the Greek tourist industry will soon come across problems in the infrastructure, especially on the islands. In some cases airport services are woefully inadequate and leave weary tourists who have arrived in the middle of the night waiting hours for a run-down baggage system to deliver their luggage, only to be faced with a coach and ferry journey of five hours or more to their resort. Representatives often have to work very long shifts on changeover day due to the long transfer times and airport problems. Michelle, who worked for Manos Holidays (now part of MyTravel), claims that it was not unusual to start work at 8am, finish at 6pm in time to shower, change and pick up last week's guests for an airport transfer. All being well, she was back in her resort by 4am the next morning, but sometimes not until nearer 9.30am when it was time to attend a welcome meeting.

The Greek infrastructure is not always sufficiently robust in other respects to deal with the pressures put on it by the mass invasion of tourists. Camilla Lambert enjoyed her job as a bar manageress with Sunsail in Levkas except when the fridge, freezer and ice machine all packed up in a heatwave and she had to take the brunt of the guests' fury while trying to rouse someone to come and repair the faulty machinery.

As a rep 'your' villas and apartments are often located in different villages; the normal mode of transport is a bicycle or moped. (Make sure you have a crash helmet. With some tour operators it is a dismissable offence not to wear one, even if the locals scoff.) One advantage of working for a large tour operator is that you are unlikely to be posted to a small island where you will be very isolated (unless you speak fluent Greek). The disadvantage is that you will be expected to sell, sell, sell excursions. The commission is often pooled, so if you don't make the target you may incur the censure of your colleagues. Something else reps dread is the client assessment forms distributed by certain tour operators.

Some women find the legendary attention paid by prowling male Greeks intolerable; others have said this unwanted admiration is not unduly difficult to handle. Once you have established your reputation (one way or the other) you will be treated accordingly, at least by the regulars. But still, you might not want to undertake the sort of job Sharon Inge found in Khania's bars sitting around outside to attract tourists and American soldiers inside. When Nicola Sarjeant's bar at Perissa Beach on Santorini was quiet, she was expected to liven things up by dancing, to which she said 'No thanks'.

Always insist on getting paid at the end of each day's work, so no misunderstandings can arise. Laura O'Connor describes the difficulty she had with her employer on Mykonos:

The only problem was in getting our money. It's like blood out of a stone. When you go for your money there's no one around, or you wait ages then they say 'tomorrow, tomorrow'. Well, we finally got our money but not as much as promised. You haven't a leg to stand on. They'll pay if you stand up to them, especially if you are a woman since they are so shocked.

Stephen Psallidas agrees. He describes his life as a waiter on Mykonos as idyllic but did not relish the constant attempts to rip him off. His advice is to stand up for yourself from the beginning since any weakness will be exploited. He was not prepared to act in the unprofessional way his boss expected, i.e. to present 'fiddled' bills to customers and he would not stand for his tips being pinched. He recommends threatening to leave and, if necessary, carrying out the threat, as much for the sake of working travellers who come along next.

> **Safra Wightman was delighted at how easily she found work on Naxos:**
> *Finally I cashed my last travellers cheque and headed for the largest of the Cycladic islands, Naxos, to find a job. The numerous bars, cafés and tavernas seemed quite daunting at first. I decided to be choosy and approach only the places which appealed to me. I strolled the* paralia *and a café caught my eye. I marched up to a Greek guy standing in the doorway and asked him if he had a job for me. He simply said yes and I started work that evening. The Greeks appreciate a direct approach. They are kind, welcoming, generous people.*

Working in heavily touristed areas can leave you feeling jaded. Scott Corcoran describes Kavos in the south of Corfu as a 'nightmare resort town full of northerners drinking Newcastle brown ale and eating chip butties' but since it has 200 bars and restaurants there is plenty of employment. The 1,000-bedded Pink Palace on Corfu (066-53103) has been described as a cross between a Club Med for backpackers and an American summer camp, though others have reported that in the crowded high season, brawls and trouble erupt almost nightly. The hostel employs an army of foreign workers as bartenders, cooks, receptionists, etc. Michel Falardeau, a more mature traveller from Quebec, picked up work there even though November is the quiet season, and found that the wage was not much (less than €10 a day) and everybody spent their money partying.

Other possibilities for work on Corfu are the Club Barbati and the yachting centre Gouvia near Corfu town. On Paros, there are jobs in the main town of Parikia and also in the quieter town of Naoussa where the season is shorter, accommodation less expensive and wages higher. The Sani Beach Holiday Resort on the Halkidiki peninsula near Thessaloniki (www.saniresort.gr) employs a large number of trained staff and also hospitality industry trainees for a minimum of five months on what they describe as a 'training wage' (63077 Kassandra, Halkidiki; 23740-31231; hrdsa@saniresort.gr). Elsewhere on the same peninsula Philoxenia have recently been advertising abroad for summer staff for their 4-star hotel (Hotels Pefkohori, Halkidiki; tel/fax 23740-61657; info@philoxenia-hotel.gr). Further south in the Aegean, a seaside hotel on Lesbos, Hotel Vatera, wants to hire mature staff for their restaurant and cafeteria (www.vaterabeach.gr).

REGULATIONS

When EU nationals stay in any member country longer than three months, they are supposed to apply for a residence permit at least three weeks before that period expires.

To get a residence permit in Greece, take your passport, a letter from your employer and a medical certificate issued by a state hospital to the local police station. The bureaucratic procedures are still fairly sluggish and frustrating and some working travellers continue to find it easier to pop over a border and re-enter on another three-month tourist visa. Be careful not to stay longer than the three months or you risk a hefty fine when leaving; Debbie Harrison from Australia was fined the equivalent of €150 when she left Greece after her season as a rep extended beyond three months.

Non-EU nationals who find employment are supposed to have a 'letter of hire' sent to them in their home countries. In its desire to conform to EU policies, the Greek government has increased the fines for illegal workers while guilty employers are liable to jail sentences. Yet so much of the work undertaken in Greece (including by Greeks) is done 'black', many casual workers encounter no problems, in many cases with the full knowledge of the local police.

DIRECTORY REFERENCES

Most of the major tour operators have large contingents of reps in Greece. See the following entries in the Directory: Openwide International, Airtours/MyTravel, Club Cantabrica, Cosmos, CV Travel, Greek Islands Club, Mark Warner, Olympic Holidays, Setsail, Skyros Holiday Centre, Sunsail, Sunvil, Tapestry.

Ireland

According to figures published by Bord Failte (the Irish Tourist Board) the number of overseas visitors increased by 7% to almost 6 million and is predicted to rise to 10 million by 2012. The Irish tourism and hospitality industry provides an estimated 200,000 jobs nationwide. Over the past 12 years, the number of tourism businesses operating in the country has increased by nearly 50% creating massive employment possibilities. Gone are the days when Ireland was the poor cousin in the European Union. Wages and the cost of living are now among the highest in Europe.

Southern Ireland has always managed to maintain a very high tourism profile, particularly in North America, and tourism has been a mainstay of its economy. A new departure is the increased attractiveness of Northern Ireland in the current political climate. Many new jobs have been created in both Northern and Southern Ireland since the Good Friday Agreement marked a turning point in the political life of the island. Tourism Ireland (www.tourismireland.com) is now 'the official tourism website for the island of Ireland'. These moves towards marketing the island jointly can only result in an overall increase of the number of arrivals. To service this increase, a lot of investment will be needed, especially in providing accommodation in Belfast and throughout Northern Ireland.

PROSPECTS FOR WORK

Ireland is most famed for its unspoiled scenery and lack of urban bustle and development. Consequently many companies organise holidays that take advantage of Ireland's rural charms, perhaps with a bird-watching or botanical theme, or for people who fish, ride, cycle or golf. Self-catering holidays are very popular and are readily available from companies like Shamrock Cottages (13 Clifford Terrace, Wellington, Somerset TA21 8PQ). Unfortunately such holidays do not create much employment.

The beautiful scenery is undoubtedly a great attraction, but what Ireland is most appreciated for by many visitors is the friendliness of the Irish people whom they meet. Anyone who comes from outside to work will find that they have a hard act to follow. But because of the very low level of unemployment (less than 5%), vacancies can be found throughout the hospitality industry. In fact according to the National Tourism Development Agency, 8,000 vacancies were reported unfilled at the beginning of 2004.

A great many UK companies take accompanied tours to Ireland and anyone with some tour managing experience can try to get taken on as a tour director by a company like *Insight Vacations* or *Trafalgar Tours*. The websites of Tourism Ireland (www.tourismireland.com) and of the Belfast Visitor & Convention Bureau (www.gotobelfast.com) both have links to many British, American and international tour operators. The standard brochure from the Irish Tourist Board contains a list of British tour operators offering tours of Ireland. In addition to the mainstream coach tour operators like Thomson Breakaways, Shearings, Travelsphere and Saga, the following offer the best chance of employment:

12Travel, Castletownshend, County Cork (028-36008)

Applebys Super Coach Holidays, Lincolnshire (01507 357900; www.applebyscoaches. co.uk)

Cresta Holidays, Cheshire (cresta@crestaholidays.co.uk)

DA Coach & Study Tours Ltd., Williamton House, Low Causeway, Culross, Fife KY12 8HL (01383 414422; holidays@datours.co.uk)

Excelsior Holidays, Bournemouth (01202 309555)

Grand UK Holidays, Aldwych House, Bethel St, Norwich, Norfolk (01603 630803)

Whytes Coach Tours, Aberdeen (01651 862211; www.whytescoachtours.co.uk)

Yorks Tours & Holidays, Northampton (www.yorkstravel.com)

The concentration of tour coaches is so high at peak times following the same narrow roads to the same destinations (especially the Ring of Kerry) that it is essential to liaise with coach drivers working for other companies when planning the day's itinerary. Normally the level of co-operation is high with drivers agreeing times among themselves so that their groups can see castles, shop and have meals in comfort rather than have to queue because another coach has arrived at the same time.

American tours, especially student groups, employ a large number of UK-hired guides who meet the group at Heathrow, accompany them round Britain on the milk-run, cross from Fishguard to Ireland, tour Ireland, then leave on one of the northern ferry routes to Scotland. French, German, Belgian and Dutch groups are also a possible source of guiding opportunities. The ferry companies, especially Stena Line, have done a major marketing exercise to encourage continental tour operators to bring their coaches to Ireland by ferry. The giant German crane-manufacturing company Liebherr has built and converted hotels in southern Ireland suitable for such tour groups. Note that the ferry operators and airlines also act as tour operators offering coach and special interest tours, including:

Aer Lingus Holidays, 83 Staines Rd, Hounslow, Middlesex TW3 3JB (www.aerlingus.ie)

Irish Ferries, Ground Floor, Corn Exchange Building, Brunswick St, Liverpool L2 7TP (08705 171717; www.irishferries.co.uk)

Stena Holidays, Charter House, Park Street, Ashford, Kent TN24 8EX (01233 747474; www.stenaline.co.uk)

Ireland is a popular country for conferences. With the Belfast Waterfront Hall able to host major conferences, there are even more opportunities.

SPECIAL INTEREST TOURS

The superb lakes and rivers found throughout Ireland, including Lough Neagh in Northern

Ireland, the largest lake in Britain, are meccas for fishermen and boat enthusiasts (and their families). The following companies organise specialist angling holidays in southern Ireland:

Anglers Abroad, 45 Rectory Rd, Duckmanton, Chesterfield, Derbyshire S44 5JQ (01246 240836; info@anglersabroad.co.uk)

Angler's World Holidays, 46 Knifesmithgate, Chesterfield, Derbyshire S40 1RQ (01246 221717; www.anglersworld.co.uk)

Cliff Smarts Angling Holidays, The Coach House, 90g High Street, Burton Latimer, Northants. NN15 5LA (01536 725453; irish.ways@virgin.net)

Kings Angling Holidays, 27 Minster Way, Hornchurch, Essex RM11 3TH (01708 453043)

Leisure Angling Breaks, 33 Dovedale Road, Liverpool L18 5EP (0151-734 2344)

There are supposed to be more golf courses per head of population in Ireland than anywhere else in the world, so there are jobs to be found on these, especially at the times of the big tournaments. Golf holiday specialists are worth approaching by people who are involved in the sport, such as 3D Golf (www.3dgolf.co.uk) and A Golfing Experience (admin@agolfing-experience.co.uk).

Every time there is a famous horse race in Ireland, hordes of Britons fly over to attend. Some of these go in incentive travel groups, others are organised by pubs, social clubs and local coach companies who often need tour guides; watch your local press.

ACTIVITY HOLIDAYS

Experienced trek leaders and instructors may be needed by riding stables and watersports centres throughout Ireland. Anyone with experience of horses might have success by contacting stables, riding holiday centres or equestrian recruitment agencies. For example monitors and instructors are needed mainly for children at Errislannan Manor Connemara Pony Stud, Clifden, Co. Galway 095-21134; www.connemara.net/Errislannan-Manor) where pony trek leaders are needed for the summer; the minimum stay is three months and applications must be made before March)

Monitors and instructors are needed for children's activity centres, for example the holidays run by *PGL.* Children's adventure centres are a good bet for summer employment; try for example Delphi Adventure Holidays (Church Buildings, Church Lane, Main St, Rathfarnham, Dublin 14; www.delphiadventureholidays.ie) which has an adventure centre in Southwest Mayo (353-954 2336) employing many seasonal staff.

HOTELS & CATERING

The Irish employment service (FAS) recommends its website www.jobsireland.com which carries a database of existing job vacancies in the hospitality industry. Outside Dublin, the largest demand is in the southwestern counties of Cork and Kerry, especially the towns of Killarney (with well over 100 pubs) and Tralee. Vacancies are sometimes registered through EURES, for example hotel jobs paying about €250 a week plus accommodation were on offer at the time of writing to waiting staff with at least one year's experience. Write to the addresses in any guide to hotels in Ireland. When applying, you should mention any musical talent you have, since pubs and hotels may be glad to have a barman who can occasionally entertain at the piano. Directly approaching campsites, cafés, holiday centres, etc. is usually more effective than writing. Two hundred thousand people a year visit the Aillwee Cave in County Clare; the company which manages the attraction recruits seasonal guides and support staff (Aillwee Cave Co. Ltd., Ballyvaughan, Co. Clare; 065-707 7036; www.aillweecave.ie).

The Anglo-Continental Placements Agency in England (see entry) places staff, from experienced chefs to inexperienced kitchen porters, in Irish hotels. They will register anyone with an appropriate visa or Europeans with a reasonable knowledge of English.

Another specialist hospitality recruiter is the Anglo-Irish company Action Recruitment Europe with offices in London, Dublin and headquarters in Yorkshire (175 Dalton Lane, Dalton Parva, South Yorkshire S8 0GF; 0870 085 2028; www.hotjobsonline.co.uk).

The website www.irishjobsearch.com is a free up-to-date register of people looking for work in Ireland's hospitality and leisure industry. Kitchen staff, housekeepers, waiters, receptionists, office staff and gardeners are all needed for a minimum of two months.

DUBLIN

The economic renaissance of Ireland's capital has been staggering and employment opportunities in its buzzing leisure industry abound. Try the trendy spots in Temple Bar in the city centre. Writing from Dublin, the American Dan Eldridge found the city to be a land of opportunity:

> *Restaurant and pub work is still exploding in Dublin especially in Temple Bar but also north of the river on and around Grafton Street, basically anywhere you see people. For travellers who can't stand the idea of working in a pub, try the youth hostel in Temple Bar. The manager actually offered to sponsor me for a working visa for a year.*

NORTH AMERICAN JOB-SEEKERS

US nationals who can prove Irish ancestry may be eligible for unrestricted entry to Ireland and even Irish nationality (which would confer all EU rights). Enquiries should be directed to the relevant Irish Embassy or Consulate.

Full-time North American students in tertiary education or recent graduates are eligible to apply for an 'Exchange Visitor Programme Work Permit'. For American students the permit is valid for up to four months at any time of the year and for Canadians the limit is 12 months. CIEE (www.ciee.org) administer the programme in the US; and SWAP/ Travelcuts (45 Charles Street East, Suite 100, Toronto, Ontario M4Y 1S2; www.swap.ca) administer it in Canada.

Once in Ireland, the student travel service Usit Now (19-21 Aston Quay, O'Connell Bridge, Dublin 2; 01-602 1777; www.usitnow.ie) will advise on job opportunities. If you visit the Usit Now office on the south side of the River Liffey, you can inspect a large notice board with many Jobs Available notices, including for bar and café staff.

Fáilte Ireland (the Irish Tourist Board) encourages links with international organisations and educational institutes abroad to enable hospitality and tourism students experience a period of work placement in Ireland. Fáilte Ireland even runs its own placement scheme for qualified candidates normally for six months to a year (info@failteireland.ie).

WORKING CONDITIONS

Mig Urquhart from Glasgow has variously worked in an Irish hostel, bed and breakfast and for the boat taxi on the River Liffey patronised by tourists, school groups and commuters. According to her, 'Irish time' is a wonderful concept when one is doing the work, but when one is waiting for something to be finished it can be frustrating. Nevertheless she hopes that it will never disappear because it beats the uptight stressed out life in other countries where she has worked, like the United States. She goes on to point out one important exception: 'pubs have some of the best trained and fastest barmen in the world, who take great pride in their profession'.

A longstanding problem for tour guides is the resentment they encounter from coach drivers. Before European Union regulations held sway, Irish coach drivers were used to being the courier and guide as well: the roads were nearly empty and the passengers invariably fell in love with the wit and charm of their drivers. As has been mentioned elsewhere, driver-guiding is now officially banned in the EU, creating more jobs for trained guides. Note that the Irish government tourist board's training courses previously provided by CERT (88-95 Amiens St, Dublin 1; 1-855 6555; training@failteireland.ie) include excellent vocational courses in guiding, etc.

FESTIVALS AND SPECIAL EVENTS

There are innumerable festivals throughout Ireland, mostly during the summer. Big-name bands often perform at concerts near Dublin. The 'Rose of Tralee' is a large regional festival held in Tralee, Co. Kerry in the first week of September that provides various kinds of employment for enterprising workers.

DIRECTORY REFERENCES

See the following entries for companies which operate in Ireland: AA Appointments, Anglo Continental Placements, jobs.ie, Kingsbrook USA, Bike Riders, European Waterways, Expo Garden Tours, Saga Holidays and Trafalgar Tours.

Italy

Italy is the favourite country of many people working in tourism. It has good food and wine, fantastic scenery and culture and the Italians go out of their way to welcome visitors. The country is a collection of states which have been unified for a scant hundred years, of Romans, Venetians, Florentines and so on. The regional and cultural differences add to the interest and excitement of working in Italy.

Italy's tourist industry employs between 6% and 7% of the Italian workforce and on the whole is rather protectionist. There are difficulties working for a UK tour company due to legal restrictions on the hiring of non-Italian staff. Most foreign tourists head for the major cities – Florence, Rome, Venice, Pisa and so on – where there is a ready supply of well-trained, impeccably dressed and trilingual guides to look after the tourists. Some foreign companies do employ foreign staff by finding a loophole in the rules, e.g. calling themselves 'art and cultural associations.'

Even casual jobs in hospitality are difficult to land. Anyone who has had the pleasure of dining out in Italy or even buying 200 grams of cheese at a delicatessen will know that Italian standards of service are very professional and indeed people (usually men) consider waiting on tables as a career. Any openings for casual bar staff that come along are likely to be in (for example) Irish themed pubs or American-style bistros. It is also difficult

Tour managers taking groups to Italy should have a recognised qualification and carry a copy of their certificate translated into Italian and certified by the local Italian consulate. Tour managers without this documentation have been unceremoniously hauled off coaches and landed with steep fines.

PROSPECTS FOR WORK

There are tourism jobs to suit everyone, from meet and greet staff working at the major airports and ports, tour guides for coach tours of culture vultures, ski reps for school groups, reps looking after young groups holidaying on the Adriatic and older groups taking in the Italian lakes and cities, incentive tour managers at glamorous resorts like the Costa Smeralda in Sardinia and so on. Areas of the country hitherto unexplored to British tourists are being opened up by the new no-frills airline routes, e.g. Ryanair flies to Pescara, Trieste, Ancona and Bari, though so far these mainly appeal to independent travellers rather than package tourists.

British coach operators need tour guides to take groups around Italy, either by coach from Britain or flying to an airport in Switzerland or Italy, picking up their coach and then touring. The UK is the main marketplace for obtaining jobs with coach companies touring Italy. American students come over in large numbers each year to visit Italy, and many of the companies handling their travel have their European offices in London. British coach companies offer every kind of tour to Italy, from the cheap and cheerful based on one or two centres, to upmarket tours around the cultural high spots.

Most of the potential work opportunities are found in the northern half of the country, between the alpine borders and Rome. The south is poorer with high unemployment and is not as easy to visit as the north with its excellent communications with the rest of Europe. The relatively low unemployment in the Veneto region (which includes Venice, Padua and Verona) makes it a better bet than some of the other tourist regions of Italy such as the Adriatic coastal resorts of Rimini and Pescara and the Italian Riviera (Portofino, San Remo, etc.), though it may be worth trying resorts on Lake Maggiore like Stresa and Cannero. Michael Cullen worked in three hotels around Como and Bellagio and found 'a nice friendly and warm atmosphere, despite the heat and long hours'. High unemployment together with a huge population of migrant workers from poor countries in the south of Italy means that it is probably not worth trying the resorts south of Naples, viz. Capri, Sorrento and Amalfi. Even in flourishing resorts like Rimini, there seems to be nearly enough locals and Italian students to fill most of the jobs. As Stephen Venner observed, 'Although prospects appeared to be good in Rimini, café and hotel owners were unwilling to take on foreigners because of the paperwork.'

Although less well known than the seaside resorts of other Mediterranean countries, there may be seaside possibilities for foreign job-seekers, especially in the resorts near Venice, as a local resident Lara Giavi confirms. She is familiar with two holiday regions: the Lake Garda resorts like Desenzano, Malcesine, Sirmione and Riva del Garda; and the seaside resorts near Venice like Lido di Jesolo (which she says is a great resort for young people), Bibione, Lignano, Caorle and Chioggia, all of which are more popular with German and Austrian tourists than Britons so a knowledge of German would be a good selling point. Lara thinks that there are opportunities for foreigners in catering, bars and hotels in Italy, though she admits that a knowledge of Italian is necessary in most cases, apart from the job of *donna ai piani* (chambermaid).

One campsite that caters to British holiday makers is Union Lido (Il Parco delle Vacanze, 30013 Cavallino, Venezia; 04-257 5111) which has a 'Job Centre' icon on its English-language website www.unionlido.it.

FINDING A JOB

Most major British tour operators have programmes to Italy, and if you want to work in the winter they offer summer staff first pick of winter sports jobs. Italian-owned tour operator *Citalia* accepts Italian-speaking staff in the UK, as do the following operators, in addition to the ones included in the Directory (listed at the end of this chapter):

ICT (Independent Coach Travel), Studios 20-21, Colmans Wharf, 45 Morris Road, London E14 6PA (020-7538 4627; info@ictsqt.co.uk)

Italiatour, 71 Lower Rd, Kenley, Surrey CR8 5NH (0870 733 3000; www.italiatours.co.uk). Part of the Alitalia group.

Magic of Italy, now part of TUI, Greater London House, Hampstead Road, London NW1

7SD (020-7506 8598)

Sunvil Holidays, Upper Square, Old Isleworth, Middlesex TW7 7BJ (020-8758 4722; discovery@sunvil.co.uk)

Carefree Italy, Allied Dunbar House, East Park, Crawley, West Sussex RH10 6AJ (01293 552277; italy@carefreetravelgroup.com)

Ciao Travel Ltd, 76 New Bond St, London W1S 1RX UK (www.ciaotravel.co.uk)

If you can stand the pace, are young, footloose and fancy-free, there are jobs as shuttle hosts and hostesses taking groups by coach to Italy. Try *Cosmos* or any of the major coach companies. If you are less young, a more sedate pace might be preferable, working on Inghams and Saga mountains and lakes tours where the temperatures are cooler.

Contiki's coach tours for an 18-35 clientele spend some time in Italy, and staff are needed for their stopovers (e.g. Florence, Venice, Rome). Without knowing much about the company or the job she was applying for, Carolyn Edwards was interviewed by Contiki (Wells House, 15 Elmfield Road, Bromley, Kent BR1 1LS; www.contiki.com/jobs.asp) and in her first season was employed as a general assistant at their Florence stopover site (a haunted villa). The job involved everything from cleaning toilets to delivering the welcome spiel. Carolyn soon discovered that she loved standing in front of 53 people talking about the local sites.

The major camping tour operators like Eurocamp and Italian Life Holidays trading under Camping Life (see Introduction and Directory of Tour Operators) employ courier/reps and children's reps on their Italian sites, for which an ability to speak some Italian is a basic requirement. Many of these sites are on the Adriatic coast between Catolica and Rimini. Job-seekers who turn up at the gates on the off-chance of work might find some employment though at local casual rates without commission and perhaps without accommodation. Catherine Dawes enjoyed working for a UK camping tour operator near Albenga on the Italian Riviera – 'a fairly uninspiring part of Italy' – even more than she did her previous summer's work on a French campsite. In her view the Italians seem more relaxed than the French, especially under high season pressure, and would always go out of their way to help her when she was trying to translate tourists' problems to the mechanic or the doctor.

G & D Gruppo Vacanze (Via del Portonaccio 1, 47100 Forlì; 0543 26199; www.gedgruppovacanze.com) run holiday camps for which they need European young people to work as counsellors and instructors of sports, dancing, music and theatre. Pay starts at €430 per month in addition to free board and accommodation. Try also Anderson srl (Via Tevere 44, 00198 Rome; fax 06-884 4664; animazione@andersonclub.it) who hire about 100 young people for their holiday villages and tour operations.

The Alitalia Group actively recruits candidates who need not speak Italian but must have other relevant qualifications. Applications should be sent to Alitalia's Recruitment Department, Viale Alessandro Marchetti 111, 00148 Rome (www.alitalia.it/en/know/humanres/working/working.htm). EU nationals can try using official channels to find work at the beginning of the season (mid-May), i.e. the *Ufficio di Collocamento* and the local *Associazione Albergatori* (hotels association) which should know of vacancies among its members. Try to track down local hotel associations or hotel chains, for example the following along the Adriatic:

Alberghi Consorziatai, 61032 Fano (0721-827376)
Associazione Albergatori di Rimini, Viale Baldini 14, 47037 Rimini (fax 0541-56519)
Associazione Pesarese Albergatori, 61100 Pesaro (0721-67959)
Associazione Balneare Azienda Turismo – 0733-811600
Associazione Bagnini di Numana e Sirolo, 60026 Numana Ancona (0721-827376).

The Blu Hotels chain has hotels and holiday villages in Lake Garda, Sardinia, Umbria, Abruzzo, Tuscany, Rome, Palinuro and Calabria (as well as Austria); the head office is at

Via Porto Portese 22, 25010 San Felice di Benaco (Brescia); 0365-441100. The website – www.bluhotels.it – carries information (in Italian) on applying to work for the group. Another group of three hotels on Lago d'Orta has in the past hired kitchen and waiting staff (www.lagodortahotels.com).

SPECIAL INTEREST TOURS

Anyone with a degree in history, history of art, archaeology or any subject related to Italian culture may be able to find work with upmarket firms like Exodus, Explore or Inntravel (Nr. Castle Howard, York YO60 7JU; www.inntravel.co.uk) who run exclusive walking tours throughout Italy from the Amalfi coast to the Dolomites including of course the Tuscan hills. Groups often go to Rome and the Vatican on pilgrimages; your local church may have some leads. Two companies which specialise in pilgrimages to Rome (and elsewhere) are Tangney Tours (Pilgrim House, 3 Station Court, Borough Green, Kent TN15 8AF; 01732 886666; info@tangney-tours.com) and Mancunia Travel (International House, 82-84 Deansgate, Manchester M3 2ER; 0161-834 4030; info@mancunia.com).

Operators that sometimes require tour leaders with specialist knowledge and tour guides to look after their groups include:

ATG Footloose (see entry). Wild flowers, mushroom hunting, walking and cycling.

Arblaster & Clarke Wine Tours Ltd, Farnham Road, West Liss, Hants. GU33 6JQ (01730 893344; www.winetours.co.uk/ac-careers.html). Wine tours of Tuscany, Umbria, Piedmont and Veneto.

Headwater – see entry.

Voyages Jules Verne, 21 Dorset Square, London NW1 6QG (020-7616 1000; www.vjv.co.uk). Art and culture tours.

ON THE SPOT

Once you get a toehold in an Italian community you will find that a friendly network of contacts and possible employers will develop. Without contacts, it is virtually impossible to find work. Arriving in Diano Marina on the Ligurian coast to look for work, Bernie Lynes went to church on her first Sunday. The local grapevine decided she was a 'nice' girl, and she was soon offered a job with a tour operator whose rep had fallen sick.

Local sightseeing companies may need meet and greet staff; their leaflets are often displayed at tourist offices, hotels and airports. This often requires 6am pickups from hotels for a long day tour such as the Capri tour from Rome, or to meet early flights. Anyone who knows Japanese might be hired to meet the very early arrivals from Japan since local staff prefer to start work at a more civilised hour. Meet and greet staff hired locally are generally paid around €40 per transfer.

Charter yachts may need experienced sailors as crew. Harbour masters along the Adriatic coast, Italian Riviera and in Sardinia can tell you if there are yachts looking for crew.

WINTER RESORTS

Opportunities exist on-the-spot in the winter resorts of the Alps, Dolomites and Apennines. Many of the jobs are part-time and not very well paid, but provide time for skiing and in many cases a free pass to the ski-lifts for the season. Sauze d'Oulx and Courmayeur seem to be the best resorts for job hunting. Although Cortina is probably the most famous, it has a high percentage of year-round workers, and is too sophisticated and expensive. Sauze d'Oulx is particularly recommended because it hosts so many British holidaymakers that every bar and shop in the resort likes to hire an English speaker. Remember that places like this will be dead before the season. If you are job-hunting in November, choose a weekend rather than a weekday to catch some businesses open. It doesn't always work of course. Susanna Macmillan gave up her job hunt in the Italian Alps after two weeks when she had to admit that her non-existent Italian and just passable French were not getting her anywhere.

PGL Ski Holidays offer reps' jobs and instructor positions to BASI-qualified skiers, whose airfare to the resort is provided and whose salary is between £100 and £150 per week. As in other alpine resorts there are also jobs for chalet staff, though not as many as in neighbouring countries due to the very strict regulations which govern chalets in Italy.

Dog sledding is the fastest growing team sport in the Alps, with good facilities in the Trentino region. Resorts such as Madonna Di Camiglio and Passo Di Tonale have excellent dog kennels and facilities, with several teams in each resort. One of the top sledders is Armen Khatchikian who runs the Scuola Italiana Sleddog Progres (Località Case Sparse 10, 25056 Ponte di Legno (BS); info@scuolaitalianasleddog.it) and who always has two or three assistants for the season. These kennels are very small and cannot handle many enquiries from job-seekers, so if you are serious about working with the dogs, track down other kennels through the local tourist office.

CASUAL WORK

Large hotels usually recruit their staff in southern Italy and then move them en masse from the sea to the mountains in the autumn. Relatively few students and others find work serving pizzas or cleaning hotel rooms in Italy compared to other European countries, but there are cheering exceptions to the rule. Dominic Fitzgibbon from Australia spent six weeks unsuccessfully looking for a job which used up a large proportion of his travel fund. But the landlady of the flat he was renting off the magnificent Piazza Navona took a shine to him, and arranged for him to work as a night porter for one of her friends who owned a 3-star hotel off Piazza Barberina, although he had 'no work permit and practically no Italian':

When I told my landlady that perhaps I would head off to Greece, she said I was far too nice to look for dishwashing work and told me about a friend who needed help running his seasonal hotel. Within 20 minutes I was behind the counter having the telephone system explained to me and was told I would be paid a modest monthly wage for working six nights a week as a night porter. After praying the telephone wouldn't ring for the first few weeks (since I spoke virtually no Italian), everything settled down. It's quiet, a little boring, but allows me to read and study Italian, more than the few key words related to the hotel trade I knew before. My boss is even going to lend me a TV to help me improve my Italian. I now know how lucky I was to find my place and this job.

Another success was reported by Carolyn Edwards who had the advantage of having spent the summer season in Florence with Contiki. At the end of the season in October she got a job in an American-style bar in Florence called the Red Garter at Via de 'Benci 33. She worked here for four months with barely enough Italian to get by. Unlike many people in jobs like this she was legal, at least for three days of the week, when she netted the equivalent of £30 for five hours work. If she worked any extra evenings, she was paid cash.

As throughout the world, backpackers' haunts often employ travellers for short periods. Jill Weseman recommends trying the Fawlty Towers hostel at Via Magenta 39, 00184 Rome; 06-445 0374) near the Termini Station in Rome where she noticed several Antipodeans working in reception, maintenance and cleaning. Raised in New York and

largely cut off from her family's Italian roots, at age 30 Debra Fuccio decided to spend
some time in Italy.

> **By making use of www.hostels.com Debra had little difficulty pre-arranging
> a hostel job:**
> *Never in a million years did I think that watching MTV would be part of my daily
> life in Rome, Italy. But it was. I was working at a really cute, small hostel in Rome
> during April 2002. The hostel was Hostel Casanova (Via Ottorino Lazzarini, 12,
> 00136 Rome; 06-397 45228; hostelcasanova@yahoo.com). I was working 7 days
> a week (since I was a bit scared about running out of money since this was the
> first leg of the trip). The shifts would alternate from evening to morning everyday:
> one day doing the morning shift when the hostel was cleaned and the next day
> the evening shift. As well as getting to stay there for free, they paid me and my
> co-worker €20 per day in cash which was really nice. Rome was so cheap (from a
> San Francisco point of view) and with great weather, it was easy to save.*

CONDITIONS OF WORK

Tourism staff are generally treated extremely well and the industry is well regulated.
Italian employers are obliged to comply with the *Contratto Nazionale del Lavoro il
Turismo* (1999) which is a daunting 347 pages long all in Italian of course.

Hotels and restaurants usually provide tour guides and managers with the best rooms
and anything they want to eat and (within reason) drink. Groups are welcomed at shops
with gifts and treated very well. For example coaches arriving in Venice are met by a
team of public relations staff from the major glass factories. Once you tell them which
one your clients will be visiting, the company takes care of luggage and boat transport,
confirms the guide and takes you for a drink.

Pay and commission for experienced tour guides is very good. Most British coach and
tour companies offer up to £100 a day to experienced guides. Generally perks like free
coffee and drinks, taxis if you work early or late and a chance to see the best operas, etc.
flow freely, which makes up for the long hours. Tour guides should try to work for a
company that has air-conditioned coaches. The heat can easily reach more than 100°F in
high summer and sightseeing trips are often scheduled for the middle of the day.

Women don't normally have too many problems with the legendary Italian male. Once
employed, you are looked upon as an honorary cousin which can mean the locals keep a
watchful eye on you.

REGULATIONS

Unfortunately there are more red tape hassles in Italy than there are in other EU countries.
Many job-seekers have found Italians reluctant to consider hiring them because of the
bureaucratic hurdles which must be jumped. Even if working for an established tour
operator who knows the ropes, it will take about four months to get the paperwork in
order. Be prepared to be given the run-around and for delays in the processing.

If you arrive with the intention of working, you must first apply to the police *(questura)*
for a *Ricevuta di Segnalazione di Soggiorno* which allows you to stay for up to three
months looking for work. Upon production of this document and a letter from an
employer, you must go back to the police to obtain a residence permit – *Permesso di
Soggiorno*. Then in some cases you will be asked to apply for a *Libretto di Lavoro* (work
registration card) from the town hall or *Municipio,* although this should not be necessary

for EU nationals. Roberta Wedge recalls the red tape:

I had to visit three different government offices about eight times in total. Not exactly the free movement of labour! My health card arrived six months after the wheels were set in motion.

People working in the food and beverage departments of hotels will have to obtain a *Libretto sanitario* after having a free medical check-up at the local *Unita sanitaria locale* or USL.

As mentioned above, Italy is very strict about qualifications in the tourist industry. Local guides have to take a stringent course and do not welcome unqualified people taking their work. It is not unknown for a policeman to stop a foreign touring coach and order the non-Italian tour manager out of their seat if they are found giving a commentary on the mike. Italy may be part of the EU but try explaining that to the policeman who thinks you are taking work away from his cousin the guide. Make sure your company has booked a local official guide for city sightseeing, who are excellent and very helpful if there are problems in the height of the season. In general it is advisable for reps to pay a courtesy call on the local police station.

Work permits for non-EU nationals will be issued only to people outside Italy and only for jobs where the Provincial Office of the Ministry of Labour is satisfied that no Italian can do the job. The *Autorizzazione al Lavoro* must then be presented at the Italian Embassy in the applicant's home country. In other words, they are virtually impossible to obtain except for elite jobs.

DIRECTORY REFERENCES

For travel companies which operate in Italy, see entries for the following: Acorn Venture, ATG-Oxford, Bike Riders, Bolero International Holidays, Camping Life, Canvas, Casterbridge Tours, Ciclismo Classico, Citalia, Club Cantabrica, Contiki, CV Travel, Duvine Adventures, Equity, Esprit, Eurocamp, Expo Garden Tours, First Choice, Handmade Holidays, Haven Europe, Headwater, Inghams, Keycamp, King's Camps, Magic of Italy, Mark Warner, Neilson, Shearings, Total Holidays, Travelsphere, Venue Holidays.

Malta

Although small in area (30km by 15km), Malta has a flourishing year-round tourist industry. With its sister islands of Gozo and Comino, Malta hosts package tours in summer from throughout Europe (especially Britain, Scandinavia and Italy). In winter many elderly North Europeans go for an extended stay and in spring and autumn the conference season brings in high-spending visitors. Some go to Gozo, which tends to be more exclusive than the main island. Malta is not such a popular destination for families (because the beaches are rocky or sparse) so children's reps are not much in demand. Also, very few North American groups find their way to Malta.

It is a surprise to many visitors that these islands have some of the oldest archaeological sites in the world. But most people visit the islands for the climate. From the time St Paul was shipwrecked here about 60AD, the Maltese have welcomed visitors, despite having suffered incredible hardships from invaders throughout their history. The Ministry of

Tourism has been encouraging Maltese hotels to upgrade, in an attempt to attract a more mature clientele who visit for the history as much as for the sun.

In 2003 the people of Malta voted in a referendum to join the European Union in 2004, though there may be a time lag of up to seven years before employment rights become reciprocal.

Working conditions are generally good for tour operator reps working in Malta. Everyone speaks English as well as their native Maltese (a language with Arabic/Semitic origins). Among the general population, the quality of education is high, and the standard of hotel and tour administration is correspondingly good (arguably better than the standard of driving; most buses have a little shrine over the driver's compartment).

Although Malta has successfully been sold as a winter sun destination, the weather does not always live up to the promises in the brochures. So any reps working the winter season should be sure to have a warm coat and wellies (for when the roads are flooded by heavy rains) and also plenty of sunny smiles to cheer up disgruntled clients.

FINDING A JOB

Most major tour operators go to Malta, especially those catering for the older market. The Maltese government is helping hotels to upgrade and modernise, which will mean better facilities for conferences. Many incentive companies send clients to Malta, so there is work with British, Scandinavian and German companies for freelancers who go out with clients.

The Education and Training Corporation (ETC) of Malta runs an excellent online database of vacancies on www.etc.org.mt. Vacancies for chamber, kitchen and laundry staff are often posted and also higher level tourism jobs. For example one vacancy posted at the time of writing (2004) was on behalf of the Malta Tourism Authority (229 Triq Il-Merkanti, Valletta CMR02; 2291 5141; info@visitmalta.com).

Professional hotel staff may seek work in key players in Malta's hospitality industry like the Tumas Group which owns and operates the New Dolmen Hotel, Topaz Hotel, Halland Hotel and Mgarr Hotel in Gozo. It also owns the Hilton Hotel which forms part of Portomaso, a new waterfront development, also owned by the Group. Information about the human resources needs of the company may be found at www.tumas.com/job.htm and applications can be sent to the Head Office, Triq Il-Gifen, Bugibba SPB 03 (paul@tumas.com.mt).

Another hotel group with frequent vacancies is the Island Hotels Group with its HQ in Salina Bay (jobopportunities@islandhotels.com). It employs more than 800 people for its hotel and outside catering operations. This whole coastline is awash with resort hotels with ongoing recruitment needs, like the Hotel Santana and Hotel Sunflower. Locally owned Ta'Cenc in Gozo and the Corinthia group with five luxury resort hotels in Malta are among other possibilities; check the latter's website (www.corinthiahotels.com/people_careers.asp).

The student and youth travel organisation NSTS (220 St Paul St, Valletta VLT 07; 2124 6628/fax 2123 0330; nsts@nsts.org) markets English courses in conjunction with sports holidays for young tourists to Malta. NSTS run weekly vacation courses from June to August, for which they may need experienced instructors for windsurfing and other sports, as well as general catering staff.

Of the special interest holiday companies which go to Malta, ones offering scuba diving and other water sports are the most popular. For special interest and general tour operators to Malta check the links from the tourist board's website www.visitmalta.com which includes the following:

Gozo Holidays, 122 South Rd, Haywards Heath, West Sussex RH16 4LT (01444 254954;

info@gozoholidays.co.uk). Feature diving and walking as well as general touring.

Just Malta, 363a Crofton Rd, Orpington, Kent BR6 8NR (info@ctcwwt.co.uk).

Oonasdivers, 30 Church Street Old Town, Eastbourne, E. Sussex BN21 1HS (tel/fax 01323 648 924; info@oonasdivers.com). Diving holidays in Malta and Gozo.

Sunspot Tours Ltd, The Hill, Cranbrook, Kent TN17 3ST (01580 715222). Conferences and incentives, culinary tours, diving, etc.

Zenna Holidays, 118 South Ealing Rd, London W5 4QJ (0870 755 0395; fax 020 8566 1985; zenna@etsworld.com)

The Malta Youth Hostels Association (17 Triq Tal-Borg, Pawla PLA 06; +356 2169 3957; myha@keyworld.net) can put volunteers aged between 16 and 30 to work for three hours a day over a short period. A longer-term commitment of full-time work over 6, 9 or 12 months is open to EU nationals only aged 18-25 who will receive free room and board. Jobs to be done include administration, decorating, building, etc. MYHA obtains work permits for participants, a process that takes many months for long-term volunteers who should submit an application six months before they intend to go to Malta.

ON-THE-SPOT

Tourism plays such a large part in the island's economy that it may be possible to get a job on the spot. Try cafés, bars, hotels and shops in Sliema, Bugibba and beach resorts in the south. Although Robin Gray was in Malta to enjoy a holiday rather than to work, he met a number of people who were working in tourist establishments, some of whom had set up their jobs ahead of time by writing to prospective employers. Wages are far from high. Once you have connections it becomes easier to find work.

The Netherlands

The word Netherlands means low lands. The two most famous provinces are North and South Holland; when sailors from the ports of Amsterdam and Rotterdam were asked where they came from, they would give the name of their province, hence the rest of the world refers to the country as Holland.

The Netherlands is a major intercontinental gateway into Europe, particularly for groups of Americans, South Africans and people from the old Dutch colonies in Asia and South America. For such a small country, it has a high profile in tourism terms. Several mega coach companies operate huge fleets of air-conditioned coaches servicing the incoming visitors to Europe, so this is a country that is a jumping-off place for tours and for finding tour management work. More immediately, the bulb fields between Leiden and Haarlem attract an enormous number of coach tours in April and May when the flowers are in bloom, and this is a standby of any tour guide's annual calendar.

The tourism infrastructure is very sophisticated. The Dutch government recognises that tourism is an important industry and ensures that there is good access to sights, good signposting and a high standard of cleanliness and efficiency in hotels, hostels and restaurants. World class exhibition and conference venues draw in business visitors, and museums and galleries provide the framework for cultural tours. Large family theme parks, notably Efteling run their own training programme for new employees.

Any prospective employees from outside the country have to compete with people who speak more languages per head of population than any other (with the possible exception of the Swiss). Asking a Dutch person whether or not they speak English is almost tantamount to hinting that they lack a good education. German is widely spoken, although there is still some resistance with memories of the last war.

PROSPECTS FOR WORK

Although groups arriving in Amsterdam on intercontinental flights pick up their coaches at Schiphol (pronounced Skipple) Airport for their round-Europe tour, many of the companies that organise these tours are based in London, so London-based tour managers are competing on an equal footing with Dutch staff. There is a need for speakers of Japanese, Chinese and other Asiatic languages, with no requirement to speak Dutch.

Most job opportunities will be found in the twin commercial capitals of Amsterdam and Rotterdam, rather than the capital Den Haag (The Hague). In Amsterdam the giant RAI exhibition and conference hall complex hosts many of the world's major international exhibitions and conferences, with consequent demand for suitable staff and a knock-on effect for tours, etc. Hotel groups such as the NH Group (www.nh-hotels.com), Marriott and Hilton have facilities for hundreds of delegates, with similar venues in Rotterdam. However if you want to work in the hotels and catering industry, it is imperative to speak several languages or have professional training, unless you are prepared to take the lowliest jobs (see section on Casual Work below).

For leads on special interest tour operators check the Dutch tourist office site www.visitholland.com with a search facility. Cycling is the classic way to see the country, because of the Netherlands' famous network of cycle tracks and its undaunting terrain. Many Dutch companies offer bike tours for example Cycletours (020-521 8480; info@cycletours.nl) and Yellow Bike (020-620 6940). British tour operator Anglo Dutch Sports is now part of *HF Holidays* which run cycling, walking and sightseeing tours to Holland.

Although the hotel boats that ply the Rhine are mostly German-registered, many start in Rotterdam or Amsterdam where they are sometimes looking to recruit cabin crew and entertainers. English is the major language, but it helps if you speak German.

A little known opportunity for people who can communicate in German or Dutch is to work on one of the 250 *Platbodems,* traditional sailing boats that cruise the waters of Ijsselmeer and Waddensea off the north coast of the Netherlands in spring, summer and autumn. They cater mainly to school groups and are staffed by a skipper and one mate *(maat)* one of whose jobs is to offer simple instruction to the guests though he or she must also help the skipper on watch, carry out repairs and so on. Even without any background in sailing, Felix Fernandez was offered ten jobs after adding his CV to the databank *(vacature bank)* of job-seekers and ended up working the summer season on the two-masted ship *Citore*:

> *Skippers who are looking for maats can get the data about interested people from the data bank. I didn't have sailing experience before. The first week of sailing was a nightmare because of my lack of experience but I got through and now there is no problem. It is normal to work seven days a week with one day off a month. You have to be prepared to work around 70 hours a week. Having little privacy is also something one has to get used to. Nevertheless there are many advantages of the job and I met a lot of people who have returned for several seasons.*

The company that owns *Citore* is Hanzestad Compagnie, Bataviahaven 1, Postbus 300, 8200 AH Lelystad (0320-292 100; www.hanzestad.com in Dutch only).

FINDING A JOB

Tourism professionals might start by contacting a specialist hospitality recruitment and executive search agency, Courtesy Masters International

(Van Vollenhovenstraat 27, 3016 BG Rotterdam; 010-265 4327; www.courtesymasters.nl). Their website is in English as well as Dutch. If you are in the Netherlands it is worthwhile visiting the state employment service, Directoraat Generaal de Arbeidsvoorziening at Volmerlaan 1, Rijswijk ZH or any local Arbeidsbureau. To find the local address, look up *Gewestelijk Arbeids Bureau* in the local telephone directory. There is a special division of the employment service for university graduates, the Bureau Arbeidsvoorziening Academici, Visseringlaan 26, Postbus 5814, 2280 HV Rijswijk.

There is not much point looking out for ads in newspapers such as *De Telegraaf, De Volkskrant* or *Algemeen Dagblad* unless you are a Dutch speaker. Elite guide training (comparable to Blue Badge training) takes place in winter in the major towns of Amsterdam, Rotterdam, Utrecht, etc. For details contact the Dutch professional guides' association Guidor, Postbox 261, 1110 AG Diemen-Zuid/Wildenborch 6, 1112 CB Diemen-Zuid (020-624 6072; www.guidor.nl).

Because of its proximity to Britain, many school orchestras and other musical tours head for Holland each year. Try Gower Tours (2 High St, Studley, Warwickshire B80 7HJ; 01527 851410).

Centerparcs started in Holland and their recruitment of staff is carried out by the individual centres. The rising interest in green tourism has led to the rapid growth of Landal GreenParks which provide bungalow and camping holidays in the Dutch and German market. The majority of these holiday accommodation parks are dotted around the Netherlands with a sprinkling in Belgium, Germany and Austria. The company employs 2,500 people; more information can be obtained by ringing the Personnel Office in the Hague on 070-300 3560 or by emailing pz@landal.nl.

CONFERENCES AND EXHIBITIONS

For details and addresses of organisers of forthcoming conferences and conventions, contact the Amsterdam Tourism & Convention Bureau, Postbus 3901, 1001 AS Amsterdam (020-551 2570/fax 020-551 2575; info@atcb.nl/ www.amsterdamcongres s.nl) or in Rotterdam the Doelen (Postbus 972, 3000 AZ Rotterdam; 010-217 1700) or the Rotterdam Congress Bureau (010-405 4444; www.wtcrotterdam.nl) or Utrecht Fair (030-295 5911; www.jaarbeursutrecht.com).

Two major conference organisers are: Congrex, AJ Ernstraat 595K, 1082 LD Amsterdam (020-504 0200; www.congrex.com) and Eurocongres Conference Management, Jan van Goyenkade 11, 1075 HP Amsterdam (020-679 3411; www.eurocongres.com).

For details of exhibitions and the companies which are organising them, contact Amsterdam RAI, Europaplein 822, 1078 GZ Amsterdam (020-549 1212; www.rai.nl).

Some Dutch incentive conference organisers and tour operators include:

Arke Reisen, part of TUI (www.arke.nl)

Arttra, Staalstraat 28, 1011 JM Amsterdam (020-625 9303; info@arttra.nl) which specialises in art tours.

Beuk Travel, Incoming Department, Singel 259, 1012 WG Amsterdam (020-662 6322; www.beuktouringcars.nl)

Evenements Reizen – www.er-travelgroup.nl

ITB, Olympisch Stadion 14, 1076 DE Amsterdam (020-305 1350; www.itbamsterdam.nl)

Keytours, Dam 19, 1012 JS Amsterdam (020-623 5051; www.keytours.nl)

Lindbergh Excursions, Damrak 26, 1012 LJ Amsterdam (020-622 2766)

NBBS, Postbus 281, 2910 AG Nieuwerkerk a/d Ijssel (info@nbbs.nl). Field study tours.

Holland International, Postbus 157, 2280 AD Rijswijk. Part of TUI (www.tui.nl).

CASUAL WORK

Dutch hotels and other tourist establishments employ a large number of foreign workers both full time and temporarily during the tourist season. Most are from southern Europe, but a certain number are from Britain and Ireland. As usual, foreigners are the last to be hired and the first to be fired, so do not expect job security in a hotel job. Although you may be lucky enough to obtain a hotel job through an *uitzendbureau* (described below), your chances will normally be better if you visit hotels and ask if any work is available.

Adam Skuse almost succeeded in finding hotel work but not quite:

> *One very useful resource I found was the website www.visitholland.com, where I got a list of hotels and then systematically emailed them all asking for a job. Most had no vacancies, a couple told me to call them when I was in Amsterdam, and one actually arranged an interview with me. But even the knockbacks were pleasant. Quite a few offered to buy me a drink anyway.*

PRIVATE EMPLOYMENT AGENCIES

The majority of employers turn to private employment agencies (*uitzendbureaux* – pronounced and meaning 'out-send') for temporary workers, partly to avoid the complicated paperwork of hiring a foreigner directly. Therefore they can be a very useful source of temporary work in Holland. They proliferate in large towns, for example there are over 233 in Amsterdam alone.

Look up *Uitzendbureau* in the telephone directory or the *Gouden Gids* (Yellow Pages; www.goudengids.nl) and find out which ones deal with hospitality vacancies. One agency that specialises in the hotel and catering industry is JMW (www.horeca-uitzendbureau.nl) with branches in many Dutch cities. An on-line specialist recruitment database can be found at www.horecajobs.nl. Schiphol Airport's catering division often hires casual workers mainly through Amsterdam *uitzendbureaux*. Try the employment agency Adecco at the airport (020-316 3040) or indeed anywhere in Amsterdam, such as the branch on Rokin in central Amsterdam.

Among the largest *uitzendbureaux* are Randstad with about 300 branches (www.randstad.nl), Unique (www.uniquemls.com), Manpower (www.manpower.nl), Creyf's Interim, Vedior (www.vedior.nl) and Tempo Team (www.tempoteam.nl) though most of their vacancies are in business and industry.

REGULATIONS

If you intend to stay for more than three months, the first step is to acquire a sticker in your passport from the local aliens police (*Vreemdelingenpolitie*) or Town Hall, normally over-the-counter. They will expect you to provide a local address which should be used throughout your stay. The passport should then be taken to the local tax office to apply for a *sofinummer* or *'sofi'* (social/fiscal number). In Amsterdam go to the big black building outside the train station in Sloterdijk. It is also possible to apply for a *sofi* from outside the Netherlands, though this will take at least six weeks; send a copy of your passport details to Belastingdienst Particulieren/Ondernemingen Buitenland, Postbus 2865, 6401 DH Heerlen; 045-577 9100 (www.belastingdienst.nl).

DIRECTORY REFERENCES

For travel companies which operate in the Netherlands, see entries for the following: HR International, Canvas, Eurocamp, European Waterways, Expo Garden Tours, Keycamp, Travelsphere, Village Camps.

Portugal

Britain's oldest ally is a beautiful and relatively unspoilt country. Because of is situation on the furthest side of the Iberian peninsula where the sea water is colder than the Mediterranean, it has not been mobbed to the same extent as Spain, apart from the Algarve coast between Faro and Lagos which is lined with tower blocks. Other areas of Portugal such as Lisbon, Oporto and the north attract a more upmarket clientele. Hotels tend to be luxurious and self-catering villas have their own swimming pools and maids. None of the major UK camping tour operators includes Portuguese sites, partly because of the great distance for motorists.

Although Portugal's economy is reasonably healthy and the rate of unemployment among the lowest in Europe, wages are very low. The minimum wage in Portugal is €406 per month, the lowest in Europe (compared to €1,124 in Britain and France). Chances of finding work are best with tour operators or in hotels, restaurants and clubs along the Algarve coast. Portugal had a bonanza year because of the football tournament Euro 2004 taking place in eight Portuguese cities. As is commonplace at high profile international sporting events like the Olympics, the people who work on-site are normally doing so on a voluntary basis for the thrill of being part of the action. But the ancillary jobs of serving food and drink to the visiting throngs falls to paid workers.

PROSPECTS FOR WORK

Many visitors return year after year to their own villas or a resort they know well, which means that it is not easy to find jobs as these people know the country and don't need anyone to look after them. Furthermore many of the local people speak excellent English, so there are limited jobs available.

As in Italy, the Portuguese are protective of their tourist industry and this has been formalised in law. For example foreign tour managers in charge of a coach must ensure that they pick up an official Portuguese guide at major tourist venues.

FINDING A JOB

The mass-market beach resort operators (e.g. *Thomson, MyTravel, CT2* and *First Choice*) employ reps in Portugal. *Style Holidays* and *Open Holidays* both employ resort reps every year to work between April and October. Part-season short-term contracts may also be available. First Choice have about 100 staff in place who speak another language (not necessarily Portuguese). Apart from these and some of the Europe-wide tour operators like Driveline Europe, Erna Low, Headwater and Solo's, many of the tour operators which feature Portugal are specialists. The founders of the well known Travel Club of Upminster (54 Station Road, Upminster, Essex RM14 2TT; 01708 225000; www.travelclubofupminster.co.uk) virtually started tourism to Portugal from the UK when they fell in love with the country after the war. Occasionally they and other specialist tour operators like Mundi Color (276 Vauxhall Bridge Road, London SW1V 1BE: 020-7828 6021; www.mundicolor.co.uk), Caravela Tours Ltd, (Chapter House, 22 Chapter St, London SW1P 4NP; 020-7630 5148) and Destination Portugal (Madeira House, 37 Corn Street, Witney, Oxon. OX8 7BW; 01993 771555; www.destination-portugal.co.uk) who may need staff, but only if they can speak Portuguese. For links to UK tour operators to Portugal see the website of the Portuguese Trade & Tourism Office (www.portugalinsite.com).

A number of upmarket villa companies employ English staff to oversee the properties. Anyone applying for such a job would have to have a driving licence since the properties are often scattered. Note that these are plum jobs so there is little turnover:

Bonaventure Holidays, 6 Putney Common, London SW15 1HL (www.bonaventure-holidays.com)

Casas Cantabricas, 31 Arbury Road, Cambridge CB4 2JB (01223 328721; www.casas.co.uk)

CV Travel's Mediterranean World, The Manor Stables, West St, Great Somerford, Chippenham, Wilts. SN15 5EH (020-7581 0851; www.cvtravel.net)

Individual Travellers (Spain & Portugal), Manor Courtyard, Bignor, Pulborough, West Sussex RH20 1QD (01798 869485; portugal@indiv-travellers.com)

North Portugal Travel, Foxhill, Gambles Lane, Woodmancote, Cheltenham, Glos. GL52 4PU (01242 679867; www.northportugal.com)

Most tours from Brazil use Lisbon as their gateway to Europe, and people who can

"Visitors to the cellars were more interested in the free tastings than in the history of vini culture"

speak the language and know about European culture may be hired by one of these. One of the biggest is the Portuguese-owned company Abreu Travel (109 Westbourne Grove, London W2 4UW; 020-7229 9905) which handles incoming groups from Brazil.

WINE TOURS

For over 600 years the British have drunk the wines of Portugal, and many companies offer specialist wine tours of the Oporto region. Many of the families that work in this industry are of British ancestry. Henry is lucky enough to be related to one of these families and was delighted to be given a summer job as a guide showing visitors around the wine cellars. Henry soon got used to dealing with visitors who were more interested in the free tastings (even at 10am) than in the history of wine-making. He found it harder to accommodate himself to the fact that he spent most of the day underground instead of in the sunshine. Others who are not cousins of port-makers have found similar jobs. For example one guide fixed up his job when he was working for a well-known wine merchant in Britain and happened to meet a rep from one of the large port companies in the shop. The rep told him that their company often took on keen interested young students. Ask your local wine merchant for the addresses of major wine importing companies for leads.

The Douro River, lined by port wineries, is a hive of activity during the annual September barge event, when the *caravels* glide down the river. To work on these you would need to know both the language and the wine trade. There is also a hotel barge that operates on the river and occasionally needs staff.

OTHER SPECIAL INTEREST TOURS

The lush countryside makes for some wonderful golfing facilities. Anyone who has worked at a golf club in the UK or US might try to work for a specialist operator in this field. Two companies to consider are Longshot Golf Holidays (Meon Travel, Meon House, College St, Petersfield, Hants. GU32 3JN; 0870 609 0995; www.longshotgolf.co.uk) and Supertravel Golf (Sandpiper House, 39 Queen Elizabeth St, London SE1 2BT; 020-7459 2984; golf@lotusgroup.co.uk). Many others can be found via the Association of Golf Tour Operators or AIGTO (www.aigto.com).

Portugal is a highly religious country and many religious pilgrimages are made, especially to the site of Our Lady at Fatima. The enormous piazza in front of the Basilica is said to hold a million people on the two main religious festivals (May 12/13 and October 12/13, the dates of the first and last appearances of the Virgin). Catholic church newspapers carry adverts for companies organising tours. Contact them if you speak Portuguese and want to work as a tour guide.

Walking and nature holiday operators take groups to the National Park of Peneda-Geres in the remote northern Serra da Peneda, e.g. Sherpa Tours (www.sherpa-walking-holidays.co.uk).

ON THE SPOT

There is an estimated population of 12,000 expat Britons in Portugal, a great many of whom run bars, restaurants, bookshops, etc. catering mainly for an Anglophone clientele and therefore staffed by English speakers. The majority of expatriate businesses are small (and therefore have only occasional job vacancies) and located in the Algarve or on the Lisbon coast from Setúbal to Cascais. Entertainers and watersports instructors may find on-the-spot openings. Ask expatriates for help and advice in your search for a job in tourism.

Scan the advertisements in the weekly *Anglo-Portuguese News* (Apartado 113, 2766-902 Estoril; 214-66 1551; apn@mail.telepac.pt) or place your own advert in this paper, though the rates are fairly expensive. The Employment Offered section of *Algarve Resident* (on-line at www.algarveresident.com) does not usually include many useful listings. The four-star Monte do Casal Country House Hotel in Estoi on the Algarve has been seen advertising recently for a receptionist and other staff (Cerro do Lobo, Estoi, 8005-436, Faro, Algarve; 0289-991503; www.montedocasal.pt). Left over from Lisbon World Expo 98, the Frog at Expo (a popular brew pub, part of the French chain of Frog Pubs) employs English speakers as bar and waiting staff year round; applications to frog.lisboa@frogpubs.com.

The thousands of Britons and other Europeans who take their holidays on the Algarve create many job opportunities in bars and restaurants.

According to Emma-Louise Parkes, Albufeira and area is the place to head:
I arrived at Faro Airport in June last year, and went straight to the Montechoro area of Albufeira. A job hunter here will be like a kid in a sweet shop. By 12.15pm I was in the resort, by 12.30pm I had found somewhere to stay and had been offered at least four jobs by the evening, one of which I started at 6pm. All the English workers were really friendly individuals and were a goldmine of information. Jobs-wise, I was offered bar work, touting, waitressing, cleaning, packing ice cubes into bags, karaoke singing, nannying for an English bar owner, timeshare tout, nightclub dancer...I'm sure there were more. Touts can earn £16 a night with all the drink they can stomach while waitresses can expect a little less for working 10am-1pm and 6pm-10pm. Attractive females (like myself!) will be head-hunted by lively bars, whereas British men are seen by the locals as trouble and are usually kept behind bars (serving bars that is) and in cellars.

Finding somewhere to stay can be more difficult than finding employment in some cases. Not surprisingly, accommodation is quite expensive during the high season.

REGULATIONS

Portugal has always had comparatively liberal immigration policies, possibly because it has never been rich enough to attract a lot of foreign job-seekers. As throughout the EU, citizens of the European Union must apply for a residence permit if they intend to stay for more than three months. The usual documents will be needed: proof of accommodation and means of support plus adequate health insurance or proof of paying social security contributions. Wage earners must prove that they are being paid at least the Portuguese minimum monthly wage. The permit should be obtained from the nearest immigration office (*Serviço de Estrangeiros e Fronteiras*). The address of the headquarters of the *Serviço de Estrangeiros* is Rua Conselheiro José Silvestre Ribeiro 4, 1600-007 Lisbon (217-11 50 00), while the regional Lisbon office is at Avenida António Augusto Aguiar 20.

The Consular Section of the British Embassy in Portugal (Rua de S. Bernardo 33, 1249-082 Lisbon; 213 92 40 00) distributes information on taking up residence in Portugal which goes into more detail than the information from the Portuguese Consulate-General in London.

Non-EU nationals must provide the usual battery of documents before they can be granted a residence visa, including a residence visa obtained from the Portuguese Consulate in their home country, a document showing that the Ministry of Labour *(Ministerio do Trabalho)* has approved the job and a medical certificate in Portuguese. The final stage is to take a letter of good conduct provided by the applicant's own embassy to the police for the work and residence permit. There are stories of non-Europeans arranging a residence permit after finding a job on arrival, but this is difficult.

DIRECTORY REFERENCES

For companies which employ staff in Portugal, see Bike Riders, CV Travel, Open Holidays, Scott Dunn, Style Holidays, Travelsphere.

Scandinavia

Scandinavia comprises the countries of Finland, Norway, Sweden, Iceland and Denmark (which includes Greenland). In many areas there is a two-season year for tourists: winter sports from December to March/April and the relatively short summer season June to August. UK coach companies send many tours to Scandinavia, particularly to Norway. Sweden too has been doing well and recorded a steady increase in the number of visitors over recent years, most of them independent tourists and families on self-catering holidays. Although tourism is an important industry in Iceland, few foreigners are employed in it. Scandinavia is popular with student groups, and companies like EF (www.eftours.co.uk) and *ACIS UK* need tour guides (who can cope with constant moans about the high price of drinks).

The standard of living throughout Scandinavia is very high and so are prices, e.g. £4 for a soft drink in a modest café and up to £20 for a simple meal out. A tour guide's standard European wage will not go far in Scandinavia, where it is not the custom as it is elsewhere for restaurants to offer a free meal or complimentary drink. Reputable companies will pay a supplement to take account of the higher cost of living. Commission sales in the rest of Europe usually bump up a guide's salary, but prices are so high in Scandinavia that tour groups tend to choose the tours which include all excursions so there is little chance of making extra. Also clients usually have less money at the end of their holiday for tips than they would in southern Europe.

PROSPECTS FOR WORK

A few UK camping tour operators, notably *Eurocamp,* send clients (and therefore reps) to Denmark, Norway and Sweden. Self-catering and farm holidays are very popular in the region, with visitors escaping to the simple life in a log cabin in the forests or by a lake – idyllic, perhaps, but affording few work opportunities. The relevant country's tourist office can provide a list of campsites which may employ some foreign staff. It helps if you can write to such addresses in the relevant language, but don't worry if you can't find someone to translate for you; the majority of Scandinavians working in the tourist industry speak excellent English.

Winter sports companies in the UK occasionally need reps, though there are still relatively few British ski tour operators active in Scandinavia. Originally best known for cross-country skiing (sometimes called Nordic skiing or *langlauf*), Norway has developed its downhill facilities and resorts like Lillehammer, Oppdal, Geilo and Voss are excellent. Newer resorts like Hemsedal and Trysil are benefitting from huge investment because of fears that global warming in the Alps will in due course harm alpine resorts. Elsewhere in Scandinavia, the skiing is mostly cross-country. Other winter sports are available, including dog sledding. Many incentive companies offer their more adventurous clients the opportunity to take part in a short dog sledding expedition, so anyone who has worked with dogs in Alaska or the Alps should ask the local tourist board for addresses of operators featuring these holidays.

Scandinavian cities offer superb conference venues and facilities and anyone who speaks a Scandinavian language might find administrative work with the main incoming organisers such as Incoming Scandinavia (Box 6148, SE 102 33 Stockholm, Sweden, 08-34 35 05; www.incomingscandinavia.se) which is a destination management company operating throughout Scandinavia (except Iceland).

FINDING A JOB

One of the best opportunities for work is on the giant ferries that criss-cross the North Sea between the UK and Scandinavia. To attract passengers on the long crossings, many of these monster ships offer the same facilities as a cruise ship, so there are jobs in the pursers' department, catering, cabin stewards or croupiers. The two ferry companies are Fjord Line which sails between Newcastle and Stavanger and Bergen in Norway (0191-286 1313; www.fjordline.co.uk) and DFDS which also sails out of Newcastle to Kristiansand and Gothenburg as well as between Harwich and Esbjerg in Denmark. DFDS employs about 3,000 people and provide recruitment information on their website (www.dfdsseaways.co.uk). For jobs onboard, it is necessary to be English-speaking, over 20 and apply to their Danish office (Att: Anette Bech, DFDS A/S, Sundkrogsgade 11, 2100 Copenhagen). It would be more difficult to find work on the Smyril Line (345 900; www.smyril-line.fo) based in the Faroe Islands, which operates between Iceland, the Faroes, Shetland and Bergen in Norway.

Tour operators that feature Scandinavia include:

Arctic Experience, 29 Nork Way, Banstead, Surrey SM7 1PB (01737 214214; enquiries@arctic-experience.co.uk)

Canterbury Travel/Lapland Experience, 42 High St, Northwood, Middlesex HA6 1BL (01923 822 388). Very smart staff needed for day-trips to Lapland, incentives, etc.

DA Tours, Williamton House, Low Causeway, Culross, Fife KY12 8HL (01383 881700; holidays@datours.co.uk). Coach touring holidays in Scandinavia and Europe.

Headwater – see entry. Cross-country skiing holidays in Norway and Sweden.

Inntravel, Nr Castle Howard, York YO60 7JU (01653 617788; www.inntravel.co.uk). Walking, riding, cycling and skiing holidays in Norway.

Scandinavian Holidays, 8 Boreham Holt, Elstree, Herts. WD6 3QF (020-8953 8874; www.scandinavianholidays.org)

Scandinavian Travel Service/Norwegian Coastal Voyage, 3 Shortlands, London W6 8NE (020-8846 2666)

Scantours, 47 Whitcombe Street, Leicester Square, London WC2H 7DH (020-7839 2927; www.scantours.co.uk)

Taber Holidays, 30a Bingley Road, Saltaire, Shipley, West Yorkshire BD18 4RS (01274 594 656; www.taberhols.co.uk). Long-time specialist programmes to Norway and Iceland.

DENMARK

Every year thousands of families head off to the theme park at Legoland near Copenhagen to see fantastic models made out of the famous children's building bricks. A number of large campsites within range service the park and employ the usual range of seasonal staff.

As the centre of the Danish tourist industry as well as the commercial and industrial centre of the country, Copenhagen is as good a place as any to look for work. The Jobcenter in Copenhagen at Kultorvet 17 (33 55 17 14/33 55 10 20) should be able to assist EU nationals with a sought-after skill and a knowledge of Danish. They can do nothing for people who send their CVs. It is also worth looking for jobs door to door in hotels, restaurants and the Tivoli Amusement Park. The highest concentration of restaurants is located from Vesterbros Torv to Amalienborg Slot and from Sø Torvet to Christiansborg Slot. Many of the large hotels have personnel offices at the rear of the hotel which should be visited frequently until a vacancy comes up. The Mercur Hotel has a high turnover of staff and pays from kr80 per hour before tax. Also try the English Pub, the Scottish Pub and Rosie McGee's near Tivoli Gardens. Some job-seekers may have to call only once, as in the case of the Dutch traveller Mirjam Koppelaars:

My Norwegian friend Elise and I rather liked Copenhagen but realised that money was going quick again and decided to try to find some work. After filling in an application form and having a very brief interview at the Sheraton, we both got offered jobs as chambermaids starting the next day. The next five weeks I cleaned 16 rooms and 16 bathrooms a day in a very funny uniform. Although I had to pay over half in tax, I was able to save for more travels.

The attractive Danish countryside also absorbs tourists and people to look after them. Sam and Petra set off to spend the summer in Denmark and found work in the farmhouses that cater for visitors. The barman on the ferry going over told them that his aunt and uncle's farm took in paying guests and recommended they make contact on arrival. When they mentioned the nephew's name, they were greeted like long-lost friends and the aunt phoned all her friends in the farmers' network until they found one who needed two assistants.

FINLAND

Finland has had a long and uneasy association with Russia, one which at last is bringing some benefits to Finland as many tours are now combining Helsinki and St Petersburg, thereby boosting Finland's tourist industry. The Finnish Tourist Boards are actively promoting their country for holidays, especially in the high revenue sectors of conferences and incentive conferences.

Lapland has its special appeal and in fact Levi and Yllas in Lapland are being developed as ski resorts which are now among *Inghams'* top five destinations (out of about 100 in its ski brochure).

Finland offers about 1,800 short-term paid training opportunities to foreign students every year. The International Trainee Exchange programme in Finland is administered by CIMO, the Centre for International Mobility (PO Box 343, 00531 Helsinki, Finland; +358-1080 6767; www.cimo.fi); their website is in English. British tourism students and graduates who want on-the-job training in their field (e.g. tourist offices, travel agencies, hotels, restaurants) should apply directly to CIMO for a placement that will last between one and 18 months. Short-term training takes place between May and September, while long-term training is available year round. Applications for summer positions must be in to CIMO by the middle of February. To qualify for the trainee exchange, you must have studied for at least one year, preferably with a year's related experience as well. Despite the designation 'trainee', wages are on a par with local Finnish wages for the same work.

Applicants in the US should contact the American-Scandinavian Foundation (Exchange Division, 58 Park Avenue, New York, NY 10016; 212-879-9779; www.amscan.org) to find out about traineeships. If successful, work and residence permits are granted for the specific training period offered by a named Finnish employer. Immigration queries can probably be answered by looking at the English language website of the Directorate of Immigration (UVI), PO Box 18, 00581 Helsinki (09-476 5500; www.uvi.fi).

NORWAY

For both winter and summer seasons, you can try to fix up a job by emailing or writing to hotels listed on websites such as www.hotelsinnorway.com which lists 250 properties or in the accommodation brochure available each February from the Norwegian Tourist Office, Charles House, 5-11 Lower Regent St, London SW1Y 4LR (send a 9X6 envelope and 53p in stamps). There is a greater density of hotels in the south of Norway including beach resorts along the south coast around Kristiansand, and inland from the fjords north of Bergen (Geilo, Gol, Vaga, Lillehammer, and in the Hardanger region generally). Remember that even in the height of summer, the mountainous areas can be very chilly. As mentioned, winter resorts like Lillehammer, Nordseter, Susjoen, Gausdal and Voss employ a certain number of foreign workers.

The Norwegian Hotels Association sets wages and deductions for board and lodging, which are revised annually. The starting net monthly wage of an unskilled hotel worker is about 9,000 Norwegian kroner after a deduction for board and lodging. Wages are lower outside the big cities, but the work may be more pleasant. Note that the website www.hotel-jobs.no is only in Norwegian but might provide some leads for experienced hospitality workers.

Norwegian youth hostels have a steady demand for unskilled domestic staff who are willing to accept little more than a living wage. The Norwegian Hiking Association takes on some people to be caretakers at their network of mountain huts, though the only foreigner we have heard of who did this job was studying at the University of Oslo and therefore was on the spot.

If you choose to go job-hunting on spec in Norway, be prepared to pay high prices for food and accommodation while you're looking for work. First do the rounds of the hotels in a resort like Lillehammer where there are about a dozen hotels in the centre of town. Neil Tallantyre, who spent several winter seasons in Lillehammer, found that there is quite a demand for British workers. He has been amazed at the resourcefulness of travellers who have extended their time in ski resorts (primarily to ski), by doing odd jobs like snow clearing and car-cleaning, waitressing and DJing (especially common since the British are thought to know their way around the music scene).

One intriguing avenue to pursue is to work on one of the eleven working ships which cruise the fjords of Norway to the Arctic Circle, known as the *Hurtigruten*. Woden Teachout from Vermont describes how she came close to finding work on this route:

Because the trip under the midnight sun is so luxurious, a lot of staff are needed to pander to the passengers. I called the offices and asked if they needed help; they said to meet the boat in Bergen at the docks and ask the captain. I did this on three successive days and none of the captains wanted help. But they didn't laugh at me (as I'd expected) and in fact were quite encouraging, saying that chances were I'd get something within the week. I imagine the trick is to catch them quite early in the season. I don't know what the wages were but the trip is supposed to be so spectacular that it would be worth doing one 14-day run for nothing. Ask as early in the season as possible.

SWEDEN

A few UK ski tour operators like Thomson Ski, Neilson and Crystal Ski (part of TUI) are beginning to feature Sweden in their brochures but as yet the programmes are relatively small. The principal ski resort is chic Åre in northern Sweden.

It may be worth trying to find work in hotels, usually in the kitchen. The best bets are the large hotels in Stockholm and Göteborg. Elsewhere you might try areas where tourism is well established. Try the Sunshine Coast of western Sweden including the seaside resorts between Malmö and Göteborg, especially Helsingborg, Varberg and Falkenberg. Other popular holiday centres with a large number of hotels include Orebro,

Västeras, Åre, Ostersund, Jönköping and Linköping. The chances of fixing up a hotel job in advance are remote. After writing to dozens of Scandinavian hotels, Dennis Bricault's conclusion was 'Forget Sweden!'.

ICELAND

Iceland has a tiny population of about 250,000 and a low rate of unemployment 5% (January 2004). Demand is great within the tourism industry mainly during the summer, as well as the fish, farming and construction industries. Generally employers wish to hire people for at least three months but preferably 6-12.

There are eight regional Employment Offices in Iceland and the EURES Advisers can be consulted at the main VMH (Jobcentre), Firdi, Fjardarjötu 13-15, 220 Hafnarfjordur (554 7600; eures@svm.is). The VMH website www.vinnuslastofnun.is is in English and links to an application form for English-speaking foreigners. One employer posted vacancies in winter 2003 for 20 hotel staff over the age of 22 willing to spend at least two months in the summer working in country locations around Iceland.

Efforts are concentrated on recruiting workers from other Scandinavian countries primarily through the Nordjobb scheme which arranges summer jobs for Nordic citizens aged 18-25 in other Nordic countries for at least four weeks (www.nordjobb.net).

REGULATIONS

Sweden, Finland and Denmark are fully-fledged members of the EU. The Norwegian people voted against joining in a referendum; however Norway and Iceland are members of the European Economic Area (EEA) which permits the free movement of goods, services and people among the members of the European Union and the two Scandinavian members of the EEA. This means that EEA/EU citizens are now entitled to enter any Scandinavian country for up to three months to look for work. When they find a job and get a 'Confirmation of Employment' from their employer, they can then apply to the police for a residence permit.

In order to work legally, North Americans and others will have to obtain work permits before leaving home, which is very difficult. However, the American-Scandinavian Foundation mentioned above can assist 'self-placed trainees' to fix up a work permit, i.e. those who have fixed up their own job or traineeship in a Scandinavian country.

DIRECTORY REFERENCES

The travel companies listed in the Directory which have operations in Scandinavia include: Cosmos, Eurocamp, Freewheel Holidays, Headwater, Regent Holidays, Top Deck, Travelsphere.

Spain

Spain hosts a staggering 48 million visitors a year including 16.8 million Britons who have been buying second homes and taking advantage of the no frills airfares. The tourist industry employs about 11% of the Spanish population. Of the top ten package holiday destinations for Britons last year, five are Spanish: Majorca, Tenerife, Ibiza, Menorca and the Costa Blanca.

99.9% of visitors go to Spain for the sun, sand, sea, etc. and not for the history or culture. After World War II Spain was ideally placed to offer cheap holidays to the rest of Europe devastated by bombing, and the government support for their tourist industry meant boom times for farmers and fishermen lucky enough to own a few acres of land on one of the Costas. Concrete buildings grew up where once there had been scrubland, and Spain became the playground of Europe. Although not quite so booming as in the late 1980s, the coastal resorts continue to draw hordes of tourists, especially Lloret de Mar, Calella (Costa Brava), Benidorm (Costa Blanca), Torremolinos, Benalmadena, Fuengirola (Costa del Sol), Mojacar (Costa de Almeria) and Ibiza and Palma (Majorca).

First-time reps working for major tour operators, whether British, German or Scandinavian, have a 60% chance of being sent to a Spanish resort. Once, it was easy to find this work, but today competition is tougher and you will need to be able to offer a qualification even to get your first job. At the interview, you probably won't be asked questions about history, culture or language. Instead you will be asked how you would sell an excursion to a sangria evening, Flamenco show or whale-watching trip.

But even if some of these excursions make you cringe, you have to bear in mind that each year millions of satisfied holidaymakers have a wonderful time in Spain and book to return to the same resort and same hotel as soon as they arrive home. They know that the product is excellent value for money. You haven't lived until you have seen 2,000 Britons swaying to Viva España, drinking sangria and having the time of their lives.

The Spanish infrastructure is generally well organised which makes your work much easier. The hotels are of an acceptable standard, the coaches are modern, plus excursions are good value and cater well for the various nationalities. If you do well in your first posting on the Costa Brava, you may be moved mid-season to another country where there are more problems.

An example of the care that tour operators take in maintaining standards was provided by Kim who was given no choice of resort and was sent to Benidorm by a UK tour operator. She flew out a week before the season started and was immediately handed a long list of local contacts to get to know: chemist, police, doctor, clinic, hotels, car hire, windsurf and cycle hire, photo developer, ground handlers, etc. Once she had done that she had to go round the hotels checking everything from swimming pool depth to fire exits, door widths for wheelchairs to height of balconies. By the time the first clients arrived, Kim was already well known in Benidorm.

FINDING A JOB

Most of the British camping tour companies such as *Camping Life, Canvas Holidays, Club Cantabrica, Keycamp Holidays* and *Eurocamp* have sites in Spain. *Haven Europe* needs Spanish-speaking couriers and children's staff to work at mobile home and tent parks from early May to the end of September. If you wanted to work for smaller family businesses try *Harry Shaw City Cruiser Holidays, Solaire Holidays* or *Bolero International Holidays. MyTravel* run self-catering holidays on Spain's foremost holiday islands and provide an extensive children's programme which employ British nannies and animators. Holiday villages often employ English-speakers to serve their clientele. In some cases, a knowledge of German is more useful than Spanish since many holiday establishments cater primarily to the 13.5 million Germans who come to Spain annually.

In addition to these pile-'em-in-cheap packages, a vast array of special interest tours and upmarket villa holidays is available in Spain. For example a number of operators send their clients to *paradores,* a constantly expanding network of government-owned inns, usually in old stately homes or palaces. Companies like the following are sometimes looking for staff who speak good Spanish and know the country:

Headwater – see entry. Cycling, canoeing and hiking holidays.

Individual Travellers (Spain & Portugal), Manor Courtyard, Bignor, Pulborough, West Sussex RH20 1QD (01798 869485; spain@indiv-travellers.com)

Magic of Spain, now part of TUI, Greater London House, Hampstead Road, London NW1 7SD (020-7506 8598)

Mundi Color, 276 Vauxhall Bridge Road, London SW1V 1BE (020-7828 6021; www.mundicolor.co.uk)

Spanish Harbour Holidays Ltd, Field House (3rd Floor), Station Approach, Harlow, Essex CM20 2EW (fax 01279 642891; www.spanish-harbour.co.uk). Part of TUI.

Style Holidays, (see entry in Directory).

Other companies operate upmarket walking tours, wine appreciation tours or trips for pilgrims to Compostella in Galicia. The agency Select Spain in Reading has links to many interesting operators running cycling, hiking, yacht charter or other specialist tours (www.selectspain.com). English-speaking guides for horseback expeditions in Spain may be needed by Inntravel Riding Holidays, (Park St, Hovingham, York YO6 4JZ; 01653 629000) which takes riding tours into the Sierra di Guarda and Andalucia. Another riding holiday company is In the Saddle (01299 272997; rides@inthesaddle.com) which lead rides in the Sierra Nevada, Los Alamos, the Poqueira Valley, Dos Mares and in northern Tenerife.

After arrival in Spain, it is worth checking the English language press for the sits vac column. Many English language magazines and newspapers thrive on tourism and resident expatriates, for example, the *Costa Blanca Post & Mail* in Alicante, the *Costa Blanca News* in Benidorm (www.costablanca-news.com includes employment classifieds), *Lookout Monthly Magazine* in Fuengirola, the *Iberian Daily Sun* in Madrid, the *Majorca Daily Bulletin,* the *Lanzarote Gazette* (www.gazettelive.com) or the *Island Gazette* in Tenerife, which may occasionally carry adverts for chefs, bar staff, etc. It is usually not very expensive to place your own advert. Try also the giveaway weekly *Ibizasun* and *SUR in English* (www.surinenglish.com) which has a large employment section and is used by foreign and local residents throughout southern Spain including Gibraltar. It is published free on Fridays and distributed through supermarkets, bars, travel agencies, etc. If you want to place your own ad, contact the paper at Avenida Doctor Marañón 48, 29009 Malaga (952-264 96 00).

People have successfully found (or created) jobs in highly imaginative ways. One of the most striking examples is a Finnish student who wrote to the address on a Spanish wine label and was astonished to be invited to act as a guide around their winery for the summer. Tommy Karske returned home 'knowing a lot about wine and believing that anything is possible'.

In the vicinity of Barcelona is Salou, site of the theme park Port Aventura at which it might be worth enquiring for seasonal jobs. Universal Studios at Port Aventura employs 3,000 people (fax 977-77 90 97; recursos.humans@portaventura.es).

ACTIVITY HOLIDAYS

Acorn Adventure (22 Worcester St, Stourbridge, West Midlands DY8 1AN; 01384 446057; www.acorn-jobs.co.uk) need seasonal staff for their two watersports and multi activity centres on the Costa Brava. RYA qualified windsurfing and sailing instructors, BCU qualified kayak instructors and SPSA qualified climbing instructors are especially in demand, for the season April/May to September. *PGL* also needs staff for Spanish holiday centres and *TJM Travel* hire qualified instructors and ancillary staff for hotel and activity centres in Spain.

A number of indigenous organisations, including language schools, run summer language and sports camps for children and teenagers which require monitors, animators and instructors. The youth exchange organisation Club RCI (Relaciones Culturales Internacionales, Calle Ferraz 82, 28008 Madrid; 91-541 71 03; spain@clubrci.es) might be worth trying for this although they mainly place native speakers with Spanish families who want to practise their English in exchange for providing room and board.

Sailors from around the world congregate in the hundreds of marinas along the Spanish coast and create some opportunities for employment on yachts. Minorca Sailing Holidays (58 Kew Road, Richmond TW9 2PQ; www.minorcasailing.co.uk) hire nannies and other staff for their sailing centre in the Bay of Fornells in Minorca.

SKI RESORTS

Although Spain is not the first country to come to mind when thinking of skiing, there is a flourishing industry and a few British tour operators like *Thomson* and *First Choice* take skiers to Spanish resorts such as Cerler, La Molina or El Formigal in the Pyrenees. One UK company which has ski chalets in the Spanish resort of Baqueira is *Ski Miquel*. See below for some information about working in ski resorts in Andorra.

CANARY ISLANDS

Almost every large tour operator features the Canaries. Demand for staff is so high that a knowledge of Spanish is not always needed, while those who know Spanish have an excellent chance of finding a company to hire them. Some specialists include: Bonaventure (020 8780 1311; www.bonaventure-holidays.com); Lanzarote Leisure Ltd (020-8449 7441; www.lanzarote-leisure.co.uk); Meon Villas (01730 268411; www.meonvillas.co.uk) and Villanza (01245 262496; holidays@villanza.co.uk).

Although they belong to Spain, the Canaries are situated close to the coast of Africa and therefore have a warm climate year round. They are extremely popular with European tourists, especially Germans, Scandinavians and the British, and offer probably the best employment prospects for anyone starting in the tourism industry.

The seven main islands are remarkably different from each other and attract a different clientele. Tenerife is the Benidorm of the Canaries and most major British operators offer inexpensive holidays, either self-catering or in hotels, to this island. Gran Canaria is much greener than the other islands and attracts more upmarket tourists and 'golden oldies' to its many hotels and self-catering apartments. It is also a popular stop for cruise ships.

Lanzarote has grown at a tremendous rate yet, thanks to the council, its development is reasonably attractive with relatively few high-rise hotels. Lanzarote Villas & Apartments (25 Neptune Court, Brighton Marina, East Sussex BN2 5SL; 01273 819999 or +34 928 524275; www.lanzarote-villas.com) are one of the main specialist companies employing UK staff as reps. Most major tour operators offer holidays in the many self-catering complexes, especially the huge development in the south built by the British company Wimpey and the huge hotel resort centre of La Santa developed for sports-loving holidaymakers. Club La Santa on Lanzarote is a hotel complex with 400 apartments and 25 sports facilities, employing 300 people of many nationalities. Their website (www.clublasanta.com) has information in English for job-seekers; details from Club La Santa, Av. Krogager, 35560 Tinajo, Lanzarote (jobs@clublasanta.com). Applicants must be over 23 and willing to stay for at least nine months.

La Palma has the world's steepest ascent from sea level to mountain top, so the temperature drops sharply within a few minutes. There are a few self-catering complexes and some specialist tour operators feature the island because of its remoteness, but the majority of visitors come ashore on day-trips from cruise ships. Connie is Dutch, speaks

English and German, and is kept busy looking after arriving cruise groups. From her balcony she can see when a ship arrives, whereupon she strolls down to the quayside to welcome the clients and take them on walking tours of the charming town.

With a mainly German clientele, Fuerteventura offers job openings for German-speaking staff. Gomera has no airport so is probably the least spoilt of the islands. Traditionally Christopher Columbus's last stop before his discovery of the New World, it has an old-fashioned atmosphere and is quieter than the others. Finally, El Heirros is a small barren island with not much more than a *paradore* (national hotel).

The busy islands have attracted many entrepreneurs from abroad who wish to cash in on the Canaries' popularity. Like so many others, Peter and Roseanne Grubb were attracted to the climate and decided to settle on Lanzarote. As Peter had worked for one of the major Champagne houses and was an expert on food and wine, everyone expected him to open an upmarket restaurant. But his market research revealed that holidaymakers wanted something less grand. So he opened a fast food outlet on the beach at Puerto Carmen, decorated it with sporting memorabilia he had collected over the years and called it the Sports Bar. Every night the bar is full of young Britons who can't live without their daily fix of fast food and almost-British beer.

CASUAL WORK

It is possible to pick up work in the Canaries during the season (November to March), with Lanzarote and Tenerife providing the best chances. Along the beachfront at Puerto del Carmen in Lanzarote and Playa de las Americas in Tenerife, almost every building is a pizzeria, *hamburgeria,* etc. Just walk along the front until you come to a place whose client language you speak, and go in and ask. If you want to camp while looking for work, you will generally have to use a recognised campsite, as land is scarce and there are not many public places which allow camping.

If you can arrange to visit the Spanish coast in March before most of the budget travellers arrive, you should have a good chance of fixing up a job for the season. The resorts then go dead until late May when the season gets properly underway and there may be jobs available. Bear in mind that while working in these environments you will barely get a glimpse of genuine Spanish culture.

Year-round resorts like Tenerife, Gran Canaria and Lanzarote afford a range of casual work. Nick Crivich, who worked a season as a rep in Tenerife for a subsidiary of Thomson, observed that there were ample opportunities for bar staff, DJs, beach party ticket sellers, timeshare salesmen, etc. in these places and on the islands. Many young people make ends meet by working for a disco or bar as a 'PR' or 'prop', i.e. someone who stands outside trying to entice tourists to come in. Magaluf on Majorca is another busy resort full of English bars like Prince Williams where you can enquire about local jobs. At one time there were many jobs in the tourist industry of Ibiza but recent reports indicate that the only thing available is for young women dancing in clubs.

Although Euro-legislation has limited the kinds of selling techniques used, time share developments (or 'holiday ownership' companies which is the euphemism) continue to market their properties, and the job of OPC ('Offsite Personal Contact') is still around. For this job you have to be prepared to face a lot of rejection.

BALEARICS

A good starting point for finding out about seasonal job vacancies in Ibiza is the website of the Queen Victoria Pub in Santa Eulalia (www.ibizaqueenvictoria.com) which posts jobs and accommodation both on its site and on the pub notice board which anyone can drop by and consult (though it is more polite to buy a drink while consulting the board).

The Queen Vic itself employs a large number of European fun-seekers as well. Two other websites worth checking are www.balearic-jobs.com which covers the Balearic Islands of Ibiza, Mallorca and Minorca, and www.gapwork.com.

WORK EXPERIENCE

The Easy Way Association, C/ Gran Via 80, Planta 10, oficina 1017, 28013 Madrid (91-548 8679; www.easywayspain.com) makes hotel and restaurant placements in and around Madrid and Barcelona (for a placement fee starting at €300). Candidates are aged 18-32 and work as waiters, commis waiters or in fast food restaurants. Accommodation in shared flats can be arranged. The website gives wage ranges for staff, e.g. €602-€783 per month for a full-time waiter in Madrid.

The training organisation ONECO Global Training in Seville (member of the Global Work Experience Association) organises a Tourism in Spanish course and internship programme which lasts three months. It combines an intensive month-long Spanish language course (with an emphasis on Spanish for tourism) with an internship placement in a Spanish company operating in the Spanish History & Arts sector. It is designed for any participants who have at least a basic Spanish level (95-4224036; www.oneco.org); its website www.oneco.org gives extensive details of the kind of positions available and also the reasonably priced language courses it offers.

The Californian company Adelante LLC (601 Taper Drive, Seal Beach, CA 90740; 562-799-9133; www.adelantespain.com) places American interns in Bilbao, Madrid and Seville, some in the tourist industry for example in a travel agency helping with tour planning for tour groups, many American, or working with rural and environmental tourism. Placement fees start at around $2,000 for a one-month placement. Some language schools can arrange post-course work experience placements (mostly unwaged) in Spanish firms, for example Don Quijote (www.donquijote.org/english/courses.orientation.asp).

REGULATIONS

The procedures for regularising your status are similar to those in other EU countries. Those who intend to stay more than three months must apply for a residence card *(Tarjeta de Residencia)* within 30 days of arrival. Application should be made to the local police headquarters *(Comisaría de Policia)* or to a Foreigners' Registration Office *(Oficina de Extranjería)* which in Madrid is at C/ Madrazo 9; this office now gives out appointment times for presenting applications; ring 900 610 620. The documents necessary for the *residencia* are a contract of employment, three photos, a passport and (sometimes) a medical certificate. As soon as you start a job you should also apply to the police for an NIF (national insurance number). Further details are available from the Ministry of the Interior website (www.mir.es/extranje) in Spanish only or can be checked with the Labour & Social Affairs Counsellor's Office of the Spanish Embassy (20 Peel St, London W8 7PD; 020-7221 0098; constrab@mtas.es; www.conspalon.org/indexeng.html) and with the British Consulate-General in Spain (c/ Marqués de la Ensenada 16-2°, 28004 Madrid; 91-308 5201). Their notes *Settling in Spain* include detailed advice on sorting out red tape as well as the addresses of all 14 British Consulates in Spain.

The red tape for which Spain is famous does not stop at residence cards. One young Briton who was working for an expat British bar owner on the Costa del Sol was suddenly paid a visit by a Social Security inspector who pointed out that he had not yet applied for his *residencia* as he should have and the landlord hadn't done 'this and that'.

The rules for non-EU citizens have not changed and those who find a legitimate job working for a tour company, etc. will have to go through a complex rigmarole (unless the

Council scheme mentioned below applies). They must obtain a *visado especial* from the Spanish Embassy in their country of residence after submitting a copy of their contract, medical certificate in duplicate and authenticated copies of qualifications. In some cases a further document is needed, an *antecedente penal* (police certificate). Invariably the Spanish authorities take months to process this and when the visa (normally Type A which is for one specific job) is finally issued, it must be collected in the home country.

Americans, Canadians, Australians, etc. do sometimes find paid work as monitors in children's camps or touts for bars and discos. When their tourist visas are about to expire, they usually follow the example of others who simply cross into France or Portugal to extend their tourist visa for a further three months on their return to Spain.

ANDORRA

Andorra is a tiny country (470 sq km) with surprisingly good opportunities for finding employment. Although the principality of Andorra is a sovereign country straddling the French-Spanish border, it is not itself a member of the European Union. This means that all foreigners need work permits once they find an employer, which will involve several visits to the Immigration office in the capital, Andorra La Vella, and to the hospital for the required medical tests.

The main source of possibilities is the ski industry. There are seven or eight skiing areas in the tiny country, though the two best known are Soldeu and Arinsal. These attract a steady flow of British skiers and many English-speaking people fill the usual range of ski resort jobs. For ski tour operators which go to Andorra, try *Top Deck Ski, Skiworld, Thomson* and *Specialist Holidays Group*. Snowcoach (146-148 London Rd, St. Albans, Herts. AL1 1PQ; 01727 866177; www.snowcoach.co.uk) hire reps and chalet staff for Andorra.

The websites of the individual resorts often give recruitment information in English such as the one for Arinsal and Pal (www.palarinsal.com) which advises job-seekers to ring +376 7370000 and Ski Soldeu (www.soldeu.ad) where the relevant contact details are +376 890554; dpersonal@soldeu.ad).

GIBRALTAR

Gibraltar used to be a mecca for working travellers who, in the past, found seemingly endless possibilities to work in bars and cafés, but that is no longer the case. Even though the restriction on British nationals working in Gibraltar was lifted in 1996 and EU nationals are free to take up any offer of employment made to them in Gibraltar, locals always get the jobs ahead of Britons. Non-EU nationals will have even more difficulty and will have to find an employer willing to help them apply for a work permit from the Employment Service, Unit 76-77 Harbour's Walk, New Harbours (40408/fax 73981) after first obtaining a Terms of Engagement form. To have an application for a work permit approved, the prospective employer must prove that no Gibraltarian or EU national is available to fill the vacancy, undertake to repatriate the worker if necessary and show that suitable accommodation has been found.

Yet tourism continues to flourish, partly because of Gibraltar's tax-free status and it is said that there are 365 bars and restaurants in Gibraltar (one for every day of the year). Mark Hurley's advice to the job-seeker is to start at one end of Gibraltar and work through, systematically asking at all the bars and restaurants, which should take about two or three days. You will have a chance of work only if you look tidy and sell yourself.

The Ocean Terminal has been enlarged to cope with an increase of visitors and there may be work for cruise personnel and specialised guides for excursions to Jerez, Seville, etc.

Currently, locals tend to fill most jobs in the duty free shops that line the main street and in international hotels like the Rock Hotel (+350 73000; www.rockhotelgibraltar.com) and the Caleta Hotel (+350 76501) which hosts conferences and honeymooners as well as ordinary tourists. However, there might be work for those with the right qualifications and experience, especially in duty free retail.

DIRECTORY REFERENCES

For travel companies which employ staff in Spain, see entries for: Openwide International, Acorn Venture, Airtours/MyTravel, ATG-Oxford, Bike Riders, Bolero International Holidays, Camping Life, Canvas, Casterbridge, Citalia, Club Cantabrica, Cosmos, CV Travel, Emilio's Bar & Apartment Rentals, Eurocamp, Freewheel Holidays, Harry Shaw's City Cruiser Holidays, Haven Europe, Headwater, Keycamp, King's Camps, Magic of Spain, Open Holidays, PGL, Scott Dunn, Shearings, Siesta, Ski Miquel, Solaire Holidays, Specialist Holiday Group, Style Holidays, Tall Stories, TJM Travel, Travelsphere, Venue Holidays.

Switzerland

For centuries travellers used Switzerland's valleys as routes across the continent to France, Germany, Italy and Austria. Many of its famous buildings are monasteries built to offer shelter to pilgrims on their way to Rome. One of the most enduring of alpine legends is of the dogs from St Bernard rescuing travellers in snowdrifts. This happened, but the brandy keg around the neck is reputed to be folklore.

The Alps take up more than 60% of the territory, and provided protection from invaders. Left to themselves, the Swiss developed a fiercely nationalistic mentality which persists, although in recent years its immigration policies have been softening (see the section on Regulations below). During the time of the Grand Tour many young gentlemen travelled through Switzerland to reach Italy, although it must have been a frightening experience. To cross the mountain passes, your coach had to be dismantled and carried by mule, with you trudging along behind and, according to one diary, running to keep up with the mules as they tumbled down the other side.

The Victorians loved alpine grandeur. After Queen Victoria took a holiday in Switzerland, the country became the fashionable place to go for a holiday. Victorian gentlemen followed the fashion and came to climb the mountains, while the locals looked on in amazement. (The first recorded climbs of the 20 highest Swiss peaks were by British climbers.) Thomas Cook brought his tours here. And when skiing became popular, pioneers in winter sports like Sir Arnold Lunn (later of Lunn Poly fame) made Switzerland their second home. In 1922 the world's first skiing races were held under Lunn's direction at Murren. The British started the idea of international ski competitions, and then had to stand aside and watch the rest of the world win all the races.

Most educated Swiss can communicate in at least two of their country's three official languages, German, French and Italian, plus many also speak the unofficial language of English. The fourth language, Romansch, which derives from Latin, is spoken in and around St. Moritz and the Engadine Valley. During the Reformation, Switzerland produced the stern Calvin and Zwingli, and it is a paradox that the light-hearted French-speaking part of Switzerland today is mostly Protestant, whereas the German-speaking valleys overflow with exuberant Baroque and Rococo Catholic churches.

FINDING A JOB

Numerous British travel companies and camping holiday operators are active in Switzerland such as Canvas and Eurocamp. Venture Abroad (Rayburn House, Parcel Terrace, Derby DE1 1LY; www.ventureabroad.co.uk) hire 'carefully chosen British students,' especially those with Scouting and Guiding connections, to meet and guide youth groups around Gstaad, Grindelwald, Interlaken, Adelboden and Kandersteg.

Most ski tour operators mount big operations in Switzerland, such as *Mark Warner* and *Crystal Holidays*. The *Jobs in the Alps Agency* (enquiries@jobs-in-the-alps.com) has been placing waiters, waitresses, chamber staff, kitchen helps and hall and night porters in Swiss hotels, cafés and restaurants in Swiss resorts, 200 in winter, 150 in summer for at least a generation. A smaller outfit that hires resort reps at the end of the summer is On the Piste Holidays (2 Oldfield Court, Cranes Park Crescent, Surbiton, Surrey KT5 8AW; 020-8399 7225; skiing@otp.co.uk) that works in Champéry, Nendaz, Villars and Zermatt.

For summer work, most coach tour companies have tours that go through Switzerland but not many (apart from Lakes and Mountains specialists) have Switzerland-only tours. The two giant tour operators, Kuoni and Globus, have their headquarters in Switzerland. Upmarket Kuoni deals with the business end of travel and employs some of the best tour directors in the business. They also have very glossy long haul holidays. If you want to work for them you have to speak several languages and then compete with Swiss nationals for the work. Globus is the holding company for Cosmos Tourama (Via alla Roggia, PO Box 6919 Grancia, Lugano; www.globusandcosmos.com) which operate tours from the UK to Spain, Turkey, etc. If offered work, make sure you have all details before you leave.

The Swiss Travel Service Ltd (Bridge House, 55-59 High Road, Broxbourne, Herts. EN10 7DT; 0870 191 7170; www.swisstravel.co.uk) hires about 20 resort reps and tour guides who are talented linguists to work from April till the end of September; it is possible to apply for a job online.

Summer language and sports camps abound in Switzerland. The Swiss organisation *Village Camps S.A.* (rue de la Morache, CH-1260 Nyon; 022-990 9405) advertises widely its desire to recruit people over 21 as general counsellors, EFL teachers, sports instructors and nurses on its summer and winter camps in Leysin. In exchange for working fairly long hours, counsellors and domestic staff receive free room and board, insurance and an 'expense allowance' of €240 a week plus a ski pass in the winter.

Susanna Macmillan arrived in Crans Montana in the autumn and within three days had arranged a job as a *monitrice* at the International School there. The job, which was to teach sports and English, came with room and board plus pocket money. Adventure holiday operators often need qualified instructors, but your qualifications must be good.

Becoming part of a hot-air balloon crew is physically demanding work but would be an unusual way to work in the alpine tourism industry in January and February; details from Bombard Balloon Adventures, Chateau de Laborde, Laborde au Chateau, 21200 Beaune, France (+33-3-80 26 63 30) or from the US head office, 33 Pershing Way, West Palm Beach, FL 33401 (240-384-7107; www.bombardsociety.com/jobs).

HOTELS & CATERING
Swiss hotels and tourism courses are still the training ground and model for hoteliers

worldwide (see Directory of Training Courses). For the hotels and catering industry, a rapid short-term injection of labour is an economic necessity both for the summer and winter season – June/July to September and December to April.

Provided you have a reasonable CV and a knowledge of languages (preferably German), a speculative job hunt in advance is worthwhile. For example Katherine Jenkins wrote to several Swiss hotels in August/September and was gratified to have a choice of three definite contracts for the winter season. The *Swiss Hotel Guide* provides detailed entries in English on 2,500 hotels including the proprietor's name and can be ordered via www.swisshotels.ch for €15. Two hotel groups worth trying (provided you are a European national) are Mövenpick on www.movenpick-hotels.com (with a Jobs Online feature) and Park Hotels Waldhaus, 7018 Flims-Waldhaus (081-928 48 48; info@park-hotels-waldhaus.ch).

The Swiss Hotel Association has a department called Hoteljob which runs a placement scheme (in the German-speaking part of Switzerland only) for registered EU students from the age of 18 who are willing to spend three to four months doing an unskilled job in a Swiss hotel or restaurant between June and September. Excellent knowledge of the German language is essential (and information on the website is only in German). Member hotels issue a standard contract on which salary and deductions are carefully itemised. From the gross salary of SFr2,790 in subsidised mountain areas or SFr3,100 in the rest of Switzerland, the basic deduction for board and lodging (for any job) is SFr900 and a further 12-15% is taken off for taxes and insurance. Tips for waiting staff can bring net earnings back up to the gross. Application forms are available from the Swiss Hotel Association, Monbijoustrasse 130, 3001 Bern (+41-31-370 43 33/fax +41-31-370 43 34; hoteljob.be@swisshotels.ch; www.hoteljob.ch). The deadline for applications is 20th April.

At the more professional end of the spectrum, recruitment agencies like Gastro-S (Haus Howald, XL-Zentrum/Bahnhofstr.8, CH-5080 Laufenburg; 062-869 40 40; Jobs@gastro-S.ch) assist experienced and qualified individuals in the catering trade to find jobs in 300 hotels and restaurants throughout Switzerland plus Liechtenstein and southern Germany.

ON-THE-SPOT

Although the Swiss rate of unemployment is low by world standards, it is rising and all employers will hire a Swiss in preference to a foreigner. The very high cost of living while job-hunting means that going to Switzerland to find work can be fraught with difficulty. Yet many people do fix up their jobs in person, especially if they are able to visit resorts several months before the season begins (i.e. September for the winter season and March/April for the summer). Try Les Portes de Soleil at Champery, Les Crosets as well as the major resorts of Leysin, Verbier, Thyon and Crans Montana. This valley is a major road and rail route and is ideal for concentrated job hunting.

Surprisingly, tourist offices may be of use. Susanna Macmillan reported that the tourist office in Crans Montana issued photocopied lists of 'Jobs Available' and were advertising for summer staff in March. Always check notice boards and adverts in local papers.

Like most people, Andrew Winwood found the job hunt tough going:

All in all I asked in over 200 places for ski-season work, but eventually could have counted 10-12 possibilities. Going on that rate, it would be possible to get work after asking at 50 or 60 places, but of course the 'Grand Law of Sod' would prevail. As far as I can see, it's a simple case of ask, ask, ask and ask again until you get work. It was costing me about £80 a week to live in Switzerland, so I couldn't let up until I definitely had a way of getting the money back.

SKI RESORTS

See the introductory section on working in ski resorts. Apart from applying to all the ski tour operators for the following winter season, try *The Lady Magazine* (published Tuesdays) for classified ads for jobs as chalet maids, cooks, etc.

November is a bad time to arrive since most of the hotels are closed and the owners away on holiday. When David Loveless arrived in Verbier in mid-November, he declined an invitation to add his name to the bottom of eight sheets of people waiting for jobs. After moving on to Crans Montana, David soon found work at the Hotel de l'Etrier as a *chasseur* (messenger/odd jobs man).

Danny Jacobson's tip is to bypass the large ski stations in favour of the less tourist-filled ones. Head for the smaller stations and the surrounding villages where your presence will be more of a novelty. Joseph Tame's surprising tip is to go up as high as possible in the mountains. After being told by virtually every hotel in Grindelwald in mid-September that they had already hired their winter season staff, he despaired and decided to waste his last SFr40 on a trip up the rack railway. At the top he approached the only hotel and couldn't believe it when they asked him when he could start. Although he had never worked in a hotel before, they were willing to take him on as a trainee waiter, give him full bed and board plus a good wage (currently nearly £700 after all deductions for food and accommodation, insurance and tax). At first he found the job a little boring since there were few guests apart from Japanese groups on whirlwind European tours.

> **Things changed for Joseph Tame at Christmas:**
> *Christmas and New Year was an absolute nightmare. Three shifts a day for everyone with very little sleep and no time off. When a promised pay rise didn't materialise, I decided I had had enough and handed in my notice. But by January 5th, business had slumped and we had at least two hours off daily to ski. When my overdue pay rise came through I withdrew my notice. If you can stick the Christmas rush, things do get better. Switzerland was definitely the best thing that ever happened to me.*

Joseph enjoyed the experience so much that he returned for three more seasons and says that he is very glad that he stumbled across this 160-year old hotel in a blizzard four years before. The proprietors sometimes have trouble filling vacancies and so he recommends sending a CV with photo to Andreas von Almen, Scheidegg Hotels AG, 3801 Kleine Scheidegg (fax +41 33 855 12 94).

A recommended meeting place is Balmer's Herberge in Interlaken (Hauptstrasse 23-25, 3800 Interlaken; 033-822 19 61; balmers@tcnet.ch). They take on English-speaking staff for a minimum of six months only after a face-to-face interview. The owner is pleased to pass on information about other job openings in the area, as the hostel is often contacted by local hotels asking for workers.

In spring and summer, ski resorts take on a new guise as more and more companies look for staff to take walking tours, rambles, flora and fauna tours, birdwatching, etc. Attractive areas such as Zermatt and Saas Fee often have walking tours, so it is worth trying your luck there. LB Freedom Tours wants trilingual people to guide groups of clients on foot or bicycle in the Alps near Martigny from May to September; details from 7 Box Lane, Hemel Hempstead, Herts. HP3 0DH (tel/fax 01442 263377; info@freedomtours.com).

WORKING CONDITIONS

In Switzerland, it is a case of last in first out. As soon as the season ends or bookings drop, the foreign workers will be let go before the locals. Otherwise, working conditions are favourable, with better live-in accommodation than in most other countries. Hotels are very helpful to tour guides, and large jewellers such as Bucherer and Gübelin have dedicated departments to service tour groups. Everything is clean, clean, clean which puts tour groups in a good frame of mind. But the high cost of living means that tours do not spend long in the country. Representatives are well looked after both winter and summer. Ski reps get free ski lift passes, free or reduced hire of equipment, free drinks in the places frequented by your group and free transport passes in many places.

Steve Rout sums up the joys of working in a Swiss resort:

In my opinion Switzerland can't be recommended too highly, especially in the winter. If you are lucky, you will get fit and healthy, learn a new language, earn plenty of money, and make some great friends, all in one of the most beautiful areas of the world.

Swiss hotels are very efficient and tend to be impersonal, since you will be one in an endless stream of seasonal workers from many countries. The very intense attitude to work among the Swiss means that hours are long; a typical working week would consist of at least five nine-hour days working split shifts.

Whether humble or palatial, the Swiss hotel or restaurant in which you find a job will probably insist on very high standards of cleanliness and productivity. After working at an independent hostel and then a 3-star restaurant in Interlaken, Kathy Russell from Australia concluded that 'the Swiss are very picky to work for, so a good temperament is needed'.

On the other hand, the majority are *korrekt*, i.e. scrupulous about keeping track of your overtime and pay you handsomely at the end of your contract. Alison May summarised her summer at the Novotel-Zürich-Airport: 'On balance, the wages were good but we really had to earn them'. The main disadvantage of being hired outside Switzerland is that the wages will be on a British scale rather than on the more lucrative Swiss one; however perks often compensate.

REGULATIONS

Although Switzerland is not yet a member of the European Union, it is moving in the direction of integration. Since the Bilateral Agreement between Switzerland and the European Union on the free movement of persons came into effect in June 2002, Switzerland has been undergoing a huge shift in its immigration and employment policy. The category of seasonal worker was abolished. The system is now more in line with the rest of Europe so that EU job-seekers can enter Switzerland for up to three months (extendable) to look for work. If they succeed they must show a contract of employment to the authorities and are then eligible for a short-term residence permit, valid for up to one year and renewable. Quotas of foreign workers in each canton will be abolished in 2004 and the free movement of labour will be introduced step by step until 2007 when the movement of workers will be unfettered. At the time of writing seasonal workers are issued with the L-EC, a short-term residence permit valid for one year in the first instance but extendable year by year without an obligation to leave the country, provided the employer can prove that it is necessary for him or her to hire a foreigner because no local person is available to do the job.

"The Liechtenstein economy exists mainly on tourist shops and manufacturing false teeth"

All of these changes are of course bad news for non-EU citizens who will now find it much harder to gain access to Switzerland's labour market unless they apply in special categories like the trainee permit. If a non-European does find an employer willing to sponsor his or her application, the applicant will have to collect the documents from the Swiss Embassy in the home country.

Laws and rules in Switzerland are normally obeyed by the locals. Cross the road against the lights (even if the road is empty) and a Swiss will come running to point out in a helpful tone that you must wait for the lights to change. Arriving at the pretty mountain resort of Engelberg, Lucien and his driver were annoyed to see 'No Parking' signs by the cable car where they usually parked. Carefully removing the signs, the driver parked the coach and left it. While sitting on a café balcony on their return a couple of hours later, they watched in horror as their coach sank into a hole. The coach had been parked on top of a chasm which had been dug to install cables. Because the Swiss are so law-abiding, they had not thought it necessary to put up any explanatory notices. Lucien spent the rest of the afternoon watching while the Swiss Army made an efficient (and expensive) job of lifting the coach out of its hole.

LIECHTENSTEIN

This independent principality is represented by Switzerland abroad and is a member of the European Economic Area. Ruled by a hereditary Prince (Hans-Adam II) from his castle perched high overlooking the country, the economy exists on tourist shops and exporting false teeth and postage stamps. Tour guides love this country. Their groups can add another one to their list, it takes less than an hour to drive through, the food is excellent, there is easy parking outside the two rival tourist supermarkets which sell everything from maps and guide books (a good place to stock up) to souvenirs the group might have forgotten to buy in Switzerland. A few foreigners are employed in the shops, provided they are good linguists. There is skiing in winter, but not much work.

DIRECTORY REFERENCES

The following companies listed in the Directory employ staff in Switzerland: Büro Metro, Jobs in the Alps, Astons Holidays, Canvas, Cosmos, Esprit, Eurocamp, Freewheel Holidays, Inghams, Keycamp, Lotus Supertravel, NBV Leisure, Neilson, Scott Dunn, Shearings, Ski Activity, Ski Miquel, Skiworld, Swiss Travel Service, Total Holidays, Travelsphere, Venture Abroad, Village Camps.

Turkey

During the 1980s Turkey became the flavour of the decade and tourist development was permitted to run riot. When Spanish hotels began to increase their prices, European tour operators looked elsewhere for a cheaper alternative and Turkey was ripe for the picking. The operators offered huge contracts to a country which had previously concentrated on an upmarket and cruise market. The Turkish government offered to build tourist facilities as quickly as possible. Hotels were thrown up without much planning, and the government was not able to develop services (sewerage, electricity, communications, etc.) fast enough to keep up. A decade or two on, things have improved and the southwest coast of Turkey can offer some very sophisticated facilities.

The threat of terrorism has dogged the country, however, and the double bombing of the British Consulate and HSBC Bank in Istanbul in November 2003 marked a serious setback for tourist development, nearly eclipsing earlier anxieties about the threats of the PKK, Kurdistan Workers Party. Human rights abuses and fatal coach accidents are sometimes reported in the foreign press, making it difficult for Turkey to forge ahead in increasing its share of the package holiday market. It has an ambition to join the European Union though this possibility is still many years off.

Tourist development has been concentrated in the main Aegean resorts of Marmaris, Kusadasi and Bodrum, where many English-speaking people in the tourist industry end up working. Some people feel that this part of the Mediterranean coast has been spoiled though the Turkish government is now keeping a stricter eye on tourism development. The country is lucky that it still has one unspoilt coastline, the Black Sea, where development is proceeding very cautiously and keeping the ecology of the region in view. On the south coast local construction companies had their fingers burnt when a giant German hotel corporation tried to build a complex right on top of a loggerhead turtle breeding ground. This so inflamed the European green lobby that the resulting protest reverberated for years afterwards.

Yet the trappings of modern tourist development with all its problems have done little to diminish the extraordinary charm and hospitality of the people. Turkey remains a superb country, a cultural crossroads of immense riches. From the dawn of Biblical times, Asia Minor has been at the centre of the known world. It comes as a surprise to many holidaymakers how many famous places from the Bible and history are located in Turkey, from Tarsus (where St Paul was born) to Mount Ararat (where Noah's Ark came to rest).

PROSPECTS FOR WORK

Most British tour operators feature Turkey for the summer. Also, the upmarket tourists have not been completely driven away. There are still plenty of cruises which come into the harbours, and companies run tours to see the spring flowers, explore Hittite ruins and so on in the Anatolian interior. Those with an appropriate history or religion degree might be lucky enough to find a company that needs tour leaders and specialist lecturers. Get a list of companies that feature historical or architectural tours from the Turkish Tourist Office; 124 operators are listed on their website www.gototurkey.co.uk.

Anyone who knows the country well and a smattering of the language may eventually be employed to take tours into the heart of the old Ottoman Empire. Now that the border has been opened with Armenia and the southern Russian states, it is possible to follow the Silk Route, which so fascinated Marco Polo, and people are beginning to take tours to follow it to China.

FINDING A JOB

In addition to the standard range of tour operators, *Mark Warner* employs staff from bar staff to nannies, night watchmen to watersports instructors, for their sailing and watersports holidays and beach club hotels in Turkey. Reserve staff are employed throughout the summer season as vacancies arise. Another important tour operator to Turkey is *Savile Tours* which hire only a few reps each summer season.

Flotilla holiday companies take advantage of the many beautiful moorings along the Turkish coast. *Sunsail* (hr@sunsail.com) has many openings for skippers, hostesses, mechanics/bosuns and dinghy sailors, as well as cooks, bar staff and nannies to work in their watersports centres at Yedi Buku near Bodrum, Perili near Datca and an additional club at Marmaris. *Setsail Holidays* (boats@setsail.co.uk) have a similar range of vacancies for their flotilla and bareboat holidays in the eastern Mediterranean. Other companies like *Simply Turkey* (now part of TUI) and Blue Cruise Ltd (Cumberland House, 80 Scrubbs Lane, London NW10 6RF; gulet@bluecruise.co.uk) offer holidays on *gulets,* traditional wooden schooners, which may employ crew and cooks.

Occasionally resort jobs are advertised on the internet; try www.summerjobs.com or www.overseasjobs.com where jobs as animators, DJs, instructors, etc. at resorts like the Aegean Holiday Village in Bodrum (info@bodrumhotels.net) or the Hillside Beach Club in Fethiye may be posted.

The WOW (World of Wonders) chain of themed hotels advertises in the winter for a full range of entertainment staff including sports instructors, dancers, etc. Although WOW are looking to hire students, they want them to work for all of the June to September period (WOW Hotels, Kundu Köyü, 07110 Aksu-Antalya; 242-431 2323 ext 7074; apply@wowanimation.info; www.wowhotels.com). An entertainment agency in Izmir supplies staff to Turkish hotels and resorts: Fiesta Entertainments, Izmir 35340; 532-386 2900; www.fiesta-entertainment.net. Typically Fiesta will not consider applications unless they are accompanied by a photo. Another agency providing entertainers and dancers to the tourist industry of southwestern Turkey has the less-than reassuring name Hot Entertainment & Organisations, Ciftecesmeler Mahallesi 34 Sokak, No: 32, Beldibi-Antalya, Kemer 07040 (242-3245752). Another possibility is Club Sun (www.club-sun.co.uk) whose UK office sometimes helps to recruit resort staff for Bitez Watersports and Beach Club located on the Bodrum Peninsula (Club Sun Ltd, 79 London Road, Alderley Edge, Cheshire SK9 7DY).

Other operators which feature Turkey include:
Concept Express Ltd Travel & Tours, 19 Albemarle St, London W1S 4HS (020-7493 4243; info@concept-trv.co.uk). Turkey specialist.
Cresta Holidays, Tabley Court, Victoria St, Altrincham, Cheshire WA14 1EZ; 0870 161 0900; www.crestaholidays.co.uk)
Tapestry Holidays, One The Glassmills, Rear of 320 King St, London W6 0AX (020-8235 7777; www.tapestryholidays.com/contact/jobsoverseas)
Travelscene, 11/15 St Ann's Road, Harrow, Middlesex HA1 1LQ (0151-236 7941; admin@travelscene.co.uk)
Well-presented people have a good chance of being given jobs as reps once they have arrived in one of the big resorts. As usual, these reps who are locally hired will be paid lower wages than the UK tour company employees (and will of course be paid in Turkish lire). Furthermore they are not insured and may be sacked without pay if there is a downturn in bookings (e.g. after a terrorist attack).

The youth exchange organisation *Genctur* in Istanbul organises summer camps in Turkey at which English-speaking young people work as volunteers. Participants help with social activities, drama, music, sports, crafts and English teaching.

CASUAL WORK

'Help Wanted' signs can sometimes be seen in the windows of bars, carpet shops, etc. As elsewhere, proprietors aim to use native English speakers to attract more customers to buy their souvenirs or stay at their hotels. In the majority of cases, this sort of work finds you once you make known your willingness to undertake such jobs.

Major Turkish yachting resorts are excellent places to look for work, not just related to boats but in hotels, bars, shops and excursions. A good time to check harbourside notice boards and to ask captains if they need anyone to clean or repair their boats is in the lead-up to the summer season and the Marmaris Boat Show in May. Laura O'Connor describes what she found in Marmaris:

> *There's a large British community living there, retired and fed-up Brits who have sold their houses, bought a boat and are whooping it up. There's plenty of work opportunities in the Marina, especially for boat painting and varnishing in April. Also girls can do hostessing on the boats. I was cleaning boats with a friend for enough money to cover my accommodation and evenings in the pub. Just walk around the Marina and ask.*

Xuela Edwards is another traveller who found many opportunities in Marmaris but points out the down side:

> *Affordable accommodation is hard to find and wages are appalling. The Turkish work ethic can be difficult to handle too. Most Turkish businesses stay open from 10am to midnight, and much later for bars and clubs. You might not actually be doing anything but those are the hours. Turks have said to us that the English are strange because they always want to leave as soon as their hours are up and they want a day off. This is alien to the Turkish mentality which regards the office or shop as an extension of the home. Many other travellers we met also found the hanging around element frustrating.*

Paying and accepting commissions is the traditional way of doing business and not regarded as ripping off the tourist because these commissions are built into the basic price of everything. Therefore it is possible for talented salesmen/women (preferably multilingual) to make good money in Turkey.

Ian McArthur decided it would be an advantage while travelling in Turkey to be musical:

> *There is a great demand for musicians, particularly guitarists, in places where the 'Marlboro, Levis and Coca Cola generation' predominates. I have travelled around with my friend Vanessa and she has found work playing in bars in Istanbul, Marmaris, Olu Deniz and Patara (near Kas). Marmaris was the goldmine – £30 a night. The problem was that we both hated Marmaris – too many bloody tourists! In Patara she got a job in a bar called the Lazy Frog and played for a place to stay and food.*

See chapter on *Cyprus* for information about the Turkish Republic of Northern Cyprus.

WORKING CONDITIONS

Problems are par for the course for reps working in Turkey. Even companies like *Tapestry Holidays* with an upmarket image and presentation do sell packaged holidays at budget prices to people who sometimes complain that Turkish facilities and nightlife are not equal to those they have enjoyed in Spain.

Long transfer times of up to five hours one way are commonplace from Dalaman Airport. Often the staff accommodation is sub-standard. Mike was put in an airless windowless room until he complained. He was calm yet firm and got it changed. One of the features of the job he particularly disliked was having to explain the loo arrangements to clients, i.e. that the plumbing system cannot cope with toilet paper which must therefore be deposited in a bin. He soon became adept at the Turkish phrases for dealing with plumbers, since many clients ignored the warnings and caused blockages.

One of Mike's biggest problems was excursions. A large part of his income came from commission, but his company sold their excursions at double the rate the local operators charged. Eventually Mike solved this by inviting his clients to take a local excursion but suggested that they ask to see insurance certificates before booking. While showing them the company certificate, he told stories (all true) of what had happened to previous clients who had not been insured. They soon came back to book his tours.

Many clients suffer from gippy tummy at some point, so reps should get to know the local chemist and try to find a suitable remedy, preferably homeopathic. Sunburn is another problem. Few clients seem to believe the rep's warnings at the welcome meeting (especially when the rep has red hair and pale skin as Mike does) and soon come back lobster red.

Although Turkey is a secular state (due to the reforms introduced by the influential leader Ataturk in the first part of the 20th century), the people are Muslim and their religion should be respected. Topless sunbathing is illegal in most places and limbs and women's heads should be covered when visiting mosques. Islamic fundamentalism is gaining ground which has resulted in the enforced segregation of males and females in some municipalities. So people working in Turkey should be attentive to such things.

Although the social distortions found in stricter Islamic countries are absent in Turkey, women will not escape overtures from local men, though these normally take the form of unwanted gallantry rather than sexual harassment. The army plays an important part in Turkish life and all males aged 20 must do military service for 18 months. Soldiers are in evidence everywhere and they often carry out police duties. They are invariably friendly, but never forget that their rifles are their proudest possessions.

REGULATIONS

Without paper qualifications and a dedicated local employer, it will be very difficult to obtain a work permit and therefore a residence permit. Those who enter Turkey on a tourist visa (which costs £10 in cash at the border) and then find work must leave the country every three months (normally to a Greek island like Rhodes or to Northern Cyprus). If you do this too many times, the border officials may become suspicious.

At the time of writing the Foreign & Commonwealth Office was assessing the risk of terrorist activity as high; if considering Turkey, contact the FCO for updates (020-7008 0232; www.fco.gov.uk/travel).

DIRECTORY REFERENCES

For companies which operate in Turkey, see entries for the following: Openwide International, Airtours/MyTravel, Cosmos, Genctur, Mark Warner, Regent Holidays, Savile Tours, Setsail Holidays, Sunsail, Tapestry Holidays.

EASTERN EUROPE

Once the Iron Curtain fell, tourism chiefs in former Eastern Bloc countries expected that their end of Europe would be opened up to visitors, eager to see the wonderful scenery and beautiful buildings. To some extent this was true, with cities like Prague and Budapest almost overrun by tourists in the early boom days. But those countries gradually lost their exotic appeal and now the tourist chiefs are wondering how they can promote their countries and not just the capital cities.

A further problem is that outside the main centres, the inadequacies of the infrastructure have deterred high-spending tourists, and it will take many years before these countries can offer facilities equivalent to the west. For example the warm sandy beaches of the Black Sea coast are still sometimes to be found next to factories belching out fumes and polluting the water. Instability in the Balkans didn't help matters, although tourists need not have any hesitation in visiting Croatia or Slovenia. The latter country is joining the EU in May 2004 and already has a sophisticated tourist industry. At the same time Poland, the Czech Republic, Slovakia, Hungary and the three Baltic states are joining the European Union, though the free movement of labour across European borders will not take effect immediately.

It is only very recently that transport barriers have come down, so that the region will now be opened up to low-cost airlines. First Easyjet and bmibaby (based at East Midlands Airport) began flying to Prague and from May 2004 WIZZ Air is opening a Katowice-Stansted route with a view to linking many Polish and other Central European airports at no-frills fares.

Today many visitors to Eastern Europe are attracted by the cheap holiday prices, and end up spending relatively little in the host country. Others come on short weekend breaks to the capital cities, staying in hotels owned by international chains which take the profits out of the country. Staff to look after these visitors are mostly local. The pool of labour in these countries (where there is massive unemployment) is on the whole well educated and multilingual. A further source of competition for any work in tourism comes from all the emigrés who have returned from Europe and North America to homelands which they had fled. Having made good elsewhere and knowing the difficult languages of the east, they are ideally placed to develop tours and participate in other aspects of the expanding tourist industry. Anyone who fits this category can obtain a list of tour companies from the national tourist offices or via www.tourist-offices.org.uk.

A few coach companies run summer tours from the UK, France and Belgium for which they hire tour guides, preferably with a knowledge of the countries and the language. Bookings are more volatile in this market than in others and tours are liable to be cancelled at short notice. The long-time specialists in tours to the former Soviet Union and Eastern Europe normally employ only established experts:

Balkan Holidays, 19 Conduit Street, London W1S 2BH (020-7543 5555; www.balkanho lidays.co.uk). Holidays in Bulgaria, Croatia, Slovenia, Montenegro and Romania.

Fregata Travel, 83 Whitechapel High St, London E1 7QX (020-7247 8484; www.freg atatravel.co.uk). Part of Commodore International Travel Ltd, 19-21 Connaught St, London W2 2AY)

Holiday Options, 49 The Martlets, Burgess Hill, West Sussex RH15 9NJ (01444 876542; www.holidayoptions.co.uk). Job opportunities icon on website.

Progressive Tours Ltd, 12 Porchester Place, Marble Arch, London W2 2BS (020-7262 1676)

Regent Holidays – see entry

Spirit of Russia, Interchange House, 27 Stafford Rd, Croydon, Surrey CR0 4NG (020-8681 3612/3; www.interchange.uk.com). Tours to Russia, Ukraine, Kazakhstan, Albania, Bulgaria (including walking tours), etc.

Specialist executive recruitment companies such as *FM Recruitment, MRI* and HOCAPS International (www.hocaps.com) employ professional personnel and senior advisors for contracts in the Russian republics and worldwide.

The heady early days when people with money scrambled to invest in innovative and specialised tourism products, such as turning the beautifully kept trains of Romania into 'Orient Express' type holidays, are now over though in some quarters potential still exists to develop specialised services or tours. Those with money and/or time and/or expertise can make a worthwhile contribution to a local community and make a good living at the same time. A favourite target for investment by individuals is small hotels. The concrete monstrosities which accommodated the endless stream of Russian groups in the old days need to be brought up to European standards with fire escapes, better security, safer swimming pools, etc.

International hotel chains have by now colonised the major cities of Central and Eastern Europe. For example quite early on Hilton took over the old Athene Palace in Bucharest. All these hotels need accounts staff, head housekeepers, admin staff, etc. with experience of international hotels. Luxury boats ply the Danube and need casino staff, pursers and admin staff.

SPECIAL INTEREST TOURS

There is a wealth of cultural sites in these countries, and fantastic works of art, from the Fabergé in the Hermitage, to Queen Marie of Romania's Golden Furniture. As hotels have improved, more tour managers with specialist knowledge have been in demand. The beautiful and unspoilt provinces of these countries invite special interest nature tours such as those offered by Naturetrek & Wildlife Worldwide (Cheriton Mill, Cheriton, Alresford, Hants SO24 0NG; 01962 733051; www.naturetrek.co.uk/employment_oportunities.html). The Dalmatian coast of Croatia is becoming popular for sailing holidays such as those offered by *Setsail.*

Hunting was a very popular pastime for party officials in the days of Communism. That activity has fallen out of international favour, which has caused problems in some areas; the increase in the bear population with insufficient food for them to forage means that they have become a menace. Less squeamish than the British, Germans join hunting parties to most of the eastern bloc countries, which has necessitated the refurbishment of lodges and country villas.

Hungary, Romania and Slovenia offer potential for setting up riding holidays especially by people who have contacts with UK riding schools. At Lipica in Slovenia there is a stud which is probably the oldest in the world, set up 400 years ago to breed horses for the Habsburg armies and the Spanish Riding School in Vienna. There are tremendous possibilities for anyone who wants to offer package tours to horse lovers and riders, who can have lessons in dressage and carriage driving. There is easy access from Trieste in northern Italy.

TRANS-SIBERIAN EXPRESS

As one of the most famous rail journeys in the world, the trans-Siberian from Moscow to China continues to attract thousands of people on packaged trips as well as independent travellers. Corinna had worked as a tour manager in Europe and Britain and was offered the chance to look after a group going through Russia to Hong Kong. Although she realised there would be potential problems, mainly relieving the tedium of the journey for her clients, she wanted to add the experience to her CV in order to help her achieve her ultimate goal, to work in Asia:

> *By the third day of looking out across the deserted landscape, peope were at each other's throats. I was kept busy by all the problems I had to sort out, from lack of food because the train hadn't made the scheduled supply stop to trying to answer the frequent question 'where are we?' when I didn't have a clue. Thank goodness I had grabbed some of my nephew's puzzle books before I left. I tore these up, handed them out and organised a competition between carriages, and thereby managed to divert the aggression.*

Having survived this experience, Corinna is now a seasoned tour director and has visited over 60 countries in her working life.

WINTER SPORTS

Romania and Bulgaria in particular have fine terrain for downhill skiing and langlauf and are anxious to capture a larger share of the European ski touring market. The best known resorts are Borovets and Pamporovo in Bulgaria, Sinaia and Poiana Brasov in Romania and Bled and Kranjska Gora in northern Slovenia near the Austrian border. Prices for skiing packages here are generally lower than elsewhere, but there are drawbacks: the hire equipment tends to be decrepit, the après ski facilities limited and hotels of a poor standard. Tour operators admit that their reps do not want to be sent to these countries as conditions are difficult, the nightlife is limited and the pay is lower than in the Alps.

The only work opportunities are as reps for foreign ski tour operators like Thomson, Inghams, First Choice and the specialist *Balkan Tours Ltd*. Given the unpredictable nature of East European bureaucracies, these jobs tend to go only to seasoned reps or those fluent in the local language. One company which actively recruits reps, chalet staff and ski guides for holidays in Bulgaria and Romania is Crystal Holidays via the *Specialist Holidays Group* recruitment department.

An initial explosion of interest by British tour operators in East European ski resorts has now waned due to the number of unhappy clients. Michelle has worked for several major tour operators, and spent two winters in Borovets, Bulgaria:

> *I won't be going back. Too many complaints. Clients didn't like their dinner buffet being set out straight after lunch and left all afternoon, unreliable supply of hot water (never available when they came back cold and wet from the slopes), a four-hour wait for their luggage at Sofia airport, etc.*

The facilities are better in Romania though there are fewer jobs because there seem to be enough English-speaking ski guides, etc. locally. Working as an aid worker, Tim thought he would return as a ski guide, as he had the relevant BASI qualifications. He went up to Poiana Brasov for the weekend to look around, but decided his conscience wouldn't allow him to take work away from the people who needed it so badly, so he went back to work in Austria.

Many East European countries are dotted with luxurious villas once used as private retreats by the *nomenclatura*. For example in Croatia, many of Tito's villas on the island of Brioni were turned into very attractive villas, where wealthy Americans stayed for $800 a night, until the war frightened tourists away. Ceauşescu is reputed to have had over 160 villas, which are highly suitable for family holidays, provided the families can afford them. Lewis had a tidy nest egg from having worked in the Gulf and so bought a large farmhouse near Arbanassi, Bulgaria, which they intended to rent out to British tourists. For two years they tried to go it alone (by advertising in the UK press in magazines like *The Lady*, etc.) but encountered so many difficulties, chiefly with communication by fax and telephone, that they decided to go in with a UK firm. (Each year more and more villa companies open up as this market is expanding.) Unfortunately Lewis signed a ski tour operator's contract without consulting a lawyer familiar with the industry and ended up out-of-pocket with no bookings. He reverted to operating independently but this time used a telephone answering bureau and employed a local person to operate the fax machine.

HUNGARY

Probably the most sophisticated of the Eastern European countries, Hungary has a well-regulated tourism industry – so well-regulated that there are plenty of trained multi-lingual staff locally. Budapest is one of the top destinations for conferences and business tourism. If you contrast that with the sophisticated holiday infrastructure around Lake Balaton and the proximity of picturesque Sopron to the Austrian border, it is easy to see why this country is one of the top tourist destinations.

Work comes from tour operators and conference companies taking groups to Hungary and obviously, if you speak Hungarian you have a much better chance of finding work. Budapest is very popular with Japanese tourists so if you speak Japanese fluently companies may be interested in you as a tour manager or member of staff for their one-day tours. Some coach companies visit Hungary as part of a larger itinerary. Some companies are:

Arblaster & Clarke Wine Tours Ltd, Farnham Road, West Liss, Hants. GU33 6JQ (01730 893344; www.winetours.co.uk/ac-careers.html)

Creative Tours, Hanover Court, 5 Hanover Square, London W1S 1HE (www.creativetou rs.co.uk). Japanese speaking staff may be needed for East European tours.

Limosa Holidays, Suffield House, Northrepps, Norfolk NR27 OLZ (01263 578143; enq uiries@limosaholidays.co.uk). Birding and wildlife holidays Bulgaria and Romania as well as Hungary may require guides with specialised knowledge.

Miki Travel Ltd, 18/20 Cannon St, London EC4M 6XD (020-7398 5098; www.miki.co.uk). Need staff who speak Japanese.

Thermalia Travel Ltd, 12 New College Parade, Finchley Road, Swiss Cottage, London NW3 5EP (www.thermalia.co.uk). Hungary is well known for its spa hotels in Budapest and elsewhere.

POLAND

When the Iron Curtain came down, Poland already had a well-developed low budget tourism product. There are several coach companies providing frequent services between London Victoria and various Polish cities like Kraków. For example Acorn International Travel Ltd, 294 Gloucester Road, Horfield, Bristol BS7 8PD (0117-944 4544; www.king-creation.co.uk/acorn) runs a regular service from England to Polish destinations plus also runs coach tours of Poland, Prague, Budapest and a combination. The Polish National Tourist Office can provide a list of specialist operators. Its website (www.pnto.dial.pipex.com) links with about a dozen important ones in the UK like Inter-Pol Tours and Poltours and also with a few English-speaking providers in Poland like Tatra Tours & Travel (www.tatratravel.pl).

ROMANIA

One of the most beautiful countries in Europe, with a delightfully cultured people, Romania is a country that offers much to the visitor, except the money to build places for them to stay. Many young people have had a stint in Romania as aid workers, a few of whom, like John and Rosemary, fell in love with the country and now organise an annual tour, in their case to see the country's art treasures. They do a 'recce' each Easter to check out hotels and itinerary, use a local agent to cope with the complicated paperwork and hire a coach from a local coach company. By advertising on the company notice board, putting up notices in their local newsagents and distributing homemade leaflets done on their own computer they manage to get about 40 people to book each year. Their biggest problem is the accommodation, with its uncertain plumbing and electrics. They have managed to find enough hotels near the painted churches in Moldavia and the monasteries with their icons in Bulgaria. John and Rosemary are honest with clients about the standard of hotels, and most are not disappointed. They are also wise enough to have a good solicitor, accountant and insurance broker who has arranged for them to be bonded. They make a good profit each year, after costing in their time and expenses. Now that they have established a good client list, they may do more tours when they retire from their jobs.

Interesting placements are available at the Stefan cel Mare Horse Riding Centre in Transylvania through a British agency appealing mainly to the gap year market, Blue Dog Adventures (Amwell Farm House, Nomansland, Wheathampstead, St. Albans, Herts. AL4 8EJ: www.bluedogadventures.com). Volunteers, who must have extensive experience working with horses, spend three weeks marking trails and training young horses to be used for equestrian tourism, and then spend the final week trail riding. The cost is £70. It might be worth contacting the owners of this equine tourism business, one of the few British-run ones in the country, to see if work can be arranged directly (tel/fax +40 263 378470; www.riding-holidays.ro).

CZECH REPUBLIC

Although the number of foreign visitors to the Czech Republic tripled between 1990 and 2000, the industry took a major hit in August 2002 when the country was devastated by floods. Less tragic but also offputting for prospective tourists, the sales tax on most goods increased from 5% to 22% in 2004, so in time the country's reputation for cheap beer may have to be revised.

For companies that might need staff for tours to the Republic, contact the operators listed by the Czech Tourist Office. Unless you speak Czech there would be little chance of finding work in that country's tour companies. The parent company of Czech Holidays and also of the *Romania Travel Centre* is the CTT Group Ltd, 39 Mount Pleasant, Tunbridge Wells, Kent TN1 1PN (careers@cttgroup.co.uk). Cedok is the privatised national tourist organisation that runs coach tours, resort holidays, etc. with an office in London (www.cedok.co.uk) as well as headquarters in Prague (Na Prikope 18, 11135 Prague 1) with an incentive division.

CASUAL WORK

Young people in east European capitals embraced western culture so eagerly that American-style restaurants have sprung up everywhere. In Moscow at least they even hire English speakers, as attested by Bruce Collier whose British wife Sharon was hired by La Kantina Restaurant on Tverskaya near the Intourist Hotel and Red Square:

> *There are more and more Western businesses opening in Moscow all the time and the opportunities should continue to grow. This is especially true of the restaurant and entertainment industries. My wife was steered to a job as a waitress in, of all places, a Mexican restaurant (a joint Russian-Irish venture). Her job provided discounted meals (and the standard was equal to that of any Western country) and paid dollar wages.*

Of course as more and more Russians attain a working knowledge of English, there will be fewer jobs for foreigners in this sector.

If you are looking for some casual work, ask discreetly around the universities or among expatriates teaching English. Your services as anything from a disc jockey to a brochure editor may be in demand. English-language papers may carry relevant adverts. For example the classified section of the *The Prague Post* (Stepanska 20, 110 00 Prague 1; 02-9633 4411/4400) can be read on-line at www.praguepost.com/classifieds. For example at the time of writing, the Bacchus Group of Prague restaurants was advertising for English-speaking waiting and bar staff (bgoff@anet.cz).

DIRECTORY REFERENCES

For companies that employ staff in Eastern Europe, see FM Recruitment, First Choice, Neilson, Page & Moy, Regent Holidays, Setsail, Specialised Travel, Specialist Holidays Group, Specialtours, Steppes East, Top Deck, Travelsphere.

AUSTRALASIA

Australia

The Australian government campaign to increase tourism has been phenomenally successful and was crowned by the choice of Sydney for the Olympic Games in the Millennium year. Ever since Paul Hogan (aka Crocodile Dundee) threw another prawn on the barbie in the memorable television advertising campaign, people from the northern hemisphere have been flocking downunder. Tourism is Australia's number one growth industry, accounting for an estimated 853,500 jobs (directly and indirectly) and employing one in every ten people in the workforce. With flight prices starting at less than £500 return, many British holidaymakers are being wooed away from Europe. This has not happened to the same extent in the American market; however, as air fares across the Pacific come down, major US operators will be offering more tours to Australia.

Tourist facilities along the coast of Queensland and the Great Barrier Reef as far north as Port Douglas were developed at a breakneck rate over the 1990s, especially with an eye to the Japanese market. The Japanese have invested heavily in developments like the Gold Coast Resort Hotels. Anyone who has travelled in Japan or who has a smattering of Japanese will discover that there are some excellent jobs to be had looking after Japanese tour groups. The owner of one Sydney hostel reckons that 'people who speak Japanese usually get a job within three hours of landing in Australia.' The Queensland state capital Brisbane has been attempting to turn its airport into an international hub to relieve some of the pressure on Sydney Airport, which will give a further fillip to Queensland tourism, which suffered a significant downturn post September 11th 2001.

FINDING A JOB

In addition to asking potential employers directly (which is the method used by about a third of successful job-seekers in Australia), there are four main ways of finding work: private employment agencies (note that the government network of jobcentres closed in 2003), newspaper advertisements, the internet and notice boards.

Searching the web for hospitality employment leads is especially productive in Australia. There are dozens of routes in to finding out about job vacancies. The government's www.jobsearch.gov.au is a superb resource listing up-to-date vacancies throughout the country in an easily searchable format, including a category 'Travel Agents and Tour Guides' with contact details of a local employer or employment agency. In addition to the main recruitment websites www.seek.com.au and www.careerone.com.au with substantial numbers of job vacancies posted in hospitality and tourism (mainly chefs, but many others including travel agencies), specialist hospitality recruitment agencies post their vacancies online, though of course they can also be visited:

AA Appointments, 5C/160 Queen St, Melbourne 3000 (03-9670 2577; recruit@aaapp ointments.com.au). Also offices in Brisbane and Sydney plus London (see entry in Directory of Placement Agencies).

Alseasons Hospitality Recruitment, Level 6, 225 Clarence St, Sydney 2000 (02-9324 4666; www.alseasonsagency.com)

Australian Hospitality – www.hospitality.net.au. On-line recruitment.

Hostec Hospitality Services, 56 Kellett St, Potts Point, NSW 2011 (02-9368 0058; www.hostec.com.au)

OutReach Recruitment, Tower House , 2190 Gold Coast Highway, Miami QLD 4220 (07-5554 6811; welcome@outreachrecruitment.com.au)

Pinnacle Hospitality & Travel People – www.pinnaclepeople.com.au. Leading hospitality recruitment specialist with offices in Melbourne, Sydney, Brisbane and the Gold Coast.

Skilled Hospitality & Events, 18 Humphries Terrace, Kilkenny, South Australia 5009 (fax 08-8345 0461; clipsal500@skilled.com.au)

Terence Cox & Associates, – see entry in 'Directory of Placement Agencies'.

Travel People, Level 7, 191 Clarence S, Sydney 2000 (02-9262 1655; jobs@travelpeopl e.com.au). Encourages experienced personnel from the UK to contact them.

Travel Personnel, Level 14, 115 Pitt St, Sydney 2000 (02-9223 9955; employment@trav elpersonnel.com.au). Recruits for jobs throughout the travel industry.

Troys Hospitality Staff, Suite 1, Level 11, 89 York St, Sydney 2000 (02-9290 2955; www.troys.com.au)

V.I.P. Personnel, Level 8, 230 Collins St, Melbourne 3000 (03-9650 9206; info@vipstaff.com.au)

The main daily newspapers have job supplements once or twice a week, for example on Wednesday and Saturday in the *Sydney Morning Herald* (www.smh.com.au), the *West Australian* (Perth), *Adelaide Advertiser* or the *Courier-Mail* (Brisbane). The Monday Job Market in the Melbourne *Age* is particularly worthwhile. The agency website www.mycareer.com.au permits access to up-to-date job ads in the *SMH*, the *Age,* etc. Remember that these wide-circulation papers generate a lot of competition for jobs.

Anyone intending to work in catering and hospitality, health care, education or the pharmaceutical industry must provide a recent medical report assuring the authorities that they are fit enough to travel to Australia and back again at the end of the proposed stay. (Some GPs charge for this service.) For work in restaurants, bars or clubs in most states, a Responsible Service of Alcohol (RSA) Certificate is required which will cost about A$65 to obtain.

Colm Murphy from County Cork took a two-year leave of absence from his job in the airline industry of Ireland in order to work his way around Australia and New Zealand. He spent his first eight days after arrival in Melbourne replying to all the ads before he got occasional Sunday work catering at weddings and parties and after a further blitz of answering ads got a probationary contract as a casual drinks waiter at a suburban restaurant. There is often less competition for jobs advertised in local and suburban papers though transport late at night can be a problem for workplaces out of the city centre.

Colm Murphy describes how his subsequent jobs were much easier to find than the first one:

You have got to sell yourself. Nobody else is going to get you your first job, only your skills, experience and references and most importantly the first impression you make. The manager or human resources person who interviews you has to have a gut instinct that you will be honest and hardworking. When you get a trial or a job, it is very important to have a good attitude and create that vital first impression with work colleagues, management and, most importantly, the customers.

> *If you have a visa restriction that allows you to work for one company for no more than three months, then you hope that your boss will recommend you to another company. The majority of managers have been to college to do a hospitality course so might have old classmates in positions to hire people like you. If your manager works in hospitality his relations might do likewise and might give you a job, which is how I got my second job in Melbourne, when my manager got me a job in the café bar where his uncle was manager. Some of your colleagues will have worked in various hospitality venues (haven't we all?) and they are a good source of contacts, especially those back of house chefs. If they are getting good feedback about you from management and customers they will look after you and do things like get you tickets for a football match. One of the directors I worked for gave me a brand new Manchester United top (I hate Man U! but it was a lovely top). One manager took me down to Phillip Island and out for a meal with his friends, and another paid $50 for me to take a taxi home when we had to stay on unexpectedly late at work.*

TOURS

The Australian Tourist Commission's Traveller's Guide contains quite a few leads to specialist tour operators; request a copy by ringing 0906 863 3235 (60p a minute). Their website www.australia.com has impressively comprehensive links to all manner of tour operators.

Specialist wine tours are gaining popularity, although Australia can cater to almost any sporting or special interest. Camping tour operators proliferate in Darwin, most of them featuring Kakadu National Park; for example try Billy Can Tours (08-8981 9813).

Georgie had always wanted to follow her father into the travel business and studied an ABTA course with a view to qualifying to manage an agency. One weekend while talking to one of the grooms who worked for Kerry Packer (the now disgraced Australian media tycoon) at his polo pony stables at Stedham in Sussex, Georgie came home with an idea. With all her contacts in the world of horse-lovers, she thought there was a niche for specialist tours to Australian events like the Melbourne Gold Cup. She arranged to work at Packer's stables at Ellerston in Australia in order to make contacts. Now she returns twice a year leading groups that go to see the horse scene in Australia and buy polo ponies.

HOTELS AND CATERING

Standards tend to be high in the service industry especially in popular tourist haunts, but anyone with experience as a cook or chef will find him or herself in great demand and being well rewarded. Jobs in catering can usually be found in the major cities, especially Sydney and Melbourne. Outside ordinary restaurants and cafés, catering jobs crop up in cricket grounds, theatres, yacht clubs and (in Sydney) on harbour cruises.

Australian cooking has come out of the dark ages and is admired internationally for its emphasis on fresh fish and healthy fruit and vegetables. A stint in a top Australian restaurant is probably more impressive on a CV than one from France. Harry's catering college had an Australian tutor who helped him to fix up work experience at a top Sydney restaurant:

> *I expected to be laughed at as a Pom, but everyone was very friendly. They didn't even laugh at my accent after I learned how to say a proper 'G'day'. I enjoyed learning how to prepare (and eat) new types of fish, and brought back with me a book full of recipes for when I open my own restaurant.*

Harry had intended to use his savings to travel round Australia after he finished working but instead was offered a step-up in a restaurant in England so returned home with a healthy bank balance.

The websites mentioned above carry many leads. The Holiday Inn Group was advertising at the time of writing for hospitality staff for its hotel in Darwin (hrd@holid ayinndarwin.com.au).

DIVING

The dive industry is a major employer. Although not many visitors would have the qualifications which got Ian Mudge a job as Dive Master on *Nimrod III* operating out of Cookstown in northern Queensland (i.e. qualified mechanical engineer, diver and student of Japanese), his assessment of opportunities for mere mortals is heartening:

> *Anyone wishing to try their luck as a hostess could do no worse than to approach all the dive operators with live-aboard boats such as Mike Ball Water Sports in Townsville, Down Under Dive, etc. 'Hosties' make beds, clean cabins and generally tidy up. Culinary skills and an ability to speak Japanese would be definite pluses. A non-diver would almost certainly be able to fix up some free dive lessons and thus obtain their basic Open Water Diver qualification while being paid to do so. Normally females only are considered for hostie jobs.*

SKI RESORTS

Another holiday area to consider is the Australian Alps where ski resorts are expanding and gaining in popularity. Jindabyne (NSW) on the edge of Kosciusko National Park and Thredbo are the ski job capitals, though Mount Buller, Falls Creek, Baw Baw and Hotham in the state of Victoria are relatively developed ski centres too. The best time to look is a couple of weeks before the season opens which is usually around the middle of June though there is considerable staff turn-over mid-season. Most successful job-seekers use the walk-in-and-ask method, though as everywhere the internet is playing an increasing role. Check out www.ski.com.au/jobs/jobs.html which has a Jobs Database and links to the resorts and pertinent email addresses like jobs@perisher.com.au or recruitment@thredbo.com.au.

Anyone qualified as a ski instructor should attend the hiring clinics held in the big resorts before the season gets underway. Kosciuszko Thredbo Pty Ltd. at the Alpine Ski Village Thredbo (PO Box 92, Thredbo 2625; 02-6459 4100; recruitment@thredbo.co m.au) hire the full range of ski resort staff in three categories: on-the-mountain, hotel and instruction. Their website www.thredbo.com.au provides detailed information about recruitment procedures; applications must be in by mid-April and the names of short-listed candidates will be listed on the website shortly afterwards; interviews take place in Sydney, Brisbane and Thredbo in early May.

CASUAL WORK

If you go out to Australia to look for experience of working in tourism, possibly on a working holiday visa (described below), you may be surprised by the amount of competition from others on working holidays. For example, of the 50 replies to an advertisement placed by a company which operates tours of Sydney Harbour for waiting staff and a receptionist, 42 were from Poms. The glut of travelling workers is especially bad before Christmas.

Yet people on working holidays in Australia pick up an astonishing range of temporary jobs, from acting as a temporary warden in a Tasmanian backpackers' hostel to serving beer at a roadhouse along the nearly uninhabited road through the Australian north-west to working as a temp in a travel agency. Casual employees make up more than half of the total workforce employed in the hospitality industry.

BACKPACKERS' ACCOMMODATION

It is not only impecunious students who stay in backpackers' lodges around Australia. Many are young professionals who are taking time out from their careers to see and sometimes work in Australia. Most Sydney 'backpackers' (they are not generally referred to as hostels) are well clued up on the local job scene, especially in the three main backpackers' areas, sleazy Kings Cross, trendy Glebe and Coogee Beach. The 556-bed YHA hostel opposite the Central Railway Station (corner of Pitt and Rawson Sts) features an employment bureau among a range of state-of-the-art facilities.

The Cronulla Beach YHA (02-9527 7772; www.cronullabeachyha.com) actively assists backpackers to find local jobs as waiting staff, etc. and invites them to submit an on-line employment request form. In the beach suburb of Coogee (pronounced Coodjee) try the Wizard of Oz at 172 Coogee Bay Road (02-9315 7876) and Sydney Beachside next door. Both are regularly contacted for casual workers.

In Melbourne, the Hotel Bakpak in downtown Melbourne is attached to the Backpacker's Resource Centre which can assist people with a working holiday visa as well as provide a range of other back-up services for a fee. In Adelaide, try Rucksackers International at 257 Gilles Street (08-8232 0823) or any of the others along the same road, which try to direct travellers to relevant jobs and agencies. Another recommended Adelaide hostel is Sunny's at 139 Franklin St (08-8231 2430). In Perth, try Redbackpackers, 496 Newcastle St, West Perth (08-9227 9969; www.redbackpackers.com.au) which has strong links with local employers.

QUEENSLAND

Queensland is such a popular destination for visitors from overseas that there is a ready pool of people willing to work in these idyllic surroundings for very little money. The pay is generally so low in seasonal jobs in the Queensland tourist industry that the work does not appeal to many Australians, since they can earn nearly as much on the dole. When employers need to fill a vacancy, they tend to hire whomever is handy that day, rather than sift through applications. For example if you phone from Sydney to enquire about possibilities, the advice will normally be to come and see, which can be expensive if you have to pay for the ferry to several islands before you land a job.

P&O Australian Resorts run the resorts on Heron Island, Lizard Island, Bedarra, Brampton and Dunk Islands plus Silky Oaks Lodge in the Daintree Rainforest of North Queensland. They employ large numbers of seasonal staff, mainly with relevant experience in hospitality. Their employment website (www.poresorts.com/careers) includes detailed fact sheets on living and working in each of their resorts including number of employees, perks and accommodation (normally charged at $35-$50 a week plus $75-$80 for meals) and contact details for job-seekers, e.g. careers@heron.poresorts .com. You could also try in advance Rydges Capricorn International Resort (Farnborough Road, PO Box 350, Yeppoon, Qld 4703; www.capricornresort.com).

If you want a live-in position, you should try the coastal resorts such as Surfers Paradise and Noosa Heads and islands all along the Queensland coast where the season lasts from March, after the cyclones, until Christmas. If Cairns is choc-a-bloc with job-seekers try the huge resort of Palm Cove just north of the city. Here is a list of contacts to whom applications should be addressed to work in specific island resorts:

Fraser Island – Personnel Manager, Kingfisher Bay Resort & Village, PMB Urangan, Hervey Bay, Queensland $655 (008-07 2555).

Heron Island – Assistant Manager, Heron Island Tourist Resort, Heron Island, Via Gladstone, Queensland 4680 (079-78 1488).

Capricorn Coast – Personnel Manager, Capricorn International Resort, Farnborough Road (PO Box 350), Yeppoon, Queensland 4703 (079-39 5111).

Great Keppel Island – Central Recruitment, Australian Resorts, PO Box 1033, Brisbane, Queensland 4000 (079-39 5044).

Be warned that Queensland employers are notorious for laying off their staff at a moment's notice without compensation, holiday pay, etc. Emma Dunnage was disillusioned with one of the six backpackers hostels on Magnetic Island where she worked for ten weeks as a catamaran instructor-cum-general dogsbody. She was paid $100 a week, half of what most of the other staff were getting. In fact there is an 'Offshore Islands Award' for workers in isolated places which is a minimum of $350 a week in addition to board and lodging, though it seems that it is often ignored.

Caroline Perry was fairly confident that a commercial resort like Surfers Paradise would offer opportunities to work but didn't have much luck by filling in forms and waiting for the phone to ring. Eventually she and a friend got work in Movie World, 21km from Surfers Paradise on the Pacific Highway.

The Gold Coast has a number of theme parks with good opportunities for casual work during holiday periods, mainly in food and beverage and retail service. It will be difficult to save any money since wages are not high and you will have to pay for transport between a hostel in town. Check for adverts in the *Gold Coast Bulletin* on Saturdays or in the Brisbane's *Courier Mail*. Alternatively contact the Employment Hotline on 07-5573 8350 which services different theme parks or check the individual websites which feature employment information. They will keep your application on file for up to three months:

Dreamworld, Human Resources Dept, Dreamworld Parkway, Coomera 4209 (www.dreamworld.com.au). Welcome applications by post or in person only.

Movieworld, Human Resources Dept, Oxenford 4210 (www.movieworld.com.au).

Sea World, Sea World Drive, Main Beach, PO Box 190, Surfers Paradise 4217; 07-5588 2222 (www.seaworld.com.au).

Wet 'n' Wild Water World, PO Box 138, Oxenford 4210 (www.wetnwild.com.au).

Yet another possibility for work on the Gold Coast is Conrad Jupiters casino resort; the Recruitment Centre is at PO Box 1515, Broadbeach Island, Broadbeach, Qld 4218 (cjhrd@conrad.com.au) and the website lists current vacancies (www.conrad.com.au/jupiters).

CITIES

Function work is usually easy to come by via specialist agencies provided you can claim to have silver service experience. It is worth applying to catering companies as Fiona Cox did in Sydney, though she was not impressed with the wage of $7.40 an hour (weekly take-home pay of $200).

The best opportunities for bar and waiting staff in Perth are in the city centre, Fremantle and Northbridge, the area around William and James Streets. Rhona Stannage arrived in Perth in November and, having had chalet experience in the French Alps and restaurant experience in Cyprus en route, was in a strong position to find hospitality work:

Since there were lots of adverts in the newspapers for bar/restaurant staff we didn't go door-knocking, but we did meet a Canadian guy who had been in Perth one week and who had immediately found work in Northbridge just by asking around in the restaurants, bars and nightclubs. We both got jobs fairly quickly.

Rhona was also offered a job at the Burswood Resort Casino which often needs staff willing to work shifts (it is open 24 hours). To attract 'permanent' staff, they pay twice the going wage and offer their staff lots of perks such as free meals and a staff gym. In fact casinos are major employers elsewhere, such as the Crown Casino in Melbourne, which claims to be the biggest casino/entertainment complex in the southern hemisphere.

SPECIAL EVENTS

Special events like test matches and race meetings can be seen as possible sources of employment. If you happen to be in Melbourne in late October or early November for the Melbourne Cup (held on the first Tuesday of November which is a public holiday in Victoria) or for the Grand Prix, your chances of finding casual work escalate remarkably. If you can't fix up something in a meet-and-greet capacity, you can always join the army of sweepers and cleaners hired to go through the whole course clearing the huge piles of debris left by 15,000 race-goers. Hotels, restaurants and bars become frantically busy in the period leading up to the Cup, and private catering firms are also often desperate for staff. Last year Daniele Arena had the chance to work at the Phillip Island Racing Circuit just south of Melbourne. They are especially keen to employ casual before the Australian Motorcycle Grand Prix in October and the Superbikes in March.

All the major cities have important horse races. Rowena Caverly was hired for the Darwin Cup Races 'mainly to check that none of the Lady Members had passed out in the loos'.

THE OUTBACK

Uluru or Ayers Rock is a place of pilgrimage for more than a third of a million visitors a year. The nearest facilities are in the Ayers Rock Resort village about 20km north of the Rock. Ayers Rock Resort (formerly known as Yulara) is the fourth largest settlement in the Northern Territory and a good place to look for a job. Although the resort has a waiting list of job-seekers, many people have moved on before they reach the top of the list. The resort employs about 1,000 people in catering and cleaning and many other departments. Staff accommodation is available. It would be worth sending your CV if you have a catering qualification or two years experience in a four-star hotel (Human Resources Department, Ayers Rock Resort, PO Box 46, Yulara, NT 0872; humanresources@ay ersrockresort.com.au; www.voyages.com.au). New Apprenticeships and Certificates in Hospitality and Tourism (levels 2, 3 and 4) are also available to new employees.

WORKING CONDITIONS

Although there is very little unionism in tourist and service industries, award wages are high both in 5-star hotels and fast food restaurants like Fast Eddy's in Melbourne and Perth. The casual rate for hospitality staff is about $15 an hour. Partly because of the tradition of paying high wages in the hotel and catering industry, Australians are not in the habit of tipping much, though this is gradually changing.

REGULATIONS

WORKING HOLIDAY VISAS

The number of working holiday visas has risen sharply from 33,000 in 1995 to 88,750 in 2003/4, nearly half of which go to Britons and the rest to a wide range of nationalities to which Italy and Belgium have been added in 2004. The visa is for people intending to use any money they earn in Australia to supplement their holiday funds. Working full-time for more than three months is not permitted, though you are now permitted to engage in up to three months of studies or training. Applicants must be between the ages of 18 and 30 and without children. You are eligible for a working holiday visa only once. The working holiday visa is valid for 12 months after entry, which must be within 12 months of issue, and is non-renewable.

Britons can apply to an Australian Consulate or though a private visa agency. Since 2002, it has been possible to apply for an electronic working holiday visa. Assuming you are using the traditional paper method, the first step is to get the working holiday information sheet and form 1150 Application for a Working Holiday Makers (WHM) visa from the Department of Immigration (DIMIA) website www.immi.gov.au or a specialist agent like Consyl Publishing (3 Buckhurst Road, Bexhill-on-Sea, East Sussex TN40 1QF; 01424 223111) enclosing an A4 stamped addressed envelope (66p stamp). The non-refundable processing fee in the UK is currently £70 (A$165).

Each application is assessed on its own merits, but the most important requirement is a healthy bank balance. You must have enough money for your return fare, although it is not essential to have a return ticket at the time of entry. You must show evidence of having saved a minimum of A$5,000/£2,000. If your bank statements do not show steady saving, you may have to submit documents showing where the money came from (e.g. sale of a car, gift from a relative).

As of November 2002 a new temporary visa was introduced called the Work and Holiday visa (Subclass 462). Eventually it should be available to young professionals to work for up to 12 months but will not be subject to the same restrictions as the WH visa. However like the WH visa, this visa cannot be turned into a resident visa.

SPECIAL SCHEMES

BUNAC, 16 Bowling Green Lane, London EC1R 0QH (020-7251 3472; downunder@bunac.org). Anyone who is eligible for the working holiday visa to Australia may choose to join the BUNAC Work Australia package which costs from £1,500. This includes the group departures, organised three-day stopover, round-the-world flight, visa, orientation on arrival and back-up services.

CIEE UK, 52 Poland St, London W1F 7AB (020-7478 2020/fax 020-7734 7322; infouk@councilexchanges.org.uk; www.councilexchanges.org.uk) offers the Work and Travel Australia programme. Fees start at £320 to include initial accommodation and a post-arrival orientation at Exchange's Sydney headquarters (University Centre, Level 3, 91 York St, Sydney 2000; 02-8235 7000; info@councilexchanges.org.au) but not visa or insurance costs.

CIEE USA, 7 Custom House Street, 3rd Floor, Portland, ME 04101, USA (1-800-40-Study/ 207-553-7600; www.ciee.org). Travel & Work Australia for US citizens aged 18-30. $500 fee plus visa, etc. Look at CIEE's dedicated work-in-Australia website www.workinaustralia.net.

Kingsbrook Agency, Post Mail Box #117, 303 B Anastasia Boulevard, St. Augustine, FL 32080 (904-461-4291; www.kingsbrookusa.com). Hotel internships in Sydney, Brisbane and Melbourne for people aged 18-30 who want to train to become managers. Minimum stay 12 months. Must have fluent English and hotel, restaurant, culinary studies or associated work experience.

VisitOZ Scheme, Springbrook Farm, MS188, Goomeri, 4601 Queensland (fax 07-4168 6106; www.visitoz.org) sends participants with the working holiday visa to a station on the Queensland/NSW border for a 4-day crash course in hospitality industry skills or in outback working techniques and then guarantees employment on outback properties possibly as hospitality assistants. The cost is £595 if booked in the UK or Ireland, A$1,450 if booked by other nationalities.

Work & Travel Company, 45 High St, Tunbridge Wells, Kent TN1 1XL (01892 516164; www.worktravelcompany.co.uk) sells all-inclusive working holiday package to Australia costing £699 and another providing background assistance for independent travellers for £179.

ISPC (International Student Placement Centre), Suite 804, Level 8, 32 York St, Sydney 2000 (02-9279 0100; info@ispc.com.au). Independent internship provider for foreign trainees including positions in travel agencies and tour operators. Fees start at A$740 for up to six week placements up to A$1,790 for 6-12 month placements.

New Zealand

New Zealand is a charmingly rural country where less than four million natives host more than a million tourists every year. With excellent facilities for visitors and lower air fares, more and more tourists, especially older people, are braving the long flight to New Zealand. The astonishing success of the *Lord of the Rings* trilogy directed by the New Zealander Peter Jackson mainly on location in his native country has also boosted the country's appeal.

Air New Zealand consistently wins awards for in-flight service and this helps to spread the message that NZ is a quality destination. It is a wonderfully laid-back country with a refreshing lack of both European snobbishness and North American materialism. The rate of unemployment has fallen from 6% in 2000 to 4.3% in 2004, and the economy is looking stronger than it has for a long time. If wages are lower than in Australia, life is comparatively cheap.

FINDING A JOB

Openings in New Zealand's flourishing tourist industry generally continue to expand. Waiters and waitresses are usually paid $10-$13 an hour. Remember that tips in New Zealand are virtually non-existent. On the plus side, restaurant kitchens tend to be more relaxed places than they are in Europe. In preparation for the America's Cup of 2000, Auckland's waterfront was transformed and upmarket tourist facilities proliferated. International sporting events like these not only create employment opportunities before and during the event but for years afterwards. Colm Murphy from Ireland was looking for catering work there in 2003 and recommends cold calling at all the bars and restaurants in the Viaduct Harbour, Princes Wharf, Parnell, Ponsonby and Jervois Road areas. Contrary to popular belief, it is possible to make some tips in New Zealand (though there is little tradition of tipping) since Colm made $80-$100 a week extra, especially when foreign tourists came to dine:

> *Admittedly waiting on Kiwis is soul destroying. On numerous occasions I had big tables of 10-12 Kiwis and they never tipped me. They will thank you profusely for the service but they will not tip. To a certain type of Kiwi (especially those from south of the Bombay Hills, i.e. south of Auckland) tipping is an alien concept.*

Private agencies may be of some help in the job hunt, both to qualified tourism professionals and to people on working holidays. The former can contact, for example, Hospitality Recruitment, PO Box 90198 AMSC, Auckland (09-379 7532; www.hhes.co.nz) or in the South Island: The Hospitality People Limited, PO Box 12-242, Christchurch (03-329 9900; info@hospo.com). A Job Search service for backpackers is operated by Auckland Central Backpackers (229 Queen St; 09-358 4877;

jobs@acb.co.nz; www.acbtravel.co.nz or www.nzjobs.go.to). Registered members have access to vacancy information in the hospitality industry, among others. The ACB also sells a starter pack which includes 12 months registration with Job Search, four nights accommodation on arrival, etc. for $245.

Hotels in Paihia in the far north are reputed to be often short-staffed. The explosion of cafés, bars and boat trip companies means that someone determined to find a tourism job in this area would be likely to succeed, especially if they could conduct a job hunt in October.

Although Wellington is not the first city you think of in the context of New Zealand tourism, it has a remarkably high ratio of cafés to citizen and a booming job market. Catharine Carfoot showed up there in November with a working holiday visa (though she wasn't always asked to show it) and easily found work first and accommodation second:

> *I worked weekends driving for Wellington Cable Cars which has its ups and downs (cable car joke). Bizarrely, I ended up practising my French conversation skills more than I had done for years, both at the Cable Car and with people met on the street asking for directions. It seems very odd that even the bigger hotels here don't always have a francophone on duty.*

Note that the cable car and many tourist operations become very busy in February which marks the cruise ship season.

Despite the sophistication of New Zealand urban life, the country's tourist industry adopts many adventurous and sporting guises. You might get taken on by a camping tour operator as a cook; perhaps you could find a job on a yacht or in a ski resort (see below). New Zealand's prime attraction is its outdoor life, mostly just admiring it but also hiking, sailing, game fishing, rafting, skiing, mountaineering and so on. Anyone who has had experience of working for a rafting company in America or Europe might contact the rafting tour operators (names available from the New Zealand Tourist Office).

Visitors also go to see the bizarre geology of the country with its volcanic hot pools and geysers. Special interest tours go to see the vineyards which have made such an impact on the international market and people interested in agriculture go to visit farms. Many small specialised travel agencies in the UK now organise one New Zealand tour a year for clients. Unfortunately this is usually led by the owner, but those who know the country well might find an opening or even organise their own small-scale tour.

Tours for farmers are an unexpected source of employment. If you have worked as a tour manager, know your lambs from your hogs, and have a pair of wellies, you may be able to take advantage of farmers' interest in seeing the latest farming methods and also some traditional organic ones as well. Companies can occasionally be seen advertising in the farming press like *Valley Farmer, Farmers' Weekly* and the *Sheep Farmer*.

SKI RESORTS

The ski season lasts roughly from July to October. Of the dozen commercial ski fields in the country, the main ones on the South Island are Coronet Peak and the Remarkables (serviced by Queenstown), Mount Hutt and Treble Cone (with access from Wanaka). On the North Island, Mount Ruapehu is the main ski area, at least when its volcanic activity is dormant. The ski field at Turoa is serviced by the resort of Ohakune and the ski area of Whakapapa by the settlement called National Park.

Catering and related jobs are widely available in these resort towns. Altogether NZ ski resorts employ about a thousand seasonal staff. In addition to the hourly wage of $10-$15 you may be given a lift pass and subsidised food and drink. Matt Tomlinson enjoyed his two jobs in Ohakune as a barman in the ski resort bar and a waiter in a restaurant, though he came to the conclusion that New Zealand bosses like to get their money's worth. When there weren't many customers, he was put to work building shelves, chopping wood and cleaning drains. He found the jobs by checking notice boards (by the library in Ohakune and in the supermarket), reading the local newspapers and asking around. Altogether the Ruapehu/Ohakune area absorbs about 700 seasonal workers so there is plenty of scope. One of the main employers in the area is Ruapehu Alpine Lifts Ltd (Private Bag, Mount Ruapehu; 07-892 3738; who accept applications until mid-April and interview candidates in the first week of May; details are available on www.mtruapehu.com/employment_opportunities.asp. You will also have to keep your ears open if you are to find affordable accommodation.

QUEENSTOWN & THE SOUTH ISLAND

The lakeside resort of Queenstown is a town whose economy is booming due to tourism and whose population is largely young and transient. It is now almost as common to hear foreign accents among seasonal workers as New Zealand ones, though bear in mind that for this reason Queenstown has become a target for immigration investigations. Notice boards around town and in backpacker haunts often carry adverts for waitresses, kitchen help, etc. One of the perks of being a worker in Queenstown and therefore an honorary resident (instead of a 'loopy', the local term for tourist), is that workers can often get discounts on local activities like rafting or 'zorbing' (rolling down a hill in a plastic ball). On the other hand, the town's popularity means that there are often more people (including New Zealanders) looking for work than there are jobs, so it might be advisable to try more remote tourist areas, like sparsely populated but heavily visited Milford Sound. It is accepted practice to phone the resort hotels and ask if they have any immediate vacancies. Good resorts to phone in addition to Milford Sound are Fox Glacier, Franz Josef and Mount Cook.

REGULATIONS

Visitors from the UK need no visa to stay for up to six months. Tourists entering the country may be asked to show an onward ticket and about NZ$1,000 per month of their proposed stay (unless they have pre-paid accommodation or a New Zealand backer who has pledged support in a crisis). In practice, respectable-looking travellers are unlikely to be quizzed at entry.

New Zealand grants working holiday visas to many nationalities including Canadian, Irish and most European countries. The UK Citizens' Working Holiday Scheme allows Britons aged 18-30 to do temporary jobs in New Zealand for up to 12 months. When the scheme was introduced in 1993, the quota was 500. That number has now risen (from 2003) to 9,000 working holiday visas which are granted annually on a first come first served basis starting from September 1st. Although the literature says the quota fills quickly, the increased number means that visas should be available throughout the year (though they may run out in the summer). Information can be obtained from the New Zealand Immigration Service, Mezzanine Floor, New Zealand House, 80 Haymarket, London SW1Y 4TE (fax 020-7973 0370) in person, by phone on 09069 100100 (charged at £1 per minute) or via the internet www.immigration.govt.nz. To apply you need an Application for Work Visa form, your UK passport valid for 28 months beyond the date of application, the fee of NZ$120 (£44), a return ticket and evidence of NZ$4,200 (about £1,400).

A possible alternative to the working holiday visa for those who have contacts in New Zealand or special skills and can obtain a firm offer of employment before leaving the UK is to apply for a temporary Work Visa for a non-refundable fee of £107 (NZ$290).

Your sponsoring employer in New Zealand must be prepared to prove to the Immigration Service that it is necessary to hire a foreigner rather than an unemployed New Zealander. The work visa does not in itself entitle you to work, but does make it easier to obtain a work permit after arrival. If you are granted a work visa before departure it will allow you to stay for up to three years.

For the past couple of years it has been possible for people on working holidays to apply to extend their stay or even for residence without having to leave New Zealand. Applicants with skills in demand (e.g. chefs) may apply for a work permit that will be valid for up to nine months from the date of arrival at one of the seven Immigration Service offices in New Zealand.

Americans aged 18-30 are now eligible to apply for a 12-month work exchange visa through approved organisations like BUNAC USA (www.bunac.org), CIEE (www.ciee.org) and CCUSA (www.ccusa.com). Canadians may obtain a working holiday visa independently or may apply through the Student Work Abroad Programme or SWAP (www.swap.ca); the SWAP participation fee is C$385.

SPECIAL SCHEMES

BUNAC has a Work New Zealand programme which provides the usual range of services to students and non-students: group departures, organised 3-day stopover, round-the-world flight, visa, orientation on arrival and ongoing support from their partner International Exchange Programs (IEP) in New Zealand. The package is available for an inclusive fee of about £1,700.

CIEE UK (www.ciee.org.uk) operates a scheme for up to 12 months, which includes initial accommodation, post-arrival orientation and job assistance on arrival. The Work Experience Downunder programme from *CCUSA* (Green Dragon House, 64-70 High St, Croydon CR0 9XN; 020-8688 9051; www.ccusaweusa.co.uk) operates to New Zealand as well as Australia. The application and programme fees come to £375 plus insurance, travel and visas.

Changing Worlds (11 Doctors Lane, Chaldon, Surrey CR3 5AE; 01883 340960; www.changingworlds.co.uk) offer job placements (among others) in hotels or on a tall ship based in the Bay of Islands, primarily to gap year students. The programme fee including flights is £2,495.

Work & Travel Company, 45 High St, Tunbridge Wells, Kent TN1 1XL (01892 516164; www.worktravelcompany.co.uk) organises working holiday package to New Zealand costing £599 and another providing background assistance for independent travellers for £139.

NORTH AMERICA

United States

In a bid to reverse the post-September 11th decline in tourism to America, airfare wars between transatlantic carriers hotted up, making it almost as cheap to take a holiday in Florida or in New York as in Prague or Paris. By far the most important long haul market for the British market is the US which received over 4 million UK visitors last year.

The influx of Europeans to popular US destinations combined with the millions of Americans and Canadians who take their holidays in the United States accounts for the staggering statistic from the National Travel & Tourism Awareness Council in Washington DC that there are six million jobs in the American tourist industry. It is the second largest employer in the country after health services and generates hundreds of thousands of interesting job vacancies a year.

There is a catch however, unless you are working for a UK tour operator. It is exceedingly difficult to get an immigrant visa or 'green card' which allows foreigners to live and work in the US as 'resident aliens'. Nearly all permanent resident visas are issued to close relations of American citizens. Other possibilities are that you can offer a skill which is in short supply and have a US employer willing to sponsor your application for labour certification, or you may be eligible to participate in one of the special schemes for students, trainees, etc.

EXCHANGE PROGRAMMES

Approved organisations such as *BUNAC* and *Camp America* can assist students and some non-students to obtain a special J-1 work and travel visa. A large part of both organisations' programmes consists of placing young people on summer camps, but first we will consider BUNAC's more generalised *Work America Programme* which allows full-time university students to do any summer job they are able to find, including jobs in the tourist industry. Obviously the dates of the programme (June to October) do not allow much scope for advancing a career in tourism. However a summer spent doing a seasonal job in an American resort can be useful on your CV.

BUNAC (16 Bowling Green Lane, London EC1R 0QH; 020-7251 3472) administers three basic programmes in the US: one is the 'Work America Programme' which allows full-time university students to do any summer job they are able to find before or after arrival; the second is 'Summer Camp USA' which is open to anyone over 19 interested in working on a summer camp as a counsellor; the third is 'KAMP' (Kitchen & Maintenance Programme) which is open to students who want to work at a summer camp in a catering and maintenance capacity. All participants must join the BUNAC Club (£4), travel between June and October and purchase compulsory insurance (about £120). BUNAC runs its own loan scheme for selected programmes.

As part of the application for student-only programmes, you must submit a letter from your principal, registrar or tutor on college headed paper showing that you are a full-time student in the year of travel. Gap year students should submit evidence of an unconditional offer for the September/October after they have returned from the US. You are also required to take at least $400 in travellers cheques.

To assist Work America Programme applicants in finding work, BUNAC publishes an annual Job Directory with thousands of job listings in the US from hundreds of employers, many of whom have taken on BUNAC participants in the past. The Directory is available to all potential applicants and is free of charge. To widen your scope, you might look at job search web-sites such as www.seasonalemployment.com which lists summer jobs mainly in resorts and parks. Further contacts can be found in the annually revised book *Summer Jobs in the USA* distributed in Britain by Vacation Work at £12.99.

Camp America (37a Queen's Gate, London SW7 5HR; 020-7581 7333; www.campamerica.co.uk) runs a summer programme called *Resort America* of special interest to students of tourism and hospitality. This programme lasts between 12 and 16 weeks from June and is open to British, German and Polish students who have turned 19 by the time of departure. Participants are assigned to a summer job in a resort or hotel, given a free return flight and an end-of-contract payment of $1,3000 for 12 weeks plus an extra $175 per week up to a maximum of 16 weeks.

INTERNSHIPS

Internship is the American term for traineeship, normally unpaid, providing a chance to get some experience in your career interest as part of your academic course. These are typically available to undergraduates and recent graduates rather than to school leavers. Several organisations in the UK arrange for students and graduates to undertake internships in the US. BUNAC operates an internship programme dubbed OPT USA (Overseas Practical Training) sponsored by International Program Services of the American YMCA. The programme is open to non-students as well as students over the age of 19 and of any nationality but must be integrated into between three and 18 months of on-the-job training (and not just work experience). Programme fees vary from £190 to £440.

Another important sending agency is CIEE, 52 Poland St, London W1F 7AB (020-7478 2020; www.ciee.org.uk) which helps more than 1,500 students, graduates and young professionals arrange career-related work placements in the US. The Professional Career Training (PCT) programme permits people aged 20-40 with a professional qualification or two-year apprenticeship to spend between three and 18 months working for a US employer. Internships USA is open to students who take up a placement relevant to their careers at any time during studies, during a sandwich year or after graduating. Although you are responsible for finding your own placement, CIEE offers a job search service as part of the programme, which includes a searchable database of internships/ work placements plus job advice and CV writing feedback. In order to gain access to their database of potential employers it is necessary to pre-enrol for a fee of £30. Those who qualify for the programmes get a J-1 visa allowing them to work in the USA for up to 18 months. The programme fees start at £340.

While studying for a leisure and recreational management degree at Thames Valley University, Neil Hibberd arranged a CIEE internship at a Colorado ski resort:

The Council's policy is that they need a letter from the employer before giving you the visa. I first went out to Colorado in August. The Steamboat Ski Corporation gave me a written job offer as a lift operator on the condition that I could obtain a work visa. I returned to the UK, obtained the visa through the CIEE and went back to Steamboat in October. Travelling twice to the States and paying for the work visa and insurance came to £650, which exhausted my savings. Looking back on the process, I see that there should be an easier way to obtain such a placement.

The *Association for International Practical Training* or AIPT in Maryland (info@aipt.org) administers the UK/US Career Development Programme. This programme is for people aged 18-35 with relevant qualifications and/or at least two years of work experience in their career field. A separate section of the programme is for full-time students in Hospitality & Tourism or Equine Studies.

Cultural Cube, 16 Acland Rd, Ivybridge, Devon PO21 9UR (www.culturalcube.co.uk) runs two internship programmes, one for the hospitality industry, the other for business. Hospitality internships are available for 12 months in and around Atlanta. Programme fee £1,490; monthly stipend $400 on top of accommodation.

Work & Travel Company, 45 High St, Tunbridge Wells, Kent TN1 1XL (01892 516164; www.worktravelcompany.co.uk) places international applicants in a work-related field for work experience lasting 3-18 months. Fees from £250 to £375 depending on the length of stay in the US. Wages paid on a par with US co-workers.

The *American Hospitality Academy,* 3 Pope Avenue, Executive Park Drive, Hilton Head Island, SC 29928 (tel/fax 843-785-4368; info@AmericanHospitalityAcademy.com) is authorised to dispense J-1 visas to university students who want to participate in the Work & Travel Program. Suitable candidates will be placed at AHA resort locations in Myrtle Beach and Hilton Head Island (South Carolina) and Orlando (Florida). The fee is $500 for a 3-4 month summer internship and $1000 for a 5-12 month internship. This programme is intended to be an introduction to what a career in the hospitality industry entails.

The Dutch-based company *HRC International* (see Directory entry) which offers career opportunities worldwide to young culinary and hotel professionals in the international hospitality industry is especially strong on the USA. Its Careers USA Operations is a programme that gives trainees exposure to different departments such as banquets, restaurant, bar, room service, front desk, reservations, housekeeping, concierge and guest relations. The separate Careers USA Culinary programme involves no expense to participants apart from airfare and €45 per month for insurance; living costs are covered by wages paid and the $800 visa fee is waived.

Alliance Abroad Group Trainee Program, Barton Skyway, Suite 250, 1221 South Mopac Expressway, Austin, TX 78746 (512-457-8062/1-888-6-ABROAD; vnoel@allianceabroad.com/ www.allianceabroad.com). Professional trainee positions lasting 6, 12 or 18 months for students or recent graduates seeking further training while gaining experience. Paid positions are available in many fields, including hospitality, hotel management and culinary arts.

Kingsbrook USA Inc. PMB 117, 303 B Anastasia Boulevard, St. Augustine, FL 32080, USA (www.kingsbrookusa.com). Hotel management internships available in upscale hotels, resorts, marinas, ski resorts, country clubs and golf resorts. Training programme incorporated.

Smaller more local opportunities may crop up. For example on the website www.hospitalitynet.org, an immigration lawyer was offering to place qualified hotel, restaurant, and culinary management trainees from abroad in positions in New York and North Carolina in 2003/4 (Ms Becki Young, 2301 California St NW, Suite 101, Washington, DC 20008; 202-232-0983; youngb@blylaw.com/ www.blylaw.com).

The 750-page book *Internships* published by Peterson's Guides lists intern positions which are paid or unpaid, can last for the summer, for a semester or for a year. The book offers general advice (including a section called 'Foreign Applicants for US Internships') and specific listings organised according to field of interest, e.g. Advertising, Museums, Radio, Social Services, Law, etc. This annually revised book is available in the UK from Vacation-Work for £18.99 plus £3 postage.

TOURS

Experienced tour managers or people familiar with a popular region of the States should apply to the major UK operators like Shearings, Travelsphere, Cosmos and Titan Travel. Typically these companies offer tours of the west coast, California, Florida, the Deep South, the national parks (Grand Canyon, Yellowstone, etc.), plus possibly tours to Hawaii and Alaska too. Having worked two seasons in Europe, Robin wanted to widen her horizons so applied to join Travelsphere. As part of the interview she was videoed giving a commentary which she found somewhat daunting, but was subsequently offered a job taking groups around the States.

People who have worked in Europe for one of the major international coach tour operators based in the States may find work on their employers' domestic tours of the US. Among the most important US operators are:

Globus/Cosmos Vacations, 5301 South Federal Circle, Littleton, Colorado 80123 (800-276-1241; www.cosmosvacations.com/ www.globusjourneys.com). UK address: Cosmos Tourama, 1 Wren Court, 17 London Road, Bromley, Kent BR1 1DE (020-8464 3444; www.cosmostourama.co.uk)

Maupintour Inc, 10650 W Charleston Boulevard, Summerlin, NV 89135 (800-255-4266; fax 702-260-3787; www.maupintour.com)

Mayflower Tours, 1225 Warren Ave, PO Box 490, Downers Grove, Illinois 60515 (630-435-8500; info@mayflowerstours.com). Continental USA, Hawaii, Alaska and Canada.

Tauck World Discovery, 1 Norden Place, Norwalk, Connecticut 06855 (203-226-6911; TD_Recruitment@tauck.com for Tour Director positions and hrtauck@tauck.com for other vacancies). Plenty of recruitment information on website www.tauck.com.

Others are included on the list of active members of the National Tour Association, 546 East Main Street, Lexington, KY 40508 (859-682-4444; www.ntaonline.com).

For UK tour operators specialising in North America, see the website www.visitusa.org.uk and search its member tour operators which include the major ones such as:

Colours of America, Leisure House, Station Road, Kings Langley, Herts. WD4 8LQ (0870 900 5002; www.coloursofamerica.com)

Delta Vacations, address as above (0870 900 6002; www.deltavacations.co.uk)

Jetsave America & Canada, Sussex House, London Road, East Grinstead, W Sussex RH19 1HJ (www.jetsave.co.uk)

Statesavers, Suite 11, 33 Chapel St, Buckfastleigh, Devon TQ11 0AB (01364 644477; info@statesavers.co.uk)

United Vacations, United House, Southern Perimeter Road, Heathrow Airport, Hounslow, Middlesex TW6 3LP (020-8276 6647; www.unitedvacations.co.uk)

SPECIAL INTEREST HOLIDAYS

Americans are very enthusiastic about outdoor and activity holidays, for which suitably qualified cyclists, hikers and so on are needed, though of course most of these positions are filled by Americans. The best resource for someone with a specialised skill or interest they want to put to use in the American tourist industry is the *Specialty Travel Index* published twice a year (spring/summer and autumn/winter) for $10 per annum within North America, $22 abroad. It lists hundreds of companies worldwide, the majority American, including hiking, biking, golfing, winery, cookery, cruising and a host of others from astrology to zoology tours to following in the footsteps of Sherlock Holmes or Count Dracula. Much of the information can be found on the website www.specialtytravel.com and the hard copy is available from STI, 305 San Anselmo Avenue, San Anselmo, CA 94960 (415-459-4900).

National parks spawn a huge summer tourist industry and their recruitment needs are often publicised and filled via the internet, for example Glacier National Park in Montana near the Canadian border on www.nps.gov/glac.whatsnew/jobs.htm and Denali Park in Alaska (www.nps.gov/dena); the latter hires nearly 1,000 people each summer (early May to mid-September). Facilities in the famous national parks of Utah (Bryce Canyon, Zion Canyon and the Grand Canyon North Rim) are run by Xanterra Recreational Services (www.resortjobs.com/xanterra.html or www.coolworks.com/utahparks). Xanterra also recruit for the even more famous Yellowstone National Park in Wyoming which offers 2,500 seasonal jobs (www.yellowstonejobs.com). The Concession Services Corporation at Yosemite National Park in California can be contacted at PO Box 578, CA 95389 (209-372-1236; www.yosemitepark.com/html/jobs.html). Another splendid website for this kind of work is www.funjobs.com.

Camping tours are popular with a younger clientele; try TrekAmerica, Grange Mills, Weir Road, London SW12 0NE (0870-444 8735; www.trekamerica.co.uk). Suntrek Tours Inc (Sun Plaza, 77 West Third Street, Santa Rosa, CA 95401; personnel@suntrek.com) recruit fun-loving trek leaders and tour guides. Prospective staff, including foreigners with a J-1 visa, can enrol in a Suntrek training camp between mid-April and July and, if successful, take up a seasonal position with the company. They also sometimes need office personnel who are interested in pursing a career in the travel industry.

Wine tours are gaining popularity not only in California's famous Napa Valley but in other areas as well, often in conjunction with cycling tours.

SKI RESORTS

There is plenty of winter work in ski resorts, especially in Colorado, between December and the 'Mud Season' in May. Aspen, Vail and Steamboat Springs Colorado have all been recommended. Much of it can be investigated on-line, e.g. through www.jobmonkey.com/ski or www.skiingthenet.com/jobs.htm.

If you are prepared to travel in person, the best time to arrive is October/November when the big resorts hold job fairs. Jobs are available as lift operators, restaurant workers, ticket clerks, basket check (like left luggage for skiers) assistants, etc. The main problem in big resorts (especially Vail) is a lack of employee accommodation. Unless you arrive in August/September, you will have to be very lucky to find a room of any kind. Check adverts in the local papers for example in *Steamboat Today* and *Steamboat Pilot*. The former carries nearly 100 help wanted ads in the winter months (and even more in the summer).

Also check the resorts' websites which have links from the employment website www.coolworks.com. You should also be aware that immigration raids are frequent, which makes employers reluctant to hire people without papers even when desperate for staff. This danger is less likely at small out-of-the-way resorts like Purgatory or Crested Butte in Colorado but then of course there will be fewer jobs.

The Steamboat Springs Chamber Resort Association (PO Box 77408, 1255 Lincoln Ave, Steamboat Springs, CO 80477; 970-879-0880/fax 970-879-2543; www.steamboatchamber.com/comm/employment.htm) is helpful to job-seekers. It publishes a free leaflet 'Live, Work & Play in Ski Town USA' which includes an Employment Resource List. Job Fairs are held around the first weekend of November where employers can meet job-seekers.

It is common for one company to own all the facilities and control all employment in one resort, and in some cases provide accommodation to all staff. In Steamboat it is the Steamboat Springs Ski & Resort Corporation (907-871-5132; personnel@steamboat.com). In Vail try Vail Resorts Inc. PO Box 7, Vail, CO 81658 which also has a dedicated freephone jobs line 1-888-Ski-Job-1 and an employment website http: //skijob1.snow.com. Over in New England, the relevant company in Stowe Vermont is Stowe Mountain Resort who arrange job fairs in October and November and whose Human Resources Department sifts through job applications (5781 Mountain Road, Stowe, VT 05672; 802-253-3541; jobs@stowe.com).

Neil Hibberd worked a season as a ski lift operator for the Steamboat Corporation on a J-1 visa fixed up through CIEE's Internship Programme (described at the beginning of the chapter). According to Neil the Corporation offers subsidised rental accommodation to its employees who pay about $200 a month in rent.

Aspen is one of the wealthiest resorts and supports a large transient working population. The Aspen Skiing Company is heavily involved with the hiring of foreign workers through approved agencies. Because of the popularity of working in the resort among people with a J-1 or H2-B visa (see below), they encourage interested candidates to start the application procedures as early as May for the following ski season. The company is permitted to submit visa applications in July; the website www.aspensnowmass.com (click on the Jobs link) contains a wealth of detailed information about the recruitment procedures for non-US citizens.

SUMMER CAMPS

For anyone who has never worked in tourism, a sideways introduction is to work at summer camps, which cater to a very junior kind of tourist. Summer camps are uniquely American in atmosphere, even if the idea has spread to Europe. Almost every American kid is at some point sent to summer camp for a week or more to participate in outdoor activities and sports, arts and crafts and generally have a wholesome experience. The type of camp varies from plush sports camps for the very rich to more or less charitable camps for the handicapped or underprivileged.

It is estimated that summer camps employ nearly a third of a million people for eight or nine weeks in June, July and August. Each summer thousands of 'counsellors' are recruited in Europe to be in charge of a cabinful of youngsters and to instruct or supervise some activity, from the ordinary (swimming and boating) to the esoteric (puppet-making and ham radio). There is also a massive demand for catering and maintenance staff which may bring less status but more money.

For Europeans, the two major camp placement organisations authorised to issue J-1 visas are *BUNAC* (address earlier in the chapter) and *Camp America* (37a Queen's Gate, London SW7 5HR; 020-7581 7333; www.campamerica.co.uk). Camp America arranges for a massive 10,000 people aged 18 or over, from around the world, to work on children's summer camps in the USA. The work is for nine weeks between June and August where you could be teaching activities such as tennis, swimming and arts and crafts. Another programme is arranged by Camp Counselors USA (CCUSA, Green Dragon House, 64-70 High Street, Croydon CR0 9XN; 020-8688 9051; www.ccusaweusa.co.uk).

THEME PARKS & ATTRACTIONS

Apart from Disney's two major attractions in Anaheim California and Orlando Florida (employment at the latter is described in the next section), the United States boasts some of the most gigantic and innovative theme parks in the world, employing thousands of seasonal staff and many professionals as well. The giant Anheuser-Busch Brewery has a huge investment in tourist attractions including Sea World (500 Seaworld Drive, San Diego, CA 92109) and Busch Gardens and Adventure Island in Tampa Bay, Florida; their recruitment website is www.becjobs.com.

The International Association of Amusement Parks and Attractions (1448 Duke St, Alexandria, VA 22314; 703-836-4800) can advise on how to train for specific attractions. Some American attractions employ as many as 3,000 seasonal assistants to work on rides and games, food service, customer services, etc. Here is a small selection of major attractions:

Caesar's Palace Inc, 3570 Las Vegas Blvd S, Las Vegas, NV 89109 (702-731-7110; www.caesarsjobs.com)

Hershey Entertainment & Resort Co, Personnel Office, 75 East Derry Road, Hershey, PA 17033 (717-520-JOBS; jobs@hersheypa.com)

Knott's Berry Farm, 8039 Beach Boulevard, Buena Park, CA 90620 (714-995-6688; www.knotts.com/jobs/index.asp). Seasonal and professional openings.

Paramount Parks, PO Box 1776, Santa Clara, CA 95052 (408-986-5825; pga.jobs@par amountparks.com)

San Diego Zoo, PO Box 120551, San Diego, CA 92112-0551 (619-557-3968; www.sandiegozoo.org)

HOTELS & CATERING

Hotels in the US are mainly staffed by people who intend to make 'hospitality vending' their career. The lead body for the industry is the American Hotel & Lodging Association (AH&LA, 1201 New York Ave NW, Washington, DC 20005; 202-289-3100; www.ahla.com). The AH&LA's Information Center sends out various leaflets including a directory of hotel/motel companies and a brief list of placement firms, all of which operate at the executive level. It also overseas training through its own Educational Institute in Michigan (2113 N. High St, Lansing, MI 48906; 517-372-8800; info@ei-ahla.org).

All the major hotel chains create tens of thousands of job vacancies. The Marriott group is among the most voracious for employees and co-operates with many of the international internship programmes mentioned earlier in this chapter: Marriott International, Inc., Marriott Drive, Washington, DC 20058; 301-380-3000; http://careers.marriott.com). There are of course many jobs in catering, the majority of which are merely casual work (see section below). Try also Starwood Hotels & Resorts Worldwide, Inc. which incorporate the Sheraton, Westin and several other chains of luxury hotels (777 Westchester Ave, White Plains, NY 10604; 914-640-8100; www.star woodcareers.com).

FLORIDA

Despite some recent bad publicity over crime, the state of Florida continues to be in the top ten destinations for European tourists, and a great many UK tour operators feature it. As usual, companies normally send out only those employees who have proved their capabilities in European resorts.

The industry is centred on Orlando, gateway to Walt Disney World, which has a more user-friendly airport than Miami (where holidaymakers are given information leaflets on how to avoid being mugged). UK reps are sometimes hired by tour operators to accompany groups of holidaymakers. One of the biggest UK operators to Florida is Virgin Holidays near Gatwick (The Galleria, Station Road, Crawley RH10 1WW; www.virginholidays.co.uk) though they say that they hire only supervisory staff from the UK. Common or garden resort reps are hired on location and must therefore have the right to live and work in the US before applying.

Tony had worked one summer season in Spain when he applied for a winter job in Florida not expecting to get it. However his availability to fill a last-minute vacancy meant that he flew off to Orlando with a group. On arrival he met his resort manager and the local Disney group tour co-ordinator who told him that research proves that the longer people queue for a ride, the more their excitement and subsequent enjoyment builds up. Tony was especially grateful for the part of his information pack which listed the top ten attractions for each age group, since he was repeatedly asked for this kind of advice by his clients. He loved his six months in Florida: everyone was very friendly, there were lots of parties around the poolside and (compared to Spain) the plumbing was admirable. Like many Europeans who spend time in the US, his main complaint was that all those 'have a nice days' begin to feel a little synthetic after a while.

WALT DISNEY WORLD

The Disney Corporation is renowned both in its home country and in Europe for offering a very rigorous training programme, and a stint at Disney enhances the CV of anyone who wants to work in tourism.

The International Recruiting Department of Walt Disney's EPCOT Center (PO Box 10090, Lake Buena Vista, Florida 32830-0090) prefer to rely on the word of mouth network rather than have their six month or one year vacancies for young people to work as 'cultural representatives' widely publicised. People aged 18-28 from Britain and ten other countries are hired to represent the culture and customs of their countries; in the case of the UK this means olde worlde pubs, Scotch eggs and Royal Doulton china. Anyone applying will probably have to wait months until there is space at one of the two annual recruiting presentations which Disney organises in Britain in March and October. Any job which involves tips is usually more lucrative than others; wages can be swelled by more than $100 in a five-hour shift. The staff facilities are attractive with pools, jacuzzis, tennis courts and subsidised rent. Paul Binfield from Kent describes the process of being hired by Disney as 'a long and patient' one:

> *I initially wrote to Disney in October and started my contract in January, 15 months later. It was the most enjoyable year of my life, experiencing so many excellent things and making the best friends from all over the world. The pros far outweigh the cons, though some people did hate the work. Disney is a strict company with many rules which are vigorously enforced. The work in merchandising or the pub/restaurant is taken extremely seriously and sometimes it can be hard to manufacture a big cheesy Disney smile. There are dress codes (for example men have to be clean shaven every day), verbal and written warnings for matters which would be considered very trivial in Britain, and indeed terminations (which is a very nasty word for being fired). If you go with the right attitude it can be great fun.*

In your first week the induction course will teach you the Disney way of doing things, always smiling. You could be selling British merchandise, selling baked potatoes from a wheeled cart or working in an ersatz English pub. Moving up you graduate to being a waiter and therefore in on the 'tronc' (shared tips). The further you progress the better the money.

Outside the world of Disney, other Florida attractions include Sea World & Discovery Cove (7007 SeaWorld Drive, Orlando, FL 32821; 407-370-1562) which looks to hire college graduates and others with animal handling and scuba skills. The Sanibel Harbor Resort & Spa (17260 Harbour Pointe Drive, Fort Myers, Florida 33908; 239-418-2825) publishes vacancies in many departments on its website www.sanibel-resort.com/careerop.html.

CRUISE LINES

Miami is the cruise capital of the world which is easy to believe when you see the number of vast white hulls gliding in and out of the harbour. As described in the introductory section *Cruise Ships,* any nationality can work at sea without having to obtain a visa for working in the US. This is not the case if you work on land, though the cruise companies generate a lot of office-based employment. For example hundreds of reservations sales agents, air/sea agents and documentation agents are needed in the cruise lines' corporate offices; applicants must not only have travel training but they must be legally entitled to work in the US. See the section on *Cruise Ships* in the introduction for a list of cruise line offices and concessionaires.

CASUAL WORK

Labour demands in summer resorts sometimes reach crisis proportions especially along the eastern seaboard. However the majority of catering staff are paid the minimum wage of $5.15 an hour (higher in some states such as California where it is $6.75), although exceptions can be made in tipped positions where the legal minimum is much lower. An average weekly take in tips for a full-time waiter/waitress might be $100-$150 with possibilities of earning twice that. Bar staff earn even more in tips, as much as $200 a night (but note that bar staff have to be the legal drinking age of 21). Apparently a British accent helps.

Plenty of British and Irish people find work in Los Angeles, New Orleans (especially around the time of the Jazz Festival at the end of April) and also in the cafés of Greenwich Village New York, though you'll have to serve a great many generous tippers before you'll be able to afford accommodation in Manhattan. Live-in jobs are preferable, and are often available to British students whose terms allow them to stay beyond Labor Day, the first Monday in September, when most American students resume their studies. After working a season at a large resort in Wisconsin, Timothy Payne concluded:

> *Without doubt the best jobs in the USA are to be found in the resorts, simply because they pay a reasonable wage as well as providing free food and accommodation. Since many resorts are located in remote spots, it is possible to save most of your wages and tips, and also enjoy free use of the resort's facilities. Whatever job you end up with you should have a good time due to the large number of students working there.*

SEASIDE RESORTS

Popular resorts like Wildwood New Jersey near Atlantic City, Virginia Beach (Virginia), Myrtle Beach (South Carolina) and Atlantic Beach (North Carolina) offer thousands of jobs for young Americans. Britons will fare best in April/May or late August when Americans are back at college. Katherine Smith, who got her J-1 visa through BUNAC, describes the range of jobs she found in Ocean City, a popular seaside resort in Maryland:

> *I decided to spend my summer in Ocean Beach because I knew the job scene would be favourable. I found a job as a waitress in a steak restaurant and another full-time job as a reservations clerk in a hotel by approaching employers on an informal basis and enquiring about possible job vacancies. In my case this was very fruitful and I found two relatively well-paid jobs which I enjoyed very much. Other jobs available included fairground attendant, fast food sales assistant, lifeguard, kitchen assistant, chambermaid and every other possible type of work associated with a busy oceanside town. Ocean City was packed with foreign workers. As far as I know, none had any trouble finding work; anyone could have obtained half a dozen jobs. Obviously the employers are used to a high turnover of workers, especially if the job is boring. So it's not difficult to walk out of a job on a day's notice and into another*

one. It really was a great place to spend the summer. I would recommend a holiday resort to anyone wishing to work hard but to have a really fun time.

REGULATIONS

Any British citizens whose passport is issued after October 2003 but without bar-coded identification will have to purchase a visitors visa before arrival and be finger-printed on arrival. Otherwise, Britons can still qualify for the visa-waiver programme which allows ordinary tourists from approved countries to enter the US for a maximum of 90 days. Individuals entering visa-free or with a visitor visa for business or tourism are prohibited from engaging in paid or unpaid employment in the US. Check the Embassy website (www.usembassy.org.uk) for full visa information and application forms or request an outline of non-immigrant visas from the Visa Branch of the US Embassy (5 Upper Grosvenor St, London W1A 2JB). The application fee for non-immigrant visas is £67 ($100).

The visa of most interest to the readers of this book is the J-1 which is available to participants of government-authorised programmes, known as Exchange Visitor Programmes (EVPs). The J-1 visa entitles the holder to take legal paid employment. You cannot apply for the J-1 without going through a recognised Exchange Visitor Programme like those of BUNAC or CIEE described above and since new stricter security measures were put in place in 2003, applicants must now schedule a face-to-face interview at the US Embassy (at their own expense, naturally). Only approved organisations can issue the document DS2019 necessary for obtaining a J-1 visa.

Apart from the J-1 visa available to people on approved EVPs, there are three possible visa categories to consider, all of which must be applied for by the employer on the applicant's behalf and will take at least three months. The Q visa is the 'International Cultural Exchange Visa' which must be applied for by the prospective employer in the US (e.g. the Disney Corporation) and approved in advance by an office of the Immigration and Naturalization Service (INS). The H category covers non-immigrant work visas in special circumstances. The H2-B is for temporary or seasonal vacancies that employers have trouble filling with US citizens. For example, the chronic shortage of workers on the ski fields of Colorado means that many employers can obtain the necessary Labor Certification confirming that there are no qualified American workers available to do the jobs. The maximum duration of the H2-B visa is ten months though most come in for about six months to work at amusement parks, as lifeguards, in retail and fast food. They must work only for the employer that has petitioned for their visa. The H-1B 'Specialty Occupation' visa for professionals with a university degree is available for 'prearranged professional or highly skilled jobs' for which there are no suitably qualified Americans. The allocation of H1-B visas has been rising, mainly to alleviate the shortage of IT specialists, but is of little interest to candidates for entry level tourist jobs. The H-3 'Trainee' visa is the other possibility. Applicants must indicate in detail the breakdown between classroom and on-the-job time, and why equivalent training is not available in their own country.

By law, all employers must physically examine documents of prospective employees within three working days, proving that they are authorised to work. President Bush is proposing to bring in a new Guest Worker category from 2004, though this will apply mainly to migrant workers from Mexico and Latin America. Temporary legal workers must always produce their social security card for employers, but the application process has become more difficult as Homeland Security rules have been tightened. It is now advisable to take someone from your place of work with you to provide a reference to speed up the process.

DIRECTORY REFERENCES

The following companies listed in the Directory need staff for the United States, though many large tour operators in Europe do offer tours of the United States as well: Kingsbrook USA, BUNAC, Camp America, Camp Counselors USA (CCUSA), Collette Vacations, Disney Worldwide Services, Gunflint Lodge, Lotus Supertravel, Neilson, Ski Activity, Ski Independence, Ski Independence, Skiworld, Style Holidays, Travelsphere.

Canada

The Royal Canadian Mounted Police, Niagara Falls and the Rocky Mountains have always attracted a large number of tourists, not least from the United States. However 2003 was a dire year for the Canadian tourist industry. In the wake of tensions over world terrorism (apparently it is a widely held belief in some parts of the US that bombers can cross the Canadian border with impunity) came the SARS outbreak which devastated tourism in Toronto. Just before 2003 statistics showed that 3.7% of employed persons worked directly in tourism: 563,500 people out of a total population of 31.5 million. However the situation is slowly improving and Canada's pristine wilderness and landscapes may be valued even more highly in the decade ahead. Vancouver has been chosen as the venue for the 2010 Winter Olympics.

Canada has more square miles of land per head of population than almost any other country, yet the vast majority of people live within a few degrees of latitude of the US border, and most visitors confine themselves to the cities and countryside of the southern belt, which includes the three biggest urban areas of Vancouver, Toronto and Montréal. One exception is the ski industry which is attracting an increasing number of foreign skiers. Much investment in the tourist industry is coming from Hong Kong and centring on Vancouver where many of Hong Kong's wealthiest Chinese residents have established a colony. This is good news for people working in hotels and airlines.

While the tourist industry of French-speaking Québec is flourishing, it is difficult for non-Québecois people to find work, even if they are French-speaking. For example the French word for old, *vieux*, is pronounced 'voo'. With a French mother and English father, Cecile thought she was in a good position to find work in Québec. She was rather taken aback by the differences between Canadian French and Parisian French, but she did adapt and eventually found a job.

As usual, working for a European tour operator makes it easier to get round the visa difficulties. The regulations make it very difficult to work for a Canadian employer, both because of strictly enforced 'Canada-only' immigration policies and high unemployment (7.4% January 2004). One way of avoiding the problem is by taking advantage of the new Youth Holiday Worker Program introduced in 2004 which permits non-students up to age 35 to seek work in Canada under the auspices of BUNAC (see *Regulations* below).

The Rocky Mountain resorts of Banff, Jasper, Lake Louise, Sunshine Mountain and Waterton are among the most popular tourist destinations. The huge Banff Springs Hotel alone employs 900 people, and other grand mountain hotels like Chateau Lake Louise and the Jasper Park Lodge are ideal places to spend a season working. Several of these hotels are now owned by the Fairmont Group whose website describes its recruitment needs (www.fairmont.com).

SPECIAL SCHEMES

BUNAC can assist anyone up to age 35 with the visa and also with locating a job via its own Work Canada Vital Info booklet for members, which contains mostly jobs in hotels and tourist attractions in the Rockies. The BUNAC directory helped Linda James to fix up a six-month summer job as reception supervisor at Lake Moraine Lodge near Lake Louise. Although she was happy with the job, and found the hours relatively light, she would have preferred a waitressing job in order to earn the excellent tips of up to $100 a night. British university students have an edge over Canadian students in this sphere of employment since they don't have to return to their studies until mid to late September rather than the beginning of September, which means that they are more likely to be eligible for the substantial end-of-season bonuses paid by most seasonal employers.

CIEE (52 Poland St, London W1V 4JQ; 020-7478 2020; www.councilexchanges.org .uk) operate an Internship Canada programme on which British and Irish students who are enrolled in full-time further/higher education and candidates who are within one year of graduating undertake work experience internships in Canada lasting up to a year. Students in their gap year with a confirmed place at college and those due to graduate are also eligible. Interns must find their own work placements in their field of study before they apply, often with the advice of their tutors or via the internet. Those who qualify get an Employment Authorization from the Canadian High Commission. The programme fee is £200.

CIEE in New York operates a student work exchange in Canada for American students. US college and university students may accept employment at any time of year for a maximum of five months.

The placement organisation *Gap Challenge* (Black Arrow House, 2 Chandos Road, London NW10 6NF; www.world-challenge.co.uk) places a number of British students between school and university in resort jobs in the Rockies both summer and winter. *Changing Worlds* (11 Doctors Lane, Chaldon, Surrey CR3 5AE; 01883 340960; www. changingworlds.co.uk), like Gap Challenge, sends gap year students and others to work at hotels and ski resorts in the Rocky Mountain resorts in and around Banff. The jobs are the usual hotel jobs like housekeeping, waiting on tables and bartending. Hours are long in high season, up to 50 a week, but can drop when client numbers go down or when the snows come late, e.g. 20 hours a week which cuts into earnings. Workers earn about $9 an hour before tips and in some cases are given a free or reduced price ski pass. The minimum stay is six months with departures in November for the winter season and March for the summer. The cost of Changing World's programme (which fills up early) is £1,895 excluding staff accommodation which is deducted directly from wages at a rate of between $6 and $12 a day.

Jennie Cox from Derbyshire was unsure about what she wanted to do at the end of her degree at Durham University so consequently decided to take a year out for some time to think and to have a break before going into full-time employment. After being selected by Gap Challenge and completing a skills training course she left for Canada in September.

> **On her return Jennie Cox described her seven months in the Rockies:**
> *I always wanted to go to Canada and had heard much about the country from friends and family. It's renowned for its friendly people; and Banff, in particular, looked beautiful. I was especially keen to ski and snowboard which influenced my decision. My placement involved housekeeping at Banff Park Lodge and general room cleaning, making beds, etc. Overall I had an amazing time in Canada, and I certainly couldn't have asked for a more beautiful placement than the one I had*

> *in Banff. To wake up to vast snow-capped mountains each morning was such a luxury, that we had to be careful not to take it for granted. At times, of course, the work could be hard and exhausting, but you had to remind yourself why you were there: young friendly people to meet, lots of places to visit and days up on the slopes snowboarding, topped off by a pint of Canadian lager at night – who could ask for more? I've come back feeling relaxed, happy and refreshed and full of some great memories. Now I just have to find a job here.*

FINDING A JOB

Many British coach tour operators who have worked successfully in Europe are looking to expand to Canada. The Canadian Tourism Commission has long been working to encourage more coach tour visitors to Canada. If you are already working in the industry or studying on a tourism course you could approach some of the companies listed by the search engine accessible via the CTC website www.travelcanada.com.

As usual jobs for staff on British companies' tours of Canada go to experienced UK tour managers who have worked one or more seasons with a big company like Saga, Travelsphere or Titan. Those who already have permission to work in Canada and who have some travel and tourism or hotel experience might investigate the following companies:

British Columbia – Chateau Victoria Hotel (www.chateauvictoria.com), Crystal Lodge, Farwest Adventure, Gray Line, Grizzly Tours, Harbour Towers Hotel, Harrison Hot Springs Hotel, Hotel Georgia, Inbound Canada Tours, Listel Whistler Hotel, Maverick Tours, Ocean Point Resort, Rocky Mountaineer Railtours, Royal Northwest Holidays, Sandman Hotels and Inns, Super Natural Adventure, Westin Bayshore Hotel, Whistler Resort Association

Alberta – Banff Park Lodge (human_resources@banffparklodge.com), Brewster Tours (payroll@brewster.ca; they employ seasonal staff to operate the sightseeing gondola at Banff and to conduct driving tours of the Athabasca Glacier), Fairmont Hotels (mentioned above), Cruise Canada, Lake Louise Inn, Mountain Park Lodges

Manitoba – Frontiers North Adventures (www.frontiersnorth.com), Great Canadian Travel Co (www.greatcanadiantravel.com), North Star Tours (nortours@churchillmb.net)

Ontario – Best Western Hotels, Canadian Tours International (info@cdntoursintl.com), Cantours (www.cantours.com), Hilton, Hospitality Motels, Niagara Parks, Toronto Convention & Visitors Association (www.tourismtoronto.com)

Québec – Tourisme Montréal (www.tourisme-montreal.org)

Most of the upmarket shipping companies offer cruises up the west coast to see glaciers and wildlife. These companies need the usual cruise liner staff but also recruit experts on wildlife. Incoming tour operators sometimes advertise for seasonal staff, particularly people who are fluent in a European language, for example Jonview Canada Inc. (1300 Yonge Street, 8th floor, Toronto, Ontario M4T 1X3; fax 416-323-3980; hr@jonview.com) arranges Canadian tours for international clients and needs seasonal tour directors fluent in Dutch or German.

The eastern provinces of Canada are marketed as a holiday playground though most tourist businesses employ local people in a region where other employment is in such short supply. One possibility is a small company called Ocean Explorations that was advertising recently for assistants to stay in a traditional fishing village on the Bay of Fundy in Nova Scotia in exchange for working, possibly handling phone reservations, preparing or even guiding whale-watching trips or working in the gift shop (902-839-2417; tom@oceanexplorations.ca).

SKI RESORTS

The best known ski areas are in the Rockies of British Columbia and Alberta and include Lake Louise, Banff, Jasper and Whistler (one and a half hours from Vancouver). There are other significant resorts such as Sainte-Agathe and Mont Tremblant in the Laurentian Hills of Québec, and Collingwood in Ontario (which has Canada's biggest ski-lifts); however these eastern resorts are not much used by European tour operators.

The promotion of North American ski resorts to Britons frustrated by the queues and unreliable snowfalls of the Alps means that more and more companies are looking to the delights of Whistler, Lake Louise and Banff in particular for their clients. The *Specialist Holidays Group* (overseasrecruitment@s-h-g.co.uk; www.shgjobs.co.uk) recruits for British operators including Crystal Holidays, Thomson Ski & Lakes and Simply Travel. Openings may also be found with *Neilson Ski, First Choice, Inghams* and *Ski Miguel.*

For job-hunting independently with Canadian companies, consider Sunshine Village Resort near Banff which employs 700 staff, 200 of whom are provided with basic accommodation. Their website www.sunshinevillage.com has lots of useful information for prospective staff including dates of hiring clinics in October held at Banff International Hostel. You can contact the Human Resources department for details at PO Box 1510, Banff, Alberta T0L 0C0 (403-762-6546; sunshineHR@skibanff.com).

Moving west to the Pacific, the contact address for the Whistler/Blackcomb Resort is 4545 Blackcomb Way, Whistler, B.C. V0N 1B4 (604-938-7366; recruitmentwb@intraw est.com). Intrawest is the company that runs the ski operations at Whistler. The website www.whistlerblackcomb.com/employment also gives dates of the annual recruiting fair and allows you to apply on-line. A large number of workers leave after the Christmas rush so it is possible to get a job once the season begins even if you haven't lined anything up at the main hiring time of October/November.

A few jobs are available with UK ski tour operators though most are looking for staff who are at least 20, like the Specialist Holidays Group (overseasrecruitment@s-h-g.co.uk; www.shgjobs.co.uk) which recruits for Crystal Holidays, Thomson Ski & Lakes and Simply Travel among others; Hand Made Holidays Ltd (1st Floor, Carpenters Buildings, Carpenters Lane, Cirencester, Gloucestershire, GL7 1EE; 01285 642555; www.handmade-holidays.co.uk); Inghams Travel (10-18 Putney Hill, London SW15 6AX; 020-8780 8829) and Frontier Travel Ltd (6 Sydenham Avenue, London SE26 6UH; 020-8776 8709; www.frontier-travel.co.uk/ski/joinus.html).

CASUAL WORK

Most temporary jobs in the Canadian tourist industry are found by responding to 'Help Wanted' notices or ads in newspapers. Ana Güemes got one of her two waitressing jobs from the *Toronto Sun* while Vancouver's papers (the *Vancouver Sun* and *Province*) and the *Calgary Herald* contain job adverts, especially for dishwashers, waiting and bar staff. Wages are fairly good in Canada with statutory minimum wages, e.g. $6.85 per hour in Ontario ($6.25 for students) and $6 to $7 in most of the other provinces, $8 in British Columbia.

Banff is an expensive town in which to job-hunt but if you do land a job it will normally come with accommodation. One traveller to Western Canada reported:

While on holiday in Banff, I met a lot of Australians and Britons staying at the youth hostel. All of them were just on holiday visas, and all of them had found work in the height of the tourist season.

Other popular holiday areas are the Muskoka District of Ontario centred on the town of Huntsville (comparable to England's Lake District) and the shores of the Great Lakes, particularly Lake Huron. Since most of the holiday job recruitment in Ontario is done through Canadian universities, and the resorts are so widely scattered that asking door to door is impracticable, it is advisable to concentrate your efforts in the west.

REGULATIONS

To work legally in Canada, you must obtain an Employment Authorisation before you leave home. The Canadian government allows a certain number of UK nationals to work temporarily in Canada. If you apply independently to the Canadian High Commission you must have a firm job offer from a Canadian employer. This authorisation is valid for a maximum of 12 months and is not transferable to any other job. Details are available from the Canadian High Commission (Immigration Visa Information, Macdonald House, 38 Grosvenor St, London W1X 0AA; www.canada.org.uk/visa-info).

For more flexibility, you must apply through BUNAC either as a student with proof that you will be returning to the UK or, from 2004, as part of the Youth Holiday Worker Program for UK passport holders aged 18-35. These open employment authorisations are available only through BUNAC (16 Bowling Green Lane, London EC1R 0QH; 020-7251 3472; enquiries@bunac.org.uk). Their 'Work Canada' programme offers about 3,000 students and non-students aged 18-35 the chance to go to Canada for up to 12 months and take whatever jobs they can find. The only requirements are that applicants have a return ticket plus C$1,000 in Canadian funds. Departure for Canada can be any time between February and December and travel can be independent or on a BUNAC flight. The majority of participants go to Canada without a pre-arranged job and spend their first week or two job-hunting, though all benefit from orientations and back-up from the Canadian Federation of Students' SWAP offices in Toronto, Vancouver and Calgary. The BUNAC programme fee is £149 and compulsory BUNAC insurance costs about the same again for four months cover.

LATIN AMERICA AND THE CARIBBEAN

Two or three decades ago, when everybody was flocking east, few tourists from Britain considered South or Central America. Possibly because Britain has few colonial ties with that part of the world, it was less well known than India or Southeast Asia or Africa. With the recent decline in airfares to the Americas, the situation has changed and thousands of more adventurous travellers young and old now head to that great Spanish-speaking continent (including Portuguese-speaking Brazil). Many more Europeans are deciding to join the throngs of North Americans who had already discovered that South America has much more to offer than dictators and drugs.

Many of the national economies of Latin American nations are desperate for the hard currency that tourism can bring. Arguably it is particularly important in the Amazon Basin where only a huge injection of tourist money will persuade governments that the rainforests are worth protecting, just as the demands of tourism are a factor in the protection of wildlife in East Africa. Anyone who conducts a tour into the relevant areas will have to introduce some of these sensitive issues to their group. Most of the head offices of cruise companies which run escorted tours of the Amazon are in Rio de Janeiro.

FINDING A JOB

If you have spent time in a South American country preferably in a working capacity and can speak some Spanish (or Portuguese for Brazil), you will probably find yourself in demand by tour operators that feature South America. Many of these are based in Spain and Portugal for obvious reasons, and many more operate from the US. However an increasing number have become very active in the British market. To take just one example the number of Britons who visited Brazil increased from 62,300 in 1997 to 143,800 in 2001.

Most of the individual tourist offices in London (see *Appendix 2*) can refer enquirers to specialist tour operators. But an excellent centralised source of this information is the Latin American Travel Association (www.lata.org), a trade association to promote travel to the region with 150 members including tour operators, hotels and airlines. Its website is easily searchable by individual country. Only highly able candidates who have extensive Latin American travel experience and a knowledge of Spanish are hired as overland expedition guides with UK operators like the Australian-owned Tucan Travel (www.tucantravel.com), South American Experience (www.southamericanexpe rience.co.uk) or Journey Latin America (12-13 Heathfield Terrace, Chiswick, London W4 4JE; www.journeylatinamerica.co.uk). In most cases, the company pays food and accommodation plus a daily rate of about $25, but some companies do not cover all living expenses and tour leaders depend on being given free food and accommodation for bringing a group of clients to that particular restaurant or hotel.

Among the mainstream tour operators to Latin America, the following include information about their recruitment needs on their websites. They are invariably looking for candidates who have had extensive experience of travelling and preferably living in Latin America and who have a passion for the region as well as a familiarity with its language, environment and culture.

Audley Travel, 6 Willows Gate, Stratton Audley, Oxon. OX27 9AU (01869 276210; www.audleytravel.com)

Cox & Kings, Gordon House, 10 Greencoat Place, London SW1P 1PH (020-7873 5000; www.coxandkings.co.uk)

Exsus Travel, 23 Heddon St, London W1B 4BQ (020-7292 5050; recruitment@exsus.com; www.exsus.com)

Steppes Latin America – see Directory entry

Tucan Travel – ray@tucantravel.com. Suitable candidates can join tour leader training programme.

Veloso Tours, Ground Floor, 34 Warple Way, London W3 0RG (020-8762 0616; paulo@veloso.com).

Many of the tour leaders who take tours to the continent work in the office of the tour operator for most of the year but accompany tours when they are booked. Anyone with a background in conservation has an advantage since this is the aspect of South America in which many potential visitors are interested. The celebrated *South American Handbook* is an incredible compendium of useful information for people touring the continent. Although pitched at independent travellers, it is useful for everyone.

Tour guides accompanying groups from Europe must not only contend with jet lag (both theirs and their clients') but with the dangers of crime. According to one old hand who has been taking groups to South America more than two decades, it is essential to deliver a very stern lecture to holidaymakers about safety, not to go out alone, not to wear any jewellery (even the cheapest watch), not to wander off the beaten track in the major cities, not to drink the water, etc.

An even wider range of tour operators can be researched in the United States, many of them based in Miami, since that is the principal departure airport, including Tara Tours Inc (6595 NW 36th St, Suite 306, Miami, FL 33166; www.taratours.com) and Sol International Tours (561-826-0173; www.solintl.com). Another major operator is Sunny Land Tours (166 Main Street, Hackensack, NJ 07601; 201-487-2150; www.sunnylandtours.com).

The internet is awash with links, for example Gordon's Guide (www.gordonsguide.com) and Terra Trails (www.terratrails.com) both maintain extensive directories of eco-friendly tours, a booming area of the market. Gordonsguide.com even has a Human Resources department which will try to match job-seekers with suitable employers.

Brazil is probably the most popular country; most tours take in Rio and São Paulo, the Iguaçu Falls and a trip on the Amazon. The Mardi Gras Festival in Rio has a glamorous image, and British incentive companies often feature the event, so Portuguese-speakers may be needed during February. Work experience placements in Brazil are arranged by several mediating agencies include *CCUSA (Camp Counsellors USA).* CCUSA offers a choice of hotel/tourism placements as well as office work, sports jobs or working with children mainly in São Paulo but also in Florianópolis and Vitória (both islands) plus Rio de Janeiro. Participants get a pre-arranged job in Brazil, assistance in obtaining a Brazilian working visa, accommodation and meals with host family and US$50-$60 pocket money per month paid by your employer. If a candidate chooses hotel/tourism work, he or she might be assigned to the front desk of a hotel or to concierge/guest services for which intermediate Portuguese or Spanish is required. For placements as general assistants, there is no language requirement.

The volunteer placement company i-to-i Ventures (Woodside House, 261 Low Lane, Horsforth, Leeds LS18 5NY; 0870 333 2332; www.i-to-i.com) charges candidates for placing them in marketing and tourism for 4-12 weeks in Santa Cruz, Bolivia and Olinda,

Brazil. The fees charged start at £1,200 for four weeks excluding airfares.

Brazil also has some sophisticated conference centres and hotels catering for meetings, including Riocentro, Latin America's largest exhibition and convention centre (www.riocentro.com.br). If you have experience in this field it could be worthwhile contacting member companies of the International Association of Professional Congress Organisers (www.iapco.org) such as JZ Congressos in Rio de Janeiro (www.jz.com.br).

Argentina is among the most Europeanised countries in Latin America. Its tourism industry has been given a recent fillip by the devaluation of the currency which was very bad for Argentinians but which suddenly made the country a lot more affordable for tourists. A new cultural exchange organisation, Grupo de Intercambio Cultural Argentino, invites paying volunteers from abroad to work in Argentina's national parks. Participants will be assigned to work within the Los Glaciares and Nahuel Huapi National Parks (both in Patagonia) and Iguaçu Falls National Park in northwest Argentina. Assignments last at least eight weeks and range from helping park rangers to conduct guided visits, generally for four or five hours a day. Spanish language abilities are not required though make it easier to communicate with your host family. Accommodation is provided for a fee of US$485 or US$515 a month. Note that GICArg can also arrange short cooking courses at the Escuela Superior de Cocina de Alicia Berger in Buenos Aires followed by a short work experience placement in a four or five star restaurant. Details are available from the Cultural Exchange Group of Argentina, Lavalle 397, 1st Floor, Suite 1, Buenos Aires, C1047AAG, Argentina (+54-11-6311 3373; info@gicarg.org/ www.gicarg.org).

Unlike many other South American countries, Chile's economy is flourishing and its infrastructure much more developed than those of some of its neighbours to the north and east. With wonderful scenery, a healthy climate and good food and wine, Chile is one of the world's up-and-coming destinations.

The flourishing skiing industry of Chile and Argentina creates some openings for ski instructors but not many other openings for non-natives. A Scottish firm called Peak Leaders UK Ltd (Mansfield, Strathmiglo, Fife KT14 7QE; 01337 860079; www.peakleaders.co.uk) runs snowboard and ski instructor courses in the popular resort of Bariloche in Argentine Patagonia with trips to Chile and Buenos Aires, though this doesn't come cheap (£5,950 for nine weeks). As yet few British ski tour operators go to Chile, though this may change in due course.

The wine industry is especially buoyant, recovering some of its lost glory when it is said to have sent 20 million barrels of good red wine to Bordeaux. Wine tour companies are developing tours to this region.

Peru, Ecuador and Bolivia are generally considered to be the most authentic Andean destinations and are particularly targeted by the specialist expedition companies. Anyone interested in pursuing career possibilities in these countries or elsewhere should join the long established South America Explorers' Club, Av. Portugal 146, Brena, Postal Casilla 3714, Lima 100, Peru (511-425-0142) or Jorge Washington 311 y L. Plaza, Postal Apartado 17-21-431 El Faro, Quito, Ecuador (59-3222-5228) or 126 Indian Creek Road, Ithaca, NY 14850 (607-277-0488). In addition to travel information the club also keeps some information on job opportunities in the relevant clubhouses. Their mazagine has a classified section which could be useful.

Patricia Fernández, Internship Programme Consultant for the organisation *Amili* in Ecuador (see entry) describes the opportunities for enterprising tourism candidates:

At the moment we have a participant from Holland who just applied to work in the touristic area in one of our national parks. She will have the freedom to work to improve tourism in this part of the country as it has not been well developed so she will have all the support from the authorities from this place to improve tourism here. We have always a place to work for all our participants so I would be glad to have people interested in working in this area, as Ecuador is one of the best destinations to come to in South America. We have a beautiful country and there is so much to see.

If you get to know an area well, you may be able to act as a freelance guide though, not surprisingly, this will probably incur the locals' resentment, as Mónica Boza found when she lived in Cusco Peru:

If you have a good knowledge of the trails and want to become an outdoor guide, contact the tour agencies on arrival. But Peruvian guides are very jealous of foreign ones. I have known cases where they called the Migration Service and deportation followed. The adventure tour agencies are mainly along Plateros St or on the Main Square.

Local opportunities may crop up in one of the many places where tourism is booming. Many expat-style bars and clubs employ foreigners. For example Venezuela's Margarita Island in the Caribbean has dozens of places catering to package holiday makers; try 4th of May Avenue and Santiago Marino Avenue, particularly between June and September and again December to March.

Mónica Boza thinks that Cusco is a promising place with clubs like Mama Africa, Ukukus (which has the best bartenders in town), Eco, Up Town and Keros all near the main square. Few corners of the world have escaped the fashion for Irish pubs; in Cusco, try Paddy Flaherty and Rosie O'Gradys on Santa Catalina St. Similarly in the cities of Ecuador check at internet cafés such as Jamba, the Café Sutra or Pizza Net in Quito's 'Gringotown'.

The Chilean tourist industry also employs the odd gringo. Christine Hauser worked as a waitress in Santiago, though she found that the lack of a work visa was more of a problem than for English teachers since the authorities were wont to raid restaurants looking for illegal workers from other South American countries like Peru. She also landed a summer job at the beach resort of La Serena 500km north of the capital.

An agency called Persohotel International was seen advertising recently for resort animators to run entertainment programmes in Cancun, Playa del Carmen and Cozumel. They also recruit for cruise positions from time to time.

Foreign guides are occasionally hired by expatriate or even local tour operators. For example the Tambopata Jungle Lodge (PO Box 454, Cusco, Peru; tel/fax 084-245695; www.tambopatalodge.com) takes on guides for a minimum of six months who must have formal training in the natural sciences and (preferably) speak Spanish, all of which should be indicated on a CV. Information about the resident naturalist programme and research opportunities in the same area can be sought in the UK from TreeS, the Tambopata Reserve Society, c/o John Forrest, PO Box 33153, London NW3 4DR). Guides for the naturalist programme must be graduate biologists, environmental scientists or geographers over the age of 20. They receive free room and board throughout their stay. In general, however, indigenous companies like Magallanes Travel in Quito (www.magallanestravel.com) or Lima Tours in Cusco (Peru) would be unlikely to hire foreign guides.

CENTRAL AMERICA

Moving north to the seven countries of Central America (Panama, Costa Rica, Nicaragua, Honduras, El Salvador, Guatemala and Belize) opportunities to work in tourism are relatively scarce. Belize is rapidly becoming one of the main centres for eco-tourism. With the second biggest barrier reef in the world, the government has allowed a few outside diving companies to operate under strict control, who occasionally need staff who have studied conservation and have diving qualifications. Specialist companies offering botanical tours are also keen to expand, particularly as there are 95 different orchids in the forests. Costa Rica is another country with an impressive record on encouraging tourism that is sympathetic to the environment by protecting vast areas in national parks.

Quetzaltrekkers in the Guatemalan town of Quetzaltenango (called Xela locally) invite foreign people to volunteer as trekking guides for this small trekking agency, to help fund and support a residential home for street children.

Around Acapulco in Mexico the hundreds of hotels earn a large part of their income from incentive conferences. If you speak Spanish it is worthwhile contacting the big companies such as Maritz Travel (www.maritztravel.com) to see if they need freelance incentive conference staff. Mexico City is popular for exhibitions, and the companies that handle these sometimes need staff both in the head office for administration and freelance in the field to help set up stands. Again, a knowledge of Spanish is a prerequisite for jobs with companies like E.J. Krause & Associates, Inc. (6550 Rock Spring Drive, Suite 500, Bethesda, MD 20817; 301-493-5500).

Between January and March whales migrate from the Bering Sea to the Pacific coast of Baja to bear their young. Each year dozens of tour operators feature trips to see this magnificent spectacle.

FALKLANDS AND ANTARCTICA

Remote corners of the globe continue to increase their tourist trade. Although the Falklands and Antarctica still host only a few thousand visitors a year, each of those visitors is paying an average of £4,000. Antarctic tour operators look for conservationists with the appropriate degree. If you have mechanical knowledge and can service a Zodiac engine (the inflatable boats used by most of the passenger carrying ships) this could increase your chance of being hired. Ornithology tour operators like Orni-tholidays and Birdquest offer tours to the Falklands; other UK tour operators are linked from the Falkland Islands Tourism site (www.tourism.org.fk).

THE CARIBBEAN

From icebergs and penguins to rum punches and beaches. Perhaps the easiest jobs to find in the Caribbean are those working on the countless charter yachts, flotilla sailing vessels and cruise ships which ply the West Indian waters each winter and spring. From November until May the Caribbean becomes a hive of marine activity. Since it marks the start of the main tourist season, Christmas is a particularly good time to look for work. The main requirement for being hired is an outgoing personality more than qualifications or experience. Hours are long and wages are minimal, but most do it for the experience. Board and lodging are always free and in certain jobs tips can be high. It would not be unusual to top up a negligible wage with tips of $700.

As mentioned in the Introduction, the world's largest private yacht *Sea Cloud* sails around the Caribbean during the winter with a crew of 60 (see *Activity Holidays: Sailing*). For general information about cruise ship work see the relevant introductory chapter. Contracts are normally for six to nine months and the hours of work are long, often 14 hours a day, seven days a week living aboard the passenger ship with all onboard facilities provided by the ship owner. Most cruise ships active in the Caribbean contract their staff from Florida-based personnel agencies (known as concessionaires), some of which liaise with UK agencies.

The lack of a work permit can be a definite hindrance in the search for local work including with a charter company. Yacht charter companies such as Nicholson Yacht

Charters in English Harbour (Antigua) and Caribbean Sailing Yachts in St. Vincent are unwilling to publicise vacancies, both because they have enough speculative enquiries on the spot and also they are forbidden by their respective island governments from hiring anyone without the proper working papers. However once you are on the spot, you will have a better chance of hearing of vacancies, and there may even be a broker who matches up crew with boats, for example Captain and Crews in St. Thomas (US Virgin Islands).

Tim Pask arrived in Boston in August on the look-out for work and soon found day work on a large power boat. After a few weeks he was taken on as a deckhand/steward on a 72ft luxury charter yacht bound for the Virgin Islands:

> *My starting pay was $150 per week, all food and accommodation included. Tips were extra when on charter and could be as much as $400 each. It was very hard work and included long hours, keeping the boat clean, being involved in all aspects of sailing the yacht, maintaining the engine and serving meals and drinks to the guests.*
>
> *As far as advice for finding work, I suggest simply walking along the docks and asking skippers. This may seem rather awkward at times but it certainly is the best way. If the skipper or owner is unable to offer a position as crew he may well need an extra pair of hands to help out with varnishing, etc. Try to find out when and where boat shows are being held as people are always in a rush to get their boats looking first class. Quite often finding day work such as this can prove financially more rewarding. One can always try the numerous crewing agencies, but usually a fee is required.*

JOBS ON LAND

Around the Caribbean there is little chance of finding a job unless you or your parents are nationals of the island in question. The upmarket villa companies are strongly represented such as the Caribbean Islands Club (part of *Sunvil*) and in the US, Unusual Villas & Island Rentals, 409 F North Hamilton St, Richmond, VA 23221 (804-288-2823; www.unusualvillarentals.com). Some onshore work exists in the duty-free shops operated by companies like Nuance Global Traders (www.thenuancegroup.com/career) whose headquarters are in Switzerland, and Alpha Retail (Fairway House, Green Lane, Hounslow, Middlesex TW4 6BU; 020-8707 0300; www.alpha-retail.com/retail/recruitment). You may even be able to get some leads on hiring policies, etc. by speaking to the manager of the duty-free shops in UK airports, which are normally part of international chains.

People find work in nightclubs and hotels where British staff are considered chic. The Cayman Islands are meant to be one of the best places to look for this sort of work, with over 1,500 Americans alone working there. Check out the website http://cayman-jobs.com/caymanjobs for an idea of what might be on offer to subscribers. No expatriate is allowed to work in the Cayman Islands without a 'Gainful Occupation Licence' or work permit.

One of the most enjoyable jobs in tourism is to work in the Guest Relations department of a resort hotel. These jobs are never advertised; you have to know someone, keep your ears open or make yourself and your suitability known. It helps to be able to play tennis, bridge, etc.

MIDDLE EAST

Recent events have made it all but impossible for the tourist authorities of countries throughout the Middle East to attract tourists in large numbers. Even though many countries like Dubai, Bahrain and Jordan have remained remote from the recent conflicts and indeed largely untouched by hostility to westerners, their tourist industries have suffered terribly. Yet they have been investing heavily in publicity campaigns to attract back the lost revenue and pouring millions of dollars into providing incentives to the travel trade. The fourth global Travel & Tourism Summit co-ordinated by the World Travel & Tourism Council is being held in Qatar in 2004.

Overland and adventure operators are still conducting tours of the Middle East, for example the Imaginative Traveller, 1 Betts Avenue, Martlesham Heath, Suffolk IP5 7RH recruits tour leaders for the region (tljobs@imtrav.net; www.imaginative-traveller.com/jobs). One particular special interest group doesn't appear to have been put off visiting the Holy Land: Christian tour operators. Suitable candidates to work for one of the specialist agencies should approach Worldwide Christian Travel in Bristol (www.christian-travel.com), Fairlink Christian Travel in East London (020-8989 0331) or MasterSun/MasterSki, Thames House, 63-67 Kingston Road, New Malden, Surrey KT3 3PB (020-8942 9442; Resorts@mastersun.co.uk)

JORDAN

Jordan has some excellent ground handlers, mostly based in the capital Amman, looking for involvement with foreign specialist tour operators. The tourist information office can provide details. Jasmin Tours, part of McCabe Travel in the UK, are specialists for Jordan and have been for more than 20 years (53-55 Balham Hill, London SW12 9DR; 020-8675 6828; www.mccabe-travel.co.uk/jasmin.htm). They use the ground handler UTA, based in Amman (PO Box 35241, Amman 11180; +962 6-4641959) who may occasionally hire Arabic-speaking staff. One of the main incoming destination management operators in prosperous Dubai is Al-Tayer Travel Agency, PO Box 2623; +971 4-223 6000 (www.altayer-travel.com). To give some idea of the scale of some tourist operations in Dubai, the Marriott Hotel there has 11 restaurants employing 105 chefs.

Petra has always been an attraction and is now becoming so popular that people will probably have to walk or be bussed in instead of taking the picturesque donkey ride, which is a source of great anxiety to the donkey drivers, who are victims of Petra's success.

The Gulf of Aqaba has some excellent dive schools which sometimes need qualified PADI Open Water instructors able to take night dives.

Incentive tour operators are beginning to look at the country for incentives, so anyone who speaks Arabic and knows the country should approach the big companies.

LEBANON

Phoenix-like, Lebanon rose in the 1990s from the ashes of its 17-year conflict. At one time it was the most sophisticated Middle Eastern country with visitors coming from all over Europe to see Beirut, drink Chateau Musar wine and visit the Temple of Baalbek.

Ever since the troubles officially ended more than a decade ago, the country has been rebuilding hotels and restaurants. Several airlines now run scheduled flights to Beirut, and a few tour operators are active in the country.

Israel

Israel is not a happy country. The escalating conflict between the Israelis and Palestinians often seems beyond resolution. Not surprisingly, Israel has lost much of its appeal for tourists and therefore tour operators, and the numbers are drastically down. Personal security will be an overriding concern though in fact the statistics should be reassuring. The only foreigners killed have been peace activists (tragically) working in difficult circumstances, not tour groups visiting the Dome of the Rock or diving in Eilat.

Most tour operators to Israel rely on the staff provided by Israeli ground handlers rather than sending their own staff. This is because ground handlers normally have no difficulty finding well qualified multilingual locals to work for them.

Sue is a registered guide in the UK, and wanted to have a working holiday in Israel:

Knowing that guides can sometimes find opportunities while travelling in other countries, I thought there might be work in Israel meeting people at airports or working at conferences on reception. When I arrived with a friend we found that there was no tourism work available at all. Guides have to be licensed by the Ministry of Tourism. The only possibilities for work we could find were in restaurant kitchens and in the fields. So I went to work in a kitchen, feeling frustrated because I knew that I could have done a good job looking after visitors. But there was no chance.

The oldest established tour operator to Israel is Pullman Holidays, now part of the Globus Group and with an office at Luton Airport (Wren Court, 17 London Road, Bromley, Kent BR1 1DE; 08700 133085; www.pullmanholidays.com). Other specialists include:

All Abroad, 26 Temple Fortune Parade, London NW11 OQS

Israel Travel Service, 427-430 Royal Exchange, Old Bank St, Manchester M2 7EP (0161-839 1111; enquire@itstravel.co.uk)

Longwood Holidays, 3 Bourne Court, Woodford Green, Essex IG8 8HD (personnel@lon gwoodholidays.co.uk/ www.longwoodholidays.co.uk). Vacancies listed on website.

Mancunia Travel, 82-84 Deansgate, Manchester M3 2ER (0161-834 4030)

Superstar Holidays, UK House, 180 Oxford St, London W1N OEL (020-7957 4300; wwww.superstar.co.uk). In-house tour operator for the Israel national airline El Al.

Tangney Tours, Pilgrim House, Station Court, Borough Green, Kent TN15 8AF (01732 886666). Specialist in pilgrimages.

A major exception to the rule of employing only Israeli guides is made for Christian and pilgrims' tours. Companies such as Inter-Church Travel (part of *Saga Holidays*) have made the case to the Israeli authorities that their clients insist on being guided by people trained in customer care in the UK. Rather than lose all the business such companies bring to the country, the authorities allow them to bring in their own tour managers, though the truce between local staff and visiting guides is often an uneasy one. The other principal companies in this market are Mancunia and Tangney as above.

EILAT

Eilat is the main holiday resort on the Gulf of Aqaba, with a thriving yachting community and dive holiday clientele served by large seafront hotels and restaurants. Anyone with a diving instructor qualification should approach Eilat's many dive schools and dive cruise firms.

Sarah Jane Smith had the best time of her life in Eilat after she landed a job as a deckhand and hostess on a private charter yacht for scuba divers:

> *I was taken on cruises lasting between a week and a month to the Red Sea, Gulf of Suez, etc. to some of the best diving spots in the world. I was taught how to scuba dive and also did lots of snorkelling. I saw some of the most amazing sights of my life – the sun rising over Saudi Arabia as the moon sank into Egypt, coral reefs, sharks, dolphins, and so on. Every night was a party and I hardly know how I survived it. The only bad thing is the low wages (if you get paid at all) and the hard work. But the harder you work and longer you stay, the better the wages and perks become.*

The foreign tourist season lasts from late October to March. (Although some Israelis take their holidays in the extreme heat of the summer, workers at that time will be expected to speak Hebrew.) There is such a ready supply of itinerant workers desperate for any excuse to stay on that some employers try to get away with offering exploitative wages and working conditions. An additional problem for women is the level of hassle they must endure from male tourists from various countries who are attracted to Eilat on account of its thriving escort business.

Clean-cut looking women and couples can find work in tourist-related places by making the rounds of the hotel personnel managers as early in the season as possible. The Tourist Center near the Youth Hostel has lots of bars, restaurants and sandwich bars worth trying. Laura O'Connor describes the range of jobs she did in two months in Eilat:

> *I had a variety of jobs: sold tickets for a boat cruise and handed out fliers for a restaurant, waitressed in a fish restaurant, worked in Luna Park amusement park and cleaned in my hostel (Fawlty Towers).*

CASUAL WORK

The best places for finding casual tourism work on-the-spot are Eilat, Tel Aviv, Herzliya (a wealthy resort north of Tel Aviv) and, to a lesser extent, Haifa and Jerusalem. Many hostels around Israel, especially along Hayarkon St and Ben Yehuda St in Tel Aviv, employ two or three foreign young people to spend a few hours a day cleaning or manning the desk in exchange for a free bed and some meals. If you prove yourself a hard worker, you may be moved to a better job or even paid some pocket money.

Casual work in cafés, restaurants, bars and hotels is also easy to find. As in Greece, these jobs are much easier to get if you're female. The pay is usually low and sometimes non-existent, but you will get free food and drink, and tips. There is no accepted minimum and, as throughout Israel, the price of a day's work has to be negotiated. Most working travellers also recommend collecting your wages on a daily basis to prevent aggravation later. It is a common practice for cafés not to pay any wages and to expect their staff to exist on tips, which are enough to live on providing the restaurant is sufficiently popular.

AFRICA

Africa has so much to offer the tourist, not despite of but because large parts of the continent are undeveloped. The past 25 years have seen an explosion in the number of overland and expedition companies offering adventurous travels with a frisson of risk to people from all backgrounds.

The post-apartheid tourist boom in the Cape has had a knock-on effect in other southern African nations like Namibia and many tour operators have set up interesting programmes throughout southern Africa. The main tourism areas in Africa are the Mediterranean resorts of North Africa, Egypt, Kenya and East Africa, and South Africa, though the Gambia is now marketed as a winter sun packaged destination.

Travellers' hostels are one of the few providers of casual work in the developing nations of the African continent. People who stay any length of time at a hostel, especially in remote places, may be asked to assist the warden or even take charge temporarily while they are away on holiday or getting supplies. It is something that many independent trans-Africa travellers do for the odd week.

For overland expedition work, applicants are required to have first-hand knowledge of travel in Africa or must be willing to train for three months with no guarantee of work. Requirements vary but normally expedition leaders must be at least 23 and be diesel mechanics with a truck or bus licence. In addition to the main adventure tour operators like *Kumuka* and *Dragoman* in the Directory of Tour Operators, specialists in Africa include the following:

Absolute Africa, 41 Swanscombe Road, Chiswick, London W4 2HL (020-8742 0226; www.absoluteafrica.com).

Acacia Expeditions, Lower Ground Floor, 23A Craven Terrace, London W2 3QH (020-7706 4700; info@acacia-africa.com; www.acacia-africa.com).

Bukima Africa, 15 Bedford Road, Great Barford, Beds. MK44 3JD (01234 871329; www.bukima.com).

Economic Expeditions, 29 Cunnington St, Chiswick, London W4 5ER (020-8995 7707; www.economicexpeditions.com).

Oasis Overland, The Marsh, Henstridge, Somerset TA8 0TF (01963 363400; www.oasisoverland.co.uk).

Phoenix Expeditions, College Farm, Far St, Wymeswold, Leicestershire LE12 6TZ; www.phoenixexpeditions.co.uk).

Truck Africa, www.truckafrica.com.

Anyone with skills as a mechanic might be able to find work with an overland company, especially if based along one of the major routes. Suitably connected people might be able to run their own safaris, something Jennifer McKibben observed in Kenya:

> Some entrepreneurial travellers used to make money by hiring a jeep and taking holidaymakers on mini expeditions. This would either be to places inaccessible by public transport or would undercut the travel agencies on standard trips. They found customers by placing notices in the youth hostel and cheap hotels.

After working for several seasons in various capacities in Europe for the tour operator Contiki, Carolyn Edwards toyed with the idea of working further afield. She concentrated her efforts on Acacia since they employ tour guides as well as drivers, whereas many of the others are looking for guides who are also driver/mechanics. At a relaxed and informal interview she was told that she would have to join a training tour for up to 12 weeks before being sent out on her own.

The tour operator *Discover Adventure Ltd* (see entry) needs experienced leaders for mountain bike and trekking holidays in the Atlas Mountains while CycleActive Ltd (8 Low Mill, Langwathby, Penrith, Cumbria CA10 1NQ; www.cycleactive.co.uk) is expanding its cycling and multi activity programmes in Africa and beyond and in the past has advertised for cycling tour leaders.

NORTH AFRICA

The popular resorts of Tunisia and Morocco are normally incorporated into the Mediterranean programmes of major European tour operators. Companies like *Airtours* need French-speaking reps for resorts like Monastir in Tunisia and Agadir, Morocco. The Panorama Holiday Group (now part of the MyTravel empire) also needs French-speaking reps in Tunisia and operators in Egypt as well. *Club Med,* as its name might suggest, is a major operator here with vacancies for French-speaking GOs *(gentils organisateurs)* and other positions.

MOROCCO

The traditional destinations for tourists in Morocco (Tangier, Fez, Marrakesh) now enjoy a year-round season, with Europeans flying in for weekend breaks. Better communications are opening up in the south and in the High Atlas Mountains where there are more hiking and expedition-style holidays available each year. Experienced managers and reps who have spent time in Morocco agree that it is a fascinating country though it can be frustrating. French is widely spoken, at least it is until you are in trouble.

Most of the adventure holiday operators in Morocco are looking for well-trained personnel, as Andrew Dow discovered. When he applied to expedition companies, they all asked for qualifications, so the next winter he obtained one and took his tutor's advice to contact *Explore Worldwide*:

> *I've just done my first tour with 11 people in Morocco. The company seems to be highly regarded here, and the tour went well, although it was very hard work. I was amazed my books balanced at the end.*

TUNISIA

Tunisia is a very sophisticated country in which the French influence is apparent at every turn. From the beginning the Tunisian government developed the infrastructure in a sensible fashion, for example not allowing hotels to be built any higher than palm trees. Because of the mild winter climate, there are two main seasons, summer for families and winter for 'golden oldies' and others taking short breaks.

Hotels are of a high standard, and there is an excellent hotel school just outside Tunis. The major chains such as Hilton and Sheraton have properties here, and often transfer staff working elsewhere in their network. Banqueting and conference staff are in demand, as the Ministry of Tourism has helped to fund the development of facilities. The Port of El Kantaoui is a purpose-built complex of hotels from three star up to deluxe that thrives on family holidays in the summer and conferences and winter breaks from October to May.

Tunisia is usually a 'second season job' for known reps, though mature French-speaking candidates might be considered in their first season. Most of the work is for reps based at hotels, but some of the big operators such as *Thomson* and *Cosmos* operate short coach tours, usually allied to a week's hotel stay.

There are numerous appealing excursions from the resorts, so reps are able to earn well from commission. However the hours worked on these trips are long, involving 5am starts in order to see the desert. Ever since Indiana Jones got up to his tricks filming *Raiders of the Lost Ark* in southern Tunisia, incentive companies have loved this country. During filming, the stars stayed at the spectacular Sahara Palace at Nefta and groups now flock in to follow in their footsteps and ride camels across the desert.

One tour operator specialising in Tunisia is Wigmore Holidays (9 Kingsway, London WC2B 6YF (020-7836 4999). Since many European birds migrate here for the winter, birdwatching tours go to Tunisia in January. Cultural tour operators take groups to see the fantastic Roman Amphitheatre at El Jem and the ruins of Carthage (in a suburb of Tunis). Sports enthusiasts come to play tennis and golf, and many of the top hotels pride themselves on their sports facilities so need staff with appropriate qualifications. If you have marine and sailing qualifications, skippers in the yachting marinas at Port El Kantaoui, Sousse and Monastir may be interested in hiring you.

French is widely spoken, so a knowledge of Arabic is not needed. Although the people are very easy-going and welcoming, women should remember that Tunisia is a Muslim country: Kairouan, with its Great Mosque, is the fourth holiest city in the Islamic world. Another possible drawback is the great heat of the summer. Groups will be fascinated to see cave dwellings in the south, built as a refuge from the desert heat. Unlike the locals, tour groups resemble Noel Coward's mad dogs and Englishmen who go out in the mid-day sun in order to cover all the venues promised in the brochures. A supply of water and wide-brimmed hats is essential.

EGYPT

The two main types of holiday which Egypt can offer are cultural tours (which centre on the famous sites along the River Nile) and diving holidays on the Red Sea (which is a booming sector). Kathleen is one of the 'old hands' who has been looking after tours to Egypt for 20 years:

> *I love working here. Egypt gets to you. I prefer the small groups, often families, because then I have enough time to do things like teach them to read some hieroglyphics. The big groups are fun too but you can't get so involved. Usually they travel by Nile steamer for part of the tour and that can be a bit of a problem as people get bored, and there is nowhere to escape.*

Kathleen's advice to those who want to get started is to try to find work with a major tour operator with an Egypt programme. Once you have worked well for a season, start asking tactfully but persistently for a transfer. If they don't have vacancies leading to Egyptian tours then your experience will assist your application to specialist operators. Soliman Travel (113 Earls Court Road, London SW5 9RL; www.solimantravel.co.uk) is a specialist to Egypt with an office in Cairo. However the jobs mentioned on their website are all London-based.

DIVING HOLIDAYS

Anyone with a diver's certificate might be able to find work at Red Sea resorts like Sharm el Sheikh, Hurghada and Ras Muhammad. Many of the companies that offer diving holidays are small specialist companies; divers should check on their club notice boards for leads. The Egyptian diving firm *Emperor Divers* employs British and other diving instructors who are willing to stay for at least a year. You can sometimes get free diving lessons in exchange for filling air tanks for a sub-aqua club. It is possible to be taken on by an Egyptian operator (especially in the high season December/January); however the norm is to be paid no wage and just earn a percentage of the take.

The newest development on this coast is the Coral Beach Diving Hotel due to open late in 2004 in Port Ghalib not far from the Marsa Alam International Airport. The marina in this developing resort is the jumping-off point for live-aboard dive boats and also fishing vessels setting off for the marine parks of the Red Sea. The new Coral Beach Hotel is to be run by Millennium Hotels & Resorts so it might be worth trying for employment in this new project.

Jane Harris wrote from Dahab in Egypt to describe her experiences on the *Orionia*, a boat which plies the Red Sea:

It's great work, cruising on the Red Sea. Our boat takes tourists on four or six hour trips with a stop for swimming, a barbecue and meal on board. To get these jobs we just walked down to the Marina and asked around, and started work the following day. A word of warning: always ask the crew what the skipper is like and how hard the work is. Our skipper was great but lots of them were absolute bastards to work for.

PREPARATION

The biggest problem in Egypt is maintaining good health. It is not unusual for more than half the members of a touring group to be struck down by upset stomachs from the change in water and diet. A doctor must be summoned immediately if any client falls ill. Kathleen is adamant that you must ignore the advice of the Egyptian Tourist Board which says that there are no compulsory health precautions and consult a private health clinic about jabs, etc. well before departure (see introductory chapter *Preparation*). Also, malaria protection is needed around the Nile between June and October, and meningitis jabs if you are going to be there between November and May.

Note that there have been no terrorist attacks on tourists in Egypt since 1997 and the 368,000 Britons who visited Egypt in 2003 met with no problems of this kind.

EAST AFRICA

The countries of Kenya, Tanzania and Uganda have traditionally been countries that provided superb experiences rather than just holidays. Malaria and HIV are of concern to many potential visitors and are even more serious for those working in the tourist industry who spend long periods of time in the country. When the brother of Simon Hughes the MP died from the disease some years ago after honeymooning in Kenya (even though he had been taking the usual anti-malarial prophylactics), the public was alerted to the gravity of the disease. The most up-to-date expert advice must always be sought (see *Preparation* in the Introduction). Any company which offers work should be well informed. (If they don't show any interest in what inoculations you have had or should get, don't work for them. Ideally they will pay for all jabs and pills since these can come to hundreds of pounds)

Nevertheless thousands of visitors want to visit these beautiful countries. Most fall into three categories: those who go for sun, sand and sea, those who want a combination beach and safari holiday and thirdly serious wildlife lovers and photographers. It is difficult to find work with any of these groups. Safari tour operators and game wardens in national parks are inundated every year with undergraduates wanting to work in their vacations. As described above in the section on Egypt, those wanting to make a serious career of working in East Africa should first work for a European tour operator which

Ostrich farms often need linguists

features East Africa and apply to move when they have enough experience.

An increasing number of companies are offering honeymoon packages in this part of the world, typically involving a beach ceremony with the couple flying away in a balloon possibly to a safari lodge. These operators need efficient staff to handle the formalities and it is tempting to wonder whether there are openings for vicars and priests.

Specialist safari tour operators include:

Okavango Tours and Safaris, Marlborough House, 298 Regents Park Road, London N3 2TJ (020-8343 3283; info@okavango.com).

Somak Holidays, Somak House, Harrovian Village, Bessborough Road, Harrow on the Hill, Middlesex HA1 3EX (020-8423 7857; www.somak.co.uk). Large operations in Africa with recruitment information on website; applications to vacancies@somak.com.uk.

ON THE SPOT

People travelling through East Africa have noticed that diesel mechanics are in great demand to work as drivers for overland companies and suitably connected people might be able to run their own safaris; but in her whole year of volunteer nursing in Uganda, Mary Hall met only one foreigner who had found work on the spot and without a work permit. This woman was asked to manage a tourist lodge in the middle of nowhere and jumped at the chance since it was such a beautiful nowhere.

WORKING CONDITIONS

If you are working for a European operator, you will have the same type of accommodation as your clients. However staff who are hired locally (such as drivers) often live in very basic conditions. Those 'great white hunter' safari suits of beige cotton do not just belong in the movies. They are practical since the colour is the least likely to attract animals and the long trousers keep off mosquitoes.

One unusual scheme that has come to the attention of this book is based in Cameroon. The British-Cameroon Forum is encouraging youth exchanges in this part of Africa and, in partnership with another organisation (ICEYOM), claims to be able to arrange placements within the tourism sector (hotels, other hospitality organisations) in Cameroon, Gabon, Equatorial Guinea, Chad, Congo and elsewhere in Central Africa. Contact BritCam for further details: PO Box 156, Buea, South West Province, Cameroon; +237 958 02 92; britcamforum@yahoo.co.uk.

SOUTHERN AFRICA

With the political changes of the 1990s, the Republic of South Africa was set to become the next great holiday destination and, despite escalating crime rates, has succeeded in doing so. According to figures produced by the South African tourism minister in 2003, it is the fastest growing tourist destination in the world with a fifth more international arrivals in 2002 than the previous year. Many specialist tour operators have been exploiting this unprecedented interest by offering interesting tours concentrating on game parks, vineyards, historic rail routes, etc.

Brigitte Albrech from Germany managed to get a job in her career field with the South African Tourism Board and came away believing that anyone could find a job in the tourist industry. She recommends that on arrival job-seekers should check adverts in the Monday edition of the main dailies, the *Argus* in Cape Town, and the *Star* and *Citizen* in Johannesburg. People who can speak more than one language may find that hotels will not only hire them but help them to obtain a work permit. Brigitte also suggests that people who want to be tour guides should head for the Oudtshoorn region where ostrich farms often need linguists for the summer season. Long-term traveller Roger Blake was offered a job at Backpackers Oasis, a hostel in Oudtshoorn where he was given free accommodation and pocket money every week to run the bar and help prepare the nightly ostrich *braai* (barbecue). On his own initiative he did breakfasts for fellow travellers which was like being self-employed as he bought all the ingredients and kept all the profit, and made a 'small but worthwhile fortune'.

CASUAL WORK

Apart from the difficulties with work permits in South Africa, casual work is relatively accessible. Cape Town is the tourist capital of South Africa for backpackers as for everyone else; there are now about nine youth hostels in the city. The Oak Lodge on Breda Street (oaklodge@intekom.co.za) has been recommended as a source of job info

Everyone who has looked for a tourist job in Cape Town recommends Seapoint, a beach suburb lined with cafés, ice cream kiosks, snack bars and other places which have high staff turnovers, though wages are low. (Ice cream is also sold from cycle carts; find out whom to contact for work by asking the sellers.) Also try using the door-to-door approach in the flashy Victoria & Albert Waterfront development, Camps Bay and the beaches along the Garden Route. People who can speak more than one language will be especially in demand. Long Street in Cape Town is lined with bars and restaurants where jobs crop up.

Although Johannesburg is often maligned as a big, bad, city, it is the earning capital of South Africa with better job possibilities than many other places. Many newcomers now shun the inner city which has become dirty and crime-ridden in favour of the northern suburbs like Dunkeld West. The well known Jo'burg backpackers' lodge Rockey's of Fourways (22 Campbell Road, Craigavon A.H., Sandton; 011-465 4219; www.backinafrica.com) moved to an area where within a 5km radius there are more than 60 restaurants & bars, five huge night clubs, the new Montecasino complex and other backpackers' lodges.

The east coast stretching from Cape Town to Port Elizabeth or even as far as Ciskei provides lots of opportunities for resort jobs. George, Knysna, Jeffreys Bay, Plettenburg Bay and Port Elizabeth are crowded with tourists during the season (November to March) but especially in December and January. Short-term casual work is available during the fortnight long Arts Festival in Grahamstown in the East Cape in June/July.

Casinos are another possibility for anyone with experience as a croupier as well as for others. Sun International is the main casino operator but does not pay cash-in-hand as some do. In recent years the UK agency *Quest Elite* has been recruiting casino staff including croupiers for South Africa.

RED TAPE

Not surprisingly, the new government has tightened up on foreign workers as the high unemployment rate means it is hard enough to find jobs for its own citizens. It is still not too difficult to extend a three-month tourist visa, but increasingly difficult to get a work permit.

ASIA

Exotic destinations are becoming more accessible with each passing year The Asian continent stretching from India to Japan, taking in the ever-popular destinations of Thailand, Singapore, Malaysia, Hong Kong and China, is visited by millions every year. Many UK tour operators include these countries in their programmes. Charter airlines have been investigating the possibility of operating charter flights to Asian airports. If new charter routes are established, other tour operators will use them and the number of jobs for reps and tour managers will increase. Of course such a sudden increase in tourist traffic can harm a place as has happened to Goa since the Dabolim Airport was opened; one of its nicknames is now 'the Benidorm of the East'. The rate of tourist development in places like Goa and Bali has been too fast and too careless of environmental and other local concerns, so anyone hoping to work in a developing country should be aware of these issues.

For the present, companies employ senior tour directors and representatives. In countries where communications may be poor and transport and contractors unreliable, the tour leader must take full responsibility and have the authorisation to change plans and improvise solutions. It is helpful if the person who has arranged the tour is the one to lead it; hotel and other bookings are less likely to get 'lost' if the individual who has made prior contact is the same individual present. This means that only people who are established in the industry with appropriate qualifications and introductions stand much chance of working for a UK or US tour operator. A further source of competition for jobs comes from the thousands of Asian nationals who come to Britain each year to study tourism often in combination with English as a foreign language.

FINDING A JOB

TOURS

As mentioned above, there is little chance of finding work until you are very experienced. Asian economic problems mean less work for those looking for jobs locally, but more for those with top qualifications leading groups from the US, Europe and Britain. Prices of tours to this area are tumbling and companies look for staff with degrees in Oriental studies, history, history of art, etc. to lead groups. Probably the easiest way to break in is to do the least popular tours, i.e. the multi-centre tours which purport to give tourists a brief taste of Japan, Thailand, Malaysia and Hong Kong (though the taste they give is mostly of in-flight cuisine). Old hands do not relish the prospect of suffering permanent jet lag, so the tour operators sometimes encounter difficulties in finding staff.

Annabel White was an experienced tour manager in Europe, with a degree in European History. She wanted to take groups to Asia but discovered that most companies wanted somebody with experience. Applying to Voyages Jules Verne, they took her on to look after a group on the Trans Siberian Express:

> *The tour is a long one: experienced tour managers know that passengers get bored, frustrated and argumentative. But still, I needed this tour for my CV so that I could tell operators I had been to the region.*

The strategy worked and she went on to take upmarket but shorter tours to Asia. Others work for tour operators taking groups to Europe and ask personnel departments to put them on the list for Asia. Eventually experience counts. Work well for an operator and when someone falls out, they look for reliable staff and promote them. Annabel says operators employ local guides; you are there to act as tour administrator, so it is more important to have experience dealing with problems. She says she was a long way from the office and had much more responsibility. One compensation for the jet lag and the heat is that most tour leaders are very well looked after in Asia where service is a way of life.

Elderly travellers can be surprisingly adventurous and there are numerous Asian tours aimed at people of retirement age. One of the first tour operators to take advantage of the freedom to visit Vietnam when it opened its frontiers was *Saga Holidays* which is patronised only by people over 50. Saga like to employ more mature tour leaders (in fact they accept fit people up to the age of 75) and are keen on candidates with a nursing qualification. Another company catering to an older clientele is Elderhostel (11 Avenue de Lafayette, Boston, MA 02111-1746; 1-877-426-8056; www.elderhostel.org).

Malaysia has been spending mega-ringgits on improving and building new resort hotels. Thailand has suffered from adverse publicity about sex tourism, which has forced the Thai authorities to tackle the situation in order to entice back tour operators.

The major adventure tour companies like *Explore Worldwide, Dragoman* and *The Imaginative Traveller* have specialist tours to Southeast Asian destinations. First aid qualifications are usually mandatory to lead tours off the beaten track.

American companies that specialise in adventurous tours to Asia include:

Asian Pacific Adventures, 6065 Calvin Ave, Tarzana, CA 91356 (800-825-1680; www.asianpacificadventures.com)

Asia Trans Pacific Journeys, 2995 Center Green Court, Boulder, CA 80301 (800-642-2742; www.asiatranspacific.com)

Backroads – see entry in Directory of Tour Operators

Geographic Expeditions, 2627 Lombard St, San Francisco, CA 91423 (415-922-0448; www.geoex.com)

*Mountain Travel-Sobek,*1266 66th St, Emeryville, CA 94608, CA 94530 (510-527-8100; www.mtsobek.com)

Wilderness Travel, 1109 Ninth St, Berkeley, CA 94710 (800-368-2794; www.wildernesstravel.com).

Trekking trips in the Himalayas may offer some possibilities. World Challenge Expeditions (Black Arrow House, 2 Chandos Road, London NW10 6NF; 020-8537 7980; www.world-challenge.co.uk) take on about 300 expedition leaders to supervise school expeditions to developing countries. Trips take place in the summer and the minimum commitment is four weeks. Applicants must be at least 24, have a MLTB (Mountain Leader Training) and some experience of working with young people and preferably of travelling in the Third World. Remuneration is negotiable but at least all expenses will be covered.

A wealth of other special interest tours to Asia is available. Horse sports are popular throughout Asia, particularly in Hong Kong and Brunei (whose Sultan is mad on polo).

Speakers of Japanese normally find it easy to get jobs, particularly working in souvenir shops and hotels. If you lead a group with Japanese clients in it, be prepared to devote yourself 24 hours a day to looking after them. According to Corinna, it is a good idea to ask the hotel switchboard not to put any calls through after 11pm except in an emergency. She is not prepared to have her sleep interrupted at 2am because someone can't remember if a temple was 12th century BC or AD.

HOTELS & CATERING

Most of the major international chains have properties in Asia. Similarly, luxury Asian hotel groups such as Taj now have properties in Europe, so transfers may be possible. However be prepared for long waiting lists if you want to work in one of the hotels like the Regent or the Mandarin which are consistently voted best in the world.

Chefs are often attracted to Thailand because of the excellence and current popularity of Thai cuisine. Good catering colleges should have contacts in Bangkok.

AIRLINES

Many of the mainstream Asian airlines employ British staff such as JAL, Cathay Pacific, ANA, etc. and the Gulf airlines that criss-cross the areas such as Gulf Air and Emirates. Contact their UK or European offices to find out when they will be recruiting. British Airways will also be interested in candidates who can speak an Asian language fluently. Fiona went to an interview with the Japanese national airline JAL and was surprised and delighted to be selected. An intensive course in Japanese ensued before being sent off to Tokyo. The training course was very demanding and she had to bite her tongue repeatedly when her dress and make-up were criticised every day. She discovered that more tongue-biting was a requirement of the job:

I kept forgetting that work had to be taken very seriously. My flippant comments (made to relieve the atmosphere during the long Tokyo-Heathrow flights) did not go down well. I found that the cultural differences were too great and after a year the airline and I parted company. My recommendation is that anyone who wants to work for an Asian airline should go and live in the country first to understand the culture.

WORKING CONDITIONS

Health concerns should be pre-eminent and all the necessary precautions taken (see introductory section *Health & Insurance*). Cultural differences are also very important and you should consult a good book about what might unwittingly cause offence such as casually discarding a Japanese business card presented to you, touching people on the head, parading your feet in company, proffering your left hand, etc. But the most important thing to remember is never to lose your temper which causes you to lose face. The best way to tackle a problem is to smile and ask the official what advice they can offer.

Theft is always a possibility so be sure to keep separate photocopies of your passport, visas, credit cards, insurance documents and so on.

INTERNSHIPS

An Indian tour operator with a gap year placement partner in London (People Tree Gap Year Placements Ltd, 105 Westbourne Terrace, Fl-8, London W26QT; 020-7402-5576; www.gapyearinindia.com) promises that it can arrange internships in major resorts in India, Nepal and Sri Lanka. They even arrange specialist internships in tiger, elephant and other wildlife reserves and can arrange travel writing internships for tourist magazines in India. Placements could also be available with Indian state Tourism Departments or with a large city tour operator, helping to organise and guide tours. They will try to tailor-make an internship to fit the request of the intern, working with their holding company, long-established tour operator Timeless Excursions Pvt. Ltd. (340, Somdutt Chamber - II, 9 Bhikaji Cama Place, New Delhi 110066, India. 011-91-11-26161198; timeless@vsnl.com) with branch offices in Mumbia, Kolkata and Chennai. The fee charged is about £1,450, part of which goes to support conservation work in India.

One or two commercial placement agencies that specialise in sending volunteers abroad to teach English have branched out into placing interns in business. Teaching and Projects Abroad (Gerrard House, Rustington, Sussex BN16 1AW; 01903 859911; www.teaching-abroad.co.uk) arranges short-term workplace assignments in Kerala and Tamil Nadu, South India for a fee of between £1,195 and £1,595 excluding flights and you can request a placement relevant to tourism.

PART III

Directory of Placement & Recruitment Agencies

Directory of Tour Operators

DIRECTORIES OF EMPLOYERS

Alphabetical listing of placement agencies followed by details of tour operators worldwide which have occasional vacancies for tourism staff. The information given in this section should be checked personally when applying for a job.

DIRECTORY OF PLACEMENT AGENCIES

AboutJobs.com
Huge search engine for free on-line job vacancies which includes in its network specialised sites: www.resortjobs.com; www.summerjobs.com; overseasjobs.com and internjobs.com.

AA APPOINTMENTS
St Claire House, 30-33 Minories, London EC3N 1PQ. ☎020-7480 7506. Fax 020-7480 5467. E-mail London@aaappointments.com. Website www.aaappointments.com.
Offices also in Manchester, Birmingham, Glasgow, Woking, Dublin, Sydney, Melbourne and Adelaide.
In business for 21 years, placing candidates in retail, business travel, tour operators, airlines, hotels, incoming, groups & conferences, cruise lines and ferry companies, mainly in UK, Ireland and Australia. Vacancies are 70% permanent, 30% temporary.

ABC RECRUITMENT
3-5 Anderson Chambers, 34 Great King Street, Dumfries DG1 1BD Tel/fax 01387 270718. E-mail info@abcrecruitment.net. Website www.abcrecruitment.net.
In business for 2 years.
Specialists in temporary, contract and permanent (about half) recruitment in hospitality & catering, administration/clerical, customer service/retail, sales, etc. Vacancies in the UK, mainly in South West Scotland and Cumbria.
Most clients look for candidates with some previous experience.
Contact: Clive Rumbold (Owner).

ADMIRAL GROUP
72 Wells Street, Oxford Circus, London W1T 3QF. ☎020-7580 8446. Fax 020-7580 8447. E-mail Paschar@admiralgroup.com. Website www.admiralgroup.com.
Recruitment agency in business for 8+ years that specialises in catering and hospitality. Always looking for candidates from chefs to event staff to fill temporary or permanent

placements in central London.
All temporary staff need relevant experience and, for chef work, relevant qualifications.
All nationalities accepted provided they can speak and understand English.
Typical hourly wages: chefs earn £7-£8.50, waiters £5-£6 and Kitchen porters/general assistants £4.50-£5.
Interviews are essential.
Free Health and Hygiene and Silver Service Training for registered staff.

ALLIANCE ABROAD GROUP
Trainee Program, Barton Skyway, Suite 250, 1221 South Mopac Expressway, Austin, TX 78746, USA. ☎512-457-8062/1-888-6-ABROAD. E-mail vnoel@a llianceabroad.com. Website www.allianceabroad.com.
American exchange organisation which can place international hospitality trainees in relevant positions in the US for 6, 12 or 18 months. Candidates must speak English and be students or recent graduates. Paid positions are available in many fields, including hospitality, hotel management and culinary arts. Programme fees on request. Candidates who have found their own internship can obtain visa assistance for much lower fees.

ANGLO CONTINENTAL PLACEMENT AGENCY LTD
9 Wish Road, Hove, East Sussex RH13 8NQ. ☎01273 776660. Fax 01293 776634. E-mail sharon@anglocontinental.fsnet.co.uk.
Agency established 1995; alternative name 6 Placements Agency.
Staff placed in live-in positions in British and Spanish hotels; chefs, waiting staff, chamber staff, housekeepers, bar staff, receptionists and porters placed for 6-12 month period.
References essential. Candidates must be EU nationals or have working holiday visa from Australia, New Zealand or South Africa. Send CV, references and photos plus 4 international reply coupons to Mrs. Sharon Wolfe.

BLOOMSBURY BUREAU
37 Store St, London WC1E 7PN. ☎020-7430 2280. Fax 020-7813 4038. E-mail bloomsburo@aol.com.
In business since 1995.
Cultural exchange and au pair agency which makes hotel placements in Germany.
Hotel staff (chambermaids/kitchen helps) needed for Bavarian hotels: 30-40. Period of work from June (preferably the beginning) to the end of September or end of October.
Basic working week 45 hours. Permanent posts also available.
Qualifications needed: knowledge of German required. Must be EU nationals preferably students or school leavers over 18.
Wages: net monthly wage of £360 per month in addition to free board and lodging.
Applications to Marianne Dix, Principal.

BLUE OYSTER RECRUITMENT
50 Gosport St, Lymington, Hants. SO41 9BB. ☎01590 677533/ 677933. Fax 01590 677545. E-mail jobs@blueoyster.co.uk. Website www.blueoyster.co.uk.
Specialist travel and tourism, leisure and hospitality, and catering recruitment filling vacancies mainly in Hampshire and Dorset.

BUNAC
16 Bowling Green Lane, London EC1R 0QH. ☎020-7251 3472. Fax 020-7251 0215. E-mail enquiries@bunac.org.uk. Website www.bunac.org

BUNAC is a non-profit national student club in operation since 1962 offering work and travel programmes worldwide. It acts as an aide before and after arrival in the country of travel and acts as a 'security blanket' if situations go wrong whilst the student is abroad. Various work programmes in the USA, Canada, Australia, New Zealand, South Africa and elsewhere. Internships in America for students and non-students of any nationality on the Overseas Practical Training programme (OPT USA). BUNAC makes it possible for candidates to obtain the necessary visas and publishes its own job directories which help members to fix up short-term jobs before or after arrival in the tourist industry or any other field of employment.

Qualifications needed: For *Work America* students must have documentary evidence that they are returning to a university degree or HND course, or already be a full-time student. *Work Australia* and *Work New Zealand* are open to anyone who is eligible for the working holiday visa. From 2004, British nationals aged 18-25 are eligible for *Work Canada*. For details, see relevant country chapters.

Duration and time of placements: on Work America summer programme participants must return to a full-time course in the UK in September/October. Other programmes in other countries are more flexible and last up to a year.

Selection procedures and orientation: Students need to join BUNAC, either through the local club at university or at the time of applying. Applicants must pay the fee and (if relevant) show a job offer and/or proof of student status. In some cases, an attendance certificate from a BUNAC presentation (held throughout the winter at universities) is compulsory.

Cost: £4 BUNAC membership fee, plus programme fee from £62 for employment on summer camps to about £1,800 for *Work New Zealand*. First-time *Work America* participants must purchase BUNAC's travel package (average of £450 includes flight and airport taxes, airport collection and the first night's accommodation). Reductions are available to those applying early. Students cover living costs by working in tourist jobs or any paid jobs. Compulsory insurance for the summer costs about £120.

BUNAC USA (PO Box 430, Southbury, CT 06488; 1-800-462-8622; www.bunac.org) assists a large number of Americans to work in Britain for up to six months, Ireland and Australia for up to four months, and New Zealand up to 12 months.

BÜRO METRO
PO Box 1479, CH-8065 Zürich, Switzerland. ☎201 41 10. Fax 202 16 46. E-mail metroch@attglobal.net. Office address: Talackerstrasse 11, Glattbrugg (via bus 781 from Zürich airport or Oerlikon station to bus stop TMC).

Registered employment agency since 1948 placing professionals worldwide in the hotel and catering industry and on cruise ships. An application fee of SFr30 is charged plus extra expenses in some cases. Applicants from outside Europe have to be recommended by a person or company known to Büro Metro.

Contact: Viktor Pfaffhauser, Hospitality & Cruise Consultant.

CAMP AMERICA
37a Queen's Gate, London SW7 5HR; 020-7581 7333. E-mail brochure@campamerica.co.uk. Website www.campamerica.co.uk.

Major summer camp organisation which places 10,000 people from around the world to work on children's camps in the USA. Also run Resort America programme whereby people aged over 19 work in holiday resorts and are paid $1,300 for the minimum 12-week period starting in June. The work period may be extended to 16 weeks which would increase the earnings to $2,000 in addition to free flights to the US, free board and lodging and the possibility of tips.

Camp counsellors are needed for 9 weeks between June and August to teach activities such as tennis, swimming and arts and crafts. Counsellors receive free return flights from London to New York, free room and board and end-of-contract lump sum which will range from $460 to $910 depending on age, experience, qualifications and whether you've been on Camp America before. Students are also required to work on the Campower programme in the kitchen/laundry/maintenance departments of a summer camp.

CAMP COUNSELORS USA (CCUSA)
Green Dragon House, 64-70 High St, Croydon CR0 9XN. ☎020-8688 9051. Fax 020-8681 8168. E-mail info@ccusa.co.uk. Website www.ccusaweusa.co.uk. Northern office: 27 Woodside Gardens, Musselburgh, Scotland EH21 7LJ (0131-665 5843; 101355.257@compuserve.com). US headquarters of CCUSA are at 2330 Marinship Way, Suite 250, Sausalito, CA 94965, USA (www.campcounselors.com).
Camp counsellor placement in the US plus Work Experience in the US (4 months in summer), Australia, New Zealand (up to 12 months) and Brazil (2 or 4 months). Also placements on summer camps in Russia and Croatia.
Qualifications needed: Ages 19-30 for most programmes. Some programmes (e.g. Brazil) open only to registered students.
Cost: Camp Counselors USA fee from £245, Work Experience USA £635 or £735 including flights and insurance; Work Experience Downunder £375; Work Experience Brazil £545. First year counsellors at US summer camps aged 18 earn $400 in pocket money.

C&M RECRUITMENT LTD
6 Long Lane, London EC1A 9HF. ☎020-7796 1800. Fax 020-7796 1801. E-mail london@candm.co.uk. Website www.candm.co.uk. Offices also in Manchester (9th Floor, St James's, 79 Oxford St, Manchester M1 6FQ; 0161-238 4488; manchester@candm.co.uk) and Gatwick (Worth Corner, Turners Hill Road, Pound Hill, Crawley, West Sussex RH10 7SL; 01293 880 900; gatwick@candm.co.uk).
Member of REC (Recruitment & Employment Confederation).
Travel recruitment consultancy which invites qualified applicants to register their profiles online. Also operate www.executives4travel.com for senior jobs, www.temps4travel.com and www.train4travel.com.

CHANGING PLACES (RECRUITMENT CONSULTANTS) LTD
Cygnet House, 12-14 Sydenham Road, Croydon, CR0 2EE. ☎020-8681 1681. Fax 020-8681 1682. E-mail info@changingplacesltd.co.uk. Website www.changingplacesltd.co.uk.
In business for 19 years. Member of ABTA Travel Industry Partners and represented on ABTA Education & Skills Committee.
Specialist recruitment for the travel industry at all levels: tour operators, travel agents, cruise, hotel, airline and other reservations/ticketing, inbound operators. Many vacancies in UK for tourism graduates with European languages.
Qualifications needed: tourism qualifications or experience. European languages often needed. Ages 20/21+. Relevant Word experience an advantage.
Telephone interviews possible.
Contact: Ian McHaffie, Joint Managing Director.

DISCOVERY SELECTION
5 High St, Stockport, Cheshire SK1 1EG. ☎0161-475 0750. Fax 0161-475

0751. E-mail mail@discovery-selection.com.
Recruitment for tour operations, retail travel, business travel and longhaul reservations from trainee and managerial level. Consultants are ex-travel industry professionals.

EUROTOQUES
Winnenderstr 12, D-73667 Ebnisee/Schwäbischer Wald, Germany. ☎+49 7184 91055. Fax +49 7184 91053. E-mail office@eurotoques.de. Website www.Eurotoques.de (German language only); click on Chefköche and then on Jobbörse.
In operation since 1986.
Kitchen assistants and waiting staff needed for top restaurants and housekeeping staff for hotels throughout Germany. Opportunities to train with some of Germany's top chefs. Minimum period of work 2-3 months at any time of year.
Qualifications needed: must speak German and be willing to work 9 hours a day, 5 days a week.
Wages: none, but free room and board.

EXCELLENT ENTERTAINMENT
Suite 2, The Business Centre, 120 West Heath Road, London NW3 7TX. ☎020-8458 4212. Fax 020-8458 4572. E-mail theagency@excellententertai nment.biz. Website www.excellententertainment.biz.
Recruit entertainers for cruise ships and other businesses.

FM RECRUITMENT
Hedges House, 153-155 Regent Street, London W1B 4JE. ☎020-7287 5400. Fax 020-7287 5411. E-mail fm@fmrecruitment.co.uk. Website www.fmrecru itment.hcareers.co.uk.
In business since 1985.
Specialist recruitment service for financial management within the international hotel, catering and leisure industry. Clients comprise hotels, restaurants, event and industrial catering, casino, timeshare, resort operators, etc. looking for permanent or temporary accounting and finance staff. Opportunities worldwide including Russia and Eastern Europe.
Qualifications needed: positions normally require graduate education, language skills and relevant technical and professional training and qualifications.

FREE RADICALS
E-mail info@freeradicals.co.uk. Website www.freeradicals.co.uk.
Independent ski recruitment specialist based in the UK that works with many private and independent chalet companies searching and selecting staff for the season December-April. Applicants can register free of charge and each season about 120 are placed.
Qualifications: must hold an EU passport, be over 18 years old and have hospitality experience. Chefs and nannies must have relevant qualifications and/or experience. French and German speaking students/graduates also needed to work in French and German resorts for the summer or winter seasons.
All jobs include return travel to/from the UK, full board and accommodation, ski equipment, insurance, lift pass plus a wage.
Recruitment starts in mid-May and carries on into ski season to replace workers that have left. Interviews are essential and are mostly held in London.
Contact: Claire Stanton, Director.

GRAPEVINE INTERNATIONAL LTD
26/28 Clay Road, Caister-on-Sea, Norfolk NR30 5HB. ☎020-7430 2266. E-mail office@grapevine-int.co.uk. Website www.grapevine-int.co.uk.
In business for 15 years. Partner offices in Austria and Gibraltar. UK office handles enquiries for the Asia Pacific region.
Specialists for the hotel industry, spa and cruise lines. 80% of vacancies are overseas, the rest in the UK. All are permanent positions. Specialise in middle-ranking and senior appointments only, across all disciplines within the industry.
Qualifications needed: should be industry-skilled and have experience within the industry. All nationalities accepted.
Contact: Roger Burnay, Managing Director.

HOCAPS INTERNATIONAL
60 Ebury Street, Belgravia, London SW1W 9QD. ☎020-7730 8883. Fax 020-7730 8885. E-mail Mail@hocamps.com. Website www.hocaps.com.
In business since 1977. Offices in New York and Cairo.
Management resourcing within the hospitality industry.

HOUSE OF RECRUITMENT
Suite 3, Bridge House, 27-33 Reading Road South, Fleet, Hampshire GU52 7QP. ☎01252 673544. E-mail contact@houseofrecruitment.co.uk. Website www.houseofrecruitment.co.uk.
Specialises in the provision of permanent and temporary travel and tourism professionals.

HRC INTERNATIONAL
Hertogsingel 104, 6214 AG Maastricht, The Netherlands. ☎+31 43-351 0070. Fax +31 43-351 0057. E-mail info@hrc-international.nl. Website www.hrc-international.nl.
In business since 1995 with local representatives in the UK and Switzerland, and partner organisations in Japan, Canada and Ecuador.
Makes international placements of young culinary and hotel professionals in the international hospitality industry, particularly the US and Europe. Once a host employer has been found, agency co-ordinates the visa and insurance arrangements and provides local training materials and ongoing support throughout the programme. Visa fee of $800 may be waived for culinary candidates.

IN FOCUS
9 Riverside Court, Lower Bristol Road, Bath, Somerset BA2 3DZ. ☎01225 404050. Fax 01225 406070. E-mail cv@in-focus.org. Website www.in-focus.org.
In business for 8 years.
Consultancy and recruitment to hotels and restaurants. Recruits for permanent vacancies mainly in the UK but also in France, Spain and occasionally the Caribbean.
Qualifications needed: Minimum NVQ2 in catering, or some experience in the catering industry. EU nationals only.
Contact: Sonia Salles, Consultant.

I RECRUIT LTD
5a Westhill House, Westend, Frome, Somerset, BA11 3AD. ☎0870 990 8898. Fax 0870 990 8878. E-mail catering@irecruitltd.com. Website www.irecruitltd.com.

In business for 3 years.

Recruit solely for permanent positions in the hotel and catering industry, specialising in small/luxury hotels and restaurants, and some high-end themed brasseries. Mainly UK-based although clients also in Italy, France, Spain and Maldives.

Qualifications needed: must have appropriate skills and for catering positions be professionally qualified: 706.1&2 or NVQ1&2. Front of House, BTEC/HND Catering or practical experience in a high quality establishment. EU nationals only.

For lower skilled/junior positions interviews can be conducted by telephone. For senior posts, interviews necessary, sometimes followed up by a work trial.

Vacancy database on website updated every other day. Candidates can apply directly online, and utilise CV compilation form.

Contact: Nina Thompson, Owner.

JCR INTERCULTURAL EXCHANGE PROGRAMS

PO Box 497, Bentleigh East, Victoria 3165, Australia. ☎+61 3-9557 0300. Fax +61 3-9557 0400. E-mail sybil@jcraus.com.au. Website www.jcraus.com.au.

Placements in the hospitality industry in the UK for up to 12 months. Most positions are live-in.

Contact: Sybil Touyz, Director.

JOBS.IE

35 Wicklow St, Dublin 2, Ireland. ☎+353 1 670 3891. Website www.jobs.ie.

Online employment listings in hotels, restaurants, bars and leisure centres in Ireland. Chefs and experienced hotel receptionists are particularly in demand normally for a minimum of 6 months.

Wages: vary but start at minimum wage in Ireland of €6.80.

Contact Name: Marco Herbst, Director.

JULIANA'S LEISURE SERVICES

15-17 Broadway, West Ealing, London W13 9DA. ☎020-8567 6765. E-mail recruitment@julianas.com. Website www.julianas.com. Offices in Dubai and Hong Kong.

In business since 1966.

Agency places disc jockeys, entertainers and managers worldwide, mostly in luxury hotels and resorts.

Experienced 'personality DJs' and 'flair bartenders' needed for contracts worldwide, particularly in Middle East and Far East.

Qualifications needed: must have good presentation skills. Applicants should submit CV, demo tape (including mixing and voice overs) and photograph. Bartender training available.

Wages: wage paid in addition to free flights, accommodation, food and records/CDs.

KINGSBROOK USA INC.

PMB 117, 303 B Anastasia Boulevard, St. Augustine, FL 32080, USA. ☎ 904-461-4291. Fax 904-461-4275. E-mail ukhoteljobs@aol.com. Website www.kingsbrookusa.com.

Up to 500 live-in jobs a year in hotels all over England, Wales and Ireland and (mainly for Britons) in the USA.

Also place English-speaking candidates with EU passport in jobs on cruise ships.

Front office, food and beverages, culinary, banquets, housekeeping at all levels from entry level to management positions. Hotel management internships available in the US.

Most placements are in upscale hotels, resorts, marinas, ski resorts, country clubs and golf resorts which can provide thorough training.

Qualifications needed: should have studied course in hotel, culinary or food & beverage studies or at least had a minimum of 3 months relevant work experience.

Working week in most places is 40 hours over 5 days. Standard stay is 6-18 months.

Contact: Susan Goedhart, Manager.

L&G RECRUITMENT
6 Minories, London EC3N 1BJ. ☎020-7481 1475. Fax 020-7481 4951. E-mail bob@lgrecruitment.co.uk. Website www.lgrecruitment.co.uk.

In business for 14 years.

Temporary waiters and waitresses (silver service and plate), stewards (security staff) and bar staff for venues and functions in London such as Livery Halls, museums, Guild Hall, riverboat cruises, royal functions, film premiers, fashion shows, etc.

Qualifications: minimum age 18. Previous waiting/bar experience essential. Any nationality with a valid work permit and a good understanding of English (written and verbal).

Wages: £4.80-£6 per hour.

Interviews essential and also copies of passport, visa and references.

Contact: Bob Fortt, Catering Manager.

NAPPY VALLEYS LTD
22 Nansen Road, London SW11 5NT. ☎020-7223 9877. E-mail info@nappyvalleys.co.uk. Website www.nappyvalleys.co.uk.

Provides private qualified nannies to families staying in the French ski resort Val d'Isère.

Qualifications: must have a recognised nanny qualification e.g. NNEB/CACHE/BTEC and must be over 18.

Contact: Carla Laing, Manager.

NEW FRONTIERS
Lion House, 23 Islington High St, London N1 9LQ. ☎0845 202 2222. Fax 0845 458 8635. E-mail jobs@newfrontiers.co.uk. Website www.job-in-travel.com. Office in Manchester: The Triangle, Exchange Square, Manchester M4 3TR; 0161-838 5800; north@newfrontiers.co.uk.

In business since 1993.

One of the UK's largest travel recruitment specialists with plans to open a new branch in Newcastle. Vacancies in all sectors of the industry: business and retail travel, reservations, tour operations and wholesale travel.

Career advice and training courses at competitive prices.

OPENWIDE INTERNATIONAL LTD
7 Westmoreland House, Cumberland Park, London NW10 6RE. ☎020-8962 3400. Fax 020-8962 3440. E-mail recruitment@openwideinternational.com. Website www.openwideinternational.com.

Primarily entertainment suppliers for mainstream leisure and tourism industry. Recruit about 100 entertainers a year to work on cruise ships and in hotels; dancers, vocalists, technicians, ballroom dancing hosts, children's entertainers, comperes.

Qualifications needed: bright, enthusiastic personalities and excellent PR and communication skills to work in hotels in Spain, Cyprus, Greece, Balearics, Turkey and the Canaries. A knowledge of Spanish, German or French would be an advantage but not essential. All successful applicants will be given full training on the running of daytime and evening entertainment programmes.

Positions are available all year round; minimum period of work 6 months with salaries between £130 and £225 per week plus meals, accommodation and flight. Main season is May to November.

QUEST ELITE RECRUITMENT
4a-6a High St, Eastleigh, Southampton, Hants. SO50 5LA. ☎023 80 644933. Fax 023 80 618827. Website www.quest-elite.co.uk.

Top level international hospitality recruitment for professionals at managerial level. Opportunities only available for personnel who can demonstrate relevant experience in hotels of 4/5 star quality.

RESIDENT ENTERTAINERS
PO Box 74, Frodsham, Cheshire WA6 9XB. Tel: 01928 723387. E-mail recrui t@residententertainers.com. Website www.residententertainers.com.

Live-in entertainment jobs throughout the UK and Europe, e.g. on holiday parks, theme parks, hotels and cruise ships. Positions include general entertainers and animators, along with singers, dancers and karaoke hosts (750-1000 a year). Contracts last from 3 months to permanent though most are 6-8 months over the summer. Busy recruiting period is January-March though vacancies are filled throughout the year.

Qualifications needed: minimum age 18, UK residents and preferably with no dependants.

Wages: inexperienced hotel entertainer normally receives £120-£160 for a 6-day week plus accommodation, meals and drinks. Experienced singer/dancer for production shows receives £150-£250.

Contact: Craig Crowton, Director of Recruitment.

SKI STAFF
45 Farm View, Yateley, Hampshire GU46 6HU. ☎0870 432 8030. Fax 0870 011 1719. E-mail jobs@skistaff.co.uk. Website www.skistaff.co.uk.

Ski resort employment for qualified chefs to work in hotels and luxury chalets, for resort, hotel and chalet managers, chalet cooks, chalet couples, resort reps, ski guides, nannies and general chalet and hotel staff.

Qualifications: chefs and nannies must be qualified. Reps and managers must have a second language. Chalet cooks do not necessarily need a chef's qualification but do need to be highly organised in the kitchen.

Wages: £60-£180 a week plus ski package which includes transport to the resort, food and board, ski pass, ski insurance and equipment. Most companies require EU or British passport holders, some will employ Australians and New Zealanders with a working holiday visa.

Applications most welcome in July/August.

Contact: Michelle Smith, Director.

T&T RECRUITMENT & RESOURCING LTD
5-7 Folgate St, Bishopsgate, London E1 6BX. ☎020-7426 9370. Website www.t-trecruitment.co.uk.
In business since 1983.

Specialist recruitment agency with ten consultants for permanent and temporary jobs in the travel industry, including members of the Guild of Business Travel Agents. Placements made in the UK and Europe in the field of business travel, retail travel, tour operations, conference and incentives, and sales and marketing. All levels of positions available.

Only agency to offer in-house Virgin Atlantic VA-1 and VA-2 Fares and Ticketing plus Galileo CRS (see entry in Training Directory).

TERENCE COX & ASSOCIATES LTD
PO Box 60 229, Titirangi, Auckland, New Zealand. ☎09-837 0549. Fax 09-837 4384. E-mail terence@terencecox.com. Website www.terencecox.com.
In business since 1985.
Recruitment consultancy within the hospitality industry active in New Zealand, Australia, the Pacific Islands (including Papua New Guinea, Fiji, etc.). Specialise in the placement of chefs. Assistance given with work permits.

UK OVERSEAS HANDLING (UKOH)
PO Box 2791, London W1A 5JU. ☎020-7629 3064. E-mail cv@ukoh.co.uk or candidatures@eurogroup-vacances.com.
In business since 1991/2.
UKOH recruits young people for Eurogroup, a French tourism and property management company which owns and operates hotels and restaurants in the French Alps, on the Atlantic and Mediterranean coasts and in Paris and Montpellier. For students, Eurogroup offers a work placement scheme either in resort or in the head office in Chambéry (BP 429, 73004 Chambéry Cedex; 04-79 65 07 79). Places are available all year round, and accommodation is always provided. Applicants should have a good level of French.

VIP INTERNATIONAL
VIP House, 17 Charing Cross Road, London WC2H 0EP. ☎020-7930 0541. Fax 020-7930 2860. E-mail vip@vipinternational.co.uk.
International recruitment consultancy for the hospitality industry, including cruise lines. Head waiters, chefs, hotel managers, food and beverage managers, pursers, housekeepers, controllers and all department heads.
Qualifications needed: minimum 3 years experience with 4 or 5 star operations. Must be aged 21-40 and have good command of English.
Wages: some posts pay up to $2,500-$5,000 per month tax free.

WORLDNET
Avondale House, 63 Sydney Road, Haywards Heath, West Sussex RH16 1QD. Tel: 01444 457676. Fax: 01444 440445. E-mail info@worldnetuk.com. Website www.worldnet.uk.com.
In business for 22 years.
Chefs, kitchen assistants, cooks and general assistants placed in permanent posts in hotels, mainly in UK. Relevant training and experience needed. All nationalities considered; entry clearance/work permits can be arranged.

DIRECTORY OF TOUR OPERATORS

ACIS (AMERICAN COUNCIL FOR INTERNATIONAL STUDIES)
38 Queen's Gate, London SW7 5HR. ☎020-7590 7474. Fax 020-7590 7475. E-mail tmdepartment@acis.com. Website www.acis.com
Educational travel company, part of the American Institute for Foreign Study (AIFS). Tour managers (100) recruited to lead groups of North American high school teachers

and students on educational tours of one or more European countries. Tours are between 9 days and 2 weeks in length and run principally in March/April and June/July.

Qualifications needed: tour managers meet groups on arrival, travel with them, act as commentators and guides, keep accounts, direct bus drivers, troubleshoot etc. Fluency in French, Italian, German or Spanish is essential for trips outside the UK and Ireland. Must be familiar with the relevant country (particularly its capital city) and able to communicate a genuine interest in the people and places of Europe. Candidates must be over 21 and have a university degree or be studying for one. Previous experience preferred but not essential; full training given.

Wages: Daily salary, accommodation provided with the groups in 3/4-star hotels, generous tips, insurance and back-up provided.

Applications accepted from the autumn and can be done online.

ACORN VENTURE LTD
22 Worcester Street, Stourbridge, West Midlands DY8 1AN. ☎01384 378827. Fax 01384 378866. E-mail jobs@acornadventure.co.uk. Website www.jobs-acorn.co.uk
In business since 1982. Members of BCU, RYA, ABTA, AALA, BAHA.

Activity holiday company offering groups multi-activity camping holidays in North Wales, the Lake District, France, Spain and Italy.

300 seasonal opportunities: instructors, reps, maintenance staff, administrators, catering staff and nurses needed mid-April to September (some shorter contracts are available). Activities include sailing, canoeing, kayaking, climbing, abseiling and caving. Send a CV or apply online from October onwards; interviews start in January.

Wages: living allowance of approximately, plus supplement. Bonus subject to qualifications and experience.

ADVENTURE & COMPUTER HOLIDAYS LTD
PO Box 183, Dorking, Surrey RH5 6FA. ☎01306 881299. Fax 01306 885933. E-mail info@holiday-adventure.com. Website www.holiday-adventure.com
Children's activity day camps in Surrey every half term and school holiday for 4-14 year olds. Camp leaders always needed.

Camp leaders needed: 2. Period of work Easter and school summer holidays.

Qualifications needed: training/experience with children. Minimum age 21 for day camps.

Wages: £130-£160 per week for day camp leaders.

ADENTURE ALASKA TOURS
PO Box 64, Hope, Alaska 99605, USA. ☎907 782 3730. Fax 907 782 3725. E-mail info@adventurealaskatours.com. Website www.adventurealaskato urs.com
In business since 1987.

Operate tours in Alaska plus Yukon and Northwest Territories of Canada.

Multi day tour guides (6) and housekeeping interns (2) needed. Contract lasts from early June to late August. Applications welcome in winter/spring.

Qualifications needed: previous experience of guiding. Knowledge of French or German preferred.

AFRICAN PORTFOLIO
146 Sound Beach Avenue, Old Greenwich, CT 06870,USA. ☎800-700-3677. Fax 203-637-6813. E-mail onsafari@africanportfolio.com. Website www.onsafari.com. Also has office in Harare Zimbabwe.

Tour operators to Southern and East Africa, Seychelles, Mauritius, Madagascar, Mozambique. May require staff for sales and itinerary planning with clients, etc. Contracts for 1-2 years. Languages not necessary but ability to pay attention to detail is. Must have residency and work permit for Zimbabwe.

AIRTOURS – see MyTravel.

ALPINE TRACKS
40 High Street, Menai Bridge, Anglesey LL59 5EF. ☎0800 028 2546. Fax 01248 717441. Website www.alpinetracks.com
Organisers of skiing and mountain biking trips in France (Morzine and Champagny) and Austria (Lech).
Chefs, chalet girls and guides needed. Winter season is 5 months, summer season is 3 months. Interviews for winter take place in June and in January for summer season. Sometimes staff employed in-country.
Qualifications needed: knowledge of French preferred. Good sense of humour.

ALPOTELS
E-mail info@jobs-in-the-alps.com. Website www.jobs-in-the-alps.com
Associated with Jobs in the Alps and Free Radicals (see separate entries).
Opportunities for waiters, waitresses, chambermaids, porters, chefs and kitchen staff in German and French owned hotels. Applications by 15th September for winter, 15th April for summer.
Qualifications needed: must be alert, intelligent, hardworking, responsible and pleasant. Hotel experience valuable but not essential. Knowledge of language needed for French jobs, less so for German. Applicants must be EU nationals.
Wages approximately £500 per month in France, £400 in Germany, plus free food and lodging.

AMILI
P.O. Box: 17-1423, Quito, Ecuador. ☎+593 9-940 0851. E-mail info@amili.org. Website www.amili.com/internship.htm.
Unpaid internships in many fields including tourism and event management throughout Ecuador including the highlands, coastal areas, at lodges deep in Amazonia and the Galapagos Islands; candidate chooses location. Positions may be available in international travel agencies (selling tickets, etc.) or working for land tour operators (e.g. jungle tours, mountain biking, Galapagos tours, etc.)
Qualifications needed: good knowledge of Spanish is required. Must be able to adapt to different culture.
Duration: minimum 2 months, up to 6 months (since foreigners require no visa for stays of less than 6 months). Available any time of year.
Cost: $200 placement fee includes transfer from airport to host family. Language lessons cost $6 an hour (20 hours a week). Accommodation with host families costs $12 per day including full board.
Contact: Patricia Fernández (Internship Consultant), Patricio Fernández (General Co-ordinator).

ARDMORE LANGUAGE SCHOOL
Hall Place, Burchetts Green, Maidenhead, Berkshire SL6 6QR. ☎01628 826699. Fax 01628 829977. E-mail dos@theardmoregroup.com Website www.theardmoregroup.com.

Member of ALTO (Association of Language Travel Organisations), FIYTO (Federation of International Youth Travel Organisations) and BITOA (British Incoming Tour Operators Association).

Multi activity and English language camps mainly in London and region.

Tour guides occasionally needed in addition to 100 EFL teachers plus sports leaders aged 20-30 for summer and Easter language holidays. Must speak a European language. Group leaders and centre directors also needed.

ASTONS HOLIDAYS
Clerkenleap, Broomhall, Worcester WR5 3HR. ☎01905 829200. Fax 01905 820850. E-mail info@astons-coaches.co.uk. Website www.astons-coaches.co.uk

Ski tour operator, mainly to Austria and Switzerland.

Ski tutors/guides required 1-7 weeks through winter season, particularly New Year, February, half-term and Easter holidays. Applications processed all year. Some vacancies filled abroad with people who are qualified and already working with local ski school.

Qualifications needed: BASI/National Ski School/Alpine Ski Leader award and proven track record as a ski guide. Preferred minimum age 21. Current first aid certificate linked to outdoor education environment needed. Knowledge of foreign languages not essential.

ATG-OXFORD
69-71 Banbury Road, Oxford OX2 6PJ. ☎01865 315679. Fax 01865 315697/ 8/9. E-mail jessicag@atg-oxford.co.uk. Website www.atg-oxford.co.uk/ working.php.

In business since 1979. Upmarket independent tour operator (formerly Alternative Travel Group) offering walking and cycling tours in Europe. Member of AITO.

Tour Managers, Tour Leaders and Route Managers needed on a seasonal basis needed to look after individual clients and groups in many European countries especially Italy plus a few further afield. Extended training given (company has won National Training Awards).

Qualifications needed: minimum age 22. Must be able to converse in English plus two of Italian, Spanish, French, Portuguese, Greek, Turkish and Czech. Must have appreciation of culture (history, wine, etc.) and be able to cook.

Wages: £210-£700 per week plus expenses. Season lasts from March to October.

Interviews in February, one-week training in March. Occasionally vacancies need to be filled in August for autumn season.

BACKROADS
801 Cedar Street, Berkeley, CA 94710-1800, USA. ☎510-527-1555 ext. 560. Fax 510-527-1444. E-mail humanresources@backroads.com. Website www.backroads.com

In operation since 1979.

Leading activity travel company to worldwide destinations.

15 office staff and 60 trip leaders needed. Recruitment takes place from mid-January. Most trips are in the USA but also some in Europe.

Qualifications needed: minimum age 21. Languages preferred. Must have ability to relate to people of different ages and backgrounds, have clean driving record, good public speaking skills, be capable of solving problems independently and professionally.

Wages: $55 per day for inn trips, $73 per day for camping trips. Meals, lodging and transportation included. Bonuses and wage increases awarded annually.

BALES WORLDWIDE LTD
Bales House, Junction Road, Dorking, Surrey RH4 3HL. ☎01306 885991. Fax 01306 740048. E-mail enquiries@balesworldwide.com. Website www.balesworldwide.com.
In business since 1947.
Tours to worldwide destinations (not Europe).
Recruit permanent staff reservations executives only occasionally. Vacancies, if any, are shown on website or advertised in trade journals.
Travel and tourism qualifications or experience necessary.

BALKAN HOLIDAYS
19 Conduit Street, London W1S 2BH. ☎020-7543 5555. Website www.balk anholidays.co.uk.
Experienced children's reps needed for kids' clubs at resorts along the Black Sea. Junior reservations consultants sometimes needed for head office.

BELLE FRANCE
Spelmonden Old Oast, Goudhurst, Kent TN17 1HE. ☎0870 405 4056. Fax 01580 214011. E-mail enquiries@bellefrance.co.uk. Website www.bellefrance.co.uk.
Walking and cycling tour operator through rural France.
Member of AITO, ABTOF & ABTA.
Bike reps needed: 2. To maintain bikes, transport luggage, collect customers, etc. May to September. Applications welcomed around Christmas.
Qualifications needed: must be well organised, capable of working independently and enjoy the great outdoors. Minimum age 21. Driving experience required.
Wages: £125 per week plus accommodation.

BESTatTRAVEL
Part of Worldwide Journeys plc, 10 Berners Mews, London W1T 3AP. ☎0870 709 3095. Fax 0870 709 3088. E-mail Enquiries@bestattravel.co.uk. Website www.bestattravel.co.uk.
Tour operator in business since 1985.
Recruiting year round, specifically looking for experienced sales staff.
Contact: Carole Booth, Head of Product & Marketing.

BIKE RIDERS
PO Box 130254, Boston, MA 02113, USA. ☎617-723-2354/ 800-473-7040. Fax 617-723-2355. E-mail info@bikeriderstours.com. Website www.bikeriderstours.com.
Bicycle tour holidays in Italy, Ireland, Spain and Portugal plus New England and Canada.
Recruit 20 tour guides for full and part time work from April-October. Recruitment begins January, interviews in February.
Qualifications needed: appropriate language for each country, Must be well-travelled and organised individuals with good ability in customer service.
Contact: Ashley Harris.

BOLERO INTERNATIONAL HOLIDAYS
The Old Airfield, Master Road, Thornaby, Teesside TS17 OBE. ☎01642 767222. Fax 01642 767677. E-mail info@boleroholidays.co.uk. Website www.boleroholidays.co.uk.

In business since 1984 running family holidays by coach to a campsite in Spain (near the French border) and one in Italy on the lido near Venice.

Campsite couriers (6) to carry out cleaning and maintenance on campsites and run programmes of entertainment. Children's campsite couriers (4) for running Kids Club for ages 4-14 plus cleaning duties. Coach couriers (4) to travel on coaches to and from Spain and Italy, load bike trailer, and provide on-board entertainment, quizzes, videos, etc.

Minimum 3 months between April and October.

Qualifications needed: knowledge of Spanish or Italian required. Experience with children and craft skills preferred.

Wages: £120 per week. Lodging provided but not board.

BOURNE LEISURE GROUP
1 Park Lane, Hemel Hempstead, Herts. HP2 4YL. ☎01442 241658. Fax 01442 219031. Website www.bourneleisuregroup.co.uk

In business for over 35 years. Now owns Haven Europe (see entry) and Warner as well as Butlins and Owners Exclusive.

500+ employees in head office plus many others working for their brands.

Qualifications needed: knowledge of languages not necessary. Must have outgoing personality, be customer-oriented, have computer skills.

BOWHILLS LTD
Mayhill Farm, Swanmore, Southampton SO32 2QW. ☎01489 872727. Fax 01489 872707. E-mail enquiries@bowhills.co.uk. Website www.bowhills.co.uk.

Farmhouse and villa holidays in France.

Sometimes need reservations and admin staff.

CAMP BEAUMONT
The Recruitment Team, Camp Beaumont, West Runton, Cromer, Norfolk NR27 9NF. ☎01263 835155. Fax 01263 835192. E-mail jobs@campbeaumont.com Website www.campbeaumont.com.

Camp Beaumont Summer Camps, which have been running for 24 years at various locations across the UK.

Group Leaders (60-80) to be responsible for round-the-clock welfare of a group of children at summer camps, including overnight dormitory supervision. Also to instruct and initiate games and non-specialist activities, and to monitor the welfare needs of individual children.

Wages: £728 per month. Camps run for 8 weeks from the start of July to the end of August. Accommodation provided at a cost of £22.75 per week and food at a cost of £39.95 per week.

Qualifications needed: applicants must be aged 19-25 and have some previous experience working with children and/or a well-developed interest in sports, music, drama, art and crafts or any recreational pursuits. Foreign applicants with fluent English welcome. Part of the Kingswood Group with comprehensive training provided (see entry in Directory of Training Courses). Applications should be sent to the HR department at the above address in the spring. Telephone interviews and an assessment weekend required. Training commences first week in July.

CAMPING LIFE
Spring Mill, Earby, Barnoldswick, Lancashire, BB94 0AA. ☎0870-197 6541. Fax 0870-444 1484. E-mail overseasemployment@frenchlife.co.uk. Website www.frenchlife.co.uk.

Leading tour operator in France, Spain and Italy.
Onsite General, Children's and Senior couriers needed: 100.
Full-season contracts from March to September. Minimum period of work 8 weeks during high season. Application forms available from November.
Qualifications needed: knowledge of relevant language preferred but not essential.
Wages: from £440 per month (depending on position) plus commission, including accommodation in a chalet tent.

CANVAS HOLIDAYS
East Port House, 12 East Port, Dunfermline, Fife KY12 7JG. ☎01383 629018. Fax 01383 629071.
Self-drive tour operator founded in 1965. Operates more than 100 campsites in 8 European countries, mainly across France, but also in Spain, Italy, Germany, Austria, Switzerland, Luxembourg and the Netherlands.
Looking to fill positions of area managers, site supervisors, senior couriers, campsite couriers, children's couriers and 'wild and active' couriers for children. Complete season lasts from March until October with a small number of high season positions available from July to September. Recruitment takes place from October to March, in Dunfermline, Manchester, London and Bristol.
Applicants must be hard-working, flexible, enthusiastic and level-headed. A good working knowledge of a European language is preferred but not essential. Children's couriers, 'buzz couriers' and 'wild and active couriers' must have relevant experience. Applicants must be 19 for France, 18 otherwise. Applications are invited from mature

couples and individuals.
Wages: £101 per week (paid into UK bank account), return travel to and from UK port of entry. Uniform and tented accommodation provided.

CARISMA HOLIDAYS
Bethel House, Heronsgate Road, Chorleywood, Herts. WD3 5BB. Fax 01923 284235. E-mail personnel@carisma.co.uk.
In business since 1979. Specialises in self-drive family holidays in mobile homes on private beaches in the south-west of France. Couriers and site managers required for full season or high season. Candidates should have friendly personalities, be flexible, outgoing and have the ability to get on with people. French speakers preferred.
Full season couriers work from May 12th to September 24th and high season workers are required from July 1st to September 13th. When applying, state whether applying for full or high season work.
Wages: up to £100 a week for site managers, £95 for full-season and £90 for high-season reps.

CASTERBRIDGE TOURS
Salcombe House, Long St, Sherbourne, Dorset DT9 3BU. ☎01935 810810. Fax 01935 815815. Email chiefguide@casterbridge-tours.co.uk. Website www.casterbridgetours.com.
In business since 1979. Educational tours of Europe for schools and groups including Americans. Specialise in concert tours and trekking trips.
Tour guides needed: 25 to escort groups in Britain and Europe, mainly France, Spain and Italy, between March and July. Residents of destination countries could be considered for tours in that country.
Qualifications needed: knowledge of languages preferred but not always required. Guides must attend Casterbridge's winter training course. Applicants should be well travelled and have good standard of education.
Wages: from £280 per week with board and lodging provided.

CICLISMO CLASSICO
30 Marathon Street, Arlington, MA 02474, USA. ☎781-646-3377. Fax 781-641-1512. E-mail info@ciclismoclassico.com. Website www.ciclismoclassico.com.
Established 1988. Leading specialists in active cycling and walking vacations in Italy.
Need a few exceptional guides. Applicants must be bilingual (Italian/English) with hiking or cycling experience in Italy. Should have a strong passion for Italian culture and people, and also cycling.
To work for 2-8 months between April and November. Recruitment takes place December to February. Sometimes employ people on location.
Qualifications needed: minimum age 23. Must speak Italian, have leadership skills, knowledge of Italian culture, cycling and bike repair skills.

CITALIA HOLIDAYS LTD
Marco Polo House, 3-5 Lansdowne Road, Croydon, Surrey CR9 1LL. ☎020-8256 0271 (Overseas Human Resources). Fax 020-8686 6412. E-mail sandied@citalia.co.uk/julier@citalia.co.uk. Website www.citalia.com
In business arranging holidays to Italy since 1935 and more recently to Spain (since 2000) trading as The Real Spain.
Representatives needed. Interviews held in London, though people who are based in Italy

are also required.

Qualifications needed: applicants need to be self-motivated, flexible, pro active in problem-solving, able to deal with unexpected situations and to use excellent communication skills. Minimum age 23 for Italy, 25 for Spain. Must be fluent in the local language and hold a clean driving licence.

Contact: Sandie Devereux, Overseas Human Resources Controller.

CLUB CANTABRICA HOLIDAYS LTD.

Holiday House, 146/148 London Road, St. Albans, Herts. AL1 1PQ. ☎01717 866177. Fax 01727 843766. E-mail iona.mccabe@cantabrica.co.uk. Website www.cantabrica.co.uk.

In business since 1975. Member of AITO, ABTA and ATOL.

Camping tour operator to France, Italy, Spain and Corfu.

Couriers and resort managers needed: 80 posts. Season lasts May to October. Applications processed from January.

Qualifications needed: knowledge of languages preferred. Minimum age 18 for couriers, 21 for managers.

Work also available for children's couriers and drivers with PSV licence.

CLUB MED

Recruitment Dept, 11-12 place Jules Ferry, 69458 Lyon Cedex 06, France. ☎08453 676767. E-mail recruit.uk@clubmed.com. Website www.clubmed-jobs.com. For US applicants: resumes@clubmed.com.

In business since just after World War II.

Runs 120 Club Med villages in 37 countries and 1 luxury yacht which employ 25,000 GOs.

Mainly employ Gentils Organisateurs (GOs) and also excursion guides, nannies, sports instructors, hostesses, boutique assistants, receptionists, and cashiers. Work is seasonal up to 6 months.

Recruitment takes place August to November for winter season and December to May for summer season. Applicants must send CV and covering letter and attend a half-day or full-day assessment.

Qualifications needed: varies depending on position applied for. Minimum age 20. Applicants must speak fluent English and French (for some positions a third language is required). Sports instructors must have relevant qualifications and experience to teach sailing, water-skiing, scuba diving, tennis, windsurfing, golf and archery. Hostesses and guides should speak three European languages including German. Nannies must have childcare experience.

COLLETTE VACATIONS

162 Middle St, Pawtucket, Rhode Island 02860, USA. ☎(401) 728-3805. Fax (401) 728-1380. E-mail humanresources@collettevacations.com. UK affiliate: Adventures Unlimited Inc, Unit 11, Brook Business Centre, Cowley Mill Road, Uxbridge, Middlesex UB8 2FX; 01895 812333; www.collettevacations.co.uk).

In business since 1918. Member of Coach Tourism Council.

Deluxe motorcoach tour wholesaler to 100 destinations worldwide.

Staff needed: full-time tour managers employed in 4 offices worldwide. Sales and reservation personnel recruited year round, tour guides in spring.

Qualifications needed: knowledge of languages preferred (German, Spanish, French, Russian, Greek, Italian).

CONTIKI HOLIDAYS

Wells House, 15 Elmfield Road, Bromley, Kent BR1 1LS. ☎020-8290 6777. Fax 020-8225 4246. E-mail liesa.bissett@contiki.co.uk. Website www.contiki.co.uk.
In business since 1961 (founded by a New Zealander).
Coach and camping tour operator to Europe catering for 18-35s market.
30 Tour managers, drivers and site representatives needed. Contracts are for 30 weeks March to October/November. Interviews take place between October and March. 45-day training trip in Europe.
Qualifications needed: tour managers must have European travel experience, excellent organisational skills and interest in history, politics, etc. Tour drivers must have coach licence. Reps must be people-oriented. All must be over 23 and prepared to work hard. Knowledge of languages not necessary. Must have European passport or right to work in UK.
Wages: £130 a week plus incentive bonuses.
Work also available for cooks, bar staff and cleaners at sites throughout Europe.
Minimum period of work 4 months. Applications to Contiki Services Ltd.
Contact: Liesa Bissett, European Training Manager.

CONTINENTAL WATERWAYS

PO Box 31, Godalming, Surrey GU8 6JH. Tel/fax 01273 470076. E-mail crew @continentalwaterways.co.uk. Website www.continentalwaterways.co.uk (Recruitment). French office: Continentale de Croisières SA, 1 Promenade du Rhin, BP 41748, F-21017 Dijon, France (fax +33 3-80 41 67 73).
Continental Waterways have operated a fleet of luxury floating hotel barges on the waterways of France for the last 30 years.
Crew Members required to work from March to November in a fleet of 15 luxury hotel barges, including 3 large river boats, crewed by French, British and other EU nationalities. High standards of service and commitment to look after mainly American passengers. This is an ideal job for those who wish to improve their language skills, appreciate gourmet food, wine and cheese and who wish to immerse themselves in French culture for 7 months. Benefits include three weeks paid holiday, medical insurance, uniform and training. Applicants must have a valid permanent National Insurance number and hold a British or EU passport.
Download an application form and send it with a CV to Sarah-Jane Borradaile, Crew Recruitment at the above UK address.

COSMOS COACH TOURS LTD

Wren Court, 17 London Road, Bromley, Kent BR1 1DE. ☎(Recruitment) 020-8695 4724. Website www.cosmos-holidays.co.uk. Part of the Globus Group with headquarters in Switzerland.
Tour operator for UK clients.
Resort representatives and children's reps required for resorts in the Balearics, Canaries, Croatia, Cyprus, France, Greece, Lapland, Maldives, Malta, Spain and Turkey.
Qualifications needed: Minumum age 20/21 (19 for children's reps). Second language is desirable. 5 GCSEs including Maths and English.

COUNTRY WALKERS

PO Box 180, Waterbury, VT 05676, USA. ☎802 244 1387. Fax 802 244 5661. E-mail info@countrywalkers.com. Website www.countrywalkers.com.
In business since 1979.
Tours to Europe, South and Central America, USA, Canada.

Need 20 tour guides with appropriate languages. Work is for 10 one-week tours per year. Recruitment takes place all year. Must have detailed knowledge of the country with multi-tasking skills.

CRUSADER HOLIDAYS LTD.
Crusader Business Park, Clacton-on-Sea CO15 4HP. ☎01255 425453. Fax 01255 222683. Website www.crusader-holidays.co.uk.
In business since 1969.
Coach tour operator to European cities.
Tour escorts and tour managers needed: 20 (extra). For both summer (May to September) and winter (October to March) seasons. Staff recruited via adverts in trade press in February.
Qualifications needed: previous experience in customer care and knowledge of languages preferred.
Staff sometimes hired on location.

CRYSTAL HOLIDAYS – see Specialist Holidays Group.

CV TRAVEL
43 Cadogan St, London SW3 2PR. ☎020-7591 2800. Fax 020-7591 2802. E-mail cv@cvtravel.net. Website www.cvtravel.net. Also CV Travel, The Manor Stables, Great Somerford, Chippenham, Wilts. SN15 5EH (01249 721185/ fax 01249 721490).
In business since 1971. London office covers Italy, France and Morocco; Wiltshire office is for Spain, Portugal and Greece.
Well established upmarket villa holiday company.
Overseas representatives needed for the summer season (May-October). Must be able to speak the relevant language. Also require experienced cooks for either ad hoc appointments or seasonal vacancies. Must be able to drive.

DELTA TRAVEL
University Precinct, Oxford Road, Manchester M13 9RN. ☎0161-274 4444.E-mail products@deltatravel.co.uk. Website www.deltatravel.co.uk.
Travel agents to worldwide destinations.
Occasionally require travel consultants for permanent contracts.
Contact: Paul Newland.

DISCOVER ADVENTURE LTD
Throope Down House, Blandford Road, Coombe Bissett, Salisbury SP5 4LN. ☎01722 718444. Fax 01722 718445. E-mail darren@discoveradventure.com. Website www.discoveradventure.com.
Operates multi-activity, mountain-biking and trekking tours worldwide.
Tour leaders must speak English, be aged over 25 and hold a first aid certificate. An MBLA or MLA certificate is an advantage.
Staff also needed for field studies centre in France (see entry for Discover Ltd. below).
Wages: from £80 per week plus board and lodgings.

DISCOVER BRITAIN
International House, Pierpoint Street, Worcester WR1 1YD. ☎01905 613746. Fax 01905 613747. E-mail info@discoverbritain.co.uk.
UK tours company require 20 reservations staff in its Worcester and Edinburgh offices. Seasonal work for varying lengths between April and October. Recruitment takes place

between February and May.
Qualifications needed: knowledge of languages and office skills are useful.

DISCOVER LTD.
Timbers, Oxted Road, Godstone, Surrey RH9 8AD. ☎01883 744392. Fax 01883 744913. E-mail info@discover.ltd.uk or Eagles.Office@wandoo.fr.
In business since 1978.
Field study and personal development courses for students in the Cevennes mountains of France.
Staff needed: general kitchen assistant, assistant housekeeper, 2 cooks and maintenance person. Season lasts April to October though assistants can work for shorter periods. Interviews held in January/February.
Qualifications needed: cooks must have relevant qualifications or experience. General help must be willing and have likeable personality. No knowledge of French needed. British nationals preferred.
Contact: Sam Hillcox, Course Director.

DISNEYLAND PARIS
Service du Recruitement-Casting, Euro Disney SCA, BP 110, 77777 Marne-la-Vallée Cedex 4, France. ☎+33 1-64 74 61 47. E-mail simon.pearson@disney.com. Website http://disneylandparis.com/uk/employment/our_jobs/hotel_and_catering.htm.
Biggest theme park in Europe, in business since 1991.
Permanent or seasonal staff (known as cast members) to work in the Disneyland Paris Resort situated 30km east of Paris, consisting of 5,800 hotel rooms, an Entertainment Centre and the Theme Park, with restaurants, shops and attractions. Seasonal positions start between March and May and last until October. Opportunities exist in the Attractions, Merchandise, Food and Beverage, Reception, and Cleaning departments. Monthly gross wage is approximately £785 (€1138) for a 35-hour week. Staff contribute towards and are covered by French social security during their contract. Assistance is provided to help find accommodation and travel expenses will be reimbursed providing the contract is successfully completed.
Qualifications needed: minimum age 18. Must be of European nationality or have a valid work permit to work in France. Candidates must be friendly, cheerful and outgoing as the work involves a good deal of contact with visitors. It is also necessary to be able to communicate well in French and English and knowledge of a third European language is an asset. Applicants should write to the above address.
Contact: Simon Pearson, Casting Operations.

DISNEY WORLDWIDE SERVICES INC
International Recruiting, PO Box 10090, Lake Buena Vista, FL 32830. ☎407-828-1000 (Casting Jobline). Fax 407-824-1429. Website http://disney.go.com/DisneyCareers.
Biggest theme park in USA with much scope for international recruitment. Require people to feature in their Cultural Representative Program at the World Showcase at Epcot. Activities may include selling British merchandise or working in an English pub. Send CV to address above. Recruitment takes place twice a year in United Kingdom (March and October). For details of other countries, contact office in Florida.
Qualifications needed: Minimum age 18. Must be flexible, outgoing, willing to share a room with someone from a different country.

DRAGOMAN OVERSEAS TRAVEL & ENCOUNTER OVERLAND
Camp Green, Kenton Road, Debenham, Suffolk, IP14 6LA. E-mail kelly@dragoman.co.uk. Website www.dragoman.com or www.encounter.co.uk.
Overland expedition and adventure holiday operator to Africa, Asia, South and Central America.
Overland crew recruited. Must be resourceful and enthusiastic to drive groups of up to 24 clients around the globe in custom-built Mercedes vehicles. Trips are camping based.
Qualifications needed: minimum age 25. A mechanical background is an advantage but an interest in mechanics and a willingness to get dirty hands are sufficient. Extensive training provided in the UK.

DUVINE ADVENTURES
124 Holland St, Suite 2, Somerville, MA 02144, USA. ☎617-776-4441. Fax 617-776-1660. E-mail info@duvine.com. Website www.Duvine.com.
In business since 1994.
Luxury bicycle tours through rural France and Italy, especially Burgundy, Provence, Loire, Bordeaux and the Tour de France route.
Accommodation in inns and chateaux with emphasis on gourmet food and fine wines.
Recruit 6 staff for touring season May-October. Apply in January.
Qualifications needed: fluent French and knowledge of wine, food and biking. Excellent customer service skills.
Contact: Ed Flanagan, Operations Director.

EDWIN DORAN SPORTS TRAVEL
54 King St, Twickenham, Middlesex TW1 4SH. ☎020-8288 2949. Website www.edwindoran.com
Organisers of sports tours (rugby, lacrosse, field hockey, athletics). Good knowledge of geography and languages preferred. Good administration skills and self motivation needed.

EMILIO'S BAR & APARTMENT RENTALS
Apartado de Correos Nº880, El Puerto de Santa Maria, Cadiz 11500, Spain. ☎056-540112. E-mail mail@emiliosbar.com. Website www.emiliosbar.com.
Bar staff (6) for a café/bar in the Marina of Puerto Sherry, mainly patronised by Spanish tourists, so a sound knowledge of Spanish is essential. Must work 7 hours a day from 4pm, 6 days a week including all weekends. Minimum period of work 3 months.
Wages: €100 a week plus share of tips. Accommodation provided nearby in the Marina.
Applicants should send CV and photo.

EMPEROR DIVERS
Head office, Rosetta Hotel, PO Box 112, Sharm El Sheikh, South Sinai, Egypt. ☎+20 69-601734. Fax +20-69 601735. E-mail terry@emperordivers.com. Website www.emperordivers.com.
In business since 1992.
Diving holidays in Egypt at 6 Red Sea locations: Nuweiba, Sharm El Sheikh, Hurghada, Soma Bay, Marsa Alam and Port Sudan.
Diving instructors needed to teach holidaymakers to scuba dive. Minimum commitment one year.
Qualifications needed: minimum PADI MSDT plus BSAC OWI if possible. Knowledge of German, French, Italian and/or Spanish would be useful.

Wages: by arrangement plus commission on courses and sales.
Contact: Terry Simpson, Managing Director.

EQUITY LTD.
Dukes Lane House, 47 Middle Street, Brighton BN1 1AL. ☎01273 886901. Fax 01273 203212. E-mail recruitment@equity.co.uk. Website www.equity.co.uk.
In business since 1991. Direct-sell tour operator organising educational tours, sports tours, ski courses, etc.
Resort representatives: 5. To work with school groups on cookery, language or sports tours in France, Germany, Italy and Spain. Reps have a briefing at the Brighton office before travelling and a day in resort to set up prior to the group's arrival. Duties include liaison between the group, hotelier and coach driver; organisation of course-related excursions and interviews; translating during demonstrations and helping pupils with course-related work. Also up to 150 ski jobs; see www.equityski.co.uk/employment.
Qualifications: Applicants must be fluent in French, German, Italian or Spanish, well organised and able to work on their own initiative. They must be able to relate to children and will ideally have some experience of working with school groups or in a public service industry. Minimum age 21. A driving licence is required for some tours. Positions are available for periods varying from one week to one month between February and October.
Wages: £20-£25 per day plus full board, accommodation, travel expenses, insurance and uniform.
Contact: Carrie Husband.

ERNA LOW
9 Reece Mews, London SW7 3HE. ☎0870 750 6820. Fax 020-7589 9531. E-mail info@ernalow.co.uk. Website www.ernalow.co.uk.
Independent tour operators offering ski, summer and spa holidays.
Seasonal sales executives and administration assistants (10) for the ski department every winter to work in small busy office for 8 months. Overseas rep positions (8) with sole responsibility also available in France for the winter season (6 months).
Qualifications needed: must speak fluent French and have worked at least one season in the Alps for a UK operator. Good opportunity for ex-seasonal workers or recent graduates to get a start in the tourism industry.
Interviews in London at mutually convenient time.
Contact: Jane Hartley, Managing Director.

ESPRIT HOLIDAYS LTD.
185 Fleet Road, Fleet, Hants. GU51 3BL. ☎01252 618318. Fax 01252 618328. E-mail recruitment@esprit-holidays.co.uk. Website www.esprit-holidays.co.uk.
Winter and summer family holidays in catered chalets and hotels in alpine resorts in France (Chamonix, Tignes), Austria (Kaprun) and Italy (Val Gardena).
Resort managers (12), resort reps (16), resort child care reps (14), chalet chefs (20), chalet assistants (55), resort nursery assistants (60), snow rangers to look after children (90) plus various hotel staff (40). All needed from December to the end of April. Recruitment takes place year round. Some hiring takes place in the resorts.
Qualifications needed: resort/hotel managers require hospitality and customer service experience and excellent command of French, German or Italian. Must be a competent skier with a clean driving licence. Resort reps must have a good command of the language and be over 21. Hospitality experience an advantage. Chalet and hotel assistants need a

THE KEY TO A SUMMER IN EUROPE...
AND A CAREER IN LEISURE

If you are interested in working overseas but would like the security of being employed by an established UK Tour Operator, contact us today!

We are recruiting for vacancies in the following areas:

General Assistants	Mature Couples
Customer Service	Site Preparation*
Team Leaders	Site Closing*
Administration	Trainers
Children's Club*	Mature Singles

*Successful applicants will be asked to apply for a Standard or Enhanced Disclosure.

We will provide you with:

- RETURN TRAVEL
- UNIFORM
- FULL TRAINING
- ACCOMMODATION
- COMPETATIVE SALARY
- SUBSIDISED INSURANCE

To apply for one of these positions you will need to be:
- 18 or over, there's no upper age limit!
- Fit and healthy
- An EU passport holder
- Available to start work between March and May, contracts available until Mid July or September/October

If you think you have the qualities to provide our customers with the 'perfect family holiday' apply now!

Apply on-line at www.holidaybreakjobs.com or phone 01606 787525 for an application pack, quoting WT

*Further information about Disclosures can be found at www.disclosure.gov.uk or by phoning 0870 90 90 811

friendly and outgoing personality with excellent communication skills and the ability to work within a team. Requirements for other positions vary.
Contact: Samuel Edmonds, Senior Overseas Recruitment Co-ordinator.

EUROCAMP
Overseas Recruitment Department. ☎01606 787525. Website www.holida ybreakjobs.com.
Part of the Holidaybreak Group which includes Keycamp Holidays. Member of ABTA and AITO.
Major camping and mobile-home tour operator with hundreds of campsites in Austria, Belgium, France (mainly), Germany, Italy, Netherlands, Spain and Switzerland. Each year the company seeks to recruit up to 1,500 seasonal staff.
Campsite couriers, children's couriers, senior couriers and site managers needed. Telephone applications are preferred, from September/October. Interviews are held up until April in Hartford (Cheshire).
Qualifications needed: knowledge of local language and previous customer service or teamwork experience. Comprehensive training is provided together with a competitive salary, insurance, return travel and accommodation. Children's couriers require previous childcare experience. Applicants should apply on-line at www.holidaybreakjobs.com or telephone the above number for an application pack. Applications are accepted only from UK/EU passport holders who can attend interviews in England, Ireland, Holland, Germany, Poland or Denmark.

EUROPEAN WATERWAYS
35 Wharf Road, Wraysbury, Staines, Middlesex TW19 5JQ. ☎01784 482439. Fax 01784 483072. E-mail derek@gobarging.com. Website www.gobarging.com.
Fully crewed luxury hotel barge holidays in France (mainly), Germany, England, Ireland and Holland. Chefs, stewardesses, deckhands, tour guides and qualified barge captains needed. Employment in France is in Burgundy, Loire Valley and the South of France.
Qualifications needed: EU nationals only. Some French useful. Driving licence required. Minimum age 21 (25 for skippers and chefs).
Wages: £1,200-£1,400 a month.

EXODUS TRAVELS LTD
Grange Mills, Weir Road, London SW12 0NE (ipicken@exodus.co.uk; www.exodus.co.uk).
Overland expedition leaders needed. Suitable candidates (aged 25-32) for leader positions in Africa, Asia and the Americas can acquire the appropriate licence during the months of training. Knowledge of Italian, Spanish, French or Japanese highly valued.

EXPLORE WORLDWIDE LTD.
1 Frederick St, Aldershot, Hants. GU11 1LQ. ☎01252 760020. Fax 01252 760207. E-mail ops@exploreworldwide.com. Website www.explore.co.uk.
In business since 1981. Member of AITO.
Adventure tour operator to Europe, Africa, Asia and the Americas.
Tour leaders needed (approximately 40). Recruit mostly in the early spring.
Qualifications needed: minimum age 24 years. Must have (or be prepared to obtain) first aid certificate. French or Spanish preferred. Training given.

EXPO GARDEN TOURS
33 Fox Crossing, Litchfield, CT 06759, USA. ☎860-567-0322.

Fax 860-567-0381. E-mail info@expogardentours.com. Website www.expogardentours.com.
Specialises in garden tours in UK, Ireland, Holland, France, Italy.
Hires local guides and tour managers on a freelance basis between April and September.
Recruitment takes place July-September. Must be organised, have knowledge about gardens and their history.

FAMILY SKI COMPANY
Bank Chambers, Walwyn Road, Colwall, Herefordshire WR13 6QG. ☎01684 540333. Fax 01684 540203. E-mail enquiries@familyski.co.uk. Website www.familyski.co.uk.
Specialises in catered chalet holidays with flexible childcare in small resorts in the French Alps near Les Trois Vallées, La Plagne/Les Arcs and Les Portes du Soleil.
Chalet cooks, chalet hosts, activity leaders, ski school helpers and resort managers: 60 in all.
Qualifications needed: experience necessary, qualifications preferred. Muust have a valid UK national insurance number.
Wages: ski employment package includes food, accommodation, full season lift pass, ski or snowboard hire, uniform, return transport from Dover to resort, insurance and a weekly wage plus end-of-season discretionary bonus.
Contact: Mike Duffin, Overseas Personnel Manager.

FILOXENIA LTD
Unit 57, Bowers Mill, Branch Road, Barkisland, Halifax, West Yorkshire HX4 0AD. ☎01422 375999. Fax 01422 310340. E-mail travel@filoxenia.co.uk. Website www.escape-packages.com.
Greek island villa holiday company requires 7-9 clerical, admin and sales staff for Yorkshire office.
Qualifications needed: range from junior positions (suitable for university leavers) to senior positions for experienced staff. Some temporary positions during summer but mostly permanent. Knowledge of Greek or German would be an advantage.
Contact: Suzi Stembridge, Managing Director.

FIRST CHOICE AIRWAYS
Cabin Crew Recruitment, 7th Floor, Commonwealth House, Chicago Avenue, Manchester Airport MP0 3DP. E-mail jacqui.bastock@firstchoice .co.uk
Charter airline from January 2004 (formerly Air 2000).
Cabin crew required.
Qualifications needed: Must hold EU passport. Qualified to GCSE standard. Be able to swim a minimum of 25 meters. Minimum age 20. Minimum height 1.58 meters, with weight in proportion and excellent standard of personal presentation. Must be friendly, caring and have a realistic view of what the job entails.

FIRST CHOICE SKI, LAKES AND MOUNTAINS
First Choice Holidays, London Road, Crawley, West Sussex RH10 2GX. ☎01293 588585. Fax 01293 588277. E-mail overseas.recruitment@firstch oice.co.uk; also skijobs@firstchoice.co.uk. Website www.firstchoice4job s.com.
First Choice embraces a number of brand name holidays including JWT, Falcon, Skibound and Travelbound. As well as being a tour operator First Choice has a Hotels Division which leases and runs 25 Clubhotels and 55 Chalets in European ski lakes

and mountain resorts. Destinations include France, Austria, Italy, Andorra, Canada and Bulgaria.

Hotel Managers/Assistant Managers, Chefs (all grades), Chalet Cooks and General Assistants (500 in all).

CVs and covering letters are processed from June, group interviews held throughout the UK during September.

FLEUR HOLIDAYS
4 All Hallows Road, Bispham, Blackpool, Lancs. FY2 0AS. ☎01253 593333. Fax 01253 595151. E-mail employment@fleur-holidays.com. Website www.fleur-holidays.com

Campsite holiday operators in France.

Need campsite representatives/couriers with managerial capabilities.

Wages: approximately £630 a month plus £14 per week bonus paid on completion of contract. Contracts can be tailored to suit candidate's needs. Eager to take on staff for whom the work experience will form part of a recognised course. Knowledge of languages preferred. Must have a work visa.

FRANCE MONTGOLFIERES BALLOON FLIGHTS
La Picouliere, 41120 Valaire, France. ☎+33 2-54 44 16 41. Fax +33-2-54 44 19 18. E-mail jane@franceballoons.com. Website www.franceballoons.com.

Hot air balloon ground crew (10) needed to help with general cleaning and preparation of balloon vehicles. Season lasts April-October.

Qualifications needed: spoken French, physical strength and a driving licence that has been clean for at least two years. Must be EU national. Own transport essential.

Wages: SMIC (French minimum wage; see France chapter). Accommodation normally provided for pilots only.

Contact: Jane Janvier, Pilot/Manager.

FREEWHEEL HOLIDAYS
Temple Court, Cathedral Road, Cardiff CF11 9HA. ☎029 2078 6650. Fax 029 2034 4280. E-mail info@freewheelholidays.com. Website www.freewheelh olidays.com.

In business since 1988 offering a wide choice of gentle cycling holidays in Europe: Austria, Spain, France, Denmark, Belgium, Switzerland and England.

Freewheel hosts (10 vacancies a year) act as guides, translators, mechanic, cyclists, friends and diplomats. Must be able to relate to guests. Application deadline falls in March each year to work the summer season.

Qualifications needed: minimum age 24. Good German needed and a full driving licence. Pleasant personality and knowledge of bicycle maintenance both essential. Applications from couples welcomed.

Wages: £150 per week plus bonus and expenses.

Contact: Barbara Cray, Managing Director.

GENCTUR
Istiklal Cad. Zambak Sokak 15/5, Taksim, 34435 Istanbul, Turkey. ☎+90 212-249 25 15. Fax +90 212-249 25 54. Website www.genctur.com.

In operation since 1979.

Volunteers and counsellors with experience or enthusiasm needed for summer camps for children and teenagers. Applicants must be willing to undertake maintenance and housekeeping tasks as well as guiding and teaching, language practice and drama. Counsellors must have ability in sports, music, art, drama or handicrafts. Minimum stay

1 month between 1st April and 30th October.

Wages: work is voluntary but full board and excursions are provided.

Applications should be sent to partner agency in home country, such as UNA Exchange (www.unaexchange.org) or IVS (www.ivsgbn.demon.co.uk) in the UK.

GOING ABROAD TRAVEL
417 Hendon Way, London NW4 3LH. ☎020-8202 2080. Fax 020-8202 9105. E-mail job@gatuk.com.

Operate tours to worldwide destinations.

20-25 travel consultants and administration staff needed. Recruitment year round. Minimum length of contract 1 month. Computer skills and good telephone manner required.

Contact: John L. Slade, Managing Director.

GREEK ISLANDS CLUB
10-12 Upper Square, Old Isleworth, Middlesex TW7 7BJ. ☎020-8232 9780. Fax 020-8568 8330. E-mail info@greekislandsclub.co.uk. Website www.greekislandsclub.co.uk.

In business since 1968. Villa specialist to the Greek islands, part of Sunvil Holidays. Member of AITO.

Reps and other experienced staff needed.

GULLIVER'S SPORTS TRAVEL
Fiddington Manor, Tewkesbury, Glos. GL20 7BJ. ☎01684 293175. Fax 01684 297926. E-mail gullivers@gulliversports.co.uk. Website www.gulliversports.co.uk.

Co-ordinate and tailor-make tours to world sporting events in Australia, New Zealand, South Africa, India, North America, West Indies, etc.

Tour managers occasionally needed for 12-18 months. Sometimes staff are employed on location for major sporting events.

Qualifications needed: candidates must hold a degree. Languages are preferred and sometimes essential.

GUNFLINT LODGE
143 S. Gunflint Lake, Grand Marais, MN 55604, USA. ☎218-388-2294. Fax 218-388-9429. E-mail gunflint@gunflint.com. Website www.gunflint.com.

In operation since 1927.

Long established wilderness holiday resort, with fishing and canoeing activities.

Keen to employ overseas personnel for various positions; domestic staff, activities leaders, reception staff. Recruitment and work continues throughout the year, and contracts are a minimum of 3 months. Staff work 45 hours per week. Workers must have a work visa.

Wages: $1065 per month, plus bonuses. Shared accommodation is available for $115 per month.

HANDMADE HOLIDAYS
1st Floor, Carpenters Buildings, Carpenters Lane, Cirencester, Gloucestershire GL7 1EE. ☎01285 648518. Fax 01285 651685. E-mail travel@handmade-holidays.co.uk. Website www.handmade-holidays.co.uk.

Owners of Meriski (see separate entry).

Offers a wide range of hotels, catered chalets and apartments in many ski resorts in

France and Italy.
Chefs (6), assistant chefs (2), plongeurs (2), chalet staff (12), drivers, bar staff (8), resort managers (6), assistant resort reps (6).
Qualifications needed: chef, cookery, hospitality or childcare qualifications for relevant positions. Languages necessary for resort managers.

HARRY SHAW CITY CRUISER HOLIDAYS LTD
Mill House, Mill Lane, Binley, Coventry CV3 2DU. ☎02476 455544. Fax 02476 450774. E-mail robertshaw@harryshaw.co.uk. Website www.harryshaw.co.uk.
In business for 50 years. Arrange coach, camping and mobile home holidays in a variety of sites in France and Spain.
Campsite reps (5) to welcome clients and keep campsite clean.
Qualifications needed: French or Spanish would be an advantage.
Minimum period of work four months between April and October.

HAVEN EUROPE
1 Park Lane, Hemel Hampstead, Herts. HP2 4YL. Tel. 01442 203967; recruitment hotline 01442 203970. Fax. 01442 241473. Email joel.metcalfe@bourne-leisure.co.uk. Website www.haveneurope.com.
In business since 1974. Now part of Bourne Leisure Group.
Family camping holiday operator with 8 Owned Parcs and 23 Franchised sites across France, Italy and Spain.
Seasonal staff needed: 300 including park reps, assistant park reps, bar team members, accommodation team members, lifeguards, maintenance team members, tiger club reps, receptionists, entertainers, presenters, dancers and vocalists.
Season lasts from March to end of September. Recruitment begins in September; staff sometimes employed on location.
Qualifications needed: conversational French desirable but not essential to all positions. Minimum age 18 years. Tourism or hospitality qualification desirable. Mature couples welcome to apply. Experience of working with people, children, etc. needed. Employees must have a UK bank account and NI number.

HAYS TRAVEL
9/10 Vine Place, Sunderland, Tyne and Wear SR5 1PA. ☎0191-566 1903. Fax 0191-586 1921. E-mail personnel@hays-travel.co.uk. Website www.hays-travel.co.uk.
Largest independently owned travel agent in the UK.
Permanent employment offered in all aspects of travel consultancy: retail, telesales and homeworking. 70-100 positions.
Qualifications needed: Modern Apprenticeship schemes start at 16.
Contact: Helen Liddle, Personnel Manager.

HEADWATER
The Old School House, Chester Road, Castle, Northwich, Cheshire CW8 1LE. ☎01606 720033. Fax 01606 720001. E-mail info@headwater.com. Website www.headwater.com.
Activity holidays (walking, canoeing, cycling) in France, Italy and Spain. Cross-country skiing holidays in Austria, Norway and Sweden.
35 summer overseas reps and canoe instructors needed. Duties include meeting clients at airports and stations, supervising local transportation for clients and their luggage, hotel and client liaison, bike maintenance and on-the-spot problem solving. Contracts usually

5-7 months. Recruitment usually takes place January-February.
Cross-country ski reps (6) needed for winter season. Must be confident skiers, able to teach basics and guide groups with driving licence.
Qualifications needed: Minimum age 21. Must have good working knowledge of French, Italian or Spanish. Full, clean driving licence essential. Canoe instructors require BCU qualifications or relevant level of experience.
Wages: £115-£135 per week for summer reps, £120-£180 for winter reps plus accommodation.

HF HOLIDAYS
Redhills, Penrith, Cumbria CA10 0DT. ☎01768 899988. Fax 01768 899323. E-mail hr@hfholidays.co.uk. Website www.hfholidays.co.uk/recruitment.
Runs holidays in country house hotels across the UK.
500 positions to fill as chefs, general assistants and kitchen porters as well as a few managerial positions.
Qualifications needed: depends on position. A willingness to learn is often more important than qualifications.
Wages: £148.20-£175.50 for general assistants. Positions are available as live-in posts with £24.50 per week deducted for accommodation (single or twin) and £10 for food.
Contact: Sue Chandler (Head of HR) or Kim Hilditch (HR Administrator).

HOLIDAYBREAK – see Eurocamp and Keycamp.
Holidaybreak also encourages work experience placements for college and university students studying modern languages and other courses. For further information about college placements email overseasplacements@holidaybreak.com or phone the UK Placement Co-ordinator on 01606 787474.

HOLTS, BATTLEFIELD TOURS
HiTours House, Crossoak Lane, Salfords, Redhill, Surrey RH1 5EX. ☎01293 455300. Fax 01293 455302. E-mail info@holts.co.uk. Website www.battletours.co.uk.
In business since 1976. Member of AITO. Part of the Titan Group.
Tour operator specialising in military historical tours, taking in battlefields worldwide, from Vimy Ridge to Zululand. Expert tour leaders may be needed. Background in military history essential.

HOVERSPEED LTD
Human Resources, International Hoverport, Dover, Kent CT17 9TG. ☎0870 460 7474 (Recruitment Team). Fax 0870 460 7310. Website www.hoverspeed.com.
In business since 1981.
Runs frequent cross-Channel service (Dover-Calais, Newhaven-Dieppe) on fast car ferries and SeaCat catamarans.
Summer season staff needed: 150-200 including cabin crew (50) to work at sea looking after the safety and comfort of passengers, serving refreshments and selling duty-free goods; retail assistants (15) to work in duty-free outlets; and reservation assistants (25). Staff work various rosters at any time of the day or night, 7 days a week. Season lasts from March or June till the end of September, but some contracts are shorter. Applications accepted from January.
Qualifications needed: some knowledge of French needed; German preferred for some posts. Shop staff must have previous retail experience and reservations assistants must have keyboard experience. Cabin crew are given 3 weeks' training and must sit an

exam. Previous experience of dealing with the public an advantage. Travel and tourism qualifications desirable. Must be EU national or have permission to work in UK.
Wages: up to £7.16 an hour for cabin crew. Website carries detailed recruitment information.

IAN MEARNS HOLIDAYS
Tannery Yard, Witney St, Burford, Oxfordshire OX18 4DP. ☎01993 822655. Fax 01993 822650. E-mail enquiries@ianmearnsholidays.co.uk. Website www.ianmearnsholidays.co.uk.
Campsite tour operator to France.
Campsite representatives (18) and montage/démontage assistants (7) needed. Minimum period of work for reps is 10 weeks between Easter and mid-September. Camps are set up between March and early May, and dismantled for 3-4 weeks from the middle of September. Applications from November, giving dates of availability with s.a.e.
Qualifications needed: reps must have good knowledge of French, in good health and able to work without supervision.
Wages: from £400 per month for reps plus bonus.

THE IMAGINATIVE TRAVELLER
1 Betts Avenue, Martlesham Heath, Ipswich, Suffolk IP5 3RH. ☎01473 636066. Fax 01473 636016. E-mail tljobs@imtrav.net or liddy@imtrav.net. Website www.imaginative-traveller.com/jobs.
Operates small group, active journeys in the Middle East, Asia and Europe.
Tour leaders (80) recruited on an ongoing basis to work in Asia, the Middle East and Europe. Comprehensive training provided for those willing to work at least 13 months overseas. Minimum age 22. Must be experienced, responsible self-reliant travellers with great people skills and a positive attitude. No travel industry experience required. Good spoken English is required. Minimum 1 year contract.
Wages: vary with experience. Maximum £410 per month plus bonus and all living expenses (in 2 or 3-star hotels).
Contact: Liddy Pleasants, Head of Operations.

INGHAMS TRAVEL
10-18 Putney Hill, London SW15 6AX. ☎020-8780 4400. Fax 020-8780 8805. E-mail travel@inghams.com. Website www.inghams.co.uk.
In business since 1934. Long-established tour operator and largest independent operator of ski holidays. Operate in Andorra, Austria, France, Italy and Switzerland, plus ski resorts in North America.
Representatives (160) for client service, administration, sales, guiding of excursions and general problem solving. Salary £800-£1,200 per month including commission. Knowledge of French, German, Italian or Spanish is required. Minimum age 23.
Hotel managers (5) for staff management, budgetary control, guest and supplier liaison, problem solving and menu planning. Wages £500-£800 per month. Applicants must have good management and food and beverage experience within the hospitality industry. A good command of French or German is essential. Minimum age 24.
Hostesses (20) to waitress, clean and liaise with guests. Salary £200-300 per month. Minimum age 18. Relevant experience required.
Chefs and assistant chefs required to cater for up to 80 guests. Recognised cooking qualifications required and the ability to budget and menu plan. Salary £400-£800 per month. Minimum age 20.
Minimum period of work 3-4 months from May to September. Free board and accommodation provided. Applicants must be friendly, outgoing flexible team players with enthusiasm and a good sense of humour and must be customer care oriented and

have a liking for the country and culture.

INTERLOCKEN INTERNATIONAL
19 Interlocken Way, Hillsboro, New Hampshire 03244. ☎603-478-3166. Fax 603-478-5260. E-mail jobs@interlocken.org. Website www.interlocken.org/ general/jobs.html.
In operation since 1961. One of the first United Nations-inspired summer camps, dedicated to bringing together campers from different ethnic, religious, socio-economic and national backgrounds.
Travel Leaders (20) needed to take groups to Europe, Latin America, Africa, Asia and North America.
Camp counsellors needed (60) to work at Interlocken International on Windsor Mountain for 10 weeks during the summer, starting in mid-June. CV and covering letter should be sent between October and February.
Qualifications needed: experience working with children in a camp environment, specific skills (art, ceramics, photography, sports, sailing, camping, theatre, music, etc.), creativity and abundant enthusiasm. Minimum age 18.
Contact: David Love, Staffing Manager.

JOBS IN THE ALPS (EMPLOYMENT AGENCY)
E-mail info@jobs-in-the-alps.com. Website www.jobs-in-the-alps.com
Associated with Alpotels and Free Radicals (see separate entries). In business since 1972. Have opportunities for waiters, waitresses, chambermaids, night-porters, chefs and kitchen staff in Swiss-owned hotels. Applications by 15th September for winter, 15th April for summer.
Qualifications needed: must be alert, intelligent, hardworking, responsible and pleasant. Hotel experience valuable but not essential. Knowledge of language needed. Applicants must be EU nationals.
Wages from £500 per month plus free board and lodging.

JOURNEY LATIN AMERICA LTD.
12-13 Heathfield Terrace, Chiswick, London W4 4JE. ☎020-8622 8328. Website www.journeylatinamerica.co.uk.
In business since 1980. Member of AITO.
Overland tour operator to South and Central America.
Applicants should be familiar with Latin America and fluent in Spanish or Portuguese.

JUNIOR CHOICE ADVENTURE
14 Queensway, New Milton, Hants. BH25 5NN. ☎08705 133773. Fax 08705 133774. E-mail jcajobs@travelclass.co.uk. Website www.juniorchoiceadve nture.co.uk.
Part of Travel Class Ltd. Coastal and rural adventure activity centres in Southwest England (Devon, Cornwall, Somerset and Hampshire).
150 children's instructors (e.g. surfing, climbing, archery) and support staff needed.
Qualifications needed: enthusiasm for working with children in a multicultural community. Season lasts from March to July, application deadline February.
Wages: £180 per week. Accommodation provided in single or shared rooms.
Contact Liz Scott, Human Resources Administrator.

KEYCAMP HOLIDAYS
Overseas Recruitment Department, Hartford Manor, Greenbank Lane, Northwich, Cheshire CW8 1HW. ☎01606 787525. Website www.holidayb

reakjobs.com.
Part of the Holidaybreak Group. Member of AITO and ABTA.
Major camping and mobile-home tour operator with hundreds of campsites in Austria, France (mainly), Italy, Netherlands, Spain, Luxembourg and Switzerland. Each year the company seeks to recruit up to 500 seasonal staff.
Campsite couriers, children's couriers, team leaders and site managers needed. On-line applications are preferred, from September/October. Interviews are held up until April in Hartford (Cheshire).
Qualifications needed: Previous customer service and teamwork experience. Comprehensive training is provided together with a competitive salary, insurance, return travel and accommodation. Children's Couriers require previous childcare experience. Applicants should apply on-line at www.holidaybreakjobs.com or telephone the above number for an application pack. Applications are accepted only from UK/EU passport holders who can attend interviews in England, Ireland, Holland, Germany, Poland or Denmark.

KING'S CAMPS
The Manor House, Ecclesall Road South, Sheffield S11 9PS. ☎0870 345 0782. Fax 0870 345 0783. E-mail staff@kcjobs.org. Website www.kcjobs.org.
Registered charity that runs sports camps for children during the Easter and summer holidays in the UK for children aged 4-14. Also entertainment programme offered to children aged 10-16 on holiday at campsites in France, Italy and Spain.
Coaches and carers needed (about 600 positions in total). Must have childcare and/or sports coaching experience and qualifications. Minimum age 17. Managers should have a teaching qualification; senior coaches need 3 National Governing Body qualifications; group coaches need one NGB qualification; swimming teacher needs ASA Full Teacher or equivalent. For Europe, team leaders need 3 NGBs and couriers need 1 NGB. Period of work is 6 weeks in UK, 4 months in Europe. UK posts are non-residential, European posts come with tent accommodation.
Contact: Recruitment & Training Team.

KUMUKA EXPEDITIONS
40 Earls Court Road, London W8 6EJ. ☎020-7937 8855. E-mail humanreso urces@kumuka.com. Website www.kumuka.co.uk/employment.asp.
In business since 1987.
Overland tour operator to Africa, South America, Asia, the Middle East and Europe.
Drivers and tour leaders recruited. Must hold a PCV or HGV driving licence, have a good mechanical knowledge and be over 23.
Contact: Brian Hamilton.

LOTUS SUPERTRAVEL
Sandpiper House, 39 Queen Elizabeth Street, London SE1 2BT. ☎020-7295 1650. E-mail ski@lotusgroup.co.uk. Website www.supertravel.co.uk.
Ski tour operator specialising in upmarket chalet holidays in the Trois Vallées, Val d'Isère, St. Anton, and Zermatt, plus Canadian and American ski resorts.
Resort and chalet managers (5), chalet hosts (40), nannies (4), carpenters/plumbers, electricians (2) and resort managers needed mainly for Méribel, Courchevel and Val d'Isère.
Qualifications needed: applicants must have EU passports, be over 21 and have cooking or NNEB qualifications. All candidates must have relevant experience. Managers must

speak good French or German.

MAGIC OF ITALY/MAGIC OF SPAIN/MAGIC OF PORTUGAL – Part of TUI Group; see Specialist Holidays Group.

MALTA YOUTH HOSTELS ASSOCIATION
17 Triq Tal-Borg, Pawla, Malta PLA 06 Tel/fax +356 21-693957. E-mail myha@keyworld.net.
Independent group of Maltese youth hostels.
Volunteers needed to work 21 hours a week in youth hostels. Jobs to be done include administration, decorating, building, office work, etc. Period of work from 2 weeks to 3 months. Work permits must be obtained before beginning work, which can take 3 months, at least until the restrictions are lifted following Malta's accession to the EU. A good faith deposit must be paid.
Qualifications needed: ages 16-30.
Wages: free hostel accommodation and breakfasts provided.

MANOS HOLIDAYS – now part of MyTravel (see entry)

MARK WARNER LTD
Resorts Recruitment Department, George House, 61/65 Kensington Church St, London W8 4BA. ☎020-7761 7300 or 020-7761 7340 for Childcare Recruitment. Fax 020-7761 7301. Website www.markwarner-recruitment.co.uk.
Has 7 beachclub hotels in Corsica, Greece and Turkey and ski holidays in 10 resorts in Austria, France and Italy.
Staff needed: club managers, receptionists, chefs, bar and waiting staff, watersports and tennis instructors, pool attendants, aerobics instructors, laundry staff, handymen, drivers, gardeners, night watchmen and nannies (but not couriers or resort representatives). Must be available from mid-April to mid-October, though there is a continuous need for replacements throughout the season.
Qualifications needed: minimum age 19.
Wages: £50 and up per week in addition to free travel to resort, free food and accommodation and benefits such as use of watersports facilities, medical insurance and the potential for winter work in the Alps.
Contact: Kristina Farndell.

MATTHEWS HOLIDAYS LTD.
8 Bishopsmead Parade, East Horsley, Surrey KT24 6RP. ☎01483 284044. E-mail information@matthewsfrance.co.uk. Website www.matthewsfrance .co.uk.
In business since 1968. Campsite and mobile home holiday organiser in western France.
Campsite reps/couriers needed: 40. Season lasts from April/May to mid/late September. Applications are processed from January.
Qualifications needed: knowledge of French essential. Minimum age 20 years. Must be responsible, enthusiastic and reliable.
Wages: £120 per week plus accommodation.

MERISKI
1st Floor, Carpenters Buildings, Carpenters Lane, Cirencester, Gloucestershire GL7 1EE. ☎01285 648518. Fax 01285 651685. E-mail sales@meriski.co.uk. Website www.meriski.co.uk.

Part of Handmade Holidays. Specialise in luxury catered chalets in Méribel, France. Need chalet staff (20+), drivers (3), guest services representatives (3), nannies (8), managers (4). Season lasts early December to late April.

Qualifications needed: chef, cookery, hospitality, and nanny certificate for relevant positions. French language necessary for management positions.

MOUNTAIN LEAP
25 Eccleston Square, London SW1V 1NS. ☎020-7931 0621. Fax 020-7931 0613. E-mail info@mountainleap.com. Website www.mountainleap.com.

Luxury winter and summer tour operator to the Alps, mainly the French Alps.

Guides, chalet and resort teams (5) needed to work in Chamonix, Courchevel, Val d'Isère, Méribel, Megève, Verbier and Klosters.

Qualifications needed: minimum age 25. Hospitality, sales and resort experience useful. Period of work normally between 5 months and a year. Some jobs are part-time (e.g. 15 hours a week), others full-time.

Wages: £100-£300 a week. Comfortable private rooms in company apartments.

Contact: Adam Honey, Managing Director.

MYTRAVEL UK
Holiday House, Sandbrook Park, Sandbrook Way, Rochdale, Lancs. OL11 1SA. ☎0870-241 2642. Fax 01706 742328. Website www.mytravelcareers. co.uk.

Giant UK tour operator operating under the brands of Airtours Holidays, Direct Holidays, Panorama and Manos Holidays to worldwide destinations.

Staff needed: approximately 700 customer service reps, 150 children's reps, 20 nursery nurses, 80 transfer reps, 30 Escapades reps, 40 entertainers, 20 airport team leaders and airport reps and 40 commercial administrators needed April to October, mostly for Mediterranean resorts.

Qualifications needed: no formal qualifications are needed but experience in a sales or customer service environment is essential. Knowledge of a foreign language is not essential but is desirable for commercial administrator positions. Minimum age 21 for admin and Airport positions, 20 for Customer Service Reps, 19 for transfer reps and 18 for all other positions. Children's reps must have experience of working with groups of children and boundless energy.

NBV LEISURE LTD
PO Box 371, Bromley, Kent BR1 2ZJ. ☎0870 220 2148. Fax 020-8466 0653. E-mail personnel@nbvleisure.com. Website www.nbvleisure.com or www.skifrance.co.uk.

Specialist tour operator to the Swiss, French and Austrian Alps. Affiliated to Ski France (www.skifrance.co.uk).

Seasonal staff needed (240): admin/accounts assistants, hotel manager, chalet and resort managers, reps, chefs, chalet hosts, chalet assistants and nannies.

Qualifications needed; minimum age for reps and chalet staff is 21, for managers 24. Good customer service experience and knowledge of languages needed for some positions. Nannies need NVQ qualification or equivalent. All staff must hold permanent national insurance numbers.

Contact: Julian Banks, Personnel Manager.

NEILSON ACTIVE HOLIDAYS
Locksview, Brighton Marina, Brighton BN2 5HA. ☎01273 666130. Fax 01273 666005/0870 909 9089. E-mail recruitment@neilson.com or

skijobs@neilson.com. Website www.neilson.com/recruitment.
Neilson is a specialist brand within the Thomas Cook Group. Ski programme in winter to many resorts in Andorra, Austria, France, Italy, Switzerland, Eastern Europe, Canada and the USA.
Broad range of positions includes: ski representatives, chalet hosts, chefs (all grades), hotel managers, hospitality heads of departments, waiting and bar staff, receptionists, dinghy sailing and windsurfing instructors, PADI instructors, flotilla skippers and mates, mountain bike guides, children's club staff and nannies. Applicants must be EU citizens.
Contact: Catherine Deheer, Overseas HR Co-ordinator.

NEWMARKET PROMOTIONS
McMillan House, Cheam Common Road, Worcester Park, Surrey KT4 8RQ. ☎020-8335 4400. Fax 020-8335 4464. E-mail info@newmarket-group.co.uk.
Operates weekend breaks in Britain and Europe.
Couriers needed for pick-up points throughout the UK.
Qualifications needed: French an advantage.

NORTHUMBRIA HORSE HOLIDAYS
East Castle, Stanley, Co. Durham DH9 8PH. ☎01207 235354. E-mail rob@n orthumbriahorseholidays.com. Website www.dalehotel.freeserve.co.uk.
Equestrian tour operator.
Reps needed to take charge of parties of riders on equestrian holidays.
Qualifications needed: must be competent rider and be bright and enthusiastic.

NSS RIVIERA HOLIDAYS
288 Chemin du Caladou, 06560 Valbonne, France. Tel/fax +33 4-93 12 95 81. E-mail nss@wanadoo.fr. Website www.NSSRivieraHolidays.com.
Holiday village on 4-star site midway between St. Tropez and Cannes in the south of France.
Maintenance couples with DIY skills to act as caretakers of 28 chalets, cottages and mobile homes. Minimum age 45 years. Period of work 2 weeks or more at beginning and possibly end of summer season (April, May, September). In exchange for 3 days of work a week (e.g. joinery, plumbing, electrics, building, decorating), couples receive free self-catering accommodation. Must have own vehicle. Could lead to position as on-site representatives from March to October.
Contact: Donald Nimmo.

NST TRAVEL GROUP
Recruitment Dept, Chiltern House, Bristol Avenue, Blackpool, Lancs. FY2 0FA. ☎01253 503011. Fax 01253 356955. E-mail info@nstjobs.co.uk. Website www.nstjobs.co.uk.
In business since 1968. Two residential centres in France for educational groups.
Group co-ordinators (7) for Le Chateau to accompany guests on excursions around the French countryside. Excellent working knowledge of French required.
Activity instructors (20) for Lou Valagran to instruct a range of outdoor activities and to assist with the evening entertainment programme. Qualifications in canoeing, kayaking, caving, or climbing advantageous.
Catering assistants (5) for Lou Valagran to assist the Catering Manager and be involved in all aspects of kitchen work. No previous experience required.
Support Staff (6, for both centres), including positions for drivers, boat loaders, bar, shop,

support, cleaning and maintenance staff. No experience required though an unblemished driving licence is needed for driving positions.

Minimum period of work 2 months between January and November.

OLYMPIC HOLIDAYS LTD
c/o Interaction Ltd, 1 Torrington Park, London N12 8NN. ☎020-8492 6742. Fax 0870 429 4142. E-mail julian@olympicholidays.co.uk. Website www.olympicholidays.co.uk.

In business since 1967. Specialist package tour operator to Greece and Cyprus.

Overseas resort representatives (180) and overseas administrators (25) needed for many island resorts.

Qualifications needed: Greek language skills an advantage but not essential. Reps should have customer service experience and if possible sales experience.

Wages: £100 a week for reps, £600 a month for admin. Employees receive free travel to resort, accommodation (but not meals) and insurance.

Hand-written applications welcomed from October and regional assessments held between November and January for the start of the season in March/April. High season positions (June-September) are available.

Contact: Julian Pearl.

OPEN HOLIDAYS
The Guildbourne Centre, Chapel Road, Worthing, BN11 1LZ. ☎01903 201864. Fax 01903 201225. E-mail recruitment@openholidays.co.uk. Website www.openholidays.co.uk.

Villa and apartment holidays in the Algarve or Portugal and various locations in Spain.

Overseas Representatives required between March/April and October to look after holidaymakers, host welcome meetings and check properties.

Qualifications: Applicants must have a full driving licence and be over 21.

Wages: vary according to age and experience, but start at £750 (gross) per month, with a net accommodation allowance of £150 per month.

OPERATION EUROPE
33 Clerkenwell Close, London EC1R 0AU. ☎020-7566 5400. Fax 020-7566 5401. E-mail sales@operationeurope.com. Website www.operationeurope.com.

Wholesale incoming tour operator providing tourist services across Europe.

Staff needed in high season (March to June) and students are sometimes hired. Other staff occasionally taken on on a short term basis.

A second language is always helpful.

OXFORD SKI COMPANY
3 Barn Business Centre, Great Rissington, Cheltenham, Glos. GL54 2LH. ☎01451 810300. Fax 01451 822300. E-mail info@oxfordski.com. Website www.oxfordski.com.

Handful of luxury catered chalets in the French and Swiss Alps, staffed with a manager and assistant, qualified chef, ski guide and masseuse.

Staff needed: 15. Relevant qualifications and experience and command of French are seen as beneficial.

Wages: between £130 and £260 per week. Benefits include season lift pass, season ski and boot hire, transport to and from the resort, tips and gratuities.

Application deadline is mid-November. Interviews essential and take place in London or Gloucestershire.

Contact: Mark Gibbins, Operations Manager.

PAGE & MOY
136-140 London Road, Leicester LE2 1EN. ☎0870 832 7000. Website www.page-moy.co.uk.
Worldwide direct sell tour operator. Also run national and regional reader holiday offers and motor racing tours.
Experienced freelance tour leaders needed.
Qualifications needed: minimum age 21. Second language and experience essential.

PANORAMA HOLIDAYS – part of MyTravel.

PGL ADVENTURE
416 Alton Court, Penyard Lane, Ross-on-Wye, Herefordshire HR9 5NR. ☎0870 401 4411. Fax 0870 401 4444. E-mail pglpeople@pgl.co.uk. Website www.pgl.co.uk/people
In business since 1957. Europe's largest provider of activity holidays for children with 26 centres throughout Britain, France and Spain. Require 2,500 energetic staff to work between February and October. Opportunities exist to work directly with children as group leaders or activity instructors. Catering and support staff are also required. Qualifications needed: previous experience is not essential but a sense of fun and enthusiasm is. Minimum age 18 years. Must be able to work for a minimum of 8 weeks.
Wages: living allowance £60-£80, plus board and lodgings.

P J SCUBA DIVING CO LTD
225/274 Sumpwut Road, Bang Na, Bangkok, Thailand. ☎+66 1-864 4490. Fax +66 12-720 7520. E-mail peter@pjscuba.com. Website www.jpscuba.com.
Scuba diving training for people who want to stay on and teach diving in Thailand, Vietnam or Cambodia. Job placement scheme for 75-100 PADI dive professionals within network of shops in Southeast Asia.
Qualifications needed: no background in diving needed but must have good interpersonal skills and the ability to swim.
Inclusive cost of 6-month internship programme for complete novices including at least 200 dives is US$5,500.
Contact: Peter Scott, Managing Director.

PURPLE SKI LTD
Hamilton Cottage, Chapel Hill, Speen, Bucks. HP27 0SL. ☎01494 488633. Fax 0845 345 6633. E-mail karen@purpleski.com. Website www.purpleski.com.
Privately owned operator providing select number of catered chalet holidays in Méribel, France.
Chalet staff, chefs, drivers, general assistants and other staff (28 in total).
Qualifications needed: must be energetic, enthusiastic and professional. Chefs must be qualified to NVQ3 or equivalent and have at least 4 years' experience.
Wages: from £100 per week for drivers to £160+ for chefs.
Contact: Karen Broom Smith, Co-owner and Operations Director.

QUETZALTREKKERS
Casa Argentina Diagonal 12 8-37, Zona 1, Quetzaltenango, Guatemala. ☎(502) 761-5865. E-mail info@quetzaltrekkers.com. Website www.quetzaltrekkers.com.

Company offers guided backpacking excursions to areas of beauty in the highlands.

Opportunities for 20-30 volunteers a year to work as trekking guides leading trips throughout the Guatemalan highlands. All trip proceeds go to support Escuela de la Calle, which operates a school for 100 or so at-risk youth and a dormitory for street children. Guides also have lots of interaction and responsibility for the children. Minimum stay normally 3 months.

Qualifications: applicants should possess experience and/or education in hiking/backpacking, group leadership, medical training, cooking, and social work.

Wages: none. Some rent assistance is available, though cost of living is US$250-$325 a month.

REGENT HOLIDAYS
15 John Street, Bristol BS1 2HR. ☎0117-921 1711. Fax 0117-925 4866. E-mail regent@regent-holidays.co.uk

In business since 1970.

Special interest holiday operator to unusual countries, e.g. Albania, Baltics, Russia and other Republics, China, Cuba, Turkey, Iceland and Vietnam.

Staff needed: 1 at most (only when permanent vacancy crops up).

Qualifications needed: higher education background in tourism or in destination countries. Knowledge of languages needed.

ROMANIA TRAVEL CENTRE
39 Mount Pleasant, Tunbridge Wells, Kent TN4 1PN. ☎01892 516901. Fax 01892 511579. E-mail enquiry@romaniatravelcentre.com. Website www.romaniatravelcentre.com.

Specialist tour operator to Romania. Need reservation and administration staff occasionally. Candidates should have a good education and some experience in the travel industry.

ST PETER'S PILGRIMS
87a Rushey Green, Catford, London, SE6 4AF. ☎020-8244 8844. Fax 020-8697 2466. E-mail info@stpeter.co.uk. Website www.stpeter.co.uk.

Representatives/Pilgrimage Leaders (2) to look after pilgrims and arrange hotel bookings, transfers, excursions and daily programmes. Pilgrimages are arranged to most pilgrim destinations worldwide from Easter to October; all are accompanied by a Catholic priest. A good knowledge of Christianity is required. Representatives will be paid about £1000 and will have full board, uniform and other extras provided.

Contact: Bob & Mary Metcalf.

S&S Tours
3366 E. Trevino Drive, Sierra Vista, AZ 85650, USA. ☎520-803-1352 or 800-499-5685. Fax 520-803-1355. E-mail ss@ss-tours.com. Website www.ss-tours.com.

Small operator of naturalist tours in Mexico and Costa Rica.

May need a Spanish speaker for week-long trips throughout the year. A part-time position, ideal for a retired person. Working knowledge of bird, plant and tree identification necessary.

SAGA HOLIDAYS
The Saga Building, Enbrook Park, Folkestone, Kent CT20 3SE. ☎01303 711111. Website www.saga.co.uk.

Holidays for those aged 50+, with a very wide range of worldwide destinations.

Reps and coach couriers needed in British tourist areas and on the continent. Qualifications needed: ex-nurses especially welcome.

SANDPIPER HOLIDAYS
Walnut Cottage, Kenley, Shrewsbury SY5 6NS. ☎01746 785123. Fax 01746 785100. E-mail sandpiperhols@bigfoot.com. Website www.sandpiperhols.co.uk.
In business since 1989. Member of AITO.
Family-run camping holiday operator to west coast of France.
On-site campsite couriers needed: 12. Full season May to September or part season (May to July or June/July to September). Most applications are processed between October and December.
Qualifications needed: good French required.

SAVILE TOURS
47 Charlbert Street, St. John's Wood, London NW8 6JN. ☎020-7722 2986. Fax 020-7586 4859. E-mail info@saviletours.com. Website www.saviletours.com.
Upmarket tour operator specialising in holidays to Turkey and Northern Cyprus.
Overseas representatives (3-4) to escort clients between airport and accommodation and assist them during their holidays. Pay negotiable depending on experience.
Qualifications needed: previous experience preferred. Working hours are variable and the minimum period of work is 6 months from May to October.

SAVOY CHALET HOLIDAYS
Chalet Etoile de la Savoie, 81 Chemin du Bulle, 74170 Saint Gervais-Mont-Blanc. ☎+33 4-50 47 78 31. Fax +33 4-50 47 79 66. E-mail anna@ski-montblanc.com. Website www.ski-montblanc.com.
Catered chalet holiday company needs chalet helpers for winter and summer seasons, though the Chalet is open year round. Team live as family members so must be honest, friendly, flexible, hardworking and child-friendly.
Qualifications needed: catering, food service, housekeeping, childcare.
Wages: €7.19 per hour gross (35-39 hours a week).
Contact: Anna George, Partner.

SCENIC TOURS
Canada Operations, PO Box 807, Newcastle NSW 2300, Australia. Fax +61 2-4929 6785. E-mail employment@scenictours.com. Website www.scenictours.com.
Large Australian wholesale tour company employs tour directors and meet-and-greet staff to co-ordinate and escort passengers on extended tours worldwide. Most positions are permanent but seasonal staff needed in North America, particularly to work out of Vancouver. Looking for strong customer service background.

SCOTT DUNN
Fovant Mews, 12 Noyna Road, London SW17 7PH. ☎020-8682 5005. Fax 020-8682 5090. E-mail recruitment@scottdunn.com. Website www.scottdunn.com.
In business since 1986.
Ski tour operator to France (Courchevel 1850, Val d'Isère and Méribel), Switzerland (Zermatt). Also has summer programme.
Winter season staff needed: 12 resort managers, 2 ski hosts, 32 chalet chefs, 30 chalet

hosts, 12 drivers/maintenance people, 5 beauty therapists and 25 nannies. Period of work from early December to end of April. Applications for ski jobs are processed from end of May; interviews are held at London office.

Qualifications needed: resort managers must be over 25, speak fluent French or German, and have management experience. Chefs must be over 21, have a recognised qualification and have experience. Guides must be over 23 and have 25 weeks of skiing experience. Nannies must be over 20 and have NNEB or equivalent. All applicants must have a British passport or an EU visa.

Wages: £75-£220 per week depending on job. Staff receive full area ski pass, equipment hire, food and accommodation, 1 day off a week, medical insurance, return travel from London to resort, and staff uniform.

Summer season staff needed for Mediterranean resorts in France, Spain and Portugal: 6 resort managers, 25 chefs, 15 hosts, 50 nannies, etc. Wages £125-£220 per week.

SELECT FRANCE
Murcott, Oxon. OX5 2RE. ☎01865 331350. E-mail jobs@selectfrance.co.uk. Website www.selectfrance.com.
Member of AITO. Specialist family camping holiday operator to France.

On-site campsite representatives needed. Duties include preparation of client accommodation, hosting clients while on site, admin/paperwork, organising and running children's club and some regular social activities for clients, maintaining good working relations with campsite management.

Qualifications needed: must be self-reliant, outgoing, cheerful, careful, pragmatic, responsible and honest. Knowledge of French is preferred and applicants over 21 are at an advantage. Available to work mid-May to end of September.

Wages: approximately £476 per month, plus accommodation on site.

SETSAIL HOLIDAYS
The Business Centre, 140 Station Road, Redhill, Surrey, RH1 1ET. ☎01737 764443. Fax 01737 765985. E-mail boats@setsail.co.uk. Website www.setsail.co.uk.
Flotilla sailing and bareboat charter holidays to Greece, Turkey and Croatia.

Skippers, hostesses and engineers needed to co-ordinate and run flotillas, consisting of up to 12 yachts. Minimum period of work 7 months.

Qualifications needed: should have sailing experience and qualifications and the ability to work well with people. First Aid qualifications would be useful.

Accommodation is provided on the 'lead yacht'.

SHEARINGS
Miry Lane, Wigan, Lancs. WN3 4AG. ☎01942 244246. Fax 01942 321641. Website www.shearingholidays.com.
Established coach touring company in UK and tour operator in Europe.

Resort reps needed (Austria, France, Italy and Spain), coach tour guides and TGV couriers for France.

Qualifications needed: minimum age 21. Languages and experience preferred.

SIESTA INTERNATIONAL HOLIDAYS
156-158 Linthorpe Road, Middlesbrough TS1 3RB. ☎01642 227711. E-mail resortops@siestaholidays.co.uk. Website www.siestaholidays.co.uk/ recruit1.html. Also offices in Hull, Leeds and Birmingham.
Budget coach operator with nationwide departures to Spain (Catalunya) and France.

Various seasonal positions available: resort reps, maintenance, coach couriers/hostesses.

SILCOCK LEISURE GROUP
Pier Forecourt, Promenade, Southport PR8 1QX. ☎01704 536733. Fax 01704 531787. E-mail jobs@silcock-leisure.co.uk. Website www.silcock-leisure.co.uk/jobs.
Amusement centre in Lancashire.
Customer services and catering positions available (120).
Qualifications needed: good customer service skills or catering experience. Students welcome for summer season. Willing to work long hours (up to 12 hours a day, 5-7 days a week). All nationalities accepted; must be able to communicate in English.

SIMPLY TRAVEL – see Specialist Holidays Group.

SKI ACTIVITY
Lawmuir House, Methven, Perthshire PH1 3SZ. ☎01738 840888. Fax 01738 840079. E-mail recruitment@skiactivity.com. Website www.skiactivity.com.
Ski tour operator to France, Switzerland, USA and Canada.
Need chalet staff, resort reps and office staff. Recruitment takes place between July and December.
Qualifications needed: reps should have a knowledge of languages, customer service and skiing experience. Chalet staff must have catering and customer service experience.

SKI AMIS LTD
122-126 High Road, London NW6 4HY. ☎020-7692 0850. Fax 020-7692 0851. E-mail jobs@skiamis.com. Website www.skiamis.com.
Ski tour operator to resorts in France. Need chalet supervisor/resort reps, chalet couples and chalet hosts (15 in total).
Qualifications needed: minimum age 21. Must have had driving licence for 2 years. Ski package includes season's ski pass, uniform, accommodation and board, insurance, travel to the resort, equipment rental and varying wage.
EU nationals accepted and anyone who already holds a UK national insurance number and work permit.
Contact: Ed van Zadelhoff, Director.

SKIBOUND – see First Choice Ski, Lakes and Mountains

SKI INDEPENDENCE
Broughton Market, Edinburgh, Scotland EH3 6NU. ☎0870 555 0555. Fax 0870 550 2020. E-mail ski@ski-i.com. Website www.ski-i.com.
Upmarket ski chalet tour operator to USA and Canada. Require resort and chalet staff for season lasting from end of November to end of April. Sometimes employ people on location. Must have cooking experience, knowledge of health and safety and driving licence. 5-day training course given.
Contact: Susan Dunlop, Overseas Manager.

SKI MIQUEL
33 High St, Uppermill, Nr. Oldham, Lancs. OL3 6HTS ☎01457 820200. Fax 01457 872715. Website www.miquelhols.co.uk.
In business since 1981.
Ski tour operator to France (Alpe d'Huez, Serre Chevalier), Austria (Badgastein),

Switzerland (Lauterbrunnen) and Spain (Baqueira), Canada (Whistler).

Resort managers (5), bar person/ski guides (4), chalet people (10) and chefs (4) to work 4½-5 months for winter season.

Qualifications needed: chefs must have City & Guilds 706/1/2; resort managers need to speak appropriate language and have 2 years repping experience (minimum age 23); chalet assistants and barmen/ski guides need bubbly personalities and staying power.

Wages: chalet staff and barmen earn £60 per week, chefs £110 and resort managers £120-£140.

SKI OLYMPIC
PO Box 396, Doncaster DN5 7YS. ☎01302 328820. Fax 01302 328830. E-mail mieke@skiolympic.co.uk or info@skiolympic.co.uk. Website www.skiolympic.com.

In business since 1987. Member of AITO.

Ski tour operator to France (Courchevel, Tignes, La Plagne, La Rosière and Val Thorens).

Winter season staff needed: 35 out of total of 70 (10 ski guides, 5 chefs, 15 chalet girls, 2 nannies, 3 bar staff. Applications are processed from August.

Qualifications needed: minimum age 21 for most positions. Knowledge of French preferred but not essential. Ski guides must have BASI III (or equivalent); chefs must have good qualifications and extensive experience in restaurants or hotels; nannies must have NNEB. All must have EU passport.

SKIWORLD
Overseas Personnel Department, Skiworld House, 3 Vencourt Place, London W6 9NU. ☎0870 420 5912 (Recruitment). E-mail recruitment@skiworld.ltd.uk. Website www.skiworld.ltd.uk.

In business since 1982. Largest independent ski operator in the UK with offices in London and Bourg St Maurice (France) and 115 chalets in 26 resorts in France, Switzerland, Austria, USA and Canada.

Approximately 330 overseas positions for chalet staff, resort managers, resort reps, nannies, maintenance staff and chefs needed to work winter season. Recruitment takes place between June and December. Staff are sometimes hired on location.

Qualifications needed: minimum age 21. Reps and managers must be able to speak French and ski; management work overseas preferred. Chalet staff must be confident cooks and hard-working. Must be UK/EU nationals.

SKYROS HOLIDAYS
92 Prince of Wales Road, London NW5 3NE. ☎020-7267 4424/020-7284 3065. Fax 020-7284 3063. E-mail connect@skyros.com. Web site www.skyros.com.

Holistic holiday community on the Greek island of Skyros that offers over 200 workshops and courses from yoga to sailing. 'Work scholars' assist in the smooth running of the centre for 3 months: May to July or August to October. Flexible 5-7 hours per day in split shifts, 6 days per week.

Qualifications: minimum age 18. Qualified nurses, chefs and Greek speakers preferred. Must be hardworking, fit, exceptionally caring and thrive in a community environment.

Wages: full board, course tuition fees, plus approx £40 pocket money for some positions.

SOLAIRE HOLIDAYS
1158 Stratford Road, Hall Green, Birmingham, B28 8AF. ☎0121-778-5061. Fax 0121-778-5065. E-mail jobs@solaire.co.uk. Website www.solaire.co.uk.
Camping and mobile home tour operator to France (Brittany, Normandy, Paris region, Loire, Vendée and Mediterranean coast) and Blanes (Costa Dorada, Spain).
Site couriers (20) to look after clients and prepare accommodation at beginning of season. Knowledge of French or Spanish desirable. Children's couriers (4) to run a children's club. Previous experience of working with children is required.
Wages: £280-£400 per month. Accommodation but not food is provided as part of contract.
Choice of work period: April-October, May-September or July-August. Hours of work vary according to demand, but applicants can expect to work for six days a week, on a rota system.

SOLO'S
54-58 High Street, Edgware, Middlesex HA8 7EJ. ☎08700 720700 ext 2823. E-mail travel@solosholidays.co.uk. Website www.solosholidays.co.uk.
Large tour operator selling holidays worldwide to singles.
Staff must be good at mixing and creating a sociable atmosphere. Also need reservations staff from time to time.

SPECIALISED TRAVEL LTD
12-15 Hanger Green, London W5 3EL. ☎020-8799 8360. Fax 020-8998 7965. E-mail admin@stlon.com or ablair@stlon.com. Website www.stlon.com.
In business since 1955. Also trades as Travel for the Arts (www.travelforthearts.co.uk which has a link to Employment information). Specialises in concert and opera tours of Europe. Also incentive tour operator.
Tour leaders needed: 60-80 to accompany choirs, orchestras and bands (including American groups) on concert tours around Europe (including UK and the Russian Republics) between April and August (mainly June/July). Work involves being responsible for all daily events, reconfirming concert arrangements, accommodation, transport and leading sightseeing excursions. Applications accepted in summer and autumn for the following season. Individual contracts for various tours which last between 2 and 3 weeks each.
Qualifications needed: applicants must have excellent organisational skills, leadership qualities and initiative. A musical background and knowledge of touring are advantages. Languages necessary according to specific tour destination. All nationalities welcome.

SPECIALIST HOLIDAYS GROUP
King's Place, 12-42 Wood St, Kingston-upon-Thames, Surrey KT1 1SG. ☎0870-888 0028. E-mail overseasrecruitment@s-h-g.co.uk. Website www.shgjobs.co.uk.
Division of the giant tour operator Tui UK (see entry) which incorporates Crystal Holidays, Thomson Ski & Lakes, Simply Travel, Simply Ski plus other brands. SHG recruit winter and summer staff throughout the year for many European, American & Canadian destinations.
Qualified nannies & children's representatives, resort representatives, chalet hosts, chalet assistants, hotel chefs, hotel assistants, maintenance staff, kitchen/night porters.
Qualifications needed: positions are available for qualified and unqualified staff with a flexible and friendly attitude. Staff need a good understanding of customer requirements and the ability

to work within a busy team. Minimum age 21 for reps, 18 for some other positions.

SPECIALTOURS LTD
2 Chester Row, London SW1W 9JH. ☎020-7823 2297. Fax 020-7823 5035. E-mail info@specialtours.co.uk. Website www.specialtours.co.uk.

Arranges art and cultural tours on behalf of museum groups and similar.

Staff needed: tour planners who have hands-on experience of preparing detailed and costed programmes for art and cultural tours worldwide. London-based employees may be asked to escort overseas tours if required.

Qualifications needed: excellent planning and IT skills (Word, Excel, databases) are a pre-requisite as is knowledge of a foreign language (German and Eastern European are of particular interest). Some overseas travel accompanying tours may be required. Ability to work to deadlines and unsupervised. An art degree may be considered useful. Interviews will not be offered to those unable to offer the relevant skills.

Contact: David Robertson, Company Secretary.

SPORTSWORLD GROUP plc
New Abbey Court, Stert St, Abingdon, Oxon. OX14 3JF. ☎01235 555844. E-mail intoperations.jobs@sportsworld.co.uk. Website www.sportsworld.co.uk.

Global company providing event services with particular emphasis on major sporting events like the Summer and Winter Olympic Games, FIFA World Cup and the Commonwealth Games. Also temporary event staff needd for international event programme. Experienced tour leaders may be needed.

Contact: Ms. Virginia Mullins.

STAR HOTELS SARL
Hotel la Belle Etoile, Le Bettex, Saint Gervais, 74170 France. ☎+33 4-50 93 11 83. Fax +33 4-5- 93 14 91. E-mail kieron@belleetoile.com. Website www.belleetoile.com.

Alpine hotel open in ski season and summer.

Staff needed: 3 waitresses/waiters, 1 bar person, 1 admin/receptionist, 1 ski technician, 1 assistant chef.

Qualifications needed: preference given to applicants who speak French. All staff should have knowledge of working in the hospitality industry.

Wages £160 per week paid in euros at the end of the month for working 35-42 hours per week. Staff are accommodated in single rooms at the hotel and in one apartment. Application deadlines fall in November and June. Interviews not essential. Skis and boots supplied to staff and discounted season's ski pass.

Contact: Kieron Hatt, Hotel owner.

STEPPES TRAVEL
51 Castle St, Cirencester, Gloucestershire GL7 1QD. ☎01285 651010. Fax 01285 885888. Websites www.steppeseast.co.uk, www.steppesafrica.co.uk, www.steppeslatinamerica.co.uk.

In operation since 1989. Tour operator to worldwide destinations including Asia, Africa and South America.

Occasionally require sales staff with detailed knowledge of locations for UK office. Previous work in tour operations preferred.

Tour guides and representatives may be needed to look after clients in South America. £400 per month including board and accommodation. Minimum period of work is 6 months to a year, year round. Hours of work are flexible and there is a day off a week. Knowledge of Spanish/Portuguese required.

Applications to the Overseas Personnel department at the above address. E-mails to enquiry@steppeseast.co.uk, enquiry@steppesafrica.co.uk or enquiry@steppeslatiname rica.co.uk.

STYLE HOLIDAYS
Coomb House, 7 St. John's Road, Isleworth, Middlesex TW7 6NH. ☎0870 442 3653 (Recruitment). Website www.style-holidays.co.uk.
Resort holidays in Portugal (Algarve, Madeira), Spain (Costa Blanca, Costa del Sol, Majorca, Menorca), Cyprus and Florida.
Resort reps for seasonal work April to October. Part season short term contracts also possible.
Qualifications needed: languages preferred but not essential. Minimum age 20. Driving licence and EU passport needed. Customer service experience, initiative, teamwork, problem-solving skills and sense of humour required.

SUNSAIL LTD
HR Overseas, The Port House, Port Solent, Portsmouth, Hants. PO6 4TH. ☎023 9222 2308 or 24-hour ansaphone 023 9233 4600. E-mail hr@sunsail.com. Website www.sunsail.com.
In business since 1974 and now employ more than 1700 staff worldwide, operate a fleet of 1000 charter yachts in 36 different locations and also 9 beach clubs in the Mediterranean and one in Antigua.
Operate Flotilla and Bareboat sailing holidays and Watersports hotels in the Mediterranean.
Staff needed: more than 300, as flotilla skippers, hostesses, engineers, qualified dinghy instructors, receptionists, chefs, bar staff, qualified nannies and many others. Season lasts from March to November. Some winter work usually reserved for loyal summer employees. Website carries current available positions.
Qualifications needed: minimum age for Club position is 19, for base or flotillas 21. Knowledge of other European languages an advantage for many positions. Training and experience appropriate to job required, e.g. sailing positions require RYA/AYF/NZYF certification.
Wages: vary from £220 to £400 a month plus return flights, food, accommodation and other benefits depending on position.

SUNVIL HOLIDAYS
Sunvil House, Upper Square, Old Isleworth, Middlesex TW7 7BJ. ☎020-8568 4499. Fax 020-8568 8330. Website www.sunvil.co.uk.
Villa holiday operator to Greece and Cyprus, plus Fly Drive Islands programme. In business since 1970. Member of AITO and ABTA.
Experienced staff needed with knowledge of Greek and tourism experience.

SUSI MADRON'S CYCLING FOR SOFTIES
2-4 Birch Polygon, Rusholme, Manchester M14 5HX. ☎0161-248 8282. Website www.cycling-for-softies.co.uk.
Cycling holiday operator in France.
Company assistants needed. Minimum period of work 2 months between May and September.
Qualifications needed: must speak French and be at least 20. Non-smokers only. Full training on bicycle maintenance given.
Wages: fixed wage plus bonus.

SWISS TRAVEL SERVICE
Bridge House, 55-59 High Road, Broxbourne, Herts. EN10 7DT. ☎0870 191 7170. Fax 01992 448855. E-mail swiss@bridge-travel.co.uk. Website www.swisstravel.co.uk.
In business since 1950.
Tour operator to Switzerland.
Resort representatives needed: 20 for summer season (April-October), 10 in winter (December-April).
Qualifications needed: Graduates preferred. Must be at least 21, have a smart appearance and a responsible and friendly attitude. Applications accepted year round. Interviews in UK.
Wages: £430 per month plus free board and accommodation.
Work also available for scenic tour guides to guide rail tours in 4 or 5 Swiss resorts.

TALL STORIES
Brassey House, New Zealand Avenue, Walton on Thames, Surrey KT12 1QD. ☎01932 252002. Fax 01932 252970. E-mail tina@tallstories.co.uk. Website www.tallstories.co.uk/jobs.shtm.
In business since 1991. Adventure sports holidays in Austria, France, Spain, Corsica and Mallorca for adults and some families with teenagers.
Resort hosts needed to work in resort looking after small groups of up to 16 people. Duties include airport transfers, organising hotels, sports and restaurants, managing the evening entertainment and so on. Reps are needed from mid-May until mid-September.
Qualifications needed: applicants should have outdoor and sports interests as they will be expected to do many of the sports on offer, e.g. paragliding, rafting, mountain biking and scuba diving. Should have experience in a service industry or working with people, be very organised with crisis management experience, be aged 23 or over and hold a clean driving license. Knowledge of French, German or Spanish an advantage. PSV driving license also an advantage.
Wages: from £120 per week plus food, accommodation and travel.

TAPESTRY HOLIDAYS
The Glassmills, 322B King St, London W6 0AX. ☎020-8235 7500/7886. Fax 020-8235 7501. E-mail admin@tapestryholidays.com or kim@tapestryholidays.com. Website www.tapestryholidays.com.
In business since 1991.
Small upmarket tour operator to Turkey and Greece.
Experienced staff sometimes needed in UK.

THOMAS COOK TOUR OPERATIONS
29-31 Elmfield Road Bromley Kent BR1 1LT. ☎0870-607 0309. E-mail overseas.jobs@thomascook.com. Website www.thomascookjobs.com.
One of the biggest tour operators in ABTA. Other companies in the Thomas Cook Group include JMC, Sunset and Blue Sky Holidays Direct.
Overseas representatives to be responsible for ensuring that customers receive hassle-free holidays. Must have experience of face-to-face customer service, a genuine desire to help and stamina to work long hours. Minimum age 20 years old.
Children's representatives to supervise and entertain groups of children aged 3-16 years. Experience of working with large groups of children is essential. Minimum age 19 years old.
Crèche representatives: to look after and care for younger children aged 6-24 months; a

qualification in childcare is essential. Minimum age 19 years old.

Overseas administrators: the overseas offices are the nerve centre of Thomas Cook Tour Operations abroad. Office experience and people used to working under pressure are required. Sound knowledge of Microsoft word, Excel and Outlook is essential. Minimum age 19 years old.

Contracts run from March to October with a possibility to continue through the winter. All applicants must have a valid UK or EU passport.

THOMSON HOLIDAYS – see Tui UK and Specialist Holidays Group

TJM TRAVEL
Penhalveor East, Redruth, Cornwall TR16 6NL. ☎01209 860000. Fax 01209 860998. E-mail jobs@tjm.co.uk. Website www.tjm.co.uk/jobs.

TJM run hotels and activity centres in France, Spain and Newquay in the summer months, and they operate ski holidays from Alpine hotels in the winter.

Many positions from resort reps to mountain bike leaders to chamber staff. Qualified sailing, canoe, windsurfing, snorkelling, climbing, mountain biking instructors and hotel staff for activity centres in France, Spain and the UK,

Wages: vary between £300 and £700 per month according to job and experience. Board and lodging provided.

Applications with photos, CVs and relevant certificates are accepted year round.

TOP DECK
Level 2, William House, 14 Worple Road, Wimbledon, London SW19 4DD. ☎020-8879 6785. Fax 020-8944 9474. E-mail ops@topdecktravel.co.uk. Website www.topdecktravel.co.uk.

In business since 1972.

Youth budget tour operator taking coach tours throughout Europe including Eastern Europe and Scandinavian countries. Also tours to Turkey and Egypt. Camping tours as well as hostel/cabin tours.

Coach drivers needed: most work available March-October.

Applications processed November-February. Occasional on-site opportunities in July. Qualifications needed: full PCV coach licence. Knowledge of European languages an advantage (must be fluent in English).

Tour managers for coach tours around Europe March-October. No formal qualifications required, but must have good knowledge of European history and current affairs and proven people skills. Training given (to be paid by applicant) March/April. Knowledge of European languages an advantage.

Cooks are also hired. Chef experience desirable.

TOTAL HOLIDAYS LTD.
3 The Square, Richmond-Upon-Thames, Surrey TW9 1DY. ☎01252 618309. Fax 01252 618328. E-mail recruitment@skitotal.com. Web: www.skitotal.com.

Ski holidays with catered chalet accommodation in France (e.g. Val d'Isère, Courchevel), Austria (St Anton), Italy (Selva/Val Gardena), Switzerland (Verbier) and Canada (Whistler).

Resort managers (14), resort representatives (14), chalet chefs (20), chalet hosts/cooks (58), chalet assistants (52), resort drivers & handymen (2). Qualifications needed: resort managers must have hospitality and customer service experience with management or supervisory skills plus an excellent command of French, German or Italian. Be a competent skier with a full clean driving licence, age 23 years and over. Lesser requirements for other jobs. All must have friendly, outgoing personalities and enough experience to play their part in the running of a chalet or resort. All staff required to work the full season from mid-November to late April, although also opportunities to start in early to mid January. Applicants must be in possession of a UK or EU passport and a permanent National Insurance number. For positions in Canada, applicants must provide their own work visa (see Canada chapter).

Contact: Samuel Edmonds, Senior Overseas Recruitment Co-ordinator (Esprit & Total Holidays).

TRACKS TRAVEL LTD
The Flots, Brookland, Romney Marsh, Kent TN29 9TG. ☎01797 344164. Fax 01797 344135. E-mail info@tracks-travel.com. Website www.tracks-travel.com.

In business since 1971. Overland camping tour operator operating throughout the UK and Europe.

Tour managers, cooks and drivers with valid UK PCV licence needed. Applicants must be good with a microphone and confident when dealing with large groups.

TRAFALGAR TOURS
15 Grosvenor Place, London SW1X 7HH. Tel: 020-7235 7090. E-mail trafalgartravel@aol.com. Website www.ttuk.trafalgartours.com.

Major tour operator in Europe, Ireland and the UK.

Meet and greet staff needed to work at London airports and hotels. Seasonal vacancies.

TRAVELBAG PLC
3-5 High St, Alton, Hampshire GU34 1TL. ☎01420 547800. Website www.travelbag.co.uk.

Specialist travel consultancy with a number of branches in England, selling tailor-made itineraries to long-haul destinations including; Australia, Asia, Far East, South Pacific, South Africa, USA, South America.

Require 200 staff for mostly permanent staff (some 1 year contracts available for students). Benefits include high level of training and travel concessions.

Qualifications needed: sales, customer service and travel experience/knowledge. HND Leisure and Tourism (or equivalent).

TRAVELBOUND/SKIBOUND – see First Choice.

TRAVELCOAST LTD
First Floor, Fraser House, 15 London Road, Twickenham, Middlesex TW1 3ST. ☎0870 887 0123. E-mail recruit@onlinetravel.com. Website www.captivating-holidays.com.

In business since 1986. Subsidiary company of Online Travel Company (www.onlinetravel.com/about/jobs.asp).

Resort holidays in Cuba, Cayo Largo, Cayo Coco, Croatia, etc.

Need resort reps for Cuba for 1 year contract. Interviews take place March-August. Sometimes employ people on location. Also hire people as reservations consultants and ticketers for Twickenham office.

Qualifications needed: minimum age 21. Fluency in Spanish and experience in customer service industry may be necessary. Candidates must be self-reliant. EU nationals only.

TRAVELSPHERE LTD
Compass House, Rockingham Road, Market Harborough, Leics. LE16 7QD.

☎01858 410456. Website www.travelsphere.co.uk.
Major coach tour operator in Europe, UK, North America and worldwide, specialising in 45+ age group.
Tour managers needed to escort groups throughout Europe, including Belgium, Netherlands, Italy, France, Germany, Spain, Portugal, Austria, Switzerland, Czech Republic, Russia and Norway. To work long hours for a minimum of 3 months.
Qualifications needed: ages 20-55. Previous tour manager experience not essential but must have a friendly outgoing personality, be reliable, hardworking, organised and have an ability to deal with people. Experience of travelling in Europe and a second European language useful.
Wages: daily rate plus commission on excursions sold. Half-board accommodation usually provided plus full insurance, travel costs and training. Work may also be available for people familiar with long haul destinations.
Contact: Jon Henley, Manager (UK & Overseas Representation).

TUI UK
Human Resources Overseas, Greater London House, Hampstead Road, London NW1 7SD. ☎020-7387 9321. Website www.tui-uk.co.uk/jobopps.
Giant tour operator to worldwide destinations, incorporating many mainstream travel brands including Thomson Holidays, Crystal Holidays, Simply Travel, Magic of Italy. Also extensive ski programme. Luton-based charter airline Britannia Airways are also owned by Tui UK.
Overseas and children's reps needed to work in European and worldwide resorts for summer season April to October and ski placements available in the winter. Applications for summer work preferred in preceding September. Possibility of winter work for chalet reps and ski rangers (applications should be sent in June). Entertainment staff needed to organise a varied programme of daytime and evening events.
Qualifications needed: applicants must have pleasant outgoing nature, initiative and a strong sense of responsibility. Fluency in English is needed; a second language such as Spanish, Greek, German, Italian or Portuguese is a plus.
Representatives need minimum of 1 year's experience in a customer service role along with an empathy with all kinds of people. Minimum of 5 GCSEs including Maths and English, and the ability to converse in another European language is desirable. Minimum age 23 years.
Children's representatives should have an NNEB or similar childcare qualification along with at least 6 months practical work experience with children. Minimum age 18 years. For those without a childcare qualification the company has an in-house NVQ programme.
Entertainment staff must be educated to minimum GCSE level and have previous experience of entertaining an audience in a similar role in the leisure industry. Minimum age 21 years

UNIJET TRAVEL – see First Choice

UPTRIPS
2-4 Godwin St, Bradford, West Yorkshire BD1 2ST. ☎01274 387693. Fax 01274 387742. E-mail Joanne.ball@uptrips.com. Website www.club18-30.co.uk; www.culturatrips.com; www.uphospitality.com.
Includes Club 18-30 and other brands, all part of Thomas Cook Tour Operations.
Overseas representatives and administration jobs for Club 18-30 (180). Also personal advisor roles and sales and administration roles within the UP group. Cultura (which is a year round product) and Up Market employs about 40 annually and UP Hospitality 20.

Qualifications needed: minimum age 19. Looking for people who have sales experience, have worked with the public in customer service, and are educated to a good standard. Most contracts run for 5 months.

Wages: starting salary for a club rep is £300 a month which can be supplemented with commission. Free flights and accommodation. Recruitment runs from June to the end of October for the following summer.

Contact: Joanne Ball, UK Events & Overseas Liaison Manager.

VENTURE ABROAD
Rayburn House, Parcel Terrace, Derby, DE1 1LY. ☎01332 342050. Fax 01332 224960. E-mail charlottel@rayburntours.co.uk. Website www.ventureabroad.co.uk.

Holidays for scout and guide groups to Switzerland and sometimes Belgium.

Summer jobs for students, especially German speakers. Must have excellent people skills and problem-solving ability. Minimum age 19.

Wages: £180 per week. Accommodation and a uniform are provided.

Contact: Charlotte Lovegrove.

VENUE HOLIDAYS
1 Norwood St, Ashford, Kent TN24 8DP. ☎01233 649950. Fax 01233 634494. E-mail info@venueholidays.co.uk. Website www.venueholidays.co.uk.

In business since 1985. Camping tour operator to Italy (Venetian Riviera, Lake Garda, Tuscany), France (Vendee, Dordogne, Roussillon) and Spain (Costa Brava).

Resort reps needed (32) and senior reps (2) needed in Italy. Season lasts April to end of September though minimum period of work is 3 months between May and August. Applications are processed from October onwards.

Qualifications needed: knowledge of second European language advantageous. Should have excellent communication skills, initiative, common sense and good organisational skills, with friendly and cheerful personality. Minimum age 18. No children's club staff needed.

Wages: start from £100 per week (paid monthly) with accommodation provided.

VILLAGE CAMPS
rue de la Morache, 1260 Nyon, Switzerland. ☎+41 22-990 9405. Fax +41 22-990 9494. E-mail personnel@villagecamps.ch. Website www.villagecamps.com/personnel.

In business since 1972. Multi-activity language camps for children in Switzerland (Leysin), Austria (Zell-am-See), France, Holland and England. Most are summer camps, but also winter camps in ski resorts.

Children's counsellors, EFL teachers, sports instructors, nurses and domestic staff needed. Minimum age 21. Minimum period of work is 4 weeks.

Wages: pocket money, accommodation and insurance provided.

Work also available for ski counsellors (up to 100) and other staff in ski season.

VOYAGES ILENA
1 Old Garden House, The Lanterns, Bridge Lane, London SW11 3AD. ☎020-7924 4440. Fax 020-7924 4441. E-mail holidays@voyagesilena.co.uk . Website www.voyagesilena.co.uk.

Tour operators to Corsica, Sardinia and Provence.

Occasionally recruit selling, ticketing, administration staff, programme managers.

Qualifications needed: French and Italian speakers desired. Candidates must have a degree and preferably experience in the travel industry.

VOYAGES JULES VERNE
21 Dorset Square, London NW1 6QG. ☎020-7616 1000. Fax 020-7723 8629. E-mail sales@vjv.co.uk. Website www.vjv.co.uk.
Upmarket tours to unusual destinations, train tours, art and culture tours, etc. Experienced tour directors only.

WEXAS INTERNATIONAL
45-49 Brompton Road, London SW3 1DE. ☎020-7589 3315. Fax 020-7589 8418 Website www.wexas.com.
Telesales consultants offering travel and related products for worldwide destinations. Require travel consultants. Candidates must be well-travelled, educated to minimum 'AS' level standard, have knowledge (preferably) of SABRE GDS and have experience in retail and/or tailormade travel.

APPENDIX 1

UK TOURISM TRAINING COURSES

The following colleges and institutes offer courses in tourism at a variety of levels, mainly National Vocational Qualifications or BTEC Certificates and Diplomas in Travel & Tourism (or both). Some centres offer specialised courses in Resort Representatives or ABTA-approved travel agency courses. Note that a great many of these colleges also run catering and other relevant courses. For a comprehensive listing of relevant courses, search the website of the educational publisher Hobson's (www.studyuk.hobsons.com) which has links to 1,500 Tourism courses in the UK and Ireland plus 800 Catering courses.

Aberdeen College, Gallowgate, Aberdeen AB25 1BN (01224 612000; enquiry@abcol.ac.uk)

Abingdon and Witney College, Northcourt Road, Abingdon, Oxon. OX14 1NN (01235 555585; inquiry@abingdon-witney.ac.uk)

Academy of Professional Studies, 114/115 Tottenham Court Road, Westminster, London W1P 9HL (020-7388 8126; admin@apslondon.co.uk)

Accrington and Rossendale College, Sandy Lane, Accrington, Lancs. BB5 2AW (01254 389933; info@accross.ac.uk)

Alton College, Old Odiham Road, Alton, Hants. GU34 2LX (01420 592200; enquiries@altoncollege.ac.uk)

Amersham and Wycombe College, Stanley Hill Centre, Amersham, Bucks. HP7 9HN (01494 735555; info@amersham.ac.uk)

Angus College, Keptie Road, Arbroath, Fife DD11 3EA (01241 432600; marketing@angus.ac.uk)

Anniesland College, Hatfield Drive, Glasgow G12 0YE (0141-357 3969; reception@anniesland.ac.uk)

Aquinas College, Nangreave Road, Stockport, Cheshire SK2 6TH (0161-483 3237; enquiries@aquinas.ac.uk)

Armagh College of Further Education, Lonsdale St, Armagh, Northern Ireland BT61 7HN (028 3752 2205; armagh-fe@rmplc.co.uk)

Aylesbury College, Oxford Road, Aylesbury, Bucks. HP21 8PD (01296 588588; www.aylesbury.ac.uk)

Ayr College, Dam Park, Ayr KA8 0EU (01292 265184; information@ayrcoll.ac.uk)

Banff and Buchan College of Further Education, Henderson Road, Fraserburgh, Aberdeenshire AB43 9GA (01346 586100; info@banffbuchan.ac.uk)

Barking College, Dagenham Road, Barking and Dagenham, Essex RM7 0XU (01708 770000; admissions@barking-coll.ac.uk)

Barnet College, Wood Street, Barnet, Herts.EN5 4AZ (020-8440 6321; info@barnet.ac.uk)

Barnfield College, Luton New Bedford Road, Luton, Beds. LU2 7BF (01582 569700)

Barnsley College, PO Box No 266, Church St, Barnsley, Yorks. S70 2YW (01226 216171; programme.enquiries@barnsley.ac.uk)

Barry College, Colcot Road, Barry, Cardiff CF62 8YJ (01446 725000; enquiries@barry.ac.uk)

Barton Peveril College, Cedar Road, Eastleigh, Hants. SO50 5ZA (023 8036 7200; enquiries@imail.barton.ac.uk)

Basingstoke College of Technology, Worting Road, Basingstoke, Hants. RG21 8TN (01256 354141; info@bcot.ac.uk)

Bedford College, Cauldwell St, Bedford MK42 9AH (01234 291000)

Belfast Institute of Further and Higher Education, The Gerald Moag Campus, 125-153 Millfield, Belfast BT1 1HF (028 9026 5265; information@belfastinstitute.ac.uk)

Berkshire College of Agriculture, Hall Place, Burchetts Green, Maidenhead, Berks. SL6 6QR (01628 824444; enquiries@berks-coll-ag.ac.uk)

Bexhill College, Turkey Road, Bexhill, E Sussex TN39 5HF (01424 214545; enquiries @bexhillcollege.ac.uk)

Bexley College, Tower Road, Bexley, London DA17 6JA (01322 442331; courses@bexley.ac.uk)

Bishop Auckland College, Woodhouse Lane, Bishop Auckland, Co. Durham DL14 6JZ (01388 443000; www.bacoll.ac.uk)

Bishop Burton College, Bishop Burton, Beverley, E Yorkshire HU17 8QG (01964 553000; enquiries@bishopb-college.ac.uk)

Blackburn College, Feilden St, Blackburn, Lancs. BB2 1LH (01254 55144; studentserv ices@blackburn.ac.uk)

Bolton Community College, Manchester Road, Bolton, Lancs. BL2 1ER (01204 453838; info@bolton-community-college.ac.uk)

Boston College, Skirbeck Road, Boston, Lincs. PE21 6JF (01205 365701) Bournville College of Further and Higher Education, Bristol Road South, Northfield, Birmingham B31 2AJ (0121 483 1111; info@bournville.ac.uk)

Bracknell and Wokingham College, Church Road, Bracknell, Berks. RG12 1DJ (01344 460200; study@bracknell.ac.uk)

Bradford College, Great Horton Road, Bradford, Yorkshire BD7 1AY (01274 753004; admissions@bilk.ac.uk)

Braintree College, 1 Church Lane, Braintree, Essex CM7 5SN (01376 321711

Bridgend College, Cowbridge Road, Bridgend, Wales CF31 3DF (01656 302302; admissions@bridgend.ac.uk)

Bridgwater College, Bath Road, Bridgwater, Somerset TA6 4PZ (01278 455464; inform ation@bridgewater.ac.uk)

Brockenhurst College, Lyndhurst Road, Brockenhurst, Hants. SO42 7ZE (01590 625555; enquiries@brock.ac.uk)

Bromley College of Further and Higher Education, Rookery Lane, Bromley Common, Bromley, Kent BR2 8HE (020 8295 7000; info@bromley.ac.uk)

Brooklands College, Heath Road, Weybridge, Surrey KT13 8TT (01932 797700)

Broxtowe College, Nottingham High Road, Chilwell, Nottingham NG9 4AH (0115 917 5252; learn@broxtowe.ac.uk)

Burnley College, Shorey Bank, Ormerod Road, Burnley, Lancs. BB11 2RX (01282 711200; student.services@burnley.ac.uk)

Burton College, Lichfield St, Burton upon Trent, Derbyshire DE14 3RL (01283 494400)

Bury College, Market St, Bury, Lancs. BL9 0BG (0161-280 8280; information@buryc ollege.ac.uk)

Calderdale College, Francis St, Halifax HX1 3UZ (01422 357357) *Cambridge Regional College,* King Hedges Road, Cambridge, Cambs. CB4 2QT (01223 418200)

Cannock Chase Technical College, The Green, Cannock, Staffs. WS11 1UE

(01543 462200)

Canterbury College, New Dover Road, Canterbury, Kent CT1 3AJ (01227 811111; admissions@cant-col.ac.uk)

Cardiff Tertiary College, Trowbridge Road, Rumney, Cardiff CF3 8XZ (029 2025 0250; enquires@glan-hafren.ac.uk)

Cardinal Newman College, Lark Hill Road, Preston, Lancs. PR1 4HD (01772 460181)

Cardonald College, 690 Mosspark Drive, Glasgow G52 3AY (0141 272 3333; enquirie s@cardonald.ac.uk)

Carlisle College, Victoria Place, Carlisle, Cumbria CA1 1HS (01228 819000; marketin g@carlisle.ac.uk)

Carmel College, Prescot Road, St Helens, Merseyside WA10 3AG (01744 452214)

Carshalton College, Nightingale Road, Sutton, Surrey SM5 2EJ (020-8770 6800)

Castlereagh College of Further Education, Montgomery Road, Belfast BT6 9JD (028 9079 7144)

Causeway Institute of Further and Higher Education, Union St, Coleraine, BT52 1QA, Northern Ireland (01265 54717; info@causeway.ac.uk)

Central College of Commerce, 300 Cathedral St, Glasgow G1 2TA (0141-552 3941)

Chelmsford College, Moulsham St, Chelmsford, Essex CM2 0JQ (01245 265611; info@chelmsford-college.ac.uk)

Chesterfield College, Infirmary Road, Chesterfield, Derbyshire S41 7NG (01246 500500)

Chichester College, Westgate Fields, Chichester, Sussex PO19 1SB (01243 786321; info@chichester.ac.uk)

Cirencester College, Fosse Way Campus, Stroud Road, Cirencester Glos. GL7 1XA (01285 640994; principal@cirencester.ac.uk)

City and Islington College, The Marlborough Building, 383 Holloway Road, Islington, London N7 0RN (020 7700 9200)

City College Brighton and Hove, Pelham St, Brighton BN1 4FA (01273 667788; info@ccb.ac.uk)

City College Coventry, Butts, Coventry CV1 3GD (024 7652 6700; info@covcollege.ac.uk)

City College Manchester, 141 Barlow Moor Road, West Didsbury, Manchester M20 2PQ (0161 957 1790; admissions@ccm.ac.uk)

City College of Higher Education, University House, 53-55 East Road, Islington, London N1 6AH (020 7253 1133)

City of Bath College, Avon St, Bath BA1 1UP (01225 312191; enquiries@citybathcoll. ac.uk)

City of Bristol College, College Green Centre, St George's Road, Bristol BS1 5UA (0117 904 5000; enquiries@cityofbristol.ac.uk)

City of London College, Neil House, 71 Whitechapel High St, Tower Hamlets, London E1 7PL (020 7247 2166; Registry@clc-london.ac.uk)

City of Sunderland College, Bede Centre, Durham Road, Sunderland SR3 4AH (0191-511 6060)

City of Wolverhampton College, Paget Road, Wolverhampton WV6 0DU (01902 317700)

Clackmannan College of Further Education, Branshill Road, Alloa Clackmannanshire FK10 3BT (01259 215121; learning@clacks.ac.uk)

Colchester Institute, Sheepen Road, Colchester, Essex CO3 3LL (01206 518000; info@colch-inst.ac.uk)

Coleg Ceredigion, Cardigan Campus, Park Place, Aberystwyth SA43 1AF (01239 612032)

Coleg Gwent, Crosskeys Campus, Risca Road, Crosskeys NP1 7ZA (01495 333456;

info@gwent-tertiary.ac.uk)

Coleg Gwent (Usk Campus), Usk NP5 1XJ (01495 333333; info@gwent-tertiary.ac.uk)

Coleg Llandrillo, Llandudno Road, Rhos-on-Sea, Colwyn Bay LL28 4HZ (01492 546666; admissions@llandrillo.ac.uk)

Coleg Meirion, Dolgellau, Gwynedd LL40 2SW (01341 422827; coleg@meirion-dwyfor.ac.uk)

Coleg Menai, Bangor, Gwynedd LL57 2TP (01248 370125; student.services@menai.a c.uk)

Coleg Morgannwg, Ynys Terrace, Rhydyfelin, Pontypridd Mid-Glamorgan CF37 5RN (01443 662800; college@pontypridd.ac.uk)

Coleg Powys, Llanidloes Road, Newtown, Powys SY16 4HU (01686 622722; enquiries@coleg-powys.ac.uk)

College of North East, London High Road, Haringey, London N15 4RU (020 8802 3111; admissions@staff.conel.ac.uk)

College of North West, London Willesden Centre, Dudden Hill Lane, Brent, London NW10 2XD (020 8208 5000; course.enquiries@cnwl.ac.uk)

College of Richard Collyer in Horsham, Horsham, W Sussex RH12 2EJ (01403 210822)

College of West Anglia, Tennyson Avenue, King's Lynn, Norfolk PE30 2QW (01553 761144; enquiries@col-westanglia.ac.uk)

Coulsdon College, Place House Lane, Croydon, Surrey CR5 1YA (01737 551176)

Craven College, High St, Skipton, York. BD23 1JY (01756 791411; enquiries@craven-college.ac.uk)

Crawley College, College Road, Crawley, Sussex RH10 1NR (01293 442200; information@crawley-college.ac.uk)

Croydon College, Fairfield, Croydon, Surrey CR9 1DX (020 8686 5700; info@croydon.ac.uk)

Darlington College of Technology, Cleveland Avenue, Darlington DL3 7BB (01325 503050)

Daventry Tertiary College, Badby Road West, Daventry, Northants. NN11 4HJ (01327 300232; irs@davcoll.ac.uk)

Dearne Valley College, Manvers Park, Wath upon Dearne, Rotherham, Yorks. S63 7EW (01709 513333; enquiries@dearne-coll.ac.uk)

Deeside College, Kelsterton Road, Connah's Quay, Clwyd CH5 4BR (01244 831531; enquiries@deeside.ac.uk)

Derby College, Wilmorton London Road, Wilmorton, Derby DE24 8UG (01332 757570; enquiries@derby-college.ac.uk)

Derwentside College, Park Road, Consett, Durham DH8 5EE (01207 585900)

Dewsbury College, Halifax Road, Dewsbury, West Yorks. WF13 2AS (01924 465916/ 436221; info@dewsbury.ac.uk)

Dudley College of Technology, The Broadway, Dudley, W. Midlands DY1 4AS (01384 363000; student.services@dudleycol.ac.uk)

Dundee College, Kingsway Campus, Old Glamis Road, Dundee DD3 8LE (01382 834834; enquiries@dundeecoll.ac.uk)

East Devon College, Bolham Road, Tiverton, Devon EX16 6SH (01884 235200; admiss ions@admin.eastdevon.ac.uk)

East Down Institute of Further and Higher Education, Market St, Downpatrick, Northern Ireland BT30 6ND (028 44615815; director@eastdown.prestel.co.uk)

East Durham and Houghall Community College, Burnhope Way, Peterlee, Durham SR8 1NU (0191 518 2000; enquiry@eastdurham.ac.uk)

East Riding College, St Mary's Walk, Bridlington, Yorks. YO16 5JW (01262 852000; enquiries@east-yorks-coll.ac.uk)

Eastleigh College, Chestnut Avenue, Eastleigh, Hants. SO50 5HT (023 8091 1000; goplaces@eastleigh.ac.uk)

Easton College, Easton, Norwich, Norfolk NR9 5DX (01603 731200)

Eccles College, Chatsworth Road, Eccles, Manchester M30 9FJ (0161 789 5876; admin @ecclescollege.ac.uk)

Edinburgh's Telford College, Crewe Toll, Edinburgh EH4 2NZ (0131-332 2491)

Enfield College, 73 Hertford Road, Enfield, Middlesex EN3 5HA (020 8443 3434)

Epping Forest College, Borders Lane, Basildon, Essex IG10 3SA (020 8508 8311; informationcentre@epping-forest.ac.uk)

Esher Colleg, Weston Green Road, Thames Ditton, Surrey KT7 0JB (020 8398 0291; eshercollege@esher.ac.uk)

Evesham College, Cheltenham Road, Evesham. Worcs. WR11 6LP (01386 712600; enquiries@evesham.ac.uk)

Exeter College, Victoria House, 33-36 Queen St, Exeter EX4 8QD (01392 205222; admissions@exe-coll.ac.uk)

Fakenham College, Wells Road, Fakenham, Norfolk NR21 9HP (01328 851039; Colleg e.highfield@fakenhamhigh.norfolk.sch.uk)

Falkirk College of Further and Higher Education, Grangemouth Road, Falkirk FK2 9AD (01324 403000; info@falkirkcollege.ac.uk)

Farnborough College of Technology, Boundary Road, Farnborough, Hants. GU14 6FB (01252 407040; info@farn-ct.ac.uk)

Fermanagh College, Fairview, 1 Dublin Road, Enniskillen, Northern Ireland BT74 6AE (028 66322431; admissions@fermanaghcoll.ac.uk)

Filton College, Filton Avenue, Filton, Bristol BS34 7AT (0117 931 2121; admin@filton-college.ac.uk)

Frome Community College, Bath Road, Frome, Somerset BA11 2HQ (01373 465353; sch.527@educ.somerset.gov.uk)

Furness College, Howard St, Barrow in Furness, Cumbria LA14 1NB (01229 825017; course.enq@furness.ac.uk)

Gateshead College, Durham Road, Gateshead, Newcastle NE9 5BN (0191-490 0300)

Glasgow College of Food Technology, 230 Cathedral St, Glasgow G1 2TG (0141-552 3751)

Gloucestershire College of Arts and Technology, Brunswick Campus, Brunswick Road, Gloucester, Glos. GL1 1HU (01452 426505; info@gloscat.ac.uk)

Godalming College, Tuesley Lane, Godalming, Surrey GU7 1RS (01483 423526; college@godalming.ac.uk)

Goole College, Bartholomew Centre, Boothferry Road, Goole, S. Yorks. DN14 6SR (01405 762420)

Grantham College, Stonebridge Road, Grantham, Lincs. NG31 9AP (01476 400200; enquiry@grantham.ac.uk)

Great Yarmouth College, Southtown, Great Yarmouth, Norfolk NR31 0ED (01493 655261; info@gyc.ac.uk)

Greenwich Community College, 95 Plumstead Road, Greenwich, London SE18 7DQ (020 8488 4800; info@gcc.ac.uk)

Greenwich School of Management, Meridian House, Royal Hill, Greenwich, London SE10 8RD (020 8516 7800; enquiry@greenwich-college.ac.uk)

Grimsby College, Nuns Corner, Grimsby DN34 5BQ (01472 311222; infocent@grimsby.ac.uk)

Guernsey College of Further Education, Route des Coutanchez, St Peter Port, Guernsey C.I. (01481 727121)

Guildford College of Further and Higher Education, Stoke Park, Guildford, Surrey GU1 1EZ (01483 448500; info@guildford.ac.uk)

Guildford Secretarial and Business College, 17 Chapel St, Guildford, Surrey GU1 3UL (01483 564885; mail@g-s-c.co.uk)

Halesowen College, Whittingham Road, Halesowen, West Midlands B63 3NA (0121 602 7777; halesowen@dial.pipex.com)

Harlow College, Velizy Avenue, Town Centre, Harlow, Essex CM20 3LH (01279 868000; fulltime@harlow-college.ac.uk)

Harrow College, Lowlands Road, Harrow, Middlesex HA1 3AQ (020 8909 6100; enquiries@harrow.ac.uk)

Hartlepool College of Further Education Stockton St, Hartlepool TS24 7NT (01429 295111; enquiries@hartlepoolfe.ac.uk)

Havant College, New Road, Havant, Hants. PO9 1QL (023 9248 3856; enquiries@havant.ac.uk)

Havering College of Further and Higher Education, Ardleigh Green Road, Havering, Essex RM11 2LL (01708 455011; ciac@havering-college.ac.uk)

Haywards Heath College, Harlands Road, Haywards Heath, Sussex RH16 1LT (01444 456281; admin@hnc.ac.uk)

Henley College, Deanfield Avenue, Henley on Thames, Oxon. RG9 1UH (01491 579988)

Henley College, Coventry Henley Road, Bell Green, Coventry CV2 1ED (024 7662 6300)

Herefordshire College of Technology, Folly Lane, Hereford HR1 1LS (01432 352235; enquiries@hereford-tech.ac.uk)

Hertford Regional College (Broxbourne Centre), Turnford, Broxbourne, Herts. EN10 6AE (01992 411400; info@hertreg.ac.uk)

High Peak College (University of Derby), Harpur Hill, Buxton, Derbyshire SK17 9JZ (01298 71100)

Hopwood Hall College (Rochdale Campus), St Mary's Gate, Rochdale, Lancs. OL12 6RY (0161 643 7560)

Huddersfield New College, New Hey Road, Huddersfield HD3 4GL (01484 652341; info@huddnewcoll.ac.uk)

Hugh Baird College, Balliol Road, Bootle, Merseyside L20 7EW (0151 353 4444; info@hughbaird.ac.uk)

Hull College, Queen's Gardens, Hull HU1 3DG (01482 329943; tbarber@hull-college.ac.uk)

IHMES International Hotel School, Windsor House, Port Erin, Isle of Man IM9 6LA (01624 832836; office@ihmes.com)

International Studies Centre, 73 Newman St, Westminster, London W1P 4PG (020 7580 7759)

Inverness College, 3 Longman Road, Inverness IV1 1SA (01463 273000; admissions – officer/IC@uhi.ac.uk)

Isle of Man College, Homefield Road, Douglas, Isle of Man IM2 6RB (01624 648200; enquiries@iomcollege.ac.im)

Isle of Wight College, Medina Way, Newport, Isle of Wight PO30 5TA (01983 526631; info@iwcollege.ac.uk)

John Ruskin College, Selsdon Park Road, Croydon CR2 8JJ (020 8651 1131; info@johnruskin.ac.uk)

Joseph Priestley College, Alec Beevers Centre, Burton Avenue, Leeds LS11 5ER (0113 307 6000; helpline@joseph-priestley.ac.uk)

Keighley College, Cavendish St, Keighley, Yorks. BD21 3DF (01535 618555; guidance@keighley.ac.uk)

Kendal College, Milnthorpe Road, Kendal, Cumbria LA9 5AY (01539 724313; enquiries@kendal.ac.uk)

Kidderminster College, Market St, Kidderminster, Worcs. DY10 1LX (01562 820811; admissions@kidderminster.ac.uk)

Kilmarnock College, Holehouse Road, Kilmarnock, Ayrshire KA3 7AT (01563 523501)

Knowsley Community College, Rupert Road, Roby, Merseyside L36 9TD (0151 477 5700)

Lambeth College, Brixton Centre, Brixton Hill, Lambeth, London SW2 1QS (020 7501 5010; courses@lambethcollege.ac.uk)

Lancaster and Morecambe College, Morecambe Road, Lancaster LA1 2TY (01524 66215)

Lancaster University, Bailrigg, Lancaster LA1 4YW (01524 65201; ugadmissions@lancaster.ac.uk)

Leicester College, Freeman's Park Campus, Aylestone Road, Leicester LE2 7LW (0116 224 2000; info@leicestercollege.ac.uk)

Lincoln College, Monks Road, Lincoln LN2 5HQ (01522 876000; nlc@nlincs-coll.ac.uk)

Liverpool Community College, Old Swan Centre, Broadgreen Road, Liverpool L13 5SQ (0151 252 3000)

London City College, Royal Waterloo House, 51-55 Waterloo Road, Southwark, London SE1 8TX (020 7928 0029/0938/0901; lcclist@aol.com

Loughborough College, Radmoor Road, Loughborough, Leics. LE11 3BT (01509 215831; info@loucoll.ac.uk)

Lowestoft College, St Peter's St, Lowestoft, Suffolk NR32 2NB (01502 583521; info@lowestoft.ac.uk)

Ludlow College, Mill St, Ludlow, Shropshire SY8 1GU (01584 872846)

Macclesfield College, Park Lane, Macclesfield, Cheshire SK11 8LF (01625 410000; info@macclesfield.ac.uk)

Merton College, Morden Park, London Road, Sutton, Surrey SM4 5QX (020 8408 6400; info@merton.ac.uk)

Mid-Cheshire College (Hartford Campus), Northwich, Cheshire CW8 1LJ (01606 74444; info@midchesh.ac.uk)

Mid-Kent College of Higher and Further Education, Horsted, Maidstone Road, Chatham. kent ME5 9UQ (01634 830633; course.enquiries@midkent.ac.uk)

Middlesbrough College, Roman Road, Linthorpe, Middlesbrough TS5 5PJ (01642 333333)

Milton Keynes College (Chaffron Way Campus), Woughton Campus West, Leadenhall, Milton Keynes MK6 5LP (01908 684444; info@mkcollege.ac.uk)

Neath Port Talbot College, Afan Campus Margam, Port Talbot, West Glamorgan SA13 2AL (01639 648000; admissions@nptc.ac.uk)

NESCOT, Reigate Road, Epsom, Surrey KT17 3DS (020 8394 3038; info@nescot.ac.uk)

New College Durham, Framwellgate Moor Centre, Durham DH1 5ES (0191 375 4000; helpdesk@newdur.ac.uk)

New College Nottingham, Pelham Avenue, Mansfield Road, Nottingham NG5 1AL (0115 910 0100; enquiries@ncn.ac.uk)

New College, Pontefract Park Lane, Pontefract, Yorks. WF8 4QR (01977 702139)

Newcastle College, Rye Hill Campus, Scotswood Road, Newcastle upon Tyne NE4 7SA (0191 200 4000; enquiries@ncl-coll.ac.uk)

Newcastle under Lyme College, Liverpool Road, Newcastle under Lyme ST5 2DF (01782 715111; enquiries@nulc.ac.uk)

North Area College, Buckingham Road, Heaton Moor, Stockport, Cheshire SK4 4RA (0161 442 7494; nac@nacstock.ac.uk)

North Devon College, Old Sticklepath Hill, Barnstaple, Devon EX31 2BQ (01271 345291; postbox@ndevon.ac.uk)

North East Institute of Further and Higher Education, Trostan Avenue, Ballymena, Co. Antrim, N. Ireland BT43 7BN (01266 652871)

North Hertfordshire College, Monkswood Way, Stevenage, Herts. SG1 1LA (01462 424242; enquiries@nhc.org.uk)

North Lindsey College, Kingsway, Scunthorpe, Lincs. DN17 1AJ (01724 281111; info@northlindsey.ac.uk)

North Nottinghamshire College, Carlton Road, Worksop, Notts. S81 7HP (01909 504504; contact@nnc.ac.uk)

North Tyneside College, Embleton Avenue, Wallsend, Tyneside NE28 9NJ (0191 229 5000; infocent@ntyneside.ac.uk)

North West Institute of Further and Higher Education, Strand Road, Londonderry, N. Ireland BT48 7BY (028 71 266711)

North West Kent College, Oakfield Lane, Dartford DA1 2JT (0800 074 1447; course.en quiries@nwkcollege.ac.uk)

Northumberland College, College Road, Ashington, Northumberland NE63 9RG (01670 841200; thecollege@northland.ac.uk)

Norton Radstock College, South Hill Park, Radstock, Bath BA3 3RW (01761 433161)

Norwich City College, Ipswich Road, Norwich NR2 2LJ (01603 773311; information@ccn.ac.uk)

Oaklands College, St Albans City Campus, St Albans, Herts. AL1 3RX (01727 737273; help.line@oaklands.ac.uk)

Oldham College, Rochdale Road, Oldham OL9 6AA (0161 624 5214; info@oldham.ac.uk)

Orpington College of Further Education, The Walnuts, High St, Bromley, Kent BR6 0TE (01689 899700; hx89@dial.pipex.com)

Palmers College, Chadwell Road, Grays, Essex RM17 5TD (01375 370121)

Pembrokeshire College, Haverfordwest, Dyfed SA61 1SZ (01437 765247; info@pembrokeshire.co.uk)

Pendleton College, Dronfield Road, Salford M6 7FR (0161 736 5074)

Penwith College, St Clare St, Penzance, Cornwall TR18 2SA (01736 335000; courses@penwith.ac.uk)

Peterborough Regional College, Park Crescent, Peterborough PE1 4DZ (01733 767366; Info@peterborough.ac.uk)

Plymouth College of Further Education, Kings Road, Devonport, Plymouth PL1 5QG (01752 305300; : pic@pcfe.ac.uk)

Portsmouth College, Tangier Road, Portsmouth PO3 6PZ (023 9266 7521)

Preston College, St Vincent's Road, Fulwood, Preston, Lancs. PR2 9UR (01772 225000; marketing@preston.ac.uk)

Priestley College, Loushers Lane, Warrington, Cheshire WA4 6RD (01925 633591; www.priestleycollege.ac.uk)

Queen Mary's College, Cliddesden Road, Basingstoke, Hants. RG21 3HF (01256 417500; postman@qmc.ac.uk)

Reading College and School of Art & Design, Crescent Road, Reading RG2 0AE (0118 967 5000; enquiries@reading-college.ac.uk)

Redbridge College, Little Heath, Redbridge, Essex RM6 4XT (020 8548 7400; info@re dbridge.essex.sch.uk)

Regent College, Regent Road, Leicester LE1 7LW (0116 255 4629)

Reid Kerr College, Renfrew Road, Paisley PA3 4DR (0141 581 2222)

Reigate College, Castlefield Road, Reigate, Surrey RH2 0SD

(01737 221118; enquiries@reigate.ac.uk)

Richmond upon Thames College, Egerton Road, Twickenham, Middlesex TW2 7SJ (020 8607 8000; courses@rutc.ac.uk)

Ridge Danyers College, Hibbert Lane, Marple, Stockport, Cheshire SK6 7PA (0161-484 6600; info@theridge.ac.uk)

Rotherham College of Arts and Technology, Eastwood Lane, Rotherham, Yorks. S65 1EG (01709 362111; info@rotherham.ac.uk)

Runshaw College, Langdale Road, Leyland, Preston, Merseyside PR25 3DQ (01772 622677)

Salford College, Worsley Campus, Walkden Road, Worsley, Manchester M28 7QD (0161 211 5001; centad@salford-col.ac.uk)

Saltash College, Church Road, Saltash, Cornwall PL12 4AE (01752 848147; info@salt coll.demon.co.uk)

Sandwell College of Further and Higher Education, Woden Road South, Sandwell, West Midlands WS10 0PE (0121-556 6000; enquiries@sandwell.ac.uk)

Selby College, Abbot's Road, Selby, Yorks. YO8 8AT (01757 211000)

Shipley College, Exhibition Road, Saltaire, Shipley, Yorks. BD18 3JW (01274 327222; enquiries@shipley.ac.uk)

Shrewsbury College of Arts and Technology, London Road, Shrewsbury, Shropshire SY2 6PR (01743 342342; prospects@s-cat.ac.uk)

Solihull College, Blossomfield Road, Solihull, W. Midlands B91 1SB (0121 678 7001/2; enquiries@staff.solihull.co.uk)

Somerset College of Arts and Technology, Wellington Road, Taunton, Somerset TA1 5AX (01823 366331; somerset@somerset.ac.uk)

South Devon College, Newton Road, Torquay, Devon TQ2 5BY (01803 400700; courses@s-devon.ac.uk)

South Downs College, College Road, Purbrook Way, Havant, Hants. PO7 8AA (023 9279 7979; college@southdowns.ac.uk)

South East Derbyshire College, Field Road, Ilkeston, Derbys. DE7 5RS (0115 849 2000; admissions@sedc.ac.uk)

South East Essex College, Carnarvon Road, Southend, Essex SS2 6LS (01702 220400; marketing@southend.ac.uk)

South Kent College, Shorncliffe Road, Ashford, Kent CT20 2TZ (01303 858200; admissions@southkent.ac.uk)

South Leicestershire College, Station Road, Wigston Magna, Leics. LE18 2DW (0116 288 5051; sgs@wigston-college.co.uk)

South Nottingham College, Greythorn Drive, West Bridgford, Nottingham NG2 7GA (0115 914 6464; enquiries@south-nottingham.ac.uk)

South Trafford College, Manchester Road, West Timperley, Altrincham, Cheshire WA14 5PQ (0161 952 4600)

Southampton City College, St Mary St, Southampton SO14 1AR (023 8048 4848; information@southampton.ac.uk)

Southgate College, Southgate High St, Enfield, Middlesex N14 6BS (020 8982 5050; admiss@southgate.ac.uk)

Southport College, Mornington Road, Southport, Lancs. PR9 0TT (01704 500606)

Southwark College, The Cut, Southwark, London SE1 8LE (020 7815 1600; info@southwark.ac.uk)

Spelthorne College, Church Road, Ashford, Middlesex TW15 2XD (01784 248666)

St Helens College, Brook Street, St Helens, Merseyside WA10 1PZ (01744 733766; enquire@sthelens.ac.uk)

St Mary's College, Shear Brow, Blackburn, Lancs. BB1 8DX (01254 580464)

Stafford College, Earl St, Stafford ST16 2QR (01785 223800; enquiries@staffordcoll.a c.uk)

Stanmore College, Elm Park, Harrow, Middlesex HA7 4BQ (020 8420 7700)

Stephenson College, Bridge Road, Coalville, Leics. LE7 3PW (01530 836136; services @stephenson.ac.uk)

Stevenson College, Bankhead Avenue, Edinburgh EH11 4DE (0131 535 4600; info@stevenson.ac.uk)

Stockport College of Further and Higher Education, Wellington Road South, Stockport SK1 3UQ (0161 958 3100; stockcoll@cs.stockport.ac.uk)

Stockton Riverside College, Harvard Avenue, Thornaby, Stockton, Teesside TS17 6FB (01642 865400; info@stockton.ac.uk)

Stoke-on-Trent College, Cauldon Campus, Stoke Road, Shelton, Stoke on Trent, Staffs. ST4 2DG (01782 208208; info@stokecoll.ac.uk)

Stourbridge College, Hagley Road, Stourbridge, W. Midlands DY8 1QU (01384 344344; info@stourbridge.ac.uk)

Stroud College of Further Education, Stratford Road, Stroud, Glos. GL5 4AH (01453 763424; enquire@stroudcol.ac.uk)

Suffolk College, Ipswich, Suffolk IP4 1HY (01473 255885; info@suffolk.ac.uk)

Sussex Downs College (Eastbourne Campus), Cross Levels Way, Eastbourne, E. Sussex BN21 2UF (01323 637637; eastbourne@sussexdowns.ac.uk)

Sussex Downs College (Lewes Campus), Mountfield Road, Lewes, E. Sussex BN7 2XH (01273 483188; info@lewescollege.ac.uk)

Sutton Coldfield College, Lichfield Road, Sutton Coldfield, W. Midlands B74 2NW (0121 355 5671; infoc@sutcol.ac.uk)

Swansea College, Tycoch Road, Sketty, Swansea SA2 9EB (01792 284000; recovery@swancoll.ac.uk)

Swindon College, Regent Circus, Swindon SN1 1PT (01793 491591)

Tamworth and Lichfield College, Croft St, Upper Gungate, Tamworth B79 8AE (01827 310202; enquiries@tamworth.ac.uk)

Taunton's College, Hill Lane, Southampton SO15 5RL (023 8051 1811; e-mail@tauntons.ac.uk)

Telford College of Arts and Technology, Haybridge Road, Wellington, Telford Shropshire TF1 2NP (01952 642237)

Thames Valley University, St Mary's Road, Ealing, London W5 5RF (020 8579 5000; learning.advice@tvu.ac.uk)

Thanet College, Ramsgate Road, Broadstairs, Kent CT10 1PN (01843 605040; student – admissions@thanet.ac.uk)

Thomas Rotherham College, Moorgate Road, Rotherham, Yorks. S60 2BE (01709 300600)

Totton College, Water Lane, Totton, Southampton SP40 3ZX (023 8087 4874; info@totton.ac.uk)

Tower Hamlets College, Poplar High St, Tower Hamlets, London E14 0AF (020 7510 7510)

Treloar College, Holybourne, Alton, Hants. GU34 4EN (01420 547400; admissions@t reloar.org.uk)

Tynemouth College, Hawkeys Lane, North Shields NE29 9BZ (0191-257 8414; enquiri es@tynecoll.ac.uk)

Upper Bann Institute of Further and Higher Education Portadown, 26-44 Lurgan Road, Portadown, Northern Ireland BT63 5BL (028 3839 7777; enquiries@ubi.ac.uk)

Walford and North Shropshire College, College Road, Oswestry, Shropshire SY11 2SA (01691 688000; enquiries@wncs.ac.uk)

Walsall College of Arts and Technology, St Paul's St, Walsall, W. Midlands WS1 1XN

(01922 657000; c.kemp@walcat.ac.uk)

Warrington Collegiate Institute, Winwick Road, Warrington, Cheshire WA2 8QA (01925 494494; student.services@warr.ac.uk)

West Cheshire College, Handbridge Centre, Eaton Road, Handbridge, Chester CH4 7ER (01244 670676)

West Kent Colleg, Brook St, Tonbridge, Kent TN9 2PW (01732 358101; marketing@wkc.ac.uk)

West Thames College, London Road, Richmond upon Thames, Middlesex TW7 4HS (020 8326 2000; info@west-thames.ac.uk)

Westminster Kingsway College, Battersea Park Centre, Battersea Park Road, Wandsworth, London SW11 4JR (020 7556 8001; courseinfo@westking.ac.uk)

Weston College, Knightstone Road, Weston super Mare, Somerset BS23 2AL (01934 411411; bob.hughes@weston.ac.uk)

Weymouth College, Cranford Avenue, Weymouth, Dorset DT4 7LQ (01305 761100; igs@weymouth.ac.uk)

Wigan and Leigh College, PO Box 53, Parsons Walk, Wigan WN1 1RS (01942 761600; admissions@wigan-leigh.ac.uk)

Wilberforce College, Saltshouse Road, Hull HU8 9HD (01482 711688)

Wirral Metropolitan College, Borough Road, Birkenhead, Merseyside CH42 9QD (0151-551 7777; h.e.enquiries@wmc.ac.uk)

Woking College, Rydens Way, Woking, Surrey GU22 9DL (01483 761036)

Xaverian College, Lower Park Road, Manchester M14 5RB (0161 224 1781; college@xaverian.ac.uk)

Yale College of Wrexham, Grave Park Road, Wrexham, Clwyd LL12 7AA (01978 311794; admissions@yale-wrexham.ac.uk)

Yeovil College, Mudford Road, Yeovil, Somerset BA21 4DR (01935 423921; juc@yeovil-college.ac.uk)

Yorkshire Coast College of Further and Higher Education, Lady Edith's Drive, Scarborough, Yorks. YO12 5RN (01723 372105; admissions@ycoastco.ac.uk)

Ystrad Mynach College, Twyn Road, Ystrad Mynach, Mid-Glamorgan CF8 7XR (01443 816888)

APPENDIX 2

TOURIST OFFICES IN LONDON

ANDORRA: Andorran Delegation, 63 Westover Road, SW18 2RF (020-8874 4806)

AUSTRALIA: Australian Tourist Commission, Gemini House, 10-18 Putney Hill, Putney, SW15 6AA (020-8780 2229; www.australia.com)

AUSTRIA: Austrian National Tourist Office, 14 Cork St, W1X 1PF (020-7629 0461; www.austrian-tourism.at)

BELGIUM: 225 Marsh Wall, E14 9FW (0906 302 0245; www.belgium-tourism.net)

CANADA: Tourism Section, Canadian High Commission, Macdonald House, 1 Grosvenor Square, W1X 0AB (020-7258 6600; www.travelcanada.ca)

CYPRUS: Cyprus Tourist Office, 213 Regent St, W1R 8DA (020-7734 9822)

DENMARK: Danish Tourist Board, 55 Sloane St, SW1X 9SY (020-7259 5959; www.visitdenmark.com)

EGYPT: Egyptian State Tourist Office, 170 Piccadilly, W1V 9DD (020-7493 5282)

FINLAND: Finnish Tourist Board, PO Box 33213, W6 8JX (020-7365 2512; www.finland-tourism.com/uk)

FRANCE: French Government Tourist Office, 178 Piccadilly, W1V 0AL (0906 824 4123; www.franceguide.com)

GERMANY: German National Tourist Office, PO Box 2695, London W1A 3TN (02-7317 0908; www.germany-tourism.de)

GIBRALTAR: Gibraltar Tourist Board, Arundel, Great Court, 179 Strand, WC2R 1EH (020-7836 0777)

GREECE: Hellenic Tourism Organisation, 4 Conduit St, W1R 0DJ (020-7734 5997; www.gnto.gr)

HUNGARY: Hungarian National Tourist Board, 46 Eaton Place, London SW1 8AL *020-7823 1032; www.hungarytourism.hu)*

INDIA: Indian National Tourist Office, 7 Cork St, W1X 2LW (020-7437 3677; www.indiatouristoffice.org)

IRELAND: Visitor Centre, Nations House, 103 Wigmore St, W1U 1QS (0800 0397 000l; www.ireland.travel.ie/ www.tourismireland.com)

ISRAEL: Israel Government Tourist Office, 180 Oxford St, W1N 9DJ (020-7299 1113; www.infotour.co.il)

ITALY: Italian State Tourist Board, 1 Princes St, W1R 2AY (020-7408 1254; www.enit.it)

JAPAN: Japan National Tourist Organisation, Heathcoat House, 20 Saville Row, W1S 3PR (fax 020-7734 4290; www.seejapan.co.uk)

LUXEMBOURG: Luxembourg National Tourist Office, 122 Regent St, W1B 5SA (020-7434 2800; www.luxembourg.co.uk)

MALTA: Malta Tourist Office, Unit C, Park House, 14 Northfields, SW18 1DD (020-8877 6990; www.visitmalta.com)

MONACO: Monaco Tourist & Convention Office, The Chambers, Chelsea Harbour,

SW10 0XF (020-7352 9962; www.visitmonaco.com)

NETHERLANDS: Netherlands Board of Tourism, PO Box 30783, WC2B 6DH (0906 871 7777; www.holland.com/uk)

NEW ZEALAND: New Zealand Tourism Board, 7th Floor, New Zealand House, 80 Haymarket, SW1Y 4TQ (0207-930 1662/ 09050 606060, 60p per minute; www.purenz.com)

NORWAY: Innovation Norway, Charles House, 5 Regent St, SW1Y 4LR (0906 302 2003 50p per minute; www.norway.org.uk)

PORTUGAL: Portuguese Tourism Office, 22-25a Sackville St, W1S 3LY (020-7494 5720; www.portugal-insite.pt)

SOUTH AFRICA: South African Tourism, 6 Alt Grove, (PO Box 4911) Wimbledon, London SW19 4XZ (08701 550044; www.southafrica.net)

SPAIN: Spanish National Tourist Office, 22-23 Manchester Square, W1U 3PK (020-7486 8077; www.tourspain.co.uk)

SWEDEN: Swedish Travel & Tourism Council, 11 Montagu Place, W1H 2AL (0800 3080 3080; www.visit-sweden.com)

SWITZERLAND: Switzerland Tourism, Swiss Centre, 10 Wardour St, W1D 6QF (0020-7292 1550; www.switzerlandtourism.ch)

THAILAND: Tourism Authority of Thailand, 3rd Floor, Brook House, 98-99 Jermyn St, SW1Y 6EE (020-7925 2511; www.tourismthailand.org)

TURKEY: Turkish Information Office, 170-3 Piccadilly, W1J 9EJ (020-7629 7771; www.gototurkey.co.uk)

UK: British Tourist Authority & English Tourist Board, Thames Tower, Black's Road, Hammersmith, London W6 9EL (020-8846 9000; www.visitbritain.com)

APPENDIX 3

EMBASSIES/CONSULATES IN LONDON & WASHINGTON

AUSTRALIA: Australia House, The Strand, London WC2B 4LA (www.australia.org.uk/vti.html)
1601 Massachusetts Ave NW, Washington DC 20036-2273 (202-797-3000/3145)
AUSTRIA: 18 Belgrave Mews West, London SW1X 8HU (020-7235 3731; www.austria.org.uk)
3524 International Court NW, Washington DC 20008 (202-895-6767)
BELGIUM: 103-105 Eaton Square, London SW1W 9AB (020-7470 3700; www.belgium-embassy.co.uk)
3330 Garfield St NW, Washington DC 20008 (202-333-6900)
BRAZIL: Consular Section, 6 St. Alban's St, London SW1Y 4SG (020-7930 9055; www.brazil.org.uk)
3009 Whitehaven St NW, Washington DC 20008 (202-745-2828)
CANADA: 38 Grosvenor St, London W1X 0AA (020-7258 6600; www.dfait-maeci.gc.ca/london or www.canada.org.uk)
501 Pennsylvania Ave NW, Washington DC 20001 (202-682-1740)
CHILE: 12 Devonshire St, London W1G 7DS (020-7580 1023; cglonduk@congechile uk.demon.co.uk)
1732 Massachusetts Ave NW, Washington DC 20036 (202-785-3159)
CHINA: Visa Section, 31 Portland Place, London W1N 3AG (020-7631 1430; www.chinese-embassy.org.uk)
2300 Connecticut Ave NW, Washington DC 20008 (202-328-2517)
CZECH REPUBLIC: 26-30 Kensington Palace Gardens, London W8 4QY (020-7243 1115)
3900 Spring of Freedom St NW, Washington DC 20008 (202-363-6315/6)
DENMARK: 55 Sloane St, London SW1X 9SR (020-7333 0200; www.denmark.org.uk)
3200 White Haven St NW, Washington DC 20008 (202-234-4300)
EGYPT: 2 Lowndes St, London SW1X 9ET (020-7235 9777; www.egypt-embassy.org.uk)
2310 Decatur Place NW, Washington DC 20008 (202-234-3903)
FINLAND: 38 Chesham Place, London SW1X 8HW (020-7838 6200; www.finemb.org.uk)
3216 New Mexico Ave NW, Washington DC 20016 (202-363-2430)
FRANCE: 21 Cromwell Road, London SW7 2DQ (020-7838 2000; www.ambafrance-uk.org)
4101 Reservoir Road NW, Washington DC 20007 (202-944-6200/6215)
GERMANY: 23 Belgrave Square, London SW1X 8PZ (020-7824 1300/0906-833 1166;

www.german-embassy.org.uk)
4645 Reservoir Road NW, Washington DC 20007 (202-298-4000)
GREECE: 1A Holland Park, London W11 3TP (020-7221 6467; www.greekembassy.org.uk)
2221 Massachusetts Ave NW, Washington DC 20008 (202-232-8222)
HONG KONG: 6 Grafton St, London W1X 3LB (020-7499 9821). c/o Chinese Embassy
HUNGARY: 35b Eaton Place, London SW1X 8BY (020-7235 2664/09001-171 204; http://dspace.dial.pipex.com/huemblon)
3910 Shoemaker St NW, Washington DC 20008 (202-362-6730)
ICELAND: 1 Eaton Terrace, London SW1W 8EY (020-7730 5131)
2022 Connecticut Ave NW, Washington DC 20008-6194 (202-265 6653)
INDIA: India House, Aldwych, London WC2B 4NA (020-7836 8484)
2536 Massachusetts Ave NW, Washington DC 20008 (202-939-9839/9850)
IRELAND: 17 Grosvenor Place, London SW1X 7HR (020-7235 2171)
2234 Massachusetts Ave NW, Washington DC 20008 (202-462-3939)
ISRAEL: Consular Section, 15a Old Court Place, London W8 4QB (020-7957 9516; info@israel-embassy.org.uk)
3514 International Dr NW, Washington DC 20008-3099 (202-364-5500)
ITALY: 38 Eaton Place, London SW1X 8AN (020-7235 9371; www.embitaly.org.uk/uk)
1601 Fuller St NW, Washington DC 20009 (202-328-5500)
JAPAN: 101-104 Piccadilly, London W1V 9FN (020-7465 6500; www.embjapan.org.uk)
2520 Massachusetts Ave NW, Washington DC 20008 (202-939-6800)
KENYA: 45 Portland Place, London W1N 4AS (020-7636 2371/5)
2249 R St NW, Washington DC 20008 (202-387-6101)
LUXEMBOURG: 27 Wilton Crescent, London SW1X 8SD (020-7235 6961)
2200 Massachusetts Ave NW, Washington DC 20008 (202-265-4171/2)
MALAYSIA: 45 Belgrave Square, London SW1X 8QT (020-7235 8033)
2401 Massachusetts Ave NW, Washington, DC 20008 (202-328-2700)
MALTA: Malta House, 36-38 Piccadilly, London W1V 0PQ (020-7292 4800)
MEXICO: 8 Halkin St, London SW1X 7DW (020-7235 6393; www.mexicanconsulate.org.uk)
2827 16th St NW, Washington, DC 20009-4260 (202-736-1000)
MOROCCO: Diamond House, 97-99 Praed St, London W2 (020-7724 01719)
1601 21st St NW, Washington DC 20009 (202-462-7979)
NETHERLANDS: 38 Hyde Park Gate, London SW7 5DP (020-7590 3200/09001-171 217; www.netherlands-embassy.org.uk)
4200 Linnean Ave NW, Washington DC 20008 (202-244-5300)
NEW ZEALAND: New Zealand House, Haymarket, London SW1Y 4TE (0906 9100 100; £1 a minute)
37 Observatory Circle NW, Washington DC 20008 (202-328-4848)
NORWAY: 25 Belgrave Square, London SW1X 8QD (020-7591 5500)
2820 34th St NW, Washington DC 20008-2799 (202-333-6000)
PERU: 52 Sloane St, London SW1X 9SP (020-7838 9223; www.peruembassy-uk.com)
1700 Massachusetts Ave NW, Washington DC 20036 (202-833-9860)
POLAND: 73 New Cavendish St, London W1N 4HQ (020-7580 0476; www.poland-embassy.org.uk)
2224 Wyoming Ave NW, Washington, DC 20036 (202-8339860)
PORTUGAL: Silver City House, 62 Brompton Road, London SW3 1BJ (020-7581 8722; london@portembassy.co.uk)

2125 Kalorama Road NW, Washington DC 20008 (202-332-3307)
RUSSIAN FEDERATION: 5 Kensington Palace Gardens, London W8 4QS (020-7229 8027; www.russialink.org.uk)
1825 Phelps Place NW, Washington DC 20008 (202-939-8907/8911/8913)
SINGAPORE: 9 Wilton Crescent, London SW1X 8SA (020-7235 8315)
3501 International PLace NW, Washington, DC 20008 (202-537-3100)
SLOVAK REPUBLIC: 25 Kensington Palace Gardens, London W8 4QY (020-7243 0803; www.slovakembassy.co.uk)
2201 Wisconsin Ave NW, Suite 380, Washington, DC 20007 (202-965-5164)
SOUTH AFRICA: South Africa House, Trafalgar Square, London WC2N 5DP (020-7451 7299; general@southafricahouse.com)
3201 New Mexico Ave, Washington, DC 20016 (202-966-1650)
SPAIN: 20 Draycott Place, London SW3 2RZ (020-7917 6400)
2700 15th St NW, Washington DC 20009 (202-265-0190/1)
SWEDEN: 11 Montagu Place, London W1H 2AL (020-7724 2101; www.swedish-embassy.org.uk)
Suite 1200, 600 New Hampshire Ave NW, 1200, Washington DC 20037 (202-944-5600)
SWITZERLAND: 16/18 Montagu Place, London W1H 2BQ (020-7616 6000; swiss.e mbassy@lon.rep.admin.ch; www.swissembassy.org.uk)
2900 Cathedral Ave NW, Washington DC 20008 (202-745-7900)
THAILAND: 29/30 Queen's Gate, London SW7 5JB (020-7589 2944)
2300 Kalorama Road NW, Washington DC 20008 (202-234-5052)
TURKEY: Rutland Lodge, Rutland Gardens, London SW7 1BW (020-7589 0949; www.turkconsulate-london.com)
1714 Massachusetts Ave NW, Washington DC 20036 (202-659-0742)
UK: 19 Observatory Circle NW, Washington DC 20008 (202-986-0205)
USA: 5 Upper Grosvenor St, London W1A 2JB (09061 500590, £1.50 a minute)

Vacation Work Publications

	Paperback	Hardback
Summer Jobs Abroad	£10.99	£16.95
Summer Jobs in Britain	£10.99	£16.95
Supplement to Summer Jobs Britain and Abroad *published in May*	£6.00	-
Work Your Way Around the World	£12.95	-
Workabout Australia	£10.99	-
Taking a Gap Year	£11.95	-
Taking a Career Break	£11.95	-
Working in Tourism – The UK, Europe & Beyond	£11.95	-
Working in Aviation	£10.99	-
Kibbutz Volunteer	£10.99	-
Working on Yachts and Superyachts	£10.99	-
Working on Cruise Ships	£10.99	-
Teaching English Abroad	£12.95	-
The Au Pair & Nanny's Guide to Working Abroad	£12.95	-
The Good Cook's Guide to Working Worldwide	£11.95	-
Working in Ski Resorts – Europe & North America	£11.95	-
Working with Animals – The UK, Europe & Worldwide	£11.95	-
Live & Work Abroad – A Guide for Modern Nomads	£11.95	-
Working with the Environment	£11.95	-
The Directory of Jobs & Careers Abroad	£12.95	-
The International Directory of Voluntary Work	£11.95	-
Buying a House in France	£11.95	-
Buying a House in Spain	£11.95	-
Buying a House in Italy	£11.95	-
Live & Work in Australia & New Zealand	£10.99	-
Live & Work in Belgium, The Netherlands & Luxembourg	£10.99	-
Live & Work in France	£10.99	-
Live & Work in Germany	£10.99	-
Live & Work in Italy	£10.99	-
Live & Work in Japan	£10.99	-
Live & Work in Saudi & the Gulf	£10.99	-
Live & Work in Scandinavia	£10.99	-
Live & Work in Scotland	£10.99	-
Live &Work in Spain & Portugal	£10.99	-
Live & Work in the USA & Canada	£10.99	-
Drive USA	£10.99	-
Scottish Islands – The Western Isles	£12.95	-
Scottish Islands – Orkney & Shetland	£11.95	-
The Panamericana: On the Road through Mexico and Central America	£12.95	-
Travellers Survival Kit Australia & New Zealand	£11.95	-
Travellers Survival Kit Cuba	£10.99	-
Travellers Survival Kit Lebanon	£10.99	-
Travellers Survival Kit Madagascar, Mayotte & Comoros	£10.99	-
Travellers Survival Kit Mauritius, Seychelles & Réunion	£10.99	-
Travellers Survival Kit Mozambique	£10.99	-
Travellers Survival Kit Oman & The Arabian Gulf	£11.95	-
Travellers Survival Kit South America	£15.95	-
Travellers Survival Kit Sri Lanka	£10.99	-

Distributors of:

Summer Jobs in the USA	£12.99	-
Internships	£18.99	-
World Volunteers	£10.99	-
Green Volunteers	£10.99	-
Archaeo-Volunteers	£10.99	-

Vacation Work Publications, 9 Park End Street, Oxford OX1 1HJ
☎**01865-241978   Fax 01865-790885**

**Visit us online for more information on our unrivalled range of titles for work,
travel and gap years, readers' feedback and regular updates:**

www.vacationwork.co.uk